THE CLASSICS
OF WESTERN
SPIRITUALITY

THE CLASSICS OF WESTERN SPIRITUALITY
A Library of the Great Spiritual Masters

President and Publisher
Kevin A. Lynch, C.S.P.

EDITORIAL BOARD

RICHARD OF ST VICTOR

THE TWELVE PATRIARCHS
THE MYSTICAL ARK
BOOK THREE OF THE TRINITY

TRANSLATION AND INTRODUCTION
BY
GROVER A. ZINN

PREFACE
BY
JEAN CHÂTILLON

PAULIST PRESS
NEW YORK • RAMSEY • TORONTO

Cover Art:
The artist LESLIE FLANDERS combines a career in writing and painting. Born in Ohio she presently resides in New York. Of her cover art she says, "I saw Richard as a great mystic of the medieval period but one who because of the timeless quality of his mysticism is thoroughly modern as well. I combined a sense of the artistic forms of his time with those of our present era. . . . Richard's spirituality has everything to do with persons relating to each other and with the persons of the Divine Trinity."

Design: Barbini Pesce & Noble, Inc.

Library of Congress
Catalog Card Number: 79-83834
ISBN: 0-8091-2122-0 (paper)
ISBN: 0-8091-0241-2 (cloth)

Published by Paulist Press
Editorial Office: 1865 Broadway, New York, N.Y. 10023
Business Office: 545 Island Road, Ramsey, N.J. 07446

Printed and bound in the
United States of America

CONTENTS

Author of the Preface

JEAN CHÂTILLON, who has devoted a lifetime of study to the Abbey of St. Victor and some of its leading figures, was born in Épinal, in northeastern France, in 1912. Educated in the schools of Metz and Arcachon, he later studied in Toulouse at the Institut Catholique, in Rome at the Angelicum University, and at the Universities of Nancy and Paris. He holds the degrees of Licencié en philosophie, Docteur en théologie and Docteur ès lettres. He was ordained a priest in 1935 and was later professor in the seminary of Metz. Since 1950 he has been a member of the faculty of the Institut Catholique in Paris, where he is professor of the history of medieval philosophy. In 1961 he was Dean and is now Honorary Dean of the faculty of philosophy. Professor Châtillon began a definitive reassessment of the spirituality of Richard of St. Victor with the publication of studies considering Richard's understanding of the modes of contemplation and the degrees of charity. He has published critical Latin editions of the sermons of Achard and Walter of St. Victor, and also the *Liber exceptionum* and *L'édit d' Alexandre ou les trois processions* by Richard of St. Victor. In addition to numerous articles in such journals as *Revue d'ascétique et de mystique*, *Revue du moyen âge latin*, and *Archives d'histoire littéraire et doctrinale du moyen âge*, he has published a major study *Théologie, spiritualité et métaphysique dans l'oeuvre oratoire d'Achard de Saint-Victor* (Études de Philosophie Medievale, 58; Paris, 1969). Recently he has been a participant in a number of international conferences, including those on Bonaventure, Peter Abelard and Peter the Venerable, and Thomas Becket, as well as other colloquia and the summer sessions at the C.E.S.C.M. of the University of Poitiers. Chevalier de l'ordre national du Merite and honorary canon of Metz, Professor Châtillon resides in Paris.

Editor of this Volume

GROVER A. ZINN was born in 1937 in El Dorado, Arkansas. After taking a B.A. degree in Physics at Rice University, Houston, he studied at Duke University, from which he holds B.D. and Ph.D. degrees. He was a special student in the Faculty of Divinity, University of Glasgow, Scotland, where he served as the Assistant Minister of the Barony Church in Glasgow. Since 1966 he has been on the faculty of Oberlin College, Oberlin, Ohio, where he is presently Associate Professor in the Department of Religion. Professor Zinn is interested in twelfth-century spirituality, especially Victorine. His teaching and research activities have extended more broadly to iconography, the liturgy, Christian utopian communities, particularly nineteenth-century American communities and cross-cultural studies of mysticism and monasticism. At Oberlin he has been involved in organizing and directing several Winter Term workshop projects in meditation (with W. R. Dhiravamsa) and Benedictine Monasticism (with Fr. George Simon and, as visiting lecturer, Br. David Steindl-Rast, O.S.B.). During the years 1972–1973 he pursued research in Oxford, England, as the holder of an NEH Younger Humanists' Fellowship and a Research Status Appointment from Oberlin College. Earlier, in 1968, he was awarded an H. H. Powers Travel Grant by Oberlin and spent two months photographing major medieval sites in England and France. His articles have appeared in such journals as *Church History, History of Religions, Speculum* and the *University of Toronto Quarterly*. He is the author of articles on "Mysticism, Christian" and "Monasticism East and West" (the latter with Donald K. Swearer) in the forthcoming *Dictionary of Living Religions* (Abingdon Press). At present he is preparing a book on the thought and spirituality of Hugh of St. Victor and is also editing some of his contemplative writings. He resides in Oberlin with his wife Mary and their two children Jennifer and Andrew.

PREFACE

The lengthy introduction which Professor Grover Zinn has given us, at the very outset of this book, makes perfectly clear the reasons why the texts of Richard of St. Victor, that he here presents, merited a choice place in a collection dedicated to the great classics of Western spirituality. The preface that he has asked of me can then only express, for this project carried out so well, the sympathy, esteem and interest that everyone must feel who is familiar with the works of Richard and who has admired their richness and depth.

Richard of St. Victor is, indeed, a great spiritual figure, perhaps one of the greatest, of a Christian medieval time that included so many. He early enjoyed, in this respect, an exceptional authority of which St. Bonaventure and Dante Alighieri, both justly cited by Professor Grover Zinn, are the most prestigious witnesses. He thus exercised, for several centuries, an influence that all the historians of Christian spirituality agree upon, but whose extent they certainly have not completely delineated. It must, however, be recognized that in spite of the favorable judgments continually accorded him, the spiritual teaching of Richard in modern times has been somewhat passed over and neglected. This relative depreciation, whose causes are worth analyzing, is probably due, on the one hand, to the progressive decline of the monastery where Richard, this *Scotus* come from Scotland or from Ireland, had set his destiny. The Abbey of Canons Regular of St. Victor of Paris doubtless persisted until the French Revolution. But during the two or three last centuries of its existence, it only counted a small number of monks. These did not succeed in sustaining and bringing to fruition the intellectual and spiritual patrimony bequeathed to them by their first fathers. They often left to others, when the time came, the task of printing the works which their glorious ancestors had left, whose manuscripts they kept in their rich library. But these editions, wherever they came from, incomplete and often faulty, seem to have quite early on repelled the readers which they aimed to reach. Everything suggests that from the end of the sixteenth century, or at all events from the seventeenth, only a few theologians or a few scholars continued to familiarize themselves with the writings of the great Victorines, and above all with those of Richard.

Nevertheless, for the last few decades the spiritual works which the latter left us have emerged bit by bit from the shadows to which they had been relegated. All who have reread them, all who have studied them, and who have given them a new scrutiny, have quickly realized that it was necessary to place again before a wide public the rediscovered texts which they had begun to enjoy. Several among them, in various countries, have since undertaken, hesitantly at first, then with increasing assurance, to translate at least some passages which they more particularly appreciated, often adding to their translations, introductions, notes or comments aimed to facilitate reading and to render more easily intelligible a spiritual teaching whose virtues were far from exhausted. To confine ourselves here to the English translations, credit must first be given to the *Selected Writings on Contemplation* of Richard of St. Victor, published in London in 1957 by Clare Kirchberger. This book offered a translation of long excerpts of two treatises to which were still given the titles *Benjamin Minor* and *Benjamin Major*, but which must be identified with the treatises on *The Twelve Patriarchs* and on *The Mystical Ark*, which Professor Grover Zinn offers here. To these extracts the book of Clare Kirchberger, however, added some others, much shorter, borrowed from lesser known works, but whose variety and interest contributed to giving a more precise idea of the spiritual density and the breadth of Richard's work. Three years later, in 1960, a publishing house, founded by expatriate Ukrainians, published at Anspach in Germany an English translation of *Benjamin Minor*, preceded by a short excerpt from *Benjamin Major*, from the pen of S. V. Yankowski. This translation, elegantly presented, is a credit to those who have had the courage to undertake it and to publish it in difficult circumstances. But, printed in a small edition, without any publicity, it had an almost confidential air and has not, in consequence, reached the large public it deserved.

The proof, in any case, has been given that the spiritual writings of Richard of St. Victor not only attract the attention of a few medievalists or historians of philosophy, theology or spirituality, but also continue to exercise a kind of attraction for many minds unwilling to read the Latin texts of the ancient editions, an attraction to which a response was necessary. Professor Grover Zinn must therefore be congratulated on giving to us here, in English translation, texts that count among the most important and pregnant which Richard has left us, and on doing it in circumstances which will assure these translations a wide diffusion. Above all, it will give satisfaction to find here, in complete form, the two great treatises on *The Twelve Patriarchs* and *The Mystical Ark*. It is in these, in fact, that Richard speaks with the greatest precision and depth about contemplation, its nature and its modes. The great Victorine offers in these some astonishing analyses. He observes and describes there, with extreme care, the progressive stages of this expansion of the field of consciousness which takes place throughout the contemplative ascent and which leads to what he calls enlarging, the lifting up and finally the alienation of the spirit. He is thus led to explain to us by what interior paths the spirit is led, under the action of grace, to transcend itself, even at times to tear apart the veils which habitually limit its horizon, and to glimpse, for brief moments, the light without limits whose brightness nothing obscures.

Such descriptions and such analyses can be disconcerting, sometimes dizzying. To comprehend their sense, however, their seriousness and extent, one must first remember that they give an account of contemplative experiences whose authenticity cannot be doubted. It is not, in fact, a matter of individual experience, uncontrolled and uncontrollable, but of experiences which Richard lived and of which he was the witness and confidant in the heart of a particularly fervent community of canons, whose fidelity to an austere rule, whose practice of the most traditional of spiritual exercises, and whose assiduity in liturgical prayer certainly prevented them from falling into illusion. On the other hand one cannot forget that Richard was himself an expert exegete and theologian. His teaching, in this Abbey of St. Victor which was also a school, was always unanimously appreciated and approved. His contemporaries always considered him as a guide both enlightened and safe. If his spiritual teaching has lately been somewhat neglected, it is only because it was no longer understood. Our time, avid for spiritual reflection, will rediscover its meaning. There is no doubt that the translations here published are both an invitation and a help for that.

The treatise of Richard of St. Victor on *The Trinity* has been more often studied and better understood than *The Twelve Patriarchs* and *The Mystical Ark*. All the same we must thank Professor Zinn for having here presented Book III, not only because these admirable pages, if I am not mistaken, have never before been translated into English, but also because there is found in them a theology of love which cannot be too much emphasized if one wishes really to understand the thought of the great Victorine. Richard, in fact, is not only the doctor of contemplation, he is also that of charity. In his brief treatise on *The Four Degrees of Violent Charity*, which unfortunately has not been able to be included here, he shows with admirable clarity the specific role played by charity in the contemplative ascent. But in Book III of his treatise on *The Trinity* he shows to what point a deep pondering on the nature and demands of love can illuminate the fathomless mystery of God in three persons. Love is, in fact, gift and exchange. If then God is love, there meet in Him a plurality of persons without which there could be neither gift nor exchange. Certain theologians, it is true, have been upset by Richard's arguments. They have feared that he has been trying to demonstrate rationally a mystery which can only be known to us through revelation. But these fears are only the result of a misunderstanding. Richard, like every Christian, knows perfectly well that the mystery of the Trinity is inaccessible to human reason. The demonstration which he proposes, evoking the "necessary reasons" of which Anselm of Canterbury had spoken before him, is that of a contemplative whose meditation has so familiarized him with the three divine persons that they have become more present to him than he is to himself. It is, then, in the spirit in which Richard of St. Victor has written these pages that one must, still today, undertake their reading. They will illumine with a light not to be found elsewhere all who wish to turn their gaze to heaven and fix it on the Absolute.

Jean Châtillon

This book
is
dedicated
to

Clyde A. Holbrook
Danforth Professor of Religion, Emeritus
in Oberlin College

and

Charles T. Murphy
Graves Professor of Classics, Emeritus
in Oberlin College

friends
colleagues
fellow pilgrims

FOREWORD

In the course of bringing a work such as this to fruition many debts are incurred. Now it is my privilege to thank those persons who have rendered assistance in so many ways. To Richard Payne, Editor-in-Chief of the "Classics of Western Spirituality" I owe a great debt of gratitude. He suggested that I undertake this translation, and as the idea has become a reality I have benefitted at every stage from his professional insight, his understanding of spiritual traditions, and his valued friendship. Professor Jean Châtillon of the Institut Catholique, Paris, has honored me by providing the preface of the volume. But more than that, I, like all medievalists, am indebted to him for his exacting scholarship over the years. He has revealed to us in articles, editions, and books the riches of the Victorine tradition and twelfth-century spirituality. Professor Châtillon was kind enough to send me his critical Latin text of *The Twelve Patriarchs* which has served as the basis for my translation. His edition, with French translation, will appear soon in *Sources chrétiennes*. Professor Charles Murphy of Oberlin graciously spent many hours with me reading through the texts of *The Twelve Patriarchs* and *The Mystical Ark*. I have benefitted greatly from his profound knowledge of Latin and his felicitous phrasing of difficult passages. Over the years I have discussed the Victorines with Ewert Cousins on many occasions. I can only trust that he sees the fruit of some of those discussions in this work. In addition, he read through the translation of *The Trinity*. Dean John Leyerle of the University of Toronto made invaluable suggestions when some of the ideas in the introduction were first being formulated. From my colleagues William Hood and Allen Frantzen I received helpful suggestions at crucial junctures. Kathryn Cousins has indexed the volume with great skill. Those valiant individuals who helped read proof remain nameless here, but their names are written in the book of my memory. Linda Clarke typed the manuscript with her usual skill and speed, while Barbara Turek and Linda Miller assisted at various times. Mary Mel, whose husband I am, has provided me with many delightful conversations and much love while this book was in the process of coming to be. Jennifer and Andrew brought the delight and occasional consternation which only children can give, while Ginger, our cocker spaniel, made certain I took my daily walks.

INTRODUCTION

Richard of St. Victor (d. 1173) must by any account be seen as a major spiritual writer of the 12th century—and of any century. Saluted by Dante as being "in contemplation more than human" (*Paradiso* 11:132), Richard was recognized by Saint Bonaventure in the 13th century as the "modern" master of contemplation who equalled the greatest contemplative writer among the ancient fathers, Dionysius the pseudo-Areopagite (De reductione artium ad theologiam 5). Often overshadowed in later centuries by the figure of St. Bernard of Clairvaux and considered by some scholars, unfortunately, as more versed in the theory than the practice of contemplation, Richard has not always received his due. Any attentive reader of his works will, however, recognize in them the spirit of one who was an experienced contemplative, an exceedingly skilled theologian and preacher and an unusually sensitive guide along the spiritual journey.

During Richard's lifetime the theory and practice of contemplation (we would say mysticism today) were topics of widespread interest. New religious reforms and new orders were coming into existence with a greater emphasis upon the contemplative life, while Bernard of Clairvaux and William of St. Thierry, among others, were subjecting that life to a new analysis and exposition. Few if any periods in the history of Western religion have seen a comparable concentration of either spiritual masters or writings on the topic. Richard of St. Victor was one of the first writers to compose a systematic work intended to instruct others in the practice of contemplative asceticism. In earlier centuries Augustine, Gregory the Great, Peter Damian and other monastic authors had written, often extensively, on the discipline necessary for prayer and contemplation and also on contemplation itself. But their contributions tended to be of a more personal nature, being in the main remarks, comments, and recollections scattered in commentaries, sermons and treatises. Their writings did not systematically teach a form for discipline of self leading to interior quiet and contemplation. Nor did they subject the contemplative experience to a thorough reflective analysis. In the Western Church it remained for the 12th-century mystical writers to gather up a wealth of inherited material, combine it with their own experiences and observations, and begin a systematic literary presentation of the ascetic life and a careful analysis of contemplative experiences. In Richard's writings we find some of the best examples of this attempt to systematize and teach the discipline that leads to contemplation. Not only were they effective in the immediate context of the Abbey of St. Victor; their influence was widely felt throughout the medieval period by successive generations of contemplatives and contemplative writers.

As scholars have pointed out in recent years, the 12th century was a decisive turning point in the spirituality of the medieval period. The distinctive elements of almost all later medieval spirituality and piety were formulated then, especially such things as interiorization, affective piety, an emphasis on experience, the elaboration of patterns of contemplation and stress on the individual. Richard of St. Victor played no small role in the elaboration of these and other aspects of medieval spirituality.[1]

The Abbey of St. Victor grew out of a foundation by William of Champeaux.[2] When William retired from his position as a master in the schools of Paris in 1108 he set up a small community at the site of a hermitage on the left bank of the Seine just outside the walls of Paris. The community grew, and when William departed to become Bishop of Chalons in 1113, the community elected Gil-

---

1. See the illuminating comments and summary of past scholarship on the role of 12th-century spirituality in medieval developments in Giles Constable, "Twelfth-Century Spirituality and the late Middle Ages," *Medieval and Renaissance Studies* 5, ed. O. B. Hardison, Jr. (Chapel Hill, North Carolina, 1971), pp. 27–60.

2. A summary of what is known of Richard's life is in Gervais Dumeige, *Richard de Saint-Victor et l'idée chrétienne de l'amour* (Paris, 1952), pp. 166–167. Dumeige also has an exhaustive bibliography of editions of Richard's works and of secondary literature with some annotations.

duin as its first abbot. Under Gilduin's leadership the abbey flourished, for he was a leader capable of organizing and administering the abbey internally as well as gaining externally the support of the king and others for the new religious community. St. Victor was in the forefront of the movement to renew the life of cloistered religious discipline under the aegis of the Rule of St. Augustine. It also maintained a vigorous intellectual life, open to the new theological developments in the schools of Paris, developments that monastics, Benedictine and Cistercian alike, tended to shun. The leading intellect of the first generation of Victorines was Hugh of St. Victor. He founded the distinctive Victorine tradition, which combined a vigorous program of Bible study, serious and creative theological investigation and disciplined pursuit of contemplation, all set in the context of a community oriented towards liturgical regularity and shared experience. William of Champeaux laid the foundations, but it was with the inspired and inspiring leadership of Hugh and Gilduin that the abbey rose to the place of prominence it had in the 12th century.

Almost nothing is known about the life of Richard of St. Victor.[3] His place of birth seems to have been in Scotland, but of his early life we have no information. He came to the Abbey of St. Victor sometime in the early 1150s and one must assume he was a young man at the time. Although he was the heir to Hugh of St. Victor in the Victorine contemplative tradition, Richard's discipleship was carried on from a literary tradition, for Hugh died in 1141, some ten or more years before Richard came to St. Victor. However, it is probable that Richard arrived before the death of the first abbot, Gilduin, in 1155. If so, he had contact with one of the great founders of the Victorine tradition, a man who had been influential in forming the climate of the community.

---

3. For the most complete study of the early years of the abbey, see Jean Châtillon, *Théologie, spiritualité et métaphysique dans l'oeuvre oratoire d'Achard de Saint-Victor* (Études de philosophie médiévale 58; Paris, 1969), pp. 53–85. For the abbacy of Ernisius see Jean Châtillon in the introduction to Richard of St. Victor, *L'édit d'Alexandre ou les trois processions. Sermons et opuscules spirituels inédits* (Bruges, 1951), I, xxxvi–xl. See also Richard of St. Victor, *Selected Writings on Contemplation*, trans. Claire Kirchberger (London, 1957), 7–10. The history of the abbey by F. Bonnard is still valuable: *Histoire de l'abbaye royale et d l'ordre des channoines réguliers de Saint-Victor de Paris* (Paris, 1904–1907). The wider history of the movement of the Augustinian Canons is treated in J. C. Dickinson, *The Origins of the Austin Canons and their Introduction into England* (London, 1950).

Richard flourished at St. Victor. He rose rapidly to positions of responsibility, holding the office of subprior by the year 1159. In 1162 he was elected prior, an office he held until his death in 1173. For other reasons 1162 was to be an unfortunate year, for a new abbot, Ernisius, was elected. His abbacy can only be called a disaster. He squandered valuable resources on unnecessary projects and fomented strife within the cloister by appointing his favorites to offices and acting in prejudicial ways. In reading the Victorine *Customary* drawn up during Gilduin's time, one is struck by the power wielded in many ways, in major questions and minor details, by the abbot at St. Victor. Richard must have found it difficult on more than one occasion to be the second-ranking official in the abbey under such a person. Ernisius was finally removed from office by papal action in 1171. Richard had precious little time left to live in peace, for he died two years later.

Richard was thus something of a "second generation" figure at St. Victor and in the 12th-century renewal of spirituality generally. Bernard of Clairvaux died in 1153, which was, as we have seen, about the time that Richard entered St. Victor. At this point Hugh had been dead over 10 years, Gilduin's abbacy was drawing to a close and a new generation of Victorines was moving into the picture. The same was true of the situation in the Cistercian abbeys and in the schools of Paris. Richard quickly became the chief exponent of Victorine spirituality in the second half of the 12th century. He carried on and developed the tradition of a Biblically based, liturgically sensitive and theologically sophisticated spirituality established by Hugh. Richard also made use of the writings and insights of Dionysius the pseudo-Areopagite. Here he was again under the distinct influence of Hugh, for the earlier Victorine had brought Dionysius into the mainstream of thought with his commentary on the *Celestial Hierarchies*. [4]

Later generations saw Richard as a gifted "specialist" in mysticism. Bonaventure, writing in the 13th century, recognized him as

---

4. On the use of Dionysius in the 12th century, see M.-D. Chenu, *La théologie au douzième siècle* (Études de philosophie médiévale 45; Paris, 1957), chaps. 5, 7, 8, and 13. On the Victorine use, see Grover A. Zinn, Jr., "Book and Word, The Victorine Background of Bonaventure's Use of Symbols," *S. Bonaventure 1274–1974* (Rome: Grottaferrata, 1974), II, pp. 145–146, with bibliography. See also Kirchberger's treatment of the Dionysian influence on Richard in the introduction to *Selected Writings on Contemplation*, pp. 47–56.

the modern master, as we noted above. Richard's influence on Bonaventure and the Franciscan tradition was profound, for in the *Itinerarium mentis in Deum* the pattern of six kinds of contemplation is taken from Richard while other themes, images and essential elements reveal Victorine influences.[5] English mystical writers also owed much to Richard. *The Cloud of Unknowing* has Richard's writings as one of the major sources, along with St. Augustine, St. Bernard, and Dionysius the pseudo-Areopagite. Walter Hilton, author of *Scale of Perfection*, also appears to have known the works of Richard, but the borrowings are not so clear as they are in *The Cloud*. By the middle of the 14th century *The Twelve Patriarchs* (*Benjamin minor*) had been translated into English in the form of an abridged paraphrase. Lines of influence can also be traced in the works of German and Flemish mystics, Tauler, Ruysbroek, Denys the Carthusian, and finally Harphius (Herp).[6]

Among Spanish writers indebted to Richard was Bernardino de Laredo.[7] St. Teresa of Avila read his *Ascent of Mount Sion* in 1556 and found insights that gave her an understanding of the crisis she was experiencing in her spiritual life. The guidance offered by Laredo's book marked a turning point for St. Teresa and from this time on she grew increasingly in the contemplative life. In the first edition of the *Ascent*, published in 1535, Bernardino used Richard's treatises on *The Mystical Ark* and *The Twelve Patriarchs* as his only major sources. Revising the work for a second edition in 1538, Bernardino shifted his dependence. Richard was still quoted in important ways, but Hugh of Balma and Harphius (Herp) became major sources. These two men tended to stress the "affective way" in prayer and contemplation, as opposed to what some have called

---

5. Clues for Richard's influence on Bonaventure are indicated in Bernard McGinn, "Ascension and Introversion in the *Itinerarium Mentis in Deum*," *S. Bonaventure 1274–1974* (Rome: Grottaferrata, 1974), III, pp. 535–552. The relation of the six stages or levels in Richard and Bonaventure was shown by F. Andres, "Die Stufen der Contemplatio in Bonaventuras Itinerarium mentis ad Deum und in Benjamin major des Richards von St. Viktor," *Franziskanische Studien* 8 (1921): 189–200.

6. The influence on English mystical writers is given in Kirchberger, *Selected Writings on Contemplation*, pp. 65–74. For important comments on the influence of Richard on later medieval mystics, see Giles Constable, "The Popularity of Twelfth-Century Spiritual Writers in the Late Middle Ages," *Renaissance Studies in Honor of Hans Baron* (Florence, 1971), pp. 5–28; and "Twelfth-Century Spirituality and the Late Middle Ages."

7. See the comments on sources in the introduction to Bernardino de Laredo, *The Ascent of Mount Sion*, trans. E. Allison Peers (London, 1952), pp. 43–48.

the "intellectual approach" of Richard. The shift of dependence is clear; however the distinction between the intellectual and the affective with respect to Richard may not be as clear as some would like to think. Especially in *The Mystical Ark* there are some passages that marvelously express the affective, not intellective, approach to prayer and contemplation under the rubrics of "devotion" and "exultation."

The works that are translated in the present volume were probably written in the order in which they appear here. Most of Richard's treatises are difficult to date accurately and cannot be placed precisely in any sort of relative chronological order.[8] The best current estimates would place *The Twelve Patriarchs* and *The Mystical Ark* between 1153 and 1162, the year Richard became prior, although there is no real way to exclude a later date. The very interesting *Allegories of the Tabernacle of the Covenant* clearly depends upon *The Mystical Ark*, although there are significant additions of material dealing with the symbolic significance of the structure of the tabernacle and an interpretation of the table of shewbread. These speak to a recurring Victorine theme of the correlation of knowledge and virtue, this time set in the context of a discussion of the senses of Scripture and the responsibilities of the preacher. *On the Trinity* is accepted by Dumeige as a work of Richard's mature years.

With respect to *The Twelve Patriarchs* and *The Mystical Ark*, it seems most probable from the contents that the work on the patriarchs was written first. Certainly we find the kind of discipline outlined there to be presupposed in *The Mystical Ark* 1:2, where Jacob and Rachel are mentioned. In *De exterminatione mali et promotione boni* (3:6) there is a comment referring to an earlier interpretation of the twelve children of Jacob, a reference that surely has *The Twelve Patriarchs* in mind. However, one cannot determine with certainty if *The Mystical Ark* also preceded *De exterminatione*. The chapter on contemplation in the latter work lacks the precision of books 4 and 5 of the ark treatise. It also emphasizes the aspect of being outwardly "asleep" and inwardly "awake" in contemplation,

---

8. On chronology, see Dumeige, *Richard de Saint-Victor*, pp. 168–169; also Jean Châtillon, "De Guillaume de Champeaux à Thomas Gallus: chronique d'histoire littéraire et doctrinale de l'École de Saint-Victor," *Revue du moyen âge latin* 8 (1952): 259–60.

a motif that appears in *The Mystical Ark*, but in a subordinate role. It is not unreasonable to see *The Mystical Ark* as a more developed and mature work on the varieties of contemplative experience.

The titles we have given to these first two works are the titles by which they were commonly referred to in manuscripts of medieval authors. In the modern period *The Twelve Patriarchs* has usually been called *Benjamin minor*, while *The Mystical Ark* has been titled *Benjamin major*. In addition to their faithfulness to the medieval tradition, the titles we use herein are accurate reflections of the dominant images in the two works. The first is a tropological interpretation of the significance of the twelve sons, and one daughter, of Jacob. The second offers a subtle tropological interpretation of the Ark of the Covenant and the seraphim placed within the Tabernacle of Moses. However, the subtitles found in the Minge edition indicate the intentions of the treatises quite well. The first reads: "Of the preparation of the soul for contemplation"; the second, "Of the grace of contemplation." The first treatise does deal directly with the preparation of mind and body for contemplation through the redirection of the mind and will, the goal being the achievement of quiet and peace in both body and mind. Contemplation is treated in only the last few chapters of *The Twelve Patriarchs*, but in *The Mystical Ark* the entire treatise is a complex and brilliant analysis of the varieties of contemplation, their possible objects, and the means, human and divine, for attaining such states of awareness.

Although Richard meant his teaching for regular canons living under the Rule of St. Augustine at St. Victor, there is a universalism in what he has to say. His comments are specific, but they are directed toward individual experience and not toward the formation of a particular institutional form of disciplined life. We find out little if anything concerning specific details of life at St. Victor in *The Twelve Patriarchs*. What we do discover, however, is a very penetrating analysis of a particular scheme of discipline through which people may pass in pursuing outer and interior recollection and, ultimately, contemplation. In addition there are, as the reader will see, very pertinent comments on particularly effective means of either advancing or retarding others on this spiritual path. The works of Richard are thoroughly practical in their intent. He makes subtle and often complex sets of distinctions after the manner of the emerging contemporary scholasticism. Yet this logic of distinctions and divisions is always in the service of understanding experience. Indeed, his divisions and subdivisions are really the means to a more coherent and unified understanding of a wide range of human experiences, from the sensual perception of the world and ourselves, through mental operations, to visions and various kinds of contemplation.

In connection with the theme of universalism, we should note that our translation has followed Richard in his use of the male pronoun and the reference to "man" (*vir*) *Homo* has been usually translated "person" throughout. The translator trusts that the reader will perceive that although Richard addressed a community of men, the character of the contemplative practice he describes is open to male and female alike. In a translation of this sort the complications of changing the gender, or of avoiding it altogether, seemed likely to create more problems in the translation than were warrented.

In his concern for individual experience Richard reflects the emphasis on individual awareness that characterized much of 12th-century thought, from Peter Abelard to the troubadors. It is also clear that he was very interested in what we would call the psychological dimension of experience. He did not, however, reduce experience to mere psychological states, but rather sought to identify and clarify various psychological states one might associate with various kinds of experience.

Richard's awareness of the individual does not mean "individualism" however. He is very much concerned with the relationships between persons, as the present treatises show. Moreover he may be expressing in his own way a feature of the spirituality of regular canons that has been singled out recently as the most distinctive element in their life-style.[9] Regular canons, unlike Benedictine and Cistercian monks in the 12th century, had a deep and abiding concern for relations between persons in the cloister and the obligation of each to care about and teach the other. Bene-

---

9. For a study of the spirituality of regular canons stressing this perspective, see Caroline W. Bynum, "The Spirituality of Regular Canons in the Twelfth Century: A New Approach," *Medievalia et Humanistica* 4 (1973): 3–24.

dictines and Cistercians thought of spiritual development as a supremely individual affair between God and the person, with little reference to good for others. Canons, on the other hand, tended to stress personal example.

One of Richard's most profound expositions of the relationship of individuality and community is contained in Book 3 of *On the Trinity*. In reflecting on the nature of divine perfection and the presence of charity, he shows that not only are two persons necessary for love, but three are necessary for the fullest of all loves, charity. Unless love is not only given and received but also *shared in community* it cannot be called true charity. While Richard has in mind the nature of supreme goodness and perfect charity, he clearly has human goodness and charity in mind as well. If the ultimate perfection of God is one in which charity and a shared love among three persons are necessary, how can the perfection of the human being, who is created *ad imagem Dei*, embody less than this same ideal of shared love? Just as *one* divine person who lived as a solitary, a hermit (*On the Trinity* 3:18) could not have true fullness of charity if there were no second person to love, and no third person to share the delights of that love with, so the person who lives alone (or lives in community *as if* he or she were alone) cannot pretend to have that full charity which is love of God and neighbor.

Richard's concern for individuals in community also comes out repeatedly in *The Twelve Patriarchs*, as we shall note; in his emphasis on preaching at the conclusion of *Allegories of the Tabernacle of Moses*; in his insistence that the office of spiritual leadership demands of clerics that they be versed if possible in the superior kinds of contemplation so that they may lead the individuals under their care out of Egypt, the house of bondage, through the danger of the wilderness, and to the joys and delights of the Promised Land (*The Mystical Ark*, 4:21); and in his insistence at the conclusion of the *Four Degrees of Violent Charity* (paragraphs 42–47) that in the fourth degree of charity not only is the soul reborn, renewed and reformed to the image and similitude of God, but it now takes on the form of Christ's humility and servanthood, becoming all things to all men, seeking to bring others to spiritual maturity, and fearing nothing in this new life.

When mentioning Richard's emphasis on the individual, one

ought not to neglect a theme that was so crucial for him and for many other 12th-century writers, from Abelard in his *Ethics* to St. Bernard in his sermons: the idea of self-knowledge, coupled with notions such as the freedom of the will and the importance of personal intention. These imply a renewed focus upon the nature of the person and the development of a certain consciousness of the interior self, and they are also brought into relationship with the new ideas on love. Only if one fully knows the self can a person begin to know spiritual realities, insists Richard. Indeed, full self-knowledge is both the culmination of all discipline and the virtue that guides the others. Furthermore, this emphasis on the self and the nature of intention led to a new emphasis on the significance of interior disposition as the foundation of all right action, a development that can be seen in such diverse figures as Hugh of St. Victor and Peter Abelard. A similar point of view can be found in Richard's writings when he castigates those persons who are shamed by barbarisms in speech or by nudity of body (i.e., adherence to exterior rules) rather than being shamed by improper thoughts or poverty of spirit (i.e., interior states). He also distinguishes between the external state of being ashamed of being *caught* in the act of sin and the internal state of being ashamed of the sin itself (*The Twelve Patriarchs*, chapters 46 and 47).

In *The Twelve Patriarchs* the successive stages of awareness and discipline, as well as contemplative experience, are presented by Richard via personification allegory, a form of symbolic expression as common in the Middle Ages as it is rare today.[10] The figures for the personifications are drawn from Scripture and are interpreted according to the tropological, or moral, sense widely used in medieval Biblical interpretation. Two Biblical narratives are involved in the personification allegory in *The Twelve Patriarchs*. The first is the story of the birth of twelve sons—the twelve patriarchs—and one daughter to Jacob, his two wives and their handmaids. The second is the narrative of the disciples' experience of Jesus' transfiguration. In the first case, Richard takes the sequence of births as the basis for a sequence of stages in discipline

---

10. Some of the analysis of *The Twelve Patriarchs* and *The Mystical Ark* is drawn from my earlier article "Personification Allegory and Visions of Light in Richard of St. Victor's Teaching on Contemplation," *University of Toronto Quarterly* 46 (1977): 190–214.

and development personified by each of the children. Events associated with each birth, the child's name (traditionally a source of deeper meaning), characteristics of the person assigned in the Blessing of Jacob and events in each life provide the material for tropological interpretation. In the case of the transfiguration the experiences of the disciples in climbing the mountain, resting on the top, seeing Jesus transfigured into a being of light and then falling senseless when they hear the voice of the Father from the luminous cloud provide events in the "history" of the disciples' lives that evoke by means of symbolic interpretation certain experiences in the ascetic and contemplative quest. In each case it is the material of the historical sense that forms the basis for the deeper meaning, a point of view characteristic of Victorine exegesis.[11] Persons, actions, or other "circumstances" provide the basis for spiritual or symbolic interpretation. Richard's personifications, it should be noted, are not artificial constructions with clothing, facial expressions, demeanor and actions selected to convey "inner" characteristics, as are personifications in such excellent literary examples of Christian personification allegory as Prudentius' *Psychomachia*, written in the 4th century, and Alain de Lille's *Anticlaudianus*, written about ten years after Richard's death. Richard's personifications are Biblical characters, connected by a historical narrative that has significant relationships. A sequence of events in the external world becomes symbolic of a sequence of events in the inner life of a person. Some interpretations may seem forced to the modern reader, but on the whole the work bears the mark of intent reflection on the significance of a Biblical narrative as the symbolic embodiment of the pattern of discipline and awareness of self and God that comprises the Christian's ascent from fear of God to loving and joyful contemplation.

In the figures of Jacob, his wives, and their handmaids Richard finds an entire epistemology signified. Jacob, father of the twelve patriarchs, represents the "rational soul." His two wives represent the principle powers of the soul. Rachel is reason; Leah, affection, which includes will, emotion and sensibility. Rachel, reason, leads

---

11. On Victorine exegesis, see Beryl Smalley, *The Study of the Bible in the Middle Ages*, 2nd ed. (Oxford, 1952), esp. chap. 3. For penetrating remarks on tropology and symbolism, see Jean Châtillon in Richard of St. Victor, *Sermons et opuscules spirituels inédits*, I, pp. xlvi–l.

to all truth. From Leah, affection, comes all virtue. Rachel's hand-maid Bala signifies imagination, which links reason to the world of sense perception through the formation of images of things. Leah's handmaid Zelpha represents the five bodily senses, which connect affection with the external world. In these personifications and their relations Richard represents his epistemology, made vivid with sensible images of persons. As he works out the details of their relations he etches in basic outline his concept of the mind and will in relation to self and world. This effective and persuasive use of personification is only the beginning of what becomes in the end a magnificent *tour-de-force*. Richard's characterization of Bala as being like an old man or woman who continues to talk or tell a story even when no one is listening may not be to everyone's liking, but nevertheless it conveys in a succinct image a truth about the irrepressible nature of imagination and the difficulty of "silencing" it.

Here Richard draws inspiration from the tradition that saw Leah and Rachel as figures of the active and contemplative lives, respectively. Also, the names of the twelve sons had long been taken to have spiritual meanings, although interpretations differed. Augustine and Gregory the Great formulated the typology of Rachel and Leah for the medieval West, with Leah signifying an active life of engagement with the world in service, preaching and the like, and Rachel signifying the withdrawn life of prayer, asceticism and contemplation.[12] Richard departs from this usual typology by interpreting the two women not within a dialectic of engagement with and withdrawal from the world, but within a dialectic of the discipline of body and mind as virtues are acquired in one unified life that involves elements of both withdrawal and engagement in community.

He draws on the distinction of action and contemplation contained in the writings of the 5th-century monastic writer John Cassian, who transmitted many of the basic ideas of the early Egyptian, Palestinian and Greek monastics to the West. For Cassian, the

---

12. See Dom Cuthbert Butler, *Western Mysticism* (New York, 1966), pp. 157–188; also p. 204 on Cassian: "Cassian's actual [active] life is not the same as the active life defined by St. Gregory, though to some extent the two are coincident. The actual life is ethical training and self-discipline, and may, but does not necessarily, include the good works of the active life." On Cassian, see also Owen Chadwick, *John Cassian*, 2nd ed. (Cambridge, 1968), pp. 92–109.

active life is the pursuit of virtue, leading to an ordered and recollected life that may or may not involve service to others. The contemplative life is the pursuit of the higher states of spiritual awareness and builds upon the discipline of the active life. It is a sign of Richard's genius that he takes this twofold scheme of active and contemplative, which emerged in the context of the pursuit of individual perfection, and makes it the scheme for the pursuit of a perfection that integrates themes of individuality and community at a profound level. Indeed, for Richard the most perfect examples of "active" engagement with others in spiritual guidance, pastoral care and preaching come not as part of the discipline of the self, but as the result of the transformation wrought in contemplation, especially in its ecstatic forms.

The reader of *The Twelve Patriarchs* soon discovers that the grouping of Jacob's children according to mothers is significant, for these groups represent successive stages in the contemplative quest. The six children of Leah are virtues that discipline the will; those of Bala govern thoughts; Zelpha's children control deeds; and Rachel's two offspring, born last, respectively oversee the entire life of asceticism and signify contemplation.

It is proper that Leah's six children represent virtues governing the will, for, as Richard says, a virtue is nothing other than a properly ordered and moderated affection. Order is important, for each virtue must be acquired in proper sequence and in relationship to the others: To have hope of God's forgiveness before one possesses true fear of God and grief for sin is to have presumption, not proper hope (chapter 7). Moderation is equally necessary, since a virtue carried to excess becomes a vice: Excessive fear can become despair; unnecessary hope, dissolution; intemperate hatred of vices, fury (chapter 66).

The first four children born to Leah can be seen as representing a growing awareness of the transcendent world of spiritual reality, the beginning of moral reform and a redirection of individual intention. Ruben, the firstborn, represents Fear of God, the recognition of the distance between Creator and creature, Judge and sinner. Then come Simeon, representing Grief, and Levi, Hope of forgiveness. At this point Richard introduces a number of notions drawn from 12th-century penitential practice. Finally, Judah is born, representing Love of God (*amor Dei*), the culmination of this initial stage. In a moving and felicitous way Richard describes this first awakening of love in terms of a spiritual friendship (*amicitia*), thus drawing on the theme of friendship being revived in monastic and secular circles in the 12th century:

> *From this time on a kind of intimacy begins to arise between God and the soul, and friendship begins to be established because the soul often feels itself to be visited by God and from His advent not so much now to be consoled but on the contrary sometimes to be filled with a kind of ineffable joy. . . . The true spouse of the soul is God, who we truly join with us from this time on when we adhere to Him through true love. (chapter 11)*

A similar progression from fear through grief to love is found as the first stage of the spiritual journey in Hugh of St. Victor's *De arca Noe morali* and *De arca Noe mystica*, making it probable that Richard was inspired by his spiritual mentor in this patterning.

Now an individual has not only been awakened to the world of spirit; he or she has begun to long ardently to know God more fully and to love Him more deeply. With intention strengthened, one must undertake discipline of imagination and sensation, the handmaids of reason and affection. Only after this can the remaining two children of Leah be born, for they are virtues that represent increasing maturity in the disciplined life of contemplative longing.

Imagination, personified by Bala the handmaid of Rachel, is a very important faculty in Richard's psychology. It is a link between reason and the external world, since it conveys to reason what the bodily senses experience. In a very vivid way Richard describes how the handmaid is always rushing back and forth between her secluded mistress and the world; moreover she does not know when to be quiet or when to leave her mistress alone. Imagination is terribly difficult to silence (chapters 5 and 6). Imagination has a second function: As the faculty that presents images of the visible world, it provides the foundation for the knowledge of invisible spiritual truths via similitudes drawn from visible things (chapter 5). Richard puts it rather bluntly:

> *No one is ignorant that this [imagination] is the first way for all those*

who enter into contemplation of invisible things, unless perhaps experience has not yet instructed him with a view to this knowledge. (chapter 14)

Dan, the first son of Bala, represents the literal use of images of present things to represent other material things, without any hint of the figurative use of symbol here. Richard has particularly in mind the representation of the evils of punishment in Gehenna in eternity. But Dan also represents an especially creative use of visual images in the continual struggle against wandering and illicit thoughts and visualizations. Richard relates that there are certain holy men who, when they experience the tendency of imagination to represent illicit delights and shameful thoughts even during times of prayer, immediately visualize the images of future punishment as a counteraction of imagination to banish improper thoughts and the like (chapter 20). Here in a particularly striking passage we find Richard indicating, briefly but pointedly, a useful technique for establishing control of the imagination.

Naphtali, the second son, has a name that means comparison. He signifies the use of visible things to represent invisible, spiritual truths, especially the goods of eternal life. These representations may be by means of real things, used symbolically, or by means of fictive things such as golden streets and gates of pearl.

Two kinds of representation are distinguished: one is comparison (*comparatio*); the other, translation (*translatio*) or conversion (*conversio*) (chapter 22). In comparison a natural phenomenon, such as the brightness of the sun, leads to consideration of the much greater brightness of the light to be shared with the angels in heaven. Translation, or conversion, involves the deeper sense of Scripture. That God lives in "light inaccessible" leads to the deeper sense that such a light is properly interpreted as "the very wisdom of God." In short, by *comparison* Richard means something like our use of analogy to describe what the invisible goods of heaven must be, by reference to similar but lesser goods in this world. Conversion or translation, however, is directly related to the spiritual senses of Scripture, allegory and tropology, and it has a very distinct place in the pursuit of truth. Scripture is unique among books, for it alone has this kind of deeper sense. However, comparison is equally rooted in the Victorine conception of the universe as a kind of book in which there are manifestations of divine truth, accessible to the imagination since they are material realities, capable of carrying a deeper sense because of divine intention, but now obscured by the results of the fall and the weakness of the eye of reason. Rightly ordered and used however, the imagination can be a valuable and essential faculty in service of the pursuit of contemplation. Rather than reject material symbols, Richard finds them to be an important avenue to truth. They are the way in which all persons must begin to think about divine things. Also, they offer a way, a symbolic way, of speaking about what must otherwise remain unexpressed and uncommunicated.

The next children are born to Leah's handmaid, Zelpha, and represent discipline of the senses. Gad personifies Abstinence and Asher, Patience. The rigorous discipline they introduce results in detachment from both desires for worldly pleasure and fears of life's calamities and pains. Their purpose is to establish detachment and distance between the person and the world. In relating to the world one becomes indifferent to either pleasure or pain. Detachment, not total withdrawal, is the goal.

Together with the sons of Bala (Dan and Naphtali), Gad and Asher are called the defenders of the citadel of the soul.[11a] This theme of a castle and its defense was destined to become an important motif in later mystical writing. For Richard the defense must be both internal and external, for there are enemies within as well as without. By proper discipline and detachment, sense experience and the imagination become positive supports of and not impediments to the contemplative pursuit. In this process of discipline, control of imagination is essential and fundamental. In insisting on the priority of controlling imagination over that of controlling the body, Richard may seem to reverse much ascetic practice. However, Richard understood the basic role played by imagination and thinking. There must necessarily be a fundamental reordering of thought and inner intention before outer stillness and detachment can be effected. Indeed, outer stillness can be deceptive. In *The*

11a. The symbolic theme of the citadel of the soul and its defence as found in the Victorines and other winters is discussed in Ford Lewis Battles, "Hugo of Saint Victor as Moral Allegorist," *Church History* 18 (1949): 220–240.

INTRODUCTION

Mystical Ark 1:3 Richard points out that there are many persons who cannot be still in their minds even though they are still in their bodies.

Following the birth of the children representing discipline of imagination and sensation, three children representing the last of the seven virtues are born to Leah. As a group they personify increasing maturity in disciplined awareness of self. Issachar, Joy of Interior Sweetness, is born first. He represents fleeting experiences of stability and true joy in contemplation. Issachar lives as an exile, a wanderer. He is almost but not quite detached from the love of this world and almost but not quite ready to enter into the state of tranquillity of mind and stability of heart that is the goal of discipline. Poised between two worlds, he longs for the fatherland from which he is estranged and to which he is drawn by fervent desire.

The effective way in which Richard takes elements of the Biblical text related to Issachar and makes them the basis of a personification suggests that the personifications may function in two ways. First of all there is the obvious use of Biblical figures to express and relate various states of mind and will, a most valuable way of drawing out the dimensions of the spiritual life. There is, however, another side to this. In realizing a particular state, the initiate can view his or her state as being that of the Biblical character: The rank beginner "becomes" Ruben, Fear of God; as love of God is born, one is Judah; in beginning the ascent to knowledge of God via images, one identifies with Naphtali. The list could be lengthened, but the point should be obvious. Richard has provided archetypes for interpreting experiences, and these archetypes are drawn from the repertoire of persons who are significant in sacred history. This same use can be found in *The Mystical Ark*, where Abraham, Moses, Peter, the Queen of Sheba and others personify and represent symbolically aspects of the spiritual quest and contemplative experience.

Hatred of Vices is the sixth virtue. Personified by Zabulon whose name means "the dwelling place of fortitude," this virtue concerns not only the self and sin but also the spiritual nurture of others and a concern for community. In this virtue Richard reveals a balanced appreciation of the problem of a failure to criticize for fear of disrupting a community of brotherly love and the equally

17

serious problem of unwarranted zeal and misguided harshness in reproving vices. Above all Hatred of Vices is not meant to provide an opportunity for the self-righteous critic who destroys persons through hatred of vice. Criticism must have restoration as its final end. Furthermore it must be informed by a commitment to protect the weaker brethren from occasions of failure. Also, the effective critic must be able to take into account individual differences and varying situations. There can be no inflexible standard for all. In addition, one must always recognize that mature contemplatives as well as beginners need to be on guard against errors in thought and deed. The degree of advancement is no guarantee of proof against fault.

Leah's last child is a daughter, Dina, personifying Shame. She receives a more extensive presentation than any other child, indicating Richard's concern with this virtue (chapters 45–59). Like the others, Shame must be born at the proper time. One can have true shame only after hating vice. It is one thing to be ashamed of being caught and exposed in vice; it is quite another thing to be ashamed of the sin itself. Here Richard has put bluntly the vast difference between outward appearance and inner attitude. He also gives a penetrating analysis of the kinds of things about which one can be ashamed: ragged clothes or an impoverished moral sense; errors in speaking or worthless thoughts. We see here Richard's keen eye for spiritual deceit and false pretenses. No doubt he hit home with these comments.

Two events in Dina's life offer brilliant representations of crises in the ascetic life. First, the rape of Dina by Sichem (Love of Vain Glory), the son of Emor (Love of One's Own Excellence), provides an occasion to consider the dangers of spiritual pride and egotism. Second, the brutal murder of Sichem and his men by Simeon and Levi is the symbolic representation of inept spiritual "guides" who impose too harsh a penalty for sin and then make excessive demands on those who have strayed from the path. In both these situations Richard uses events in Dina's life as vivid representations of distortions in discipline. These complex characters contain some of Richard's best and most subtle teaching, underscoring the necessity for insight into the nature of the spiritual quest and the needs of those who pursue it. One literally has matters of life and death in hand, for a misapplication of discipline can lead to spiritual "death" or even permanent bodily injury.

Two children remain to be born after Dina: Joseph and Benjamin, Rachel's children. Joseph is Discretion or full self-knowledge. Benjamin personifies contemplation in ecstasy. Both are born of reason, for by it we know both ourselves and God. Rachel's death at the birth of Benjamin is symbolic of a basic truth of contemplative ecstasy: It transcends all reasoning. Reason is, as it were, dead when ecstasy occurs.

Joseph's birth represents the culmination of discipline through full self-knowledge. He also personifies the ordering and moderating function of reason in relation to the virtues. Without discretion, virtues become vices because of disorder or excess (chapter 66). In describing Joseph's relation to the other brothers, Richard effects one of his most engaging portraits. The character of the mature ascetic and/or the ideal spiritual guide is sketched briefly, like light pencil lines set down by a master to guide him in bringing a scene to life in vivid color. Fully self-aware, schooled in the dangers of excesses and deficiencies alike, watchful of all the brothers and their individual capacities for action, mindful of needs of body as well as mind, on guard against destructive demands as well as moral laxity masquerading as concern for peace—these go a long way toward suggesting the kind of individual inner balance and discrete yet firm direction Richard expected. The watch over the brothers has a possible double sense: Reason watches over the brothers born of affection, imagination and the senses to moderate them; the spiritual guide watches over the brothers in the abbey to restrain or exhort them as the case may be. One is tempted to see in the latter a reflection of Richard's own role in the life of the abbey.[13]

Between the states represented by Joseph and the birth of Benjamin an important transition takes place. Its most notable characteristic is the beginning of a set of new experiences that are best described as interior visions of light, divinely given. The vi-

---

13. J. Châtillon has written that Richard was "perhaps even a sort of master of novices, in any case a spiritual guide, preoccupied to instruct and to lead his listeners, that is to say his brothers in religion, to Christian perfection and contemplation" ("Autour des *Miscellanea* attribués à Hugues de Saint-Victor," *Revue d'ascétique et de mystique* 25 [1949]: 305).

sions of light have a specific name: *divina revelatio*, "divine show-ing." We translate *revelatio* as "showing" rather than the obvious word "revelation" for a specific reason. The word "revelation" tends to have many connotations linked with revealed truths or dogmas and with the subjective apprehension of truth described metaphorically as an illumination. Such connotations lead one astray from Richard's use of the word.[14] "Showing" emphasizes ideas of manifestation, of the unveiling of things otherwise hidden, and of vision, each an important aspect of *divina revelatio*.

The appearance of visions of light is associated with two sym-bolic images in *The Twelve Patriarchs*: the continual cleansing of the mirror of the soul by Joseph representing discretion, and the three disciples who experience the transfiguration of Jesus (chapters 71–82). Discretion leads to a state of full self-knowledge with increas-ing awareness of "invisible things of the self" (chapter 72). The soul discovers it is "the foremost and principal mirror for seeing God. . . . as long as we still see by a mirror and in an enigma we cannot find, as I have said, a mirror more apt for imaginative vision of Him than the rational spirit" (ibid.). This mirror is the image of God according to which man has been created. Through continued dis-cipline of mind, will and body the mature ascetic whom Joseph represents continues

> to hold it [*the mirror*] so that it does not adhere to the earth, after it has fallen down by means of love; to wipe it so that it does not become dirty from the dust of useless thoughts; to gaze into it, so that the eye of his intention does not turn toward empty pursuits. (chapter 72)[15]

Given the nature of medieval mirrors the image is apt. They were made of polished metal and gave at best a fuzzy and somewhat dim reflection. Subject to tarnishing, the accumulation of dirt and other vicissitudes of use, they needed careful attention to be useful. So it

---

14. See similar comments by Kirchberger, *Selected Writings on Contemplation*, p. 41. She uses "shewing."

15. Cleansing the mirror of the soul has striking affinities with the Eastern Orthodox tradition, particularly Gregory of Nyssa. For Gregory's ideas see G. Ladner, *The Idea of Reform* (New York, 1967), pp. 90–107.

is with the soul. Only by continual attention to discipline can the mind become still, as it were, and begin to experience a new reality, divine showings:

> *When the mirror has been wiped and gazed into for a long time, a kind of splendor of divine light begins to shine in it, and a great beam of unexpected vision appears to his eyes. . . . Therefore, from the vision of this light that it wonders at within itself, the soul is kindled from above in a marvelous way and is animated to see the living light that is above it. (chapter 72)*

This vision is *not* ecstatic contemplation. It is an experience that arouses longing for ecstasy, longing for the birth of Benjamin.

The mention of visions of light brings Richard to a new representation: a mountain. This is not an ordinary mountain, it is the mountain of Jesus' transfiguration. Interpreted tropologically the transfiguration represents four stages in the experience of ecstatic contemplation. First, the climb up the mountain, "a steep way, a secret way, unknown to many," represents the long period of discipline figured by Jacob's children, Benjamin excluded. Second, the fact that the three disciples (representing work, meditation and prayer) remain with Jesus on the mountain indicates the stability and repose of true inner peace and quiet, something reached only after long effort. Richard notes that this inner detachment and radical stillness result at first only from hard effort, but later become for some an almost spontaneous state (chapters 76 and 84–85). One recognizes resonances with Evagrius's *apatheia* and the purity of heart taught by Cassian. The third stage is Jesus' transfiguration, His manifestation as a being clothed in light. This is tropologically identified with the visions of light mentioned above. Fourth, the disciples fall on the ground senseless when they hear the voice of the Father coming from the brilliant cloud. The fainting of the three disciples represents the failure of sense, memory and reason in this highest contemplation. The parallel in the patriarchal imagery is the birth of Benjamin, which is accompanied by the death of Rachel, also interpreted as the failure of reason in the experience of contemplative ecstasy (chapter 80).

Before leaving *The Twelve Patriarchs* we should note again the positive role Richard gives to visions of light. This sets him apart from authors, medieval and modern, who either reject visions totally or consider them phenomena that are only peripheral to contemplation. We now see that Richard allows for the occurrence of visionary experiences at one of the most crucial junctures in the mystic's quest: the transition from a state of internal quiet and recollection to the state of ecstatic contemplation. However, Richard is very cautious in according visions an independent authority. He insists that Scripture is the standard by which they must be judged, for even the devil can transform himself into an angel of light. All heresies and errors come from this subversion of visions by the demonic (chapter 81).

It is interesting to note that in the long tradition of mystical experience in Eastern Orthodoxy, the transfiguration is also identified with visionary experiences of light. It is debatable whether or not Richard had much knowledge of Eastern Christian authors beyond Dionysius, but he did come to stress an aspect of mystical experience that they stressed. Emphasis on visions of light has certain similarities with phenomena in non-Christian mystical traditions as well.[16]

Further discussion of the nature of contemplation and its relation to visions is reserved for the second of Richard's major works on contemplation, *The Mystical Ark*, to which we now turn. This is an interpretation of the deeper significance of the Ark of the Covenant described in Exodus, chapter 25. Richard says immediately that he will not offer an allegorical interpretation since this has been done by others before his time; instead, he will approach the meaning of the ark tropologically. For a Victorine this meant finding not only a moral sense in the text, but also pursuing the significance it has for the contemplative life. This latter is Richard's chief interest.

For the reader about to begin *The Mystical Ark*, the most useful kind of introductory remarks are probably those which point out

---

16. On the Eastern Church, see Vladimir Lossky, *The Mystical Theology of the Eastern Church*, trans. members of the Fellowship of St. Alban and St. Sergius (London, 1957), esp. p. 227: Visionary experiences of light are the touchstone that defines orthodox spirituality, which "gains certainty of union with God in the light of the Transfiguration." For a cross-cultural study of the phenomenon of "mystic light" one can consult Mircea Eliade, *The Two and the One* (New York, 1965), pp. 19–77, "Experiences of the Mystic Light," in which most examples are non-Christian, but mention is made of Christian instances.

the special characteristics of Richard's understanding of the nature of contemplation, the kinds of objects toward which it may be directed, the modes in which it operates, and the ways it is distinguished from thinking, meditating and speculation. The reader must also pay a good deal of attention to the complex way in which Richard uses the symbolism of the Ark of the Covenant and the two seraphim that accompany it in the innermost chamber of the tabernacle. There are a number of important personifications in the text of this work. Drawn from the Biblical text, they represent certain kinds of contemplative experiences and function in a way mentioned earlier, namely to provide a concrete "example" of a particular set of experiences so that the aspiring or actual contemplative may think of himself or herself as "Abraham," "Elijah," the "Queen of Sheba," "Bezeleel," or "Moses." Finally, Biblical texts are incorporated in the text and interpreted tropologically at crucial junctures in Richard's "argument." These again provide vivid symbolic representations of aspects of the quest he is describing. Especially effective are the verses drawn from the Song of Songs in books 4 and 5.

By contemplation Richard means an attitude of mind, a state of beholding. In *The Mystical Ark* he gives a classic definition:

Contemplation is the free, more penetrating gaze of a mind, suspended with wonder concerning manifestations of wisdom. (1:4)

This use of the word *contemplatio*, although it has much that is special to Richard in its meaning, continues to retain much of the basic meaning of the word, which is an attentive or eager looking at. Above all it must be clearly understood that contemplation is not some sort of mental process. Richard, like Hugh of St. Victor before him, is careful to distinguish thinking (a rather rambling consideration of many things without purpose) and meditating (intent mental activity concentrated upon one thing or purpose, for the gaining of knowledge) from the act of contemplating (1:3–4). The same object may at various times be the object of thinking, meditating or contemplating. The contemplative act itself is an intent beholding focused upon a single object or cluster of objects presented to the mind by imagination, reason or the pure understanding that alone has access to divine things. As Richard says

23

clearly: "Contemplation always deals with things, either manifested according to their nature, known intimately by study, or made clear by divine showing" (1:3). The purpose of contemplation is not thinking about something, rational understanding, ferreting out new truths or any like mental operation. It is, rather, an "adhering with wonder to the object that brings it joy" (1:4). It is nondiscursive and unified. It enjoys rather than uses. It rests rather than acts.

Book 1 of *The Mystical Ark* contains the famous Ricardian distinction of six degrees, or kinds (*genera*), of contemplation.[17] This distinction does not introduce six different varieties of contemplation, but rather offers a sixfold division of the objects that may be contemplated. The six degrees represent an ascension in being, from the sensual world, perceived by the bodily senses and known to the mind through the imagination, through the interior world of the reason, to the transcendent world of spiritual realities, divine nature and Trinity. Anything whatsoever may be the object of contemplation, from the simplest acorn to the ineffable manifestation of the Trinity in ecstatic contemplation. Furthermore, contemplation is *not* the operation of the understanding in man (which faculty alone has access to divine realities) as opposed to reason and imagination. Understanding, reason and imagination all provide objects fit for contemplation. The analysis of the six degrees or kinds of contemplation is a presentation of the specific ways in which the objects at each level of ascension are perceived by the mind. The *mode* of contemplation, which may be suited to a specific kind of object, is a matter to which we shall return later. Suffice it to say here that ecstasy is but one of three modes of contemptation.

According to Richard the six *kinds* of contemplation may be divided thus (1:6):

1. *In imagination and according to imagination only*

---

17. For a detailed analysis of the six kinds, objects of contemplation for each and faculties for perceiving these objects, see Joseph Ebner, *Die Erkenntnislehre Richards von Saint Viktor*, Beiträge zur Geschichte der Philosophie und Theologie des Mittelalters (Münster, 1917), Band 19, heft 4, pp. 104–120. Useful comments are in Andres, "Die Stufen," pp. 189–200, and J. A. Robbilliard, "Les six genres de contemplation chez Richard de Saint-Victor et leur origine platonicienne," *Revue des sciences philosophiques et théologiques* 28 (1939): 229–233. See also B. McGinn, "Ascension and Introversion," pp. 545ff. On contemplation itself, see the very useful section in the introduction by Jean Châtillon to Richard of St. Victor, *Sermones et opuscules spirituels inédits*, I, pp. lxvii–lxxix.

2. *In imagination and according to reason*
3. *In reason and according to imagination*
4. *In reason and according to reason*
5. *Above reason but not beyond reason*
6. *Above reason and seemingly beyond reason*

In this pattern, two kinds are "in imagination," two "in reason," and two, as indicated elsewhere, are "in understanding." In the succeeding chapters of book 1, Richard weaves a rich tapestry of the interrelations and distinctions connected with these six distinct levels of knowing. Books 2–4 offer a very detailed exposition of the kinds of objects that are accessible to each of these six levels of knowing and contemplating.

Throughout the ark treatise Richard refers to the objects of contemplation at all levels by the word *spectaculum*. We have translated it as "manifestation" in the definition of contemplation offered above and at all other places in the treatise. As we have insisted above, these various *spectacula* are perceived by the individual through the imagination, the reason, the understanding (*intelligentia*) or an appropriate combination of imagination and reason or reason and understanding.

In offering his detailed analysis of the objects of contemplation at various levels, Richard constructs a complex epistemological structure, dividing and subdividing the many classes of objects suitable for contemplation. In his analysis in books 2–4 it is significant to note that he refers most frequently to various kinds of speculation (*speculatio*) rather than kinds of contemplation. The reason for this would seem to be that in his analysis Richard is concerned with classifying manifestations of divine wisdom and the ways of knowing them. Knowing is *speculatio* at first, that is, concerned with the outer world of material existence, the inner mental world of spiritual reality as mirrors that manifest the power, wisdom and goodness of the triune God, or the manifestation of divine truths in a showing. As Richard points out elsewhere, speculative men are those who still see by a mirror and in enigma; contemplatives behold directly and without any shadow or veil. Perhaps we are meant to understand that in the act of perceiving something through imagination or reason there is a "veil" or "mirror" as op-

25

posed to the experience of contemplating. The latter is without activity; it is a resting, loving, wondering apprehension of the manifestation of the divine.

The first kind of contemplation is concerned with physical things as *things*. To contemplate is simply to behold the world, or part of it, with the kind of loving wonder we have described above. It requires just as much discipline of the mind and inward quiet as any other contemplation. Only its object is "lowly" and is perceived by the lowest faculty of the mind, the imagination. The objects of this contemplation are divided and subdivided. The first division separates things, works and morals. Things are divided into matter, form and nature (or substance). The first two are knowable, the last remains always partially unknown. Works are divided into works of nature and works of human activity. Again the latter are fully understandable, the former remain in part inaccessible to human comprehension. Morals are divided into human instruction and divine instruction.

The second kind of contemplation is concerned with the rational principles of physical things. In other words, reason now enters the picture and provides analytical and abstracted knowledge of visible things according to the categories listed for the first speculation (2:10). The object of this contemplation is then one step removed from the world as immediately experienced. For that reason it is described as "in imagination but according to reason."

In discussing the first two kinds of contemplation Richard is very much concerned to contrast the work of Christian thinkers with the false ideas of the philosophers who also have built their arks of wisdom. But having inferior and insufficient materials the latter have failed in their attempts (2:2, 9).

The third contemplation is said to be in reason according to imagination. This level involves knowledge of invisible spiritual realities, but that knowledge is gained by means of similitudes drawn from the physical world. The imagination leads reason by the hand, as it were, because the knowledge is gained by reason but through the use of visible things known through imagination. This is the famous Victorine idea of the "manuductio" or guiding hand that the world provides in the quest for spiritual truth. The roots lie in the ideas of Dionysius about the world as a symbolic manifestation of divine reality and the return to knowledge of God via symbols that both reveal and hide truth.[18] Richard was clearly the heir of Hugh of St. Victor in this perception of the ascent to spiritual realities by means of visible realities, according to similitude. Richard puts it succinctly:

> *But since the investigation of this speculation cannot be led to the knowledge of invisible things without the assistance of corporeal similitudes, reason seems to be following the leading hand of imagination in this part and is shown clearly to hold on to it, the leader of the journey as it were, in the course of its search. For while imagination presents forms of visible things to reason and instructs itself from the similitude of the same things for the investigation of invisible things, in a certain manner it brings reason to that place to which it did not know how to go by means of itself. For reason would never rise up to the contemplation of invisible things unless the imagination, by means of representing the form of visible things, were to show from what it should draw a similitude to those things and form the mode of its investigation. (2:17)*

Elsewhere Richard refers to material objects as providing "a staff of corporeal similitude" that supports the third contemplation, which "lifts itself to high things by means of a ladder, so to speak, of the particular natures of corporeal things" (3:12). The ladder has a long history as a symbol of spiritual ascent, but one thinks here especially of Richard's influence on St. Bonaventure and the latter's use of the ladder theme as a symbol of ascension in the *Itinerarium mentis in Deum* (*Itinerarium* 1:2, 9; 4:2).

The Mystical Ark 2:15 offers a fivefold division of this way of knowing invisible spiritual things, based on the fivefold consideration of things used in the second kind of contemplation. These are: the particular matter of a thing; the external quality of something (form); the internal quality (nature); what is done in or by a thing by necessity; what is done according to the purpose of will, or by "artificial motion" (2:15). Richard then shows how a deeper meaning can be found in various Scriptural verses using the five

---

18. See note 4.

categories above as the way for determining a spiritual meaning. This not only reveals Richard's skill as an interpreter but also reminds us that Victorine exegesis systematically insisted that the spiritual senses of Scripture be founded upon the meaning of *things* in Scripture and could not be merely wordplay. There is a metaphysical and theological, even soteriological, rationale for the pursuit of deeper senses in Scripture and, in a more limited way, in the book of nature. Both are *spectacula*, manifestation of God's wisdom, and offer a "way" toward understanding invisible spiritual things.

To conclude book 2 Richard offers a complex consideration of the relation of divine wisdom to the salvation and damnation of humanity, dividing this wisdom into God's knowledge, foreknowledge, disposition and predestination. This is carried out as a detailed symbolic interpretation of the meaning of the rings set in the corners of the ark and the two poles that are inserted through pairs of rings in order to carry the ark. Here Richard is able to offer a rather subtle presentation of the questions of God's *permission*, which allows evil to exist, in contrast to his *working* (*operatio*), which is only for good. The consideration seems a bit out of place at this point in the ark treatise, but it is necessary to put it where it is, says Richard, because the rings and poles appear at this point in the Biblical narrative, and "the order of reason requires that some things be said briefly in this place concerning the rings and the poles, so that the same order may be followed in exposition as the author wished to follow in description [of the ark]" (2:19).

Following the third kind, which involves an incipient interiorization, Richard moves to the fourth, which is marked by complete interiorization. It is "in reason according to reason." Richard devotes the entire third book to this contemplation, indicating both the importance it held for him and the extent of his analysis of its divisions. This fourth speculation/contemplation concerns knowledge of the rational spirit only: either the soul of man or angels. The distinction between this kind of contemplation and the earlier three is strongly stressed. Here the imagination that is the reason's relation to the world is completely excluded from any participation (3:1–4). In the imagery of building the ark this work is of pure gold, having no wood (ideas from the material world derived via imagination) or contact with wood.

28

In this fourth kind the focus of consciousness turns completely within the soul. Rejecting all imaginative consciousness, the mind is aware of itself only as it explores the secret and deep things of the self. Also, at this time the pure understanding (*intelligentia*) may begin to function, thus providing some direct knowledge of things that are above not only human sense but human reason also: namely, angelic spirits and the deep things of God. This is very different from the kind of knowledge by similitude in the third level of knowing. However, the first entrance into all such matters is by way of complete and thorough knowledge of one's self.

Richard introduces images drawn from several Scripture passages to elucidate this quest for knowledge of the soul and other rational spirits. From Ecclesiastes 1:5 comes this: "The sun rises and sets, and it returns to its place, where rising again. . . ." This is taken to commend mental interiorization while also offering an opportunity to explore the ascension (the rising sun) that is associated with interiorization (3:6–7). The parable likening the kingdom of God to treasure buried in a field (Matt. 13:44) is interpreted to mean the riches of divine wisdom hidden in the depths of the human heart, especially in the *imago Dei* (3:5). The search for God's kingdom and His wisdom thus must be a quest within, to the depths of the human heart and beyond. The Pauline reference to a "third heaven" brings Richard to a distinction of three heavens, the first the imaginative, the second the rational, the third the intellectual. This corresponds to the tripartite division of mental faculties Richard uses, but more importantly it puts them into an ascending pattern and stresses the "world" to which each has access. The imaginative heaven is this world; the rational heaven is the marvelous and remarkable world of the inner self ruled over by the sun of the soul; the intellectual heaven is the awesome world of transcendent realities that circles about the true and eternal Sun, God (3:8–10). There is also an eye for each heaven: the fleshly eye, which sees the material world; the eye of reason, "with which we seek and find hidden and absent things by means of investigation or as we often understand causes by effects or effects by causes"; the eye of the understanding, "by which we see invisible things [of ourselves and of God]" (3:9). As Richard says so forcefully, this intellectual eye "grasps invisible things invisibly, to be sure, but presently and essentially," so that one sees with it in a way analogous to corporeal sight. However, in the present human condition, this intellectual eye is veiled, so that it sees nothing of divine things unless God should will to unveil this eye. This notion of the three eyes and the veiling of the third eye was formulated by Hugh of St. Victor.[19] Richard employs it with great effect to point to the soul's three ways of seeing and the spiritual blindness in the present human condition, apart from God's action of grace in restoration.

The objects of this fourth speculation/contemplation are divided by a triple distinction of "divine gifts in spiritual essences": (1) existence given in creation; (2) goodness conferred through being made just; (3) blessedness from being glorified (3:11). Like almost all of Richard's patterns, this one is concerned with progression, both cosmic from creation to consummation, and personal through varied stages of spiritual growth outlined in *The Twelve Patriarchs* and *The Mystical Ark*. Here Richard focuses especially on the soul as it advances in spiritual maturity and comes to full perfection. The goods of creation are divided into: existence, knowing and willing, with special emphasis on the freedom of human will (3:12–15). Goodness that comes through being made just is subdivided into that which comes as the gift of the Creator through aspiration and that which comes through our own action via the deliberation of the will (3:16–18). Consideration of the will in the first distinction concerns the existence of free will and its greatness; in the second, the exertion of the will, its efforts and merits (3:18). The blessedness of consummation remains always unknown, says Richard, except for the brief and fleeting experiences of spiritual joy one has in this life. These first fruits of future happiness form the substance of the object of speculation/contemplation in the third distinction.

As if to clarify things, Richard ends book 3 with a review of the five subdivisions of this kind. There is much to ponder in this conclusion, for it is a multifaceted presentation of Richard's understanding of the human soul, the apex of creation. He considers the essential nature of the soul as subsisting eternally; the marvelous

---

19. The scheme of the three eyes is found in Hugh, *De Sacramentis christianae fidei*, 1.10.2, and also in his commentary on the *Celestial Hierarchies* of Dionysius, 3 (PL 176:976A). The best analysis is in H. Weisweiler, "*Sacramentum fidei*: Augustinische und ps.-dionysiche Gedanken in der Glaubenauffassung Hugos von St. Viktor," *Theologie in Geschichte und Gegenwart* hsgb. von J. Auer und H. Volk (München, 1957), pp. 433–456.

intellectual capacity of the soul; the various states of the affections, changing almost instantly from love to hate or exultation to lamentation; the formation of virtues in the soul (recalling *The Twelve Patriarchs* on order and moderation); the gifts of the Spirit that work blessedness in this life and the next.

The concluding chapter on the gifts of the Spirit is a marvelous outpouring of praise as Richard considers the harmony of these gifts that inspire the soul and the angelic host. The work of the Spirit in the soul is likened to the work of a skillful harper who tunes his instrument carefully, stretching and loosening strings, plucking them sharply, until "a certain melody, mellifluous and sweet beyond measure, resounds from them." So the harmonious soul, with its ordered and moderated virtues inspired by the Spirit, will "resound . . . into the ears of the Lord Sabaoth as if from the playing of many harpers upon their harps" (3:24).

At this point Richard's vision shifts immediately from the harmony of one soul to the great concord that must result from the harmony of many souls with each other: "the consonant concord and concordant consonance . . . of so many . . . angels and holy souls exulting and praising Him who lives world without end" (3:24). The great Victorine theme of the concord of many souls in community, in shared knowing and loving, is sounded with great weight and effect. The book, which began with the consideration of the created soul in its individual nature, concludes with a moving vision of the eternal felicity not of one soul but of many thousands united in joy and praise. Again, as in so many passages of Richard's works, the themes of community and the place of the individual within that unity are woven into the fabric of thought. His vision is not that of the flight of the alone to the Alone but the flight of one who is recovering a sense of love and community to that ineffable Unity which is in truth Trinity in the midst of community.

The last, and highest, two kinds of contemplation are the subject of the fourth book of *The Mystical Ark*. The objects of these contemplations cannot be discovered by human reason. They are given by God through the faculty Richard calls understanding. In the fifth kind are these things which are above (*supra*) reason's power, but when known are not beyond (*praeter*) the ability of reason to comprehend. These are especially things having to do with the divine substance and its unity. In the sixth kind are those things which are not only above the power of reason to discover; they are beyond (*praeter*) comprehension by the reason and even seem to be contrary to (*contra*) all reason. Such things are what one believes about the Trinity of three persons in one God (4:2, 3). As we shall see later, the radical separation between the first four kinds and these last two is indicated by the fact that the first four are symbolized by the building of the Ark of the Covenant; the last two are symbolized by fashioning images of the two seraphim, purely spiritual beings, out of pure beaten gold. One seraph represents the fifth kind; the other the sixth.

In considering the objects of these last two contemplations, Richard makes much of the distinction between and mutually of the seraphim. The seraph on the right is the fifth kind, above but not beyond reason, the side of similitude, of knowledge of the unity of the divine. The seraph on the left is the sixth kind, beyond, even contrary to reason, the side of dissimilitude, the knowledge of the Trinity of persons in one divine nature. The truth represented by each seraph is united with the truth of the other in mutual concord, not divisive conflict (4:19). What one affirms concerning the unity of God the other must not destroy by the affirmation of Trinity and vice versa. A rather complex consideration of the unity and Trinity of God is included in this.

Here Richard insists that knowledge of God's unity and Trinity is *above* the capacity of reason to discover without divine assistance through either a divine showing or ecstatic contemplation (4:21). This "knowing" comes through the understanding, as distinct from reason or imagination. However, once God's unity is affirmed, reason can comprehend it and offer some arguments concerning it (4:17). With the Trinity, however, not only is there an absence of any proof from experience or an a priori demonstration by reasoning (these are absent in the previous case also); it is also the case that once known, the Trinity is not something that is "reasonable." It can be believed; it cannot be proved except from authorities, miracles and divine showings (4:3).

As the discussion of these two kinds of contemplation proceeds, it is clear that Richard understands them as experienced primarily in the contemplative mode of ecstasy (*excessus mentis*). Indeed, Richard points out very clearly that the first four kinds of contemplation are ordinarily experienced in nonecstatic ways, while the last two are ecstatic (4:22). However, there are some things subject to the first four kinds that nevertheless may be known in ecstasy or in a divine showing, and on occasion things known in the last two kinds can be the subject of nonecstatic contemplation. Among the several personifications used in book 4, Moses and Bezeleel apply here (4:22). Moses ascended a mountain and entered into a cloud in order to see the ark and seraphim. Hence, he saw in ecstasy the six kinds of contemplation. That Bezeleel, who constructed the ark and fashioned the cherubim, neither climbed a mountain nor entered into a cloud is symbolic of the fact that occasionally even the deepest secrets known in ecstasy may be subject to contemplation in a nonecstatic mode. Bezeleel also represents the function of *teaching* about the six kinds of contemplation to persons on the contemplative path, and in book 5 Richard represents the labor of Bezeleel in building the ark and seraphim as his own labor in the treatise (5:1).

Richard recognizes the ambiguity of the "unknowing" of ecstatic contemplation. He fully incorporates the Dionysian theme of the state of "unknowing" that characterizes ecstasy: Ecstasy takes one beyond rational consciousness, behind a veil, into darkness. However, the Victorine canon also takes account of the fact that for some there is a "memory" that gives limited and "veiled" access to the experience.

> And although we may retain in memory something from that experience and see it through a veil as it were and as though in the middle of a cloud, we lack the ability to comprehend or call to mind either the manner of seeing or the quality of the vision. And marvelously, in a way remembering, we do not remember, and not remembering, we remember; . . . (4:23)

The dreams of Nebuchadnezzar and Pharaoh exemplify respectively those who recall nothing from ecstasy and those who can remember to some degree and reflect upon what they have seen in ecstasy (5:1). In another set of Biblical images, when Abraham brings the Lord into his tent at Mamre, this represents such marvelous remembering. Failure to bring the Lord back on a second occasion represents the "not remembering" aspect (4:12). Richard's argument on this topic is rich and complex and must be read carefully, with full attention to the symbolism, to be appreciated. He clearly wants to give full scope to the variety of contemplative experiences and the objects of each within the range of human experience.

Up to this point we have been discussing the six kinds of speculation/contemplation primarily from the aspect of the characteristics of each, the faculties of mind involved and such things. We must now return to the beginning, as it were, and consider the symbols by means of which this teaching is set forth and meant to be grasped. The symbolic forms we are about to discuss are most certainly not an *addendum* for Richard. They are actually the basic foundation; the teaching is an elaboration. Richard's way of proceeding is from the symbol to the truth. The symbol is not an abstract "representation" of ideas; it is, rather, a concrete manifestation of truth.

Two separate symbolic forms are involved: the Ark of the Covenant and the pair of seraphim accompanying the ark in the innermost chamber of the tabernacle of the covenant. This tabernacle, with its furnishings, was revealed to Moses on Mt. Sinai. For Richard it represents a symbolic manifestation of the spiritual journey. Certainly the tabernacle had been interpreted "symbolically" before, but the interpretations had been allegorical, focused on Christ or His Church; Richard's new contribution is to say something on the tropological sense, thus building on clues in the writings of Augustine and Gregory the Great.

The narrative of the construction of the ark is followed carefully, with a division into four significant stages:

1. *the making of the frame from pieces of Setim wood;*
2. *the gilding of this wooden ark;*
3. *the making of a crown of pure gold; the crown encircles the ark, is attached to the wood of the ark, and goes above the top of the ark;*
4. *the making of a propitiatory, or mercy seat, out of pure gold; this provides a cover for the ark.*

The seraphim are made of pure gold, beaten and shaped into the image of the six-winged creatures who are the apex of the angelic hierarchy and are thus nearest to God. The materials and dimensions of each part of the ark are important. Wood represents knowledge derived from the senses, that is, the imaginative faculty. Gold refers to the reason, while the purest gold, of which the propitiatory and seraphim are fashioned, refers to the understanding (*intelligentia*).

Each of the four stages in building the ark refers to one of the first four kinds of contemplation. The ark of wood represents the contemplation that is "in imagination according to imagination." The gilding of the ark represents the second contemplation, since the overlay of gold indicates the function of reason in seeking out the rational principles of things. The third kind of contemplation is properly signified by the crown, which is made of pure gold but is attached at places to the wood of the ark. Pure gold indicates the dominant role played by reason. Attachment to wood means that imagination still plays a part in this contemplation in which invisible things are known by means of visible things and their similitudes. The fact that the crown rises above the gilded wooden ark indicates that in this contemplation knowledge goes beyond the world perceived by the senses. The fourth kind of contemplation is represented by the cover of the ark, the propitiatory, which is made of pure gold and in no place touches wood, for it rests on either pure gold or gilding. This level consists, as we have seen, of the complete interiorization of consciousness, as the mind begins to function "in reason, according to reason," with the occasional operation of the understanding making known things beyond the power of reason.

In addition to the significance of the materials, Richard finds the dimensions of the various elements of the ark to be significant. A clever argument proves that in existence a line logically precedes a plane surface and a plane surface, a solid. Hence in consideration of the ark, dimensions must be taken in order of length, width and height. Having established what the length, width and height of the ark, or crown, or propitiatory symbolize, Richard then finds further subdivisions of these first distinctions in the dimensions as given in cubits. Furthermore, it will be seen that the full cubit indicates fullness of knowledge of the particular thing signified, such as human activity or the form of things; a half-cubit means partial knowledge, such as in the working of nature or inner substance of something.

As noted earlier, the last two kinds of contemplation are symbolized by the seraphim. These kinds have more to do with divine things than human ability, hence they are symbolized by an angelic form. Richard emphasizes the difficulty in making these from beaten gold. Much labor must be expended, both in purifying and in shaping the material. So the contemplative must exert himself or herself in much effort to purify and shape life. As the reader will note, Richard makes much of the fact that seraphim are winged creatures, hence able to fly upward in ecstatic contemplation, and that they are associated with the ark in a *mutual* sharing.

In addition to the six *kinds* of contemplation we have been discussing, Richard also makes a very important distinction between three different *modes* in which the quality of contemplation may vary.[20] These modes are: (1) enlarging of the mind (*dilatio mentis*); (2) raising up of the mind (*sublevatio mentis*); and (3) alienation of the mind (*alienatio mentis*) or ecstasy (*excessus mentis*) (5:2). Richard offers Biblical types for these modes. Enlarging is related to building the ark; raising up, to the ark lifted up and carried behind the cloud of divine presence; ecstasy, to placing the ark behind a veil in the Holy of Holies. In another series of Biblical persons, enlarging is figured by Abraham who is told to look up and gaze round about; raising up, by Moses who ascends Mt. Nebo by his own effort and is then shown the promised land by divine grace; ecstasy, by Moses' ascent and entrance into a cloud on Sinai and also by the transfiguration (5:2).

A primary distinction between the three modes is made with respect to the relationship of human effort and grace and can be seen in the Biblical figures just mentioned. Enlarging of the mind is the result of human effort alone. It is an art that can be learned from a good master or by reading, developed by continued exercise, and

---

20. The basic study for the three modes of contemplation is Jean Châtillon, "Les trois modes de la contemplation selon Richard de Saint-Victor," *Bulletin de littérature ecclésiastique* 41 (1940): 3–26.

brought to fruition in attention, which develops one's powers of beholding even more (5:3). This mode is likened to a watchtower in a series of Biblical passages interpreted tropologically with respect to the three degrees of art, skill and attention. It cannot be stressed too much that Richard does *not* mean that this first mode of contemplation is something like meditation or that it is an extension of ordinary mental activities. It is an acquired skill, just like other arts, but it is unique in that it is the art of *contemplation* and partakes of the qualities of rest, peace, comprehensive vision and the like, which have been noted earlier.

The second mode of contemplation, raising up of the mind, comes from joining human effort with the divine grace of a showing (5:4). Thus visions of light have an explicit and necessary connection with this mode of contemplation. In it something unknown is always made manifest to the mind through what Richard calls the raising up (*sublevatio*) of the mind. There are three degrees of being raised up: (1) above one's present knowledge; (2) above what a specific individual might possibly know at some future time; (3) above all knowledge possible for human nature. In particular, certain phenomena that we might associate with extraordinary psychic experiences are grouped by Richard in the third degree of raising up. For him they are associated with aspects of prophecy, in the Biblical sense, and involve "seeing" the past, the future and events at a distance, as well as "the secrets of another's heart" and "divine things that are above sense" (5:4). In all of these forms of *sublevatio* it is very clear that the visionary experiences remain accessible to reason. They are not experienced in ecstasy. Furthermore, the divine showings in this mode of contemplation are complete in themselves. They do not lead to other experiences. In particular they do not lead to ecstasy.

When he discusses the third mode of contemplation, ecstasy or alienation, Richard discusses three causes at length. They are: (1) greatness of devotion (*magnitudo devotionis*); (2) greatness of wonder (*magnitudo admirationis*); (3) greatness of exultation (*magnitudo exsultationis*) (5:5). Before we discuss these three causes, however, let us look briefly at what Richard has to say about ecstasy in book 4 of *The Mystical Ark*.

Likened to the cherubim, the would-be ecstatic has his or her wings poised ready to fly upward and soar into the heights (see 4:10). Preparation, as one has gathered by now, is all-important. It is not merely some kind of intellectual preparation that is needed. Indeed, in some ways this is the least important. The quietness of life, of body, and especially of mind that is taught in *The Twelve Patriarchs* is crucial for anyone who longs for ecstatic contemplation.

In a long, subtle, and extremely moving presentation, Richard examines the way in which many persons put off preparation for contemplation and repeatedly ask the Lord to "command, command again; command, command again; wait, wait again; wait, wait again; a little here, a little there" (Isa. 28:10, 13) (*The Mystical Ark*, 4:13). These are the words of a spiritually unprepared soul. The penetrating and critical portrait of those who are always *wanting* to be fully reformed and perfected, who set a time for such in the future while they practice daily penance, yet who always manage to keep their time of reformation *future*, is a commentary on spiritual weakness in all generations (4:14). It is Augustine's "make me chaste and continent, but not yet" (Confessions 8:7) set in new key and fleshed out by a superb observer of human actions. One suspects that Richard knew many spiritual slackers both inside and outside the abbey.

Drawing on the famous passages in the Song of Songs (2:10ff. and 5:2ff.) that depict the call of the lover to his beloved and her yearning yet hesitant responses, Richard etches in very effective—and *affective*—language the dialectic of call and response, preparation and fruition in the contemplative quest (4:13–16). For this translator, few passages in mystical literature catch so well the subtleties of divine calling, human yearning, equally human procrastination and laziness, and the final outpouring of love in the mutual embraces of lovers that signifies mystic ecstasy for Richard. His presentations of the crowd of boisterous thoughts, purification of the outer chamber, and preparation of the innermost recess of the heart as the wedding chamber for the mystic nuptials, are extremely sensitive and show both lines of connection with Cistercian writings and also influences on later writers. Richard's appreciation of the basic quality of love that may go toward the world or God with equal force, but with radically different results, is shown in his challenge to the reader to see if the love he or she feels for God surpasses the force of love for the world (4:16; see also Richard's *Four Degrees of Violent Charity*).

In book 4 Richard offers four Biblical figures as personifications of varied experiences of ecstatic contemplation. Abraham represents the person who eagerly awaits the coming of the Lord (a showing) with longing in the heat of the day, runs from his tent (body) to meet the Lord (ecstasy), and, depending upon the occasion, may or may not be able to "bring back" something of the experience to ordinary consciousness (4:10–12). Richard's use of Abraham and the narrative of the divine manifestation at Mamre will repay close scrutiny by the reader. It is a *tour-de-force* of spiritual exegesis that exemplifies at its best Richard's use of persons, places, times and narrative structure to provide the basis for spiritual interpretation. It also offers an excellent example of the use of a Biblical figure to provide a "type" of a particular kind of experience. Rather than offering evidence from lives or legends, Richard offers his readers figures from Scripture with whom they can identify in the course of their spiritual journey. Thus the liturgical cycle and the process of salvation history find a reflection in the life of the individual, offering an ordering principle and guiding hand via symbolic realizations of experiences that might prove enigmatic, even terrifying, otherwise.

Contrasted with Abraham is Elijah, who also awaits the coming of the Lord at the mouth of a cave at Mt. Horeb. But he does not run forth; he hides his face. Such a one is unready for the divine presence (4:10).

Moses appears as a personification of many things in *The Mystical Ark*. We have already noted that he represents ecstasy in his ascent of the mountain and entrance into the cloud. Richard contrasts *this* experience, which he sees as given only as *God* wills it graciously, with the experience of Aaron who enters the Holy of Holies in the tabernacle whenever it is necessary, almost as he wills (4:23). So it is that there are people who struggle and strive for ecstasy, yet it comes only infrequently and as an unexpected gift. On the other hand there are those who are able to have ecstasy almost as they will it. It is something they can decide to have, as it were. The former persons "are" Moses; the latter, Aaron. Here we have again Richard's desire to distinguish in order to give expression to the full range of experience. The ability of Aaron to experience ecstasy almost at will is *not* merely the action of human willing; it is ultimately grounded in God's grace. But nevertheless, there are those for whom ecstasy is a much more regular thing than it is for others. Both are equally contemplatives, however.

With each of the three causes of the mode of ecstasy Richard associates a specific image and a verse drawn from the Song of Songs. Devotion is associated with kindling the fire of heavenly desire. The soul is melted like wax and vaporized like smoke that ascends upward. Wonder involves bursts of light that shock the soul and create both self-depreciation and the sense of wonder that Rudolf Otto identified as the *mysterium tremendum et fascinans* in the presence of the Holy. Exultation is described in terms of spiritual inebriation as the soul, drunk with the abundance of interior sweetness, "forgets what it is and what it has been" (5:5).

The verses from the Song of Songs are first introduced in 5:5, where Richard comments that their order in the sacred text is the same as that of the causes of ecstasy they symbolize. In each verse qualities of the experiences described above are sketched in descriptions of the bride, understood tropologically as the soul that seeks spiritual union with God through Christ, the Bridegroom.

With devotion, the primary cause is simply the loving desire for ecstasy, following upon long and attentive preparation for such. There are times when longing may be joined by the experience of a divine showing to produce ecstasy through devotion. An exemplar of such an experience is Abraham at Mamre (5:8; see also the use of Abraham at 4:10–12).

Ecstasy coming from wonder arises from the sudden shock of unexpected vision, from a divine showing. Awestruck by the suddenness and otherness of interior vision, the contemplative is caught up in wonder at what is "seen." Ecstasy follows. In attempting to convey the sense of this experience, Richard relies on two images drawn from the physical world. The first is the breaking of dawn; the second is the reflection of a ray of light by water in a container (5:9–11).

A divine showing is like dawn insofar as it is "unexpected and incredible," light mixed at first with the darkness of doubt and uncertainty. However, as the vision persists, the clouds of darkness disperse and the light becomes clearer. The dawn image comes from the verse of the Song of Songs that exemplifies this cause of ecstasy: "Who is she who comes forth like the dawn rising?" (Song of Songs 6:9). As dawn increases, it finally comes to its end in full day; in a sense, by increasing, dawn "dies." So it is with the contemplative's experience. The vision increases; the response of wonder increases until, flooded with light and wonder, the soul is cast out of and above itself in the experience of ecstatic contemplation. Ordinary consciousness is "dead"; but the immediate awareness of ecstatic contemplation is very much alive. The sun shines in full glory. This can in no way be seen as the gradual growth of illumination in the course of ecstasy. Richard thinks of dawn and day as disjunctive. One is preparation by vision. The other is ecstasy.[21]

The image of water in a container will be seen to emphasize both the qualities of interior stillness and the effect of a divine showing in carrying something of the soul "upward" in ecstasy (5:11). It is a marvelous similitude, in that it catches both of these necessary aspects of ecstasy resulting from a divine showing.

The precision of Richard's observations concerning ecstasy and the subtlety of his use of Biblical personages come out in the distinction he makes concerning two specific situations in which visions of light produce ecstasy. One takes place during a time of intense mental activity when a person is engaged in the rational activity of meditation. The vision is not an extension of meditation, but breaks into it. The other instance is during a time of spiritual darkness, a period of despair or sloth. Each situation is crystallized into a remarkable image by a Biblical figure. A divine showing leading to ecstasy in the midst of meditation is symbolized by the Queen of Sheba who asks Solomon questions and receives answers, then sees the riches of the king, and finally falls into a faint (5:12). The questioning is meditation. Seeing the riches is the sudden vision. Fainting is ecstatic contemplation.

The vision during a time of darkness is represented in the figure of Peter, imprisoned in chains. The Apostle is visited by an

---

21. Kirchberger, *Selected Writings on Contemplation*, pp. 42–43, mistakenly takes dawn as symbolizing the gradual emergence of luminosity in the dark cloud of unknowing in ecstasy.

angel of light, freed from his chains, and led forth from the prison
(5:13). Peter symbolizes the soul in despair, chained to the world
through desires or perhaps downcast because of spiritual failure.
The angel of light is a sudden showing. The freedom from chains
and prison clearly represents liberation from despair and the translation to ecstasy. The disoriented and lost soul not only regains
peace; it is impelled toward the higher unity of ecstasy.

These last two uses of Biblical figures as personifications illus-
trate again Richard's perceptive analysis—almost a psychological
analysis—of the human condition coupled with remarkable skill in
finding Biblical narratives that reveal, at a deeper level, an important "narrative event" in the history of the soul's spiritual journey.
He captures in symbols and images the aspects of experience that
are apt to be elusive and to resist reduction to mere rational
categories. In his writings a kind of symbolic consciousness can be
seen in action, striving to evoke such a consciousness in the reader.
The patriarchs, Moses, Abraham, the Queen of Sheba, Peter, and
even Elijah can become spiritual guides along a "steep way, a secret
way, unknown to many" (*The Twelve Patriarchs*, chapter 77), which
leads to that mountaintop where there is absolute stillness and the
birth of new light and ecstasy.

The third cause of ecstasy, exultation, comes from what
Richard describes as "divinely infused inner joyfulness and sweetness" (5:14). Richard offers very little analysis in the course of the
chapters devoted to this. Instead, he points to the wonderfulness of
the divine gift here and the greatness of the joy. He does, however,
offer some very striking advice to the person who has experienced
and then lost ecstasy in this mode. Quietness of spirit may again be
recovered, with the infusion of joyfulness, if the person turns to
singing and music (5:17–18). Just as Elisha recovered the prophetic
spirit at the singing of a minstrel, so the contemplative can recover
inward harmony and peace by this singing and chanting. Such
psalmody in the outer man will produce spiritual harmony within.
As a result,

the contemplative soul accustomed to spiritual contemplations begins to
dance and to make gestures in a certain way because of its excess of joy,

42

to make some unique spiritual leaps, to suspend itself above the earth and all earthly things, and to pass over completely to contemplation of celestial things by alienation of mind. (5:18)

In this we find a rare commendation of liturgical chanting as a means to interior recollection and the achievement of spiritual harmony. Again, in Richard's consciousness the paths of spiritual ascent and liturgical celebration cross in a new way.

For Richard, ecstasy is both an ascension and an introversion. It is symbolized, as we have seen, by Moses' ascent of Mount Sinai and Aaron's entrance into the tabernacle. Both movements are ultimately the same, for to go within is to go beyond, and vice versa:

Just as we understand the supreme point of the mind by the peak of the mountain, so we understand the innermost part of the human mind by the Holy of Holies. But in the human soul the supreme point is undoubtedly the same as the innermost part, and the innermost part the same as the supreme point. And so we understand the same thing by the peak of the mountain and the oracle of the tabernacle of the covenant.

Therefore, what does it mean to approach the peak of the mountain or the interior tabernacle, other than to ascend to, to take possession of, and to occupy the supreme and innermost recess of the mind? (4:23)

Whether seen as introversion or ascension, ecstasy is "beyond a veil" or "within a cloud." Here Richard shows himself to be most indebted to the Dionysian understanding of the "divine darkness" and the "unknowability" of God. And yet, the darkness of ecstasy is also an illumination, for while it is darkened with respect to the world, the soul is marvelously illumined with respect to God and divine things. Ecstasy can also be described as a "sleep" of the soul. But it is a sleep only externally. Unaware of what is taking place in the worlds of sense or rational activity, the "quiet" soul is open to a completely new level of experience. The still point, which is both a mountain peak and the innermost part of the temple, is the point of a breakthrough. As a guide to the spiritual life and to the ways of approaching and understanding ecstasy, Richard has few peers among the masters of contemplation as he continues to guide individuals through those difficult passages of interiorization and ascension which mark the contemplative quest.

The short treatise *Some Allegories of the Tabernacle*, translated into English for the first time here, is presented as an appendix to *The Mystical Ark*. It has been included in this volume for two reasons. First of all it offers a great deal of material that is drawn from the longer treatise and compressed into an interesting format. Secondly, it sets this material in a context that is wider in terms of symbolism and application.

As published in the Migne edition (vol. 196, cols. 191C–202B) this work appears to be ordinary prose. In manuscript form it has a very different format. It is arranged in columns on a page, which is not unusual, but each column is so written that one line contains one sentence. Thus the text is actually broken up into small fragments, both in terms of thought and more importantly in terms of presentation and visual impact. Our present translation, which usually presents each sentence in the form of a two-line verse, is an attempt to capture in English what Richard was able to do more compactly in Latin. No ordinary argument or prose narrative is presented. Rather, individual ideas or images are being stated and portrayed in series. One is tempted to say we have something like a series of polished stones, or better carefully shaped *tesserae*, which fit into a surface to make a complete pattern. Perhaps this format was meant to assist the memory by breaking and compacting the material of the ark treatise into small fragments. This would certainly agree with Hugh of St. Victor's idea that in order to "store" things in the memory they ought to be broken up into small units for ease of memorizing; these can later be recalled and "reconnected" to form the whole.[22]

Part of the wider context that *Some Allegories* provides for material from *The Mystical Ark* involves the extension of symbolism to include the tabernacle with its outer atrium and two inner chambers, along with various furnishings such as the candelabrum, table

---

22. See Hugh of St. Victor, *Didascalicon*, 3.11, and comments in Grover A. Zinn, Jr., "Hugh of St. Victor and the Art of Memory," *Viator* 5 (1974): 211–234, esp. pp. 217–218 and 222.

of shew-bread, and so forth. The significance of the tabernacle is stated in the first sentence: It is the state of perfection. An atrium (courtyard) open to the sky surrounds it and represents the discipline of the body, which is visible for all to see. The tabernacle represents interior discipline, and as Richard insists elsewhere, both disciplines are declared to be essential. The first chamber of the tabernacle is the state of returning to one's self, similar to the fourth degree of contemplation. The second and innermost chamber of the tabernacle, containing the Ark of the Covenant, represents ecstasy. A number of succinct tropological interpretations of the furnishings of the tabernacle are presented, all keyed to the process of spiritual discipline and advancement. The central portion of the work then gives a very abbreviated resumé of the essential materials of the first four books of *The Mystical Ark*, stressing the symbolism of ark and seraphim and outlining the six kinds of contemplation.

Rather than concluding with Richard's analysis of the three modes of contemplation, *Some Allegories* turns to the senses of Scripture, the fruit they bear in doctrine and morals, and the duty incumbent upon the preacher to communicate truth and virtue drawn from Scripture. The table of shew-bread in the tabernacle symbolizes Scripture, which is food for the soul in the way bread feeds the body. The table has physical characteristics that are identified with each of the four senses of Scripture (history, allegory, tropology and anagogy). Four rings, one at each corner, represent the proof of truth, reproof of falsehood, exhortation to justice and opposition to injustice. Through these rings are passed the poles that carry the table, symbolizing the transfer of such proof, exhortation, and so forth, from preacher to hearer. The four legs of the table offer Richard the opportunity to analyze four kinds of divine injunctions that guide life: precepts, prohibitions, admonitions and concessions. In his usual style of comparison involving sameness and difference, Richard constructs a brief but effective exposition of the significance of each of these.

With this return to Scripture and preaching at the conclusion of a work on contemplation we find Richard stressing the roots of the Victorine climate and its means of continuing existence. The

Bible was a constant focus of study, source of inspiration and essential element in the liturgy at St. Victor. Richard's writings, like Hugh's before him, are permeated with Biblical texts and persons that are there not as *addenda* but as foundational elements in the text and argument. Preaching also was essential at St. Victor. Richard preached, and so did many others, in liturgical settings and at the daily chapter meetings. There sermons were undoubtedly the source of a good bit of Victorine teaching, as one can see by examining the collections of sermons we possess.

To conclude this volume we present Book III of *The Trinity*.This section, translated in full into English for the first time, is presented not so much for the contribution it makes to Trinitian theology or speculation, but rather for the eloquent statement it makes about the nature of true charity, community, and individuality. This statement is made in the context of a discussion of the necessary plurality of persons in God, but the interpersonal Trinitarian theology Richard develops has a significant bearing on the concept of love between persons and in a community. As Ewert Cousins has pointed out, Augustine's conception of the individual soul as an image of the Trinity provided the guidelines for a spirituality of the "inner way" emphasizing the individual's ascent to union, while Richard suggests in his Trinitian thought the possibility of a spirituality that involves "interpersonal community."[23]

In *The Trinity* Richard proposes to discover necessary reasons for God's unity and Trinity (book 1, chapters 4–5). It is also a work that expounds and interprets a primary statement of faith, the Athanasian Creed, which the brothers at St. Victor recited daily. Thus reason and faith may seem to collide in this work. We must keep in mind Richard's own perspective, however. While God's unity and Trinity are beyond independent proof by reason, human reason can offer lines of reasoning that support and explicate what faith declares. Such is the role of "necessary reasons" in *The Trinity* as they are coupled with faith and experience.[24]

To consider the plurality of persons in the divine, Richard first turns to divine goodness, which is supreme goodness. But, he

---

23. Ewert Cousins, "A Theology of Interpersonal Relations," *Thought* 45 (1970): 59.
24. Ibid., pp. 61–64.

points out, supreme goodness cannot lack charity.[25] To support this, he calls upon human experience:

> Let each person examine his consciousness; without doubt and without contradiction he will discover that just as nothing is better than charity, so nothing is more pleasing than charity. Nature herself teaches us this; many experiences do the very same. (chapter 3)

But this charity of which Richard speaks requires another who is loved. Self-love, says Richard emphatically, cannot be charity. To the person who objects that God can love his creation, Richard replies that such love of creation is not charity either. For charity, as the supreme kind of love, must be properly ordered and directed; it must be between equals. The creation is not equal to the Creator. Only another divine person can be the object of charity in the divine (chapter 2).

Not only must charity be love directed toward an equal. It must also be a shared love: Each must love and be loved by the other. It is not enough to have an object of love that draws one away from self-love. The "object" of love must return love. Charity is not only given; it is received, a theme that is echoed in this century in Charles Williams's fundamental notion of "coinherence" (*The Descent of the Dove* [London, 1939]). That love must be mutual is required by the fact that supreme happiness cannot exist without the mutuality of love. Happiness requires plurality, just as charity requires the rejection of self-love.

Thus far we have seen Richard affirming the *plurality* of divine persons. But as Richard himself admits, plurality can mean only *two*, and faith declares that God is one substance in three persons (chapter 11). A further analysis of the nature of true charity reveals that three persons, not two, are necessary. For charity to be excellent, as well as perfect, it must desire that the love it experiences be

---

25. On charity, in addition to ibid., pp. 65–82, see Dumeige, *Richard of Saint-Victor*, chap. 3, and Fernand Guimet, "Notes en marge d'un texte de Richard de Saint-Victor," *Archives d'histoire littéraire et doctrinale du moyen âge* 14 (1943–1945): 361–394, and "*Caritas ordinata* et *amor discretus* dans la théologie trinitaire de Richard de Saint-Victor," *Revue du moyen âge latin* 4 (1948): 225–236. For the treatise *De Trinitate* in general one may consult A.-M. Éthier, *Le "De Trinitate" de Richard de Saint-Victor*, Publications de l'Institut d'Études médiévales d'Ottawa, 9 (Paris-Ottawa, 1939).

a love shared with another (chapters 13–20). In other words, the beloved wishes to share the love given to him or her with a third. Thus charity is not only mutual love between two; it is fully shared love among three.

Richard admits that he has drawn at times upon very human language and experience to explore the nature of love in the Trinity (chapter 18). Yet he offers no apology. It is necessary to draw not only upon authority but also experience to penetrate effectively such lofty matters of faith.

The interior life of God is thus marked by supreme goodness in which charity, happiness, sharing and excellence all demand that there be a fully personal Trinity. In the supreme source of life, the Creator, one finds full personhood understood in terms of union and individuality; of loving, being beloved and sharing love. Such a pattern suggests that in the *imago Dei* that is man, the reflection of this life should lead to a renewed appreciation of charity as a love lived in community with others, involving interpersonal sharing of the deepest kind. One may not be far wrong to suggest that the life led by the canons at St. Victor had some of the marks of this Trinitarian theology as they led a daily round of shared liturgical observance and heard Richard, among others, preach and commend to them a kind of mutual spiritual itinerary culminating in an experience of the supreme Trinity. Furthermore, as we noted earlier, it has been recently pointed out that the spirituality of the Victorines is not put in individualistic terms but has notes of concern for the other and mutual regard in ascetic and contemplative pursuits.

A Note on Texts and Translation

This translation of *The Twelve Patriarchs* has been made from a critical text prepared by Professor Jean Châtillon. The text will appear soon in the series *Sources chrétiennes*. The translations of *The Mystical Ark* and *Some Allegories of the Tabernacle of the Covenant* have been made from the texts in Migne's *Patrologiae latinae*, volume 196, columns 63B–192C and 191C–202A, respectively. Migne's text has been emended only where it seemed absolutely necessary.

Generally such changes have been made only when it seemed to be a case of misreading or a misprint. *The Trinity* has been translated from the critical text prepared by Jean Ribaillier, Richard de Saint-Victor, *De Trinitate* (Paris, 1958).

The translations presented in this volume have been made with an eye toward being as true to the Latin as is possible while also giving a readable and intelligible English version. In particular, certain Latin words such as *contemplatio*, *speculatio*, *spectaculum*, *revelatio* and the like have been translated by a consistent English word rather than perhaps varying the translation in context. The reader is called upon to make interpretations in context, if any are called for. I have also tried to be true to Richard's style where possible. A great deal depends upon the way in which he has arranged parallels, antitheses, clauses and the like. It has not always been an easy thing to be faithful, but I hope that the reader will benefit from this undertaking.

Translations of Biblical texts follow the form in which Richard uses them. His text frequently differs from the received Vulgate. Since Richard's interpretations often turn upon the specific wording of a passage from Scripture, it is necessary to be faithful to this version of the Biblical texts. Chapters and verses are cited according to the Vulgate. Generally, Biblical names have been given in their Vulgate form.

THE TWELVE
PATRIARCHS

BENJAMIN MINOR

CHAPTER I

Concerning the pursuit of wisdom and its excellence

"Benjamin a young man in ecstasy of mind" (Ps. 67:28). Let young men hear a discourse about youth; let them awaken to the voice of the Prophet: "Benjamin a young man in ecstasy of mind" (ibid.). Who is this Benjamin? Many know, some by knowledge, others by experience. Let those who know by teaching listen patiently; let those who have been taught by experience listen gladly. For a discourse concerning him—no matter how lengthy—can never satisfy anyone who has been able to know him even once by means of the teaching of experience (and I speak confidently). But who suffices to speak worthily of him? For he is more handsome of form when compared with all the sons of Jacob, as was proper for Rachel to beget. In fact, although Leah had more children, she could not have had more beautiful ones. For as we read, Jacob is known to have had two wives. One was called Leah; the other, Rachel. Leah was more fruitful; Rachel, more beautiful. Leah was fruitful but with poor eyesight. Rachel was nearly sterile but of singular beauty. Now let us see what these two wives of Jacob are so that we may more easily understand what their sons are. Rachel is teaching of truth; Leah, discipline of virtue. Rachel is pursuit of wisdom; Leah, longing for justice. But we know that Jacob served seven years for the sake of Rachel, and yet the days seemed few to him because of the greatness of love. Why do you marvel? The greatness of love was according to the greatness of beauty. Certainly, if I wish to attempt something in praise of wisdom, it will be too little however much I shall say. For what is loved more ardently

53

or is sweeter to possess than wisdom? For her comeliness surpasses all beauty, and her sweetness exceeds all pleasure. For as someone says, "She is more beautiful than the sun, and above the whole ordering of the stars; when compared with light, she is found before it" (Wisd. 7:29). For night follows day, but evil does not overcome wisdom: "She reaches powerfully from one end to the other and she sets all things in order pleasantly. I have loved and sought her out since my youth; I have desired to take her as my bride, and I have been made a lover of her beauty" (Wisd. 8:1–2). Why marvel if Jacob burned with love for such a bride, if he was unable to govern the flames of such a fire and so much love? O how much he loved, O he burned in his love who said: "I have loved wisdom above health and all beauty" (Wisd. 7:10). For, as we have said, nothing is loved more ardently or is sweeter to possess than wisdom. For this reason all wish to be wise, yet few are able to be wise.

CHAPTER II

Concerning longing for justice and its nature

Can we speak similarly concerning justice? Do we all equally wish to be just, but perhaps we are not able to be just? No— certainly we could all be just, if we perfectly wished to be just. For to love justice perfectly is already to be just. You can love wisdom greatly and you can be without it. Always and without doubt, the more you love justice, the more just you will be. But now let us see what the teachings of true justice are, and we shall discover why men so greatly detest marriage with Leah. Indeed it should be asked why nearly all who long so much for the embrace of Rachel shrink back so much from union with Leah. Perfect justice commands us to love our enemies; to leave our parents, property and other goods; to bear patiently evils inflicted on us; and everywhere to shun honor offered to us. But by the lovers of the world what can be thought to be more foolish or more laborious? For this reason they think Leah has poor eyesight and they call her "laborious." For indeed, Leah does mean "laborious." For truly it seems to them that it is a great labor, and no lesser an error, to rejoice in tribulation and to flee the good fortune of the world as if it were a plague. But because she does not reject the resources of the world that are necessary and yet does not admit them for the sake of pleasure, they say Leah has poor eyesight but is not blind and think she errs in judgment of things. Therefore, if longing for justice is understood by Leah and pursuit of wisdom by Rachel, then the reason is evident why Leah is despised by nearly everyone, while Rachel is loved so much.

CHAPTER III

Concerning the two sources of all good: reason and affection

But it is pleasing just now to inquire more carefully concerning these two wives of Jacob, and to explain more openly whatever the mind suggests. A certain kind of twofold power has been given to every rational spirit by that Father of lights from whom comes every good gift and every perfect gift. (Cf. James 1:17.) Reason is one thing. Affection is another thing. Reason, by which we distinguish things; affection, by which we love. Reason, resulting in truth; affection, resulting in virtue. These are those two sisters betrothed by the Lord: Oolla and Oolibamba, Jerusalem and Samaria. These are the two wives of the rational spirit, from whom honorable offspring and heirs of the kingdom of heaven are born. Right counsels are born from reason; holy longings, from affection. From the former, spiritual senses; from the latter, ordered affections. In short, from the latter, all virtue; from the former, all truth. Accordingly, it should be known that affection truly begins to be Leah at the time when it endeavors to form itself according to the pattern of justice. And reason is undoubtedly declared to be Rachel when it is illumined by the light of that highest and true wisdom. But who does not know how laborious the former is and how joyous the latter is? Certainly the affection of the soul is not drawn away from pleasurable things to proper things without great effort. Such a wife is rightly called Leah (that is, laborious). What can be sweeter or more joyful than to raise up the eye of the mind to contemplation of highest wisdom? When reason is extended for this contemplating it is deservedly honored with the name of Rachel. Rachel is interpreted "beginning of vision" or "a sheep." Therefore, so that he may be worthy of such a name, let a person fulfill what is found written: "Think of the Lord in goodness, and seek Him in simplicity of heart" (Wisd. 1:1). Certainly, he who thinks of the Lord in goodness already sees, with the eye of faith, Him who is the beginning of all things. But he truly is a sheep, if he seeks in simplicity. Do you not see how it is not just any wisdom, but the highest wisdom, pursued simply, that makes one to be Rachel? Indeed, I think, do you not marvel that Rachel is loved so much, when her handmaid (I speak of the wisdom of the world, which compared with her mistress is considered foolishness) is sought after, as we see, with so much love by the philosophers of the world?

CHAPTER IV

How through pursuit of wisdom the soul is often secretly drawn to the exercise of justice

Those who have been taught by experience rather than by hearing easily recognize how often it happens that Leah is substituted when Rachel is hoped for. It often happens that a soul that is by no means cleansed from the sordidness of a previous way of life and is not yet fit for contemplation of heavenly things, while placing itself in the bedchamber of Rachel and preparing itself for her embraces, while supposing itself to possess her already, suddenly and unexpectedly discovers itself to be in the embrace of Leah. For what do we call sacred Scripture except the bedchamber of Rachel, in which we do not doubt that divine wisdom is hidden beneath the veil of attractive allegories? Rachel is sought in such a chamber as often as spiritual understanding is sought out in sacred reading. But so long as we are incapable of penetrating sublime things, we do not find the long-desired, diligently sought Rachel. Therefore, we begin to groan and sigh and not only to bewail but also to be ashamed of our blindness. So while we grieve and seek the source of this blindness, we become mindful of the evils we have done. On the contrary, this divine reading frequently makes us aware of our foulness and pricks our hearts with compunction, when we consider it while we are unwilling and even seeking something else in it. Therefore, as often as we find compunction rather than contemplation in divine reading, without doubt we have found not Rachel but Leah in the bedchamber of Rachel. Just as it belongs to Rachel to meditate, to contemplate, to distinguish and to understand; so certainly it pertains to Leah to weep, to groan, to grieve and to sigh. For Leah, as was said, is affection inflamed by divine inspiration; Rachel is reason illumined by divine showing. Leah is affection forming itself according to the pattern of justice; Rachel, reason raising itself up in contemplation of celestial wisdom. But enough of this. Now let us consider their handmaids.

Chapter V

How imagination serves reason, and sensation, affection

Each of them receives her handmaid: affection, sensation; reason, imagination. Sensation submits to affection; imagination serves reason. Each of these handmaids is known to be necessary to her mistress to such a degree that without the former all of the world seems unable to confer anything upon the latter. For without imagination, reason would know nothing; without sensation, affection would have sense of nothing. For why is Leah so vehemently affected by the love of perishable things, except that she is in many ways delighted by these things through the service of her handmaid, who is sensation. Again, as it is written: "Since the invisible things of God from the creation of the world are clearly seen, being understood by means of those things which are made" (Rom. 1:20). From which it is manifestly concluded that reason never rises up to cognition of the invisible unless her handmaid, imagination, represents to her the form of visible things. For through the appearance of visible things she rises to knowledge of invisible things, as often as she draws a kind of similitude from the one to the other. But it is certain that without imagination she would not know corporeal things, and without knowledge of these things she would not ascend to contemplation of celestial things. For the eye of the flesh alone looks at visible things, while the eye of the heart alone sees invisible things. The sense of the flesh is totally outward; the sense of the heart, totally inward. Reason is not able to go out externally.

Corporeal sense is not able to enter into the reason. It is not proper for a delicate, tender and singularly beautiful daughter to run abroad through the streets, but neither is it suitable for the servant to burst irreverently into the most secret inner room of his mistress. Therefore the imagination (inasmuch as she is a handmaid) runs between mistress and servant, between reason and sense. And whatever it imbibes from outside through the sense of the flesh, it represents inwardly for the service of reason. Thus imagination always assists reason, never in fact withdrawing itself from her service for a single moment. For even when sense fails, imagination does not cease to provide. For when I am placed in darkness, I see nothing, but if I wish I am able to imagine anything. So always and in all things, imagination is ready, and reason can employ her service everywhere. But sensation none the less has her hands full: She is concerned about frequent service and having herself to provide always and everywhere service for her mistress Leah. It is sensation who is accustomed to season foods of carnal delights, to serve them to affection, to invite enjoyment of them before the proper time and to provoke beyond measure. Who is it other than sensation that inflames the affection of the soul with longing for carnal pleasures and inebriates her with their delight? It is she who goes before her mistress and leads her here and there when that laborious person goes out. Since Leah has poor eyesight and sees very little, she is not ashamed to follow the guidance of sensation. It is for this reason that Leah (namely the affection of the soul) now loves what should be despised and now despises what should be loved because as long as the eye is dimmed in the judgment of things she does not feel ashamed to follow the appetite of the flesh. These are the two handmaids of Jacob's two wives. Scripture names them Zelpha and Bala; Bala for Rachel, and Zelpha for Leah.

CHAPTER VI

Concerning the vice of imagination and sensation

We have seen their service, but I do not think it necessary to be silent concerning their vice. Bala is garrulous; Zelpha, drunken.

For not even Rachel, her mistress, can suppress Bala's loquacity, and not even the generosity of her mistress can completely quench Zelpha's thirst. The wine that Zelpha drinks is the joy of pleasures. The more of it she drinks, the greater is her thirst. For the whole earth does not suffice to satisfy the appetite of sensation. Since she always holds her mouth open for drinking, no matter how much she drinks she is rightly called Zelpha, that is "gaping mouth," the thirst of which is never quenched. Now the imagination makes noise in the ears of the heart with so much importunity, and so great is its clamor, as we have said, that Rachel herself can scarcely, if at all, restrain her. It is for this reason that often when we say psalms or pray we wish to banish phantasies of thoughts or other sorts of images of things from the eyes of the heart, but we are not able to do so. Since even unwillingly we daily suffer a tumult of resounding thoughts of this sort, we are taught by daily experience of what sort and how great is the garrulity of Bala. She calls to memory everything, whether seen or heard, that we ourselves have done or said at some time or another. And she does not cease repeating over and over again the same things she has already set forth in a full explanation. And often when the will of the heart does not give assent to hearing her, she herself nevertheless unfolds her narrative although, as it were, no one listens. So, in any case, decrepit old men and inveterate old women are accustomed to talk continually about something without any hearer and as if some people were present, to hold a conversation with them. Therefore she who imitates the habits of inveterate persons is not undeservedly called Bala (that is, "inveterate"). But who does not know about the garrulity of Bala and the drunkenness of Zelpha except perhaps one who does not know himself?

CHAPTER VII

What the principal affections are and in what order or manner they are brought back to virtues

Now it seems we should speak about their sons, and first about the sons of Leah, for she is read to have given birth first. As we have said, the sons of Jacob from Leah are nothing other than ordered affections. Whereas certainly if they are disordered, they cannot in any case be called his sons. And so, the seven offspring of Leah are seven virtues since a virtue is nothing other than an ordered and moderated affection of the soul: ordered when it is directed to that toward which it ought to be; moderated when it is as great as it ought to be. Thus there are seven principal affections that rise by turns from the one affective disposition of the soul: Hope and fear; joy and grief; hatred, love and shame. All of these can be ordered at one time and disordered at another. But only when they have been ordered are they then to be counted among the sons of Jacob. If there were no disordered fear the divine word would never have said: "They trembled from fear in that place, where there was no fear" (Ps. 13:5). Again, if there were no ordered fear it would not have been written: "Fear of the Lord is holy, enduring for all ages" (Ps. 18:10). Again, if love were not ordered at one time and disordered at another sacred Scripture would neither teach the former nor prohibit the latter: "You shall love your God with all your heart, and with all your mind, and with all your strength, and your neighbor just as yourself" (Deut. 6:5; Matt. 22:37, 39). And elsewhere, "Love neither the world nor things that are in the world" (1 John 2:15). We should understand similarly concerning the other affections: sometimes ordered and for that reason good; sometimes disordered and for that reason evil. However, concerning the good ones, which we have said are the sons of Jacob, now let us see in what order they are begotten.

CHAPTER VIII

How and from what ordered fear is born

It is written: "The fear of the Lord is the beginning of wisdom" (Ps. 110:10). Therefore this offspring is the first of the virtues. Without it you are not able to have the others. He who desires to have such a son should consider not only frequently but also carefully the evil that he has done: on one side, the magnitude of his crimes; on the other side, the power of the judge. From such consideration fear is born. Of course, this is the son who is rightly called Ruben, that is, "son of vision." In a way and as a matter of fact, he is blind and sees nothing who does not fear to sin, does not foresee future evils, is not ashamed of his depravity and is not terrified of divine power. But if he should begin to see, he will begin at the same time to fear, and the more perfectly he knows, the more strongly he will fear. You see, I think, how rightly he who is engendered from such vision is called Ruben. At his birth his mother rightly exclaims "God has seen my abasement" (Gen. 29:32) because from that time she should begin to see and to be seen; to know God and to be known by God; to see God through the intuition of dread; to be seen by God through the regard of kindness.

CHAPTER IX

How grief is born and is ordered

After the first son has been born and gradually has grown up, the second is born because it is necessary that grief follow great fear. For the more vehemently a person fears the punishment he deserves, the more sharply he laments the fault he has committed. But it should be known that, at whatever hour a sinner shall have been converted and shall have mourned, he will be saved, according to this: "A contrite and humbled heart, O God, you will not despise" (Ps. 50:19). How does it seem to you? Is it not right for such a son to be called Simeon, that is "granting"? For he who truly repents and truly grieves will receive indulgence without doubt and without delay. A prayer that is offered from a contrite and humbled heart is more quickly heard with favor. A heart is humbled through fear, contrite through grief. It is humbled by Ruben, made contrite by Simeon, and in weeping it is pricked with compunction: "Blessed are they that mourn for they shall be comforted" (Matt. 5:5).

CHAPTER X

How hope is born and is ordered

But, I ask, what consolation can there be for those truly repenting and bitterly weeping except the hope of forgiveness? This is that third son of Jacob who, for that reason, is called Levi, that is "added" or "addition," because he is added to those earlier two who were given first. The divine word does not call this son "given" but calls him "added" lest anyone presume to have hope of forgiveness before fear and grief worthy of repentance. For whoever compliments himself with impunity after committing crimes without satisfaction is not so much raised up by hope as he is thrown down by presumption. From such a name divine Scripture wishes to convince us that certainly we are not able to have this son before the two earlier sons nor can this third son be missing after the preceding two. For truly and without any doubt, the more frequently and the more vehemently anyone is afflicted with internal grief concerning his guilt, the more certain, the more secure he is made by the forgiveness of indulgence: "According to the multitude of my griefs in my heart, your comforts have given joy to my soul" (Ps. 93:19). For this is the reason that the Holy Spirit, the Paraclete, is called the Comforter, because often and freely it consoles the soul afflicted with tears of repentance. The Holy Spirit frequently visits that soul, freely comforts, and fully restores confidence of forgiveness as much as it observes that the soul condemns its sins with weeping and weeps when condemning.

CHAPTER XI

How love is born and is ordered

From this time on a kind of intimacy begins to arise between God and the soul, and friendship begins to be established because the soul often feels itself to be visited by God and from His advent not so much now to be consoled but on the contrary sometimes to be filled with a kind of ineffable joy. Unless I am mistaken, Leah had a presentiment of this bond of friendship when after Levi's birth she exclaimed with great exultation: "Now my husband shall be joined to me" (Gen. 29:34). The true spouse of the soul is God, whom we truly join with us from this time on when we adhere to Him through true love. Or rather from this time on God truly joins Himself to us when by a kind of inner communication He incites us to love Him and binds us more tightly. What heart is so unfeeling and hard that divine piety cannot soften it by His presence and cannot attract it by His sweetness? Therefore it happens that the one whom he used to fear greatly, afterward he begins to love more ardently. You see already, I think, that just as after fear increases daily, of necessity grief rises up repeatedly; so certainly after hope is born and makes progress through daily increments, love is born. And so this is that son of Jacob who is born in the fourth place and in Scripture is called Judah, that is "confessing." If we seek the reason for this name we shall find it quickly. For we know that whatever a person approves, that he loves, and the more he loves, the more he approves. And what is approval except praise? By all means that truly is praise which arises from chaste love and that is pure confession which proceeds from the admiration of praise. Do you wish to know more openly and more excellently than all the rest what is the voice of exultation and confession that Judah alone knew?

Chapter XII

What the nature of love is

Pay attention to a soul loving someone excessively and burning with an excessive love. Pay attention to what it feels, to what it says to itself about the one whom it loves so much and greatly admires. What does it say? What does it say quietly to itself? It says, "O how good, how liberal! O how pleasant, how sweet, how lovable, how embraceable, how wholly admirable, how wholly desirable! O blessed is the one he loves! O happy is the one he judges worthy of his love. Happy am I if I am permitted to enjoy him; blessed am I, if I should happen to possess him!" If I am not mistaken, this is that voice of exultation and confession which always resounds from the mouth of Judah into the ears of divine kindness. What do you say, Leah? What do you exclaim for Judah? What do you pay to the Lord? What do you give back for such a son? Now, she says, I shall confess to the Lord: "I shall confess abundantly to the Lord with my mouth" (Ps. 108:30). Surely and without doubt, you truly confess to the Lord not only frequently, but also unceasingly, if you love Him perfectly: "I will bless the Lord at all times; His praise shall always be in my mouth" (Ps. 33:2). Indeed, you always praise if you always love and always long. For you would not love if you did not approve. As it has been said, what is approval except praise? And praise itself is confession itself. But do not think that it would suffice for Judah to confess so much with the heart unless he also confessed with the mouth. For Judah wishes both to commend Him to others and to kindle them to love of Him whom he judges to be worthy of the love of all and who longs to be loved by all. All these things are said concerning the confession of praise. But what shall we say concerning the confession of crimes? Perhaps Judah ignores the latter, however much he so excellently recognizes the former. I do not think so, because I know the latter and the former both pertain very much to the honor of God. And I know that he who loves more truly does more freely whatever he knows to serve the honor of God. Not only His generosity but also our iniquity greatly commends the goodness of God. For if it is a great thing to grant many things freely to those who deserve nothing, how much greater will it be to give good things to those who deserve evil things? O what sort of kindness, which even our impiety is not able to overcome. There are some things that He mercifully forgives; there are other things that He abundantly bestows. For He forgives our evils; He gives his goods generously. Always quick to forgive; always ready to give generously. The former is kind; the latter, generous. In both cases beneficent; always good. Therefore let us confess our evils to Him. Let us confess our goods to Him. Let us confess our evils to be from us, so that He may in kindness forgive them. Let us confess our goods to be from Him so that He may preserve and increase them. Judah is incessantly engaged in these things in order not to appear ungrateful for either forgiveness conferred or grace granted. Therefore I think this son is rightly called

Judah, that is "confessing," because true love always confesses. Finally, since it is written that "God is truth," it is shown clearly that God does not love whoever is ashamed to confess the truth. Scripture says: "In the beginning the just man is an accuser of himself" (Prov. 18:17). Therefore the man who believes or desires himself to be a lover of God knows what to do unless perhaps he thinks loving God is other than loving the justice of God. Behold, we now have the fourth of the first sons of Leah. The first is fear of punishment; the second, sorrow of penance; the third, hope of forgiveness; the fourth, love of justice. After these she ceases to give birth. For she thinks that she is able to be sufficient for herself since she considers herself to love truly the true good.

CHAPTER XIII

How the mind is incited to investigation of invisible things by love of invisible things

But what do you think goes on in the heart of Rachel; by what heat of longings is she excited when she sees her sister Leah the joyful mother of sons while she remains sterile? Let us hear what she says, and let us know why she grieves. What does she say to Jacob her husband: "Give me children, otherwise I shall die" (Gen. 30:1). Without doubt, if the pursuit of wisdom does not make progress, it soon fails. Let us inquire diligently how it can be that after the birth of Judah, Rachel burns more than usual with love of offspring. We said above that just as it pertains to Leah who is affection of the soul to love, so it is for Rachel who is reason to know. Indeed, from the former every ordered affection is born; from the latter, mental sense or pure intellect. But what do we understand by Judah, if not ordered love, love of celestial things, love of God, love of the highest good? And so, at the birth of Judah—that is when longing for invisible goods rises up and ferments—Rachel begins to burn with desire for children because she begins to want to know. Where there is love, there is seeing. We gladly look at one whom we greatly love. No one doubts that since he can love invisible goods, he will want immediately to know and to see them through the understanding. So the more Judah grows (that is, the affection called loving), the greater there burns in Rachel the desire to give birth, which is the pursuit of knowing.

Chapter XIV

What the first way is for everyone entering into the contemplation of invisible things: namely through the imagination

But who does not know how difficult it is—or rather how well-nigh impossible it is—for the carnal mind, as yet unskilled in spiritual pursuits, to rise up to knowledge of invisible things and to fix the eye of contemplation on them? Certainly up until now it knows nothing except corporeal things; nothing else occurs to one thinking except only the visible things he is accustomed to think. He seeks to see invisible things, but nothing occurs except forms of visible things. He longs to see incorporeal things, and he dreams nothing except the images of corporeal things. Therefore, what should he do? Is it not better to think of those things by any mode whatever than to commit them to oblivion and neglect? Indeed, if the mind loves well it does not easily forget these things. Nevertheless, with much more difficulty is it raised up to contemplation of these things. Yet it does what it can, it considers them insofar as it is able. It thinks by means of imagination because it does not yet have the power to see by means of purity of the understanding. This, I think, is the reason why Rachel must first have children from her handmaid rather than giving birth from herself because it is sweet for her to retain, at least by means of imagination, the memory of those things while she does not yet have the power to grasp by the reasoning process an understanding of them. Just as by Rachel we understand reason, so by her handmaid we understand imagination. Therefore reason urges that it is more suitable to think about true goods in any mode whatever and at least to kindle the soul to a longing for them by a kind of imaginary beauty rather than to fix thought on false and deceptive goods. And this is the reason why Rachel wished to give her handmaid to her husband. No one is ignorant that this is the first way for all those who enter into contemplation of invisible things unless perhaps experience has not yet instructed him with a view to this knowledge.

CHAPTER XV

How divine Scripture refers to the speculation of weak persons

We should not overlook how divine Scripture refers to this speculation and condescends to human infirmity. For it describes invisible things through the forms of visible things and impresses the memory of them upon our minds through the beauty of certain very desirable appearances. This is the reason that now they promise a land flowing with milk and honey; at one time they mention flowers; at another, odors; at one time they indicate the harmony of celestial joys by means of human singing; at another, by means of a chorus of birds. Read the Apocalypse of John and you will find the adornment of heavenly Jerusalem described in various ways by means of gold and silver, by means of pearls or other kinds of precious gems. In fact we know that none of these things exists there, where nevertheless nothing can be missing altogether. For indeed, no such thing exists there through appearance, where nevertheless everything exists through similitude. In all these things Bala has that from which she may usefully serve her mistress since she willingly represents to her the memory of all these things where and when she wishes. For we are able to imagine these things immediately whenever we wish. Imagination is never able to be more useful to the reason than when it is devoted to it in such service.

CHAPTER XVI

That one kind of imagination is bestial, the other, rational

However, in order to continue with what has been said concerning the sons of Bala, it should be known that one kind of imagination is bestial, another kind is rational. However, the bestial should not be numbered among the sons of Jacob, nor will Rachel wish at anytime to take such an adopted son to herself. And so imagination is bestial when with a wandering mind we run about here and there without any usefulness, without any deliberation concerning those things which we have just seen or done. Surely this is bestial for a beast is able to do it. However, that imagination is rational when from those things which we know by means of bodily sense we fabricate something else in the imagination. For instance: We have seen gold, we have seen a house, but we have never seen a gold house. Nevertheless, if we wish we are able to picture to ourselves a gold house. In any case a beast cannot do this. It is possible for a rational creature only. We often use such an imagination when we more diligently seek what are the goods and evils of the future life. For no things here in this world are good only; no things here are evil only; but good and evil are mixed together. And although there are many among both kinds, nevertheless they are never found alone. There in that other world can be found both goods without an admixture of evils and, no less, evils without an admixture of goods. Here in this world just as we find none alone, so also we do not find the highest. We do not doubt that there in the future life are both highest and unmixed good and evil. Therefore as often as from the many goods and evils that bodily sense experiences in this life we gather what kind and how great that highest good or evil of the future life is able to be, and from imagination of these things a kind of image of future things is formed; surely in such a case it is easily proven that this is rational imagination, and it appears that this pertains to Bala and to Rachel. It pertains to Bala inasmuch as it is imagination; to Rachel, inasmuch as it is rational. Such an offspring is of the imagination through birth and of the reason through adoption. For one bears such an offspring; the other educates it. He is born from Bala but is governed by Rachel.

CHAPTER XVII

We interpret in various ways that which we call imagination, reason, or will

Let no one be thrown into confusion because I call both mother and offspring "imagination." But I mean for that to be between mother and son which is between instrument and act; or that between mother and her offspring which is between genus and species. For by joining difference to itself genus brings forth species from itself, just as union with a man impregnates a woman with offspring. Also, we often call an instrument and its action by one name: for that which we see and that by which we see, we call "sight." So when reason, or will or intellect is mentioned, sometimes the instrument, other times its action is understood. And we know in fact that the instrument is always prior to its action and is able to exist without it. Therefore action has its existence from instrument, not instrument from action. For this reason it is not inappropriate to understand the mother by instrument and her son by action. Therefore when imagination signifies an instrument, it is that power of the soul by which it is able to picture to itself anything whatsoever, whenever it wishes. When the mind uses this instrument for imagining something, without doubt a kind of action is accomplished that similarly is called imagination. I wanted to mention these things briefly, but it is not necessary to dwell for long on them. Now let us return to the order of the explanation.

CHAPTER XVIII

Concerning the twofold speculation that arises from imagination

We have said that the rational imagination alone seems to pertain to Rachel and what is not rational is judged absolutely unworthy for adoption by her. However, rational imagination is one thing when ordered by reason and another thing when mixed with understanding. We use the former when according to a known appearance of visible things we order another similar thing in the mind and yet from that we do not think of something invisible. We use the latter, then, when we exert ourselves to rise by means of the appearance of visible things to knowledge of invisible things. In the former imagination is not without reason. In the latter understanding is not without imagination. These are the two sons of Bala, of whom the firstborn is called Dan, and the second, Naphtali. To Dan especially pertains consideration of future evils; to Naphtali, speculation of future goods. Dan knows nothing except corporeal things, but nevertheless he examines things that are far removed from bodily sense. Naphtali rises to the understanding of invisible things by means of the form of visible things. We do not doubt that infernal torments are far removed from bodily sense because we are not able to see where and what kind they are, but nevertheless as often as we wish we have these things before the eyes of the heart through the service of Dan. None of the faithful who reads in holy Scripture about hell, the flames of Gehenna and the outer darkness believes that these things have been said figuratively, but he does not doubt that these things exist somewhere truly and bodily. From the foregoing it is certain that although someone may place these things before the eyes of the heart by means of imagination he ought not to seek the signification of these immediately by means of spiritual understanding because he does not doubt these things are said not figuratively but literally. As we have already rightly said, consideration of these especially pertains to Dan, where we work by imagination alone although we cannot deal with it in such labor without the ordering of reason. But when we read about a land flowing with milk and honey or heavenly Jerusalem having walls of precious stones, gates of pearl and streets of gold, what person of sane sense would wish to interpret these things according to the literal sense? Therefore immediately he has recourse to spiritual understanding, and he seeks what is contained there mystically. Do you not see how such description as this of future things seems to pertain more to Naphtali, where without understanding, imagination alone cannot suffice, as is well known? Therefore it has been rightly said that consideration of future evils pertains especially to Dan while on the other hand speculation of future goods pertains especially to Naphtali. Nevertheless, many things, even those that have been written concerning the torments of evil persons, must be interpreted mystically. Similarly, many things concerning goods of the future life, although described corporeally, must be understood simply.

Chapter XIX

Concerning the first speculation and its nature

It should be known—indeed one is not able to ignore it—that the consideration that is in imagination alone occurs more easily to a person meditating. For that which is mixed with understanding alone, being more subtle, is more difficult to discover. This is the reason that Dan is born first and Naphtali, second. In this twofold consideration it is especially notable that Dan represents a made-up imagination of future things according to an actual imagination of present things. Certainly Naphtali often rises to true understanding through the made-up imagination of a description of things. In fact, one may not fashion anything false concerning future and invisible goods through spiritual understanding, although it is without fault to perceive through imagination the torments of the wicked as other than they are. In fact, who suffices to contemplate in this life all these things as they are? But anyone by the decision of the mind describes these things not as they are but of such sort as he knows how to fabricate, in a figure. Therefore perhaps such a son as this is called Dan, that is "judgment," because in such a representation he follows not the lesson of experience but the decision of his discretion. For since Dan forms the representation of future things in each person's mind from that person's own judgment, I think anyone rightly calls Dan, that is judgment, the artificer of such things.

Chapter XX

Concerning the function of the first speculation

Nevertheless there is another reason for this name, which, perhaps being more subtle, is found to be more useful. For as often as holy men feel themselves to be beset by shameful thoughts and to be spurred on to illicit delights, so often are they accustomed in the very approach of temptation to place future torments before the eyes of the mind and from such consideration to blot out whatever illicit thing the mind suggests, before shameful delight arises. Therefore, in this way immediately they punish themselves through consideration of punishment and destroy the allurements of sin. Therefore, because through the function of Dan we perceive, reprove, condemn and punish seductive thoughts, we rightly call him Dan, that is judgment. But why do we say this concerning only shameful thoughts, since perfect men seriously detest vain and useless thoughts, according to that which is found written: "Woe to you who think useless thoughts" (Mich. 2:1)? And, "The Holy Spirit of discipline will flee from that which is made-up and will withdraw himself from thoughts that are without any understanding" (Wisd. 1:5). What will happen, I ask, concerning these things that we feel with an illicit affection, when the Holy Spirit withdraws himself even from those that are without any understanding? Often it happens that having been established in prayer, we must bear certain phantasies of thought throwing themselves at the heart with great importunity. But ought we to overlook such things without our reprehension? Is it not necessary to reprove these things more quickly, and as it has been said, by means of the representation of punishment to restrain the irritation of sin and to chasten it by our thoughts? Therefore it is written: "Dan shall judge his people just as the other tribes of Israel do" (Gen. 49:16). Certainly, to the sons of Zelpha pertains discipline of works; to the sons of Leah, disposition of the will; to the sons of Rachel, judgment of assertions; to the sons of Bala, surely, governing of thoughts. Thus any thought is judged in its tribe, as it were, when every error is corrected by its parallel, when will is corrected by will, when work is chastened by work, and assertion is corrected by assertion. As often as we think anything false, as often as we will anything unjust, as often as we do anything disordered, immediately we are in no way ignorant that we are blamable. But do all persons equally judge that they are worthy of blame when they think a useless or disordered thing? There are many who blame themselves for a perverse work or a depraved will. There are few who judge themselves for a disordered thought. But because perfect men do this and because it is necessary that those who wish to be perfect do this, therefore Jacob foretells and teaches, saying: "Dan shall judge his people just as the other tribes of Israel do."

CHAPTER XXI

Concerning the usefulness of the first speculation

If Dan watches over his people strictly, if he exercises his judgment diligently, it will happen that in other tribes those things will rarely be found which rightly should be condemned. For the mind that immediately cuts off a seductive thought in the very suggestion will not be easily carried away in depraved delight, just as the sin that is stopped before depraved consent never passes into act. Therefore more than all the others Dan should be alert and severe in judgment so that it may be granted for others to live for the greater part without contention and dispute. Dan always will find in his tribe what he ought to examine, what he ought rightly to reprehend, although in the others it may happen that sometimes some of them might be found without fault. For the fault of these others is in the will, while his disorder is often because of necessity. For I never approve evil, never give consent to evil, never accomplish evil, except I myself shall have willed it. However, it is possible for evil to occur by thought, even against one's will. But when evil rises up, when it strikes by means of thought, it immediately pertains to Dan to bring it to judgment, to crush it diligently, to condemn it when apprehended, and to strike a deceptive thought out of any other consideration, and to extinguish evil temptations by means of the recollection of torments. You see, I think, how rightly this son is called Dan, that is judgment, concerning whom alone there is hesitation whether he should have to judge his people since he alone, if it is possible, ought to judge not only assiduously but also strictly, so that the others do not have anything they ought to judge.

Chapter XXII

Concerning the second speculation and its nature

Just as it pertains to the office of Dan to restrain upsurging vices by the representation of punishment, so then it pertains to Naphtali to kindle good longings through the consideration of rewards. For Naphtali marvelously kindles our soul with longing for these things as often as he brings the image of eternal goods before the eyes of the mind, which he is accustomed to do in two modes. For sometimes he uses translation, other times, comparison. It is comparison when from the multitude or magnitude of present goods he gathers how many or how great those joys of the future life may be. For example: Looking often at the brightness of the sun (which, to be sure, is corporeal light), he considers how great that future spiritual light will be if this corporeal light is so large and so marvelous. For how great do you think that light will be, which will be in common with us and the angels, if this light that we have in common with the beasts is so great! Of what kind will be the future light of the blessed if this present light of the miserable is such! Again, he infers the multiplicity of invisible goods from the multitude of visible goods. Therefore how many shall we suppose them to be? But who is able to count them? How many delights of the eyes, how many delights of the ears and other senses are there? How many colors, how many odors, how many flavors are there? Therefore if there are so many delights of bodies, how many delights of spirits will there be? If we possess so much in this temporal life, how great will be those things which we expect in eternity? Therefore, in this mode, he uses comparison. Nonetheless, he uses translation, as has been said, when he transfers any description whatever of visible things to the signification of invisible things. For example: He hears light mentioned in Scripture, as when it has been written concerning God: "Because he lives in light inaccessible" (1 Tim. 6:16). So he inquires what is this incorporeal light that the invisible and incorporeal nature of God inhabits, and he discovers that this light is the very wisdom of God because it is the true light. For just as this exterior light illuminates the eyes of the body, so without any doubt, that incorporeal light is accustomed to illuminate the eyes of the heart. Behold how Naphtali rises up by means of the quality of visible things to knowledge of invisible things. Therefore it is evident how rightly he is called Naphtali according to both interpretations. For Naphtali is interpreted as either "comparison" or "conversion." For he is accustomed to convert any known nature of visible things to spiritual understanding. Therefore because he converts to spiritual understanding almost everything he finds written, he rightly receives the name of conversion. And also because he assiduously uses comparison, as has been said, no less rightly is he named Naphtali, that is comparison.

CHAPTER XXIII

What is familiar and even special to the second speculation

However, it should be known that the kind of contemplation that occurs in pure understanding is known to be more subtle as it certainly is more excellent than a speculation of the kind that is designated by Naphtali. Nevertheless, a speculation of this kind has something singular and very notable. For in the case of other minds as yet certainly unskilled and untrained, it is easier to understand and more enjoyable to listen to. Indeed this presents itself more easily to one who meditates and affects more sweetly one who listens. It is clear and very ready in meditation and very affable in speaking. For this reason it is said of Naphtali by Jacob: "Naphtali is a hind sent forth, giving words of beauty" (Gen. 49:21). For he is called "hind" on account of facility for running; "sent forth" on account of eagerness for running. The hind, a swift animal, is able to run very fast, and he who has been sent out desires to run fast. Therefore, unless I am mistaken, Naphtali is rightly called "a hind sent forth," since by the grace of contemplation he has the ability to run through many things, and on account of the sweetness of contemplation it pleases him to run fast. For in such speed Naphtali now raises the contemplative soul (still trained very little in such an exercise) to the heights, now casts it headlong into the depths, now snatches it through innumerable things so that the soul that experiences these things often marvels in itself, having been taught by a successful master, how aptly our Naphtali is called a hind sent forth. Certainly it should be noted how rightly he may be compared not to a bird flying but to a hind running. For indeed a bird when flying is suspended far above the earth, while a hind when making a jump begins from the earth and is not separated very far from the earth in these jumps. So certainly Naphtali, when he seeks the nature of invisible things by means of the form of visible things, is accustomed to make a sort of leap, not however to gain strength for full flight, since to the degree that he raises himself to the heights he never entirely leaves the depths, carrying with him the shadow of corporeal things.

CHAPTER XXIV

How great the joy of the second speculation is

Behold how he is "a hind sent forth." But how is he "giving words of beauty"? Perhaps the more evidently we show this by an example, the more completely we can persuade. You wish to hear words of beauty, words of pleasantness, full of beauty, full of sweetness, such as Naphtali is accustomed to form, or such as he agrees to form. "Let him kiss me with the kiss of his mouth" (Song of Songs 1:1). "Stay me with flowers, comfort me with apples, for I am sick with love" (ibid. 2:5). "Your lips, O my spouse, drip like a honeycomb; honey and milk are under your tongue; and the smell of your garments is like an aromatic odor" (ibid. 4:11). What, I ask, is found sweeter or more joyful than such words? What is heard more gladly or more avidly than such words? These words seem to sound like something carnal, but nevertheless spiritual things are described by means of them. Thus Naphtali knew to mix carnal things with spiritual things and to describe incorporeal things by means of corporeal things so that the twofold nature of man finds in his words that from which he who consists of both corporeal and incorporeal nature might marvelously refresh himself. Perhaps it is for this reason that they taste so pleasantly to man because in a way, as has been said, they refresh his twofold nature. However, in his words, that is marvelous and worthy of wonder which almost always pleases more delightfully, when according to the literal sense they seem to mean nothing. This is of such sort: "Your hair is like a flock of goats that ascend from Mount Gilead. Your teeth are like a flock of shorn sheep that come up from the washing" (Song of Songs 4:1–2). "Your nose is like the tower of Lebanon which looks toward Damascus. Your head is like Carmel" (ibid. 7:4–5). When we hear or read these and other such things, they seem to be very delightful. Nevertheless in all of these, if we follow only the sense of the letter, we find nothing in them at which we may worthily marvel. But perhaps in such words this is what we so gladly embrace: that from a kind of pleasing silliness, so to speak, of the literal sense, we are forced to take refuge in spiritual understanding. If, therefore, we think how quick our Naphtali is in meditation, how pleasing he is in speaking, the more speedily we will perceive how rightly Scripture proclaims concerning him: "Naphtali a hind let loose, giving words of beauty" (Gen. 49:21).

CHAPTER XXV

Concerning the twofold offspring of virtues, which is born from conquered sensation

But meanwhile we want these words to suffice for the sons of Bala. Now it remains that we should say something concerning the sons of Zelpha. Leah, seeing that her sister Rachel now rejoices in adopted offspring, is herself provoked to give her handmaid to her husband, so that she may be able to exult with her sister in adopted sons. Therefore if, as has been said above, we ought to understand the senses by means of Zelpha, I ask what other offspring of virtue is she herself able to bear except that she learns to live temperately in prosperity and to have patience in adversity? These are Gad and Asher, the two sons of Zelpha: namely, the rigor of abstinence and the vigor of patience. And so Gad is born first, and Asher is born second, because first we must be temperate toward our own goods; afterward we must be strong to endure alien evils. This is the twofold offspring of virtues that Zelpha indeed bears in pain, but nevertheless to the great blessedness of her mistress. Indeed, by abstinence or patience the flesh certainly is afflicted, but the soul is quieted, resulting in great peace and tranquillity. This is the reason why when Gad was born, Leah cried out, saying "Happily"; and again, when Asher was being born she spoke out, saying: "This is for my blessedness" (Gen. 30:11, 13). "For my blessedness," she said, not "for hers." For when sense experience through the external flesh is weakened, then affection of the heart is restored to the integrity of purity.

CHAPTER XXVI

Concerning the rigor of abstinence, the vigor of patience, and the nature of both

For how great do you think is the peace of heart or tranquillity to crave none of the pleasures of the world, to fear none of its adversities? One of these is acquired through Gad; the other is obtained through Asher. For what should he who by love of abstinence rejects proffered delights crave from the pleasures of this world? Or what should he, who when strengthened by the virtue of patience conquers even those who cause evils, fear concerning the adversities of this world? As it has been written about the apostles: "And the apostles departed from the presence of the council, rejoicing that they were counted worthy to suffer abuse for the name of Jesus" (Acts 5:41). And as it is taught by Paul: "Rejoicing in tribulation" (Rom. 12:12). Therefore what would diminish the joy of that one who exults even about injury that is inflicted or any sort of tribulation? He looks to beatitude of the soul, whatever harshness the flesh endures for the love of God. Therefore the body is bruised, conscience is made glad. And the more unhappy he seems to be externally, the more blessed he is internally. For there are two things of which the joy of beatitude consists: to be free of that which you do not wish and to have what you do wish. For we call him happy who suffers nothing he does not wish, and we judge that one blessed for whom those things which he desires are present. Therefore, whoever hates the pleasures of the world on account of longing for heaven will certainly be able to avoid his enemies everywhere by means of abstinence. Therefore, rigor of abstinence is rightly called Gad, that is happiness, who everywhere tramples underfoot the allurements of the world that he despises. Likewise: Where, I ask, will he who loves affliction of the body for the love of God not discover something from whence he is able to be afflicted? Therefore if he who everywhere finds what he loves is rightly thought to be blessed, then vigor of patience is rightly called Asher, that is "blessed," who meets everywhere what he desires. Behold two lovers: the one a lover of God, the other a lover of the world. The former loves temporal afflictions on account of God; the latter desires an abundance of temporal goods. In fact, the former is able to find everywhere what he loves on account of God; the latter is able on no occasion to take hold of the abundance of good things for which he thirsts. Which of these is the more blessed? Again— behold two others, of whom one hates the adversity of this world, while the other despises worldly delight. But where, I ask, will the former be able to avoid his enemy; or should the latter not be able to trample his enemy? Which of these, I ask, is the happier? Scripture says: "Blessed is the man that has not gone after gold, nor put his trust in chests of money" (Ecclus. 31:8). And again: "Blessed is the man that endures temptation: for when he is tried, he will receive the crown of life" (James 1:12). These are Gad and Asher: the first of whom tramples worldly glory while the second gladly endures the tribulation of the world on account of God. It should be especially noted and profoundly remembered that sacred Scripture wished to name the labor of abstinence not a calamity but happiness, and determined to call the rigor of patience not misery but blessed. Here we wish to recall this: that we ought to understand by Gad not only that abstinence which is found in food and drinks. Quite the contrary: By Gad and Asher we understand abstinence from all superfluous delight and patience in any affliction of the body, in all things that by the five senses either delight or torment the flesh.

Chapter XXVII

That appetite of sensation cannot be governed if wandering of imagination is not restrained

But when, I ask, would Leah have given her handmaid to her husband or would she have adopted such sons unless she had been provoked by the example of her sister? For it always happens that the handmaid of Rachel, rather than Leah's, is brought under the power of the man first. For if wandering of imagination that takes place by means of useless thoughts is not curbed, without doubt the immoderate appetite of sensation cannot be governed at all. Therefore whoever wants to govern longing for corporeal pleasures must first become accustomed to think never—or rarely— about carnal delights. For example, doubtless the more rarely you may have thought about such things, certainly the more rarely, the more tepidly you will desire them. Unless I am mistaken, this is the reason why Bala bows down under the dominion of the man before Zelpha. Nonetheless, it is known that Leah would never have made adoptive sons from Gad and Asher, that is abstinence and patience, unless she had continually seen the adopted children of her sister Rachel. For who would ever be able to persuade the affection of the heart to despise the prosperity of this world and not to fear its adversities unless by the suggestions of Dan and Naphtali it were compelled to look not only frequently but almost unceasingly at the torments or eternal rewards of future life? Now, however, through assiduous consideration of future evils, he is easily persuaded to despise present goods. And again, by continual contemplation of eternal happiness, he is kindled to a willing endurance of temporal tribulation. This is, I think, why Dan and Naphtali should be born first, and why Gad and Asher should be begotten second.

Chapter XXVIII

How the soul is strengthened for all obedience by means of abstinence and patience

After Gad and Asher are born, the time now approaches when Ruben should discover the mandrakes, if only he is not loathe to go forth outside. But why do we doubt that he wishes to go out, when we already know that he is able to go in or out? It should be believed that after his mother has borne so many children, after so many children of Bala and Zelpha, he is already mature and is able and wishes to go out and enter his father's kingdom. But if by Ruben, as has been said above, we understand fear of God, what ought we to understand by his going in and going out? What does it mean that he either is within or goes outside? Ruben is within when in the secret place of the heart, in the presence of God, we fear concerning our conscience. Ruben then goes forth when on account of God we bend even ourselves to all obedience to men. And so, fearing God on account of himself and fearing men on account of God, Ruben at one time stays within and at another time goes forth. Ruben goes out at the time of the harvest of wheat when from a command he exercises himself in works of justice. But when, do you think, does Ruben grow stronger in perfect obedience except when Gad and Asher (i.e., the love of abstinence and of patience) animate him to despise pleasure or to tolerate tribulation? For there are two things that are accustomed to hinder the perfection of obedience, namely lest we be forced either to abandon what is loved or to tolerate what is adverse. But if the soul has once been inflamed with love of abstinence and perfection of patience, then Ruben continually submits himself to all obedience without any objection. For what difficulty will be able to diminish any further the obedience of one who has decided of himself to endure adversities as well as not to delight in prosperity? For if on account of the love of God I strive after every kind of hard and harsh thing for myself, why shall I not endure these things more completely from added obedience for the glory of greater merit? Therefore Ruben is rightly said to go forth after the birth of Gad and Asher, because from voluntary abstinence and patience, fear of the Lord is strengthened for all obedience.

Chapter XXIX

How human praise rises up from abstinence, and how carefully the appetite for it ought to be governed

But how much and what kind of an odor of good opinion of himself is scattered all around by one who is not hindered from the pursuit of obedience by any trouble or by any need? These are the mandrakes that Ruben found and that his mother Leah received from him. For what except the fame of good opinion should we understand by means of the mandrakes, which are accustomed to scatter widely their odor? Certainly Leah receives them when praise that has been offered touches affection, when the soul is affected in the proclamation of her own praise and is delighted in the perverse aura of popular favor. Rachel begs a part of these. Leah complies, so that she who burns with a greater desire for offspring may receive a husband. In fact, the Holy Spirit in no way makes fruitful a mind that, when advised by reason, does not moderate appetite for vain praise. And so it is one Spirit who enriches each sister with an abundance of offspring since the same Spirit both illumines reason for cognition of truth and inflames affection for love of virtue. Therefore reason urges affection to moderate appetite for human favor under reason's guidance if it desires to rejoice for multiplying the offspring of virtues from a marriage bond with the divine Spirit. And so possession of the mandrakes is brought under the power of Rachel when appetite for praise is moderated under the rule of reason.

It should be noted, of course, how temperately Rachel begged not all the mandrakes but only part of them: for this is not hidden from reason, that it is very difficult for the soul, although it struggles, not to rejoice on account of praise which has been offered. Love of human praise first ought to be moderated; afterward, if it is possible, it ought utterly to be cut off. This is why it is read that Rachel begged part of the mandrakes. In fact, Leah, speaking to

Jacob afterward, does not boast of a part only: "You must come in to me for I have hired you for a fee with my son's mandrakes" (Gen. 30:16). "With the mandrakes," she says; not "with part of the mandrakes of my son." With the husband absent, Leah scarcely gives up a part until now, but inflamed more fully with longing for him at his arrival she wishes nothing at all from them to be reserved for her. So, of course, the mind of man when it is touched with spiritual sweetness gladly forgets whatever it craved earlier from human praise. In this way the mandrakes are taken from Leah's possession and are placed under Rachel's control. For Rachel knows better than Leah how to use the mandrakes. For whatever the affection of the heart acquires for praise of itself, reason more rightly turns it back to the glory of God. But what are we to say is the reason that Ruben was able to find the mandrakes of good opinion before the other sons of Leah?

CHAPTER XXX

From what source praise most particularly ought to be accustomed to rise up; and that true praise ought to be from right will

We know that the works of the virtues that nourish all the other virtues almost always extinguish humility. For the things done by Gad and Asher—viz., the works of abstinence and patience—are accustomed, when men marvel at them, to render the worker not fearful but arrogant; to make him not so much humble as obstinate. What should be more marvelous, what more greatly proclaimed by praise of all, than that the respect of fear is not diminished but is increased in things divine although in other things it is often extinguished? Therefore, because we are accustomed to extol with extraordinary praise a person whom we see to be disturbed not a little by small offenses not only concerning God but also concerning man, Ruben is rightly said to have found mandrakes after the births of Gad and Asher since we marvel at anyone advancing from the above-mentioned works to fear rather than arrogance.

Of course it should be noted that these mandrakes about which we have been speaking are read to have been found neither after Leah had borne so many offspring nor after the two offspring of Bala but immediately after the birth of the sons of Zelpha. In fact, wills pertain to the sons of Leah; thoughts, to the sons of Bala; actions, to the sons of Zelpha. And so how can we marvel at wills or thoughts, however much right, how much soever useful? When shall we praise those wills or thoughts that we cannot see at all? And although there should be praise for right will, nevertheless we do not praise it unless it is evident in work. For by means of good work a good will becomes known so that justly it is able to find the praise of good opinion like certain widely fragrant mandrakes. Therefore just as after Zelpha gives birth the offspring of Leah is thought to find the mandrakes, so when good will has been made manifest by means of good work it is honored everywhere by an admiring proclamation of praise.

CHAPTER XXXI

How the discipline of the heart, like that of the body, is strengthened by the above-mentioned virtues

However, concerning sons of these two handmaids, this ought not to be omitted negligently but ought to be retained joined together in the memory, that from their watchfulness and alert guard the city of our conscience is wonderfully guarded and much defended. For the firstborn of Bala pacifies it internally. The firstborn of Zelpha strengthens it externally. Evils rising up internally are restrained by Dan. Evils rising up externally are repelled by Gad. Indeed we all know that every temptation arises either externally or internally: internally through thought; externally through sense. For it disturbs inwardly only through thinking. It contrives to break in from the exterior only through the senses. Without doubt, the enemy is accustomed now to provide counsels of error from within, now to direct incitements of delight from without. But since discipline of thoughts pertains to Dan while discipline of the senses looks to Gad, surely Dan ought to be vigilant for the judgment of discretion and Gad, to fight strongly by means of the exercise of abstinence. It is the part of one to quiet civil discord; it is the part of the other to repel a hostile action. The former watches for a betrayal of the citizens; the latter, for an invasion of enemies; the former, against perfidy; the latter, against violence. For when Dan is negligent the mind is easily deceived. When Gad moves more slowly the mind is suddenly rushed toward foul delight. But of what importance is it whether the city of our heart is destroyed by power or by fraud; whether civil discord or the hand of the enemy overthrows it?

CHAPTER XXXII

That discipline of thinking cannot be maintained without discipline of the senses

However, it is necessary to understand that discipline of the body, without discipline of the heart, is doubtless useless. Truly, discipline of thinking cannot be kept at all without discipline of the senses. Therefore it is sufficiently known that without the assistance of Gad who ought to watch against exterior things, Dan labors vainly within in arranging the peace of the citizens. For what use is it when Dan judges his people continually to cut off the cause of discord, unless Gad strives not to admit the irritations of the vices (which surely are like a hostile army) through the portals of the senses? For however much Dan may remain on the throne of judgment, however much he may continually quiet the quarrels of disputing thoughts, he exerts himself in vain especially in quieting the discord of citizens unless Gad with the same zeal guards our city by discipline of the senses and eagerly kills the hostile army of the vices by a contest of abstinence. So it is written: "Gad, having been girded, shall fight before him" (Gen. 49:19). For then Dan on the inside usefully watches against the faithlessness of traitors while Gad on the outside keeps out and drives away attacking armies. And so first of all Gad is girded so that afterward he may fight bravely. Gad doubtlessly girds himself when he restrains by means of discipline the dissoluteness of the senses. Gad fights in brave battle when he slaughters carnal desires by means of mortification of the flesh. For a great overthrow of the armies is effected and that hated army of the vices is quickly turned to flight when the sense of the body is restrained from wandering by means of discipline, and the appetite of the flesh is curbed from pleasure by means of abstinence. And so in this way, as we are all able to experience, Dan quiets our city on the inside, and Gad defends it on the outside.

CHAPTER XXXIII

How the above-mentioned virtues cooperate with each other by turns in the protection of the heart

Moreover, their brothers assist them, certainly rushing not slowly to aid them: Naphtali inside with Dan, in arranging the peace of the citizens; Asher outside with Gad, in subduing the violence of enemies. And so Gad and Asher watch against enemies; Dan and Naphtali are full of care for the citizens. On one side Dan threatens; on the other side, Naphtali coaxes. Dan frightens with threats; Naphtali encourages with promises. The former punishes evil persons; the latter rewards good persons. The one frightens hearts with terror of Gehenna; the other soothes souls with hope of eternal happiness. How much do you think Naphtali himself, giving eloquence of beauty, helps his brother in such a matter — Naphtali who inclines the souls of listeners in any direction he wishes by means of the sweetness of his eloquence delivered almost without a pause? Asher helps his brother externally nonetheless, and they both defend the city against an invasion of enemies. The latter protects one side; the former defends the other. Gad contends on the right; Asher fights on the left. The prosperity of this world ambushes Gad; worldly adversity pursues Asher. But Asher easily makes sport of his enemy; while he gazes at a part, he sees from the lofty rock of patience the fortified place that he defends, and for that reason from the safe location of his station he laughs at and despises his enemies who struggle vainly and from the bottom. This is the reason that his enemies do not so much harass him with their attacks as continually provide the material for a triumph. Hence it is that, after having scorned his attackers (that is, worldly adversaries), he is totally carried away against his brothers' perse-cutors (that is, the carnal delights) and pursues them with great denunciations. However, such terror suddenly seizes the attackers of Gad when Asher himself aids him in the struggle of his own battle that without delay they all turn themselves to flight, since they dare not resist for even an hour when the brothers are bringing aid to each other. Assuredly the true enemies of the soul are carnal delights. But what place, I ask, is left for perverse delights among the torments that our Asher himself is assenting not only to bear patiently on account of God but to desire ardently? O how rightly is he called Asher, that is "blessed," according to that sentence of the Lord: "Blessed are those who suffer persecution for the sake of justice" (Matt. 5:10).

Chapter XXXIV

That mercy always accompanies perfect patience

Who is able so excellently to fulfill that precept of the Lord: "Forgive, and you will be forgiven"? (Luke 6:37). Who is able to forgive injuries offered himself as easily or as much from the heart as one who has learned more to exult than to be saddened concern-ing the crucifixion of his body? So why should he not love enemies, why should he not freely yield to those who offer him that which he desires? He has more compassion for his persecutors than for his body, so that he is blessed repeatedly: For, "Blessed are the merci-ful, for they shall receive mercy" (Matt. 5:7). O glorious man, O three and four times blessed! Blessed because of hunger for justice; blessed because of voluntary suffering; blessed because of clem-ency; blessed because of merciful compassion. For just as those are blessed who hunger and thirst for justice; just as those are blessed who suffer persecution on account of justice itself; so nonetheless blessed are the gentle, blessed are the merciful. And this our Asher, so that he may be truly and many times over blessed, thirsts ar-dently for justice, suffers freely on account of it, knows nothing of anger, easily has compassion. For although he may hunger much for the bread of justice, nevertheless he scorns eating it unless it is sprinkled with the oil of mercy. Even from the great abundance of riches that superabound from the spoils of the enemies by virtue of frequent victory there is a very delightful result: indeed, now no bread, however fine, has any taste to him unless it is sprinkled with oil, to such an extent that Scripture clearly declares concerning him, saying that: "Asher, his bread shall be plump" (Gen. 49:20). Who do you think so abounds in pleasures as he so that he is truly able to sing: "I have delighted in the way of your commandments just as in all riches" (Ps. 118:14).

Chapter XXXV

The excellence of perfect patience

For example, how much do you think Asher himself abounds in the riches of spiritual consolations, and how much he does over-flow with the delights of spiritual joys? Any adversity whatsoever is accustomed not so much to diminish as to augment his riches, and no torment at all is able to alter his delights. For the more severely he is pressed externally, the more delightfully he glories within. These are those delights which they thirst for so much, which they receive so gratefully—I say, not only the poor and the unknown, but even kings and princes. I lie if Scripture itself does not speak of this: It says, "Asher, his bread is plump, and he shall offer delights to kings" (Gen. 49:20). For as we think they are nourished pleasantly, so we believe they are delighted marvelously; not just any kings but certainly in truth those kings to whom that King of kings and Lord of lords has restored the rule of His body and to whom He has distributed the kingdom of his Father. We think, I say, how sweet it is to such kings, how intimately they savor it when they see a man not fearing torments because of love of justice and not losing peace of heart and tranquillity of soul in the midst of persecutions themselves. For, if "there is joy in heaven over one sinner who does penance" (Luke 15:7), then how much celebration will there be over any just person who gladly dies for justice? Truly, Asher, his bread is plump and he shall offer delights to kings. O what kind of bread is his bread! O what kind of delights are his delights, which taste so very good for kings, for such kings. Surely those kings have now entered into the wedding of the Lamb, now they have taken seats at that eternal banquet, now they feed upon that bread of angels and eternal delights, now they are intoxicated by a torrent of pleasure, and still they hunger insatiably for the delights of this Asher. Hungering and thirsting for justice, even until today, they are unable to quiet either their hunger or their thirst in such a great abundance of celestial joys. Asher, his bread is plump and he shall offer delights to kings. How liberal do you think he can be for the necessities of the poor who has an abundance to prepare delights for kings? How greatly do you think those marvel who are crushed by their weakness while they still live in a vale of tears? How much are they grateful for his constancy, if even those whom that eternal happiness has already engulfed delight so much in his works? Asher, his bread is plump and he shall offer delights to kings. And from whence comes so great an abundance of riches to him, such an ample supply of delights, except, as it has been said, from the spoils of the enemies in such frequent victory? For it is certain that the more the enemies of justice are destroyed, the more fully the joys of conscience are increased: "Glory and riches are in his house," says the Psalmist (Ps. 111:3). And as if explaining about this same glory and riches, the Apostle says, "Our glory is this: the witness of our conscience" (2 Cor. 1:12). This is that house or city, viz., our conscience, in which the riches of spiritual goods abound when the sons of the above-mentioned handmaids guard it with alert care: that is, when Dan and Naphtali are extremely busy with establishing the peace of the citizens and when Gad and Asher courageously work in overcoming enemies. For by the prudence of the former the citizens are pacified, while by the constancy of the latter enemies are overcome.

CHAPTER XXXVI

How and in what order true joy is born

After the enemies have been put to flight and the citizens have been pacified, I think nothing now stands in the way but that the city of ours might expect that which is the "peace" of God "which passes all understanding" (Phil. 4:7). And "how great" is "the multitude of sweetness, which God has hidden for those who love him" (Ps. 30:20). "He has hidden," it says. Therefore, why marvel if any lover of the world does not know that which God has hidden for those who love Him? For those who fasten hope on false and deceptive goods are not able to find out what are true goods. So it is that they say: "Who shows us goods?" (Ps. 4:6). For it is manna, hidden and completely unknown except to those who taste it. For it is such sweetness of the heart, and not of the flesh, that no carnal person whomever is able to have known it. "You have put joy in my heart" (Ps. 4:7). Corporeal delights, like the body itself, can be seen by the bodily eye; eyes of the flesh cannot see the delights of the heart and also not even the heart itself. Therefore by what way could he know spiritual delights unless he makes a point of entering into his heart and dwelling within? Therefore it is said to him: "Enter into the joy of your Lord" (Matt. 25:21). This inner joy is for spiritual persons. That sweetness which is felt within is that son of Leah who is born in the fifth place. For joy is one of the principal affections, as I have said above. However, when it has been set in order, this can rightly be numbered among the sons of Jacob and Leah. For we certainly have ordered and true joy when we rejoice concerning true and inner goods. The Apostle wished to animate us to the desire for such offspring when he said: "Rejoice in the Lord always, again I say rejoice" (Phil. 4:4). And the Prophet: "Rejoice in the Lord and exult you just, and glory all you with an upright heart" (Ps. 31:11). For such offspring Leah gladly despised the mandrakes so that she would be able to have such a son. In fact, the mind that delights in the praise of men does not deserve to experience what inner joy is. However, after the birth of Gad and Asher, Leah rightly gave birth to such a son because except by means of abstinence and patience the human mind cannot reach true joy. Therefore it is necessary that he who wishes to rejoice concerning the truth exclude not only false pleasure but also vain disquiet. For he who until now delights in the lowest things is especially unworthy of inner enjoyment, and he who is disquieted by vain fear is not able fully to enjoy spiritual sweetness. Truth condemned false joy when he said: "Woe to you who now laugh" (Luke 6:25). He extirpated vain disquiet when he admonished his hearers, saying: "Do not fear those who kill the body, for they are not able to kill the soul" (Matt. 10:28). We rise above one of these by abstaining. We trample the other by being patient. And so by means of Gad false delight is extirpated; by means of Asher, vain disquiet. These are Gad and Asher who exclude false joy and introduce true joy. Now I think, following this there will be no question why this particular son is called Issachar if Issachar is certainly interpreted "reward." For what else do we seek with so many and so great labors? What, I say, other than true joy do we await with such persevering forbearance? We receive as it were a kind of pledge, like a kind of first fruits of this reward, as often as we enter into that inner joy of our Lord and taste it partially.

CHAPTER XXXVII

The comparison of interior and exterior sweetness

Sacred Scripture calls this tasting of inner sweetness now a tasting, now intoxication, so that whether it appears small or great, it is certainly small in comparison to future fullness but great in comparison to any earthly enjoyment. In fact, the present delight of spiritual men, however much it grows, is found small when compared to the joys of future life; nevertheless in comparison with it the pleasantness of all outer delights is nothing. O marvelous sweetness, sweetness so great, sweetness so small! In what way are you not great? You exceed all earthly sweetness. In what way are you not small? You enjoy scarcely a modest drop from that fullness. You instill in minds a certain small portion from so great a sea of happiness. Yet you fully intoxicate the mind that you fill. Certainly so little from so much is deservedly called a taste. That which alienates the mind from itself is no less deservedly called intoxication. Therefore it can rightly be called both a taste and intoxication. "Taste," says the Prophet, "and see that the Lord is sweet" (Ps. 33:9). And the Apostle Peter: "If nevertheless you taste that the Lord is sweet" (1 Pet. 2:3). And concerning intoxication, the Prophet again: "You have visited the earth, and you have intoxicated it" (Ps. 64:10). Listen to a man overflowing with this intoxication and ignorant of everything that is happening around him: "Whether in the body or outside the body, I do not know; God knows" (2 Cor. 12:3). In what way do you think he became intoxicated; in what way did he forget the world—he who did not know himself?

Chapter XXXVIII

What is accustomed to impede that inner joy

In any case, those who until now are disturbed by the fluctuations of carnal desires do not deserve to be intoxicated by this sweetness. "You have visited the earth, and you have intoxicated it" (Ps. 64:10). What do you think is the reason that the Lord is said to have intoxicated the earth only? Why not also the sea? But we know that the mind that fluctuates through various desires, which the tumult of worldly cares still disturbs, is not admitted to that inner joy and is not drinking from that torrent of pleasure. How much less is it intoxicated? We know that the sea always fluctuates while the earth is immovable forever. Thus the other elements are always in motion; the earth alone is immovable; the others do not know how to be immovable. Therefore what should we understand by "earth" except fixed stability of the heart? Therefore he who desires or believes he is to be intoxicated by that cup of true sobriety ought to restrain the fluctuation of the heart and to gather together the movement of the affections and thoughts with a view to the longing for one true joy. This truly is that blessed earth, viz., tranquil stability of mind, when the mind is totally gathered within itself and is unalterably fixed on the one longing for eternity. This is that earth which Truth promised when he said: "Blessed are the gentle for they themselves shall possess the earth" (Matt. 5:4). This is that land of which the Psalmist reminded when he promised and promised when he reminded: "Inhabit the land, and you will feed on its riches" (Ps. 36:3). This is that land which Issachar himself, a strong ass, saw and craved, and he was marvelously inflamed with a craving for it. "Issachar, a strong ass, living between boundaries; he saw rest, that it was good, and the land, that it was best; and he set his shoulder to bearing and became one serving for tribute" (Gen. 49:14–15). Hence it is necessary for us to cross over from land to land, from an alien land to our own land, from exile to the fatherland, from people to people, and from a kingdom to another people, from the land of the dying to the land of the living, if we wish by experience to know true and inner joy. Let us crave that land which Issachar himself saw and craved. For if he had not seen he would not have known; and if he had not known he would not have craved.

CHAPTER XXXIX

How inner sweetness is accustomed both to strengthen the soul for brave things and to incline it toward humble things

After having been made an ass for this land and having been made strong, he gladly set his shoulder to bearing and became one serving for tribute. Suddenly he became very vile to himself, as he considered himself an ass, viz., an animal almost more vile in comparison to all others. He very much craved the land that he saw, for which he strongly endured in all sorts of labor. Certainly he saw that compared to the beauty of that land, "all our justices" were "like the cloth of a menstruating woman" (Isa. 64:6). Nonetheless, he saw "that the sufferings of this time are not worthy to compare with the future glory, which will be revealed in us" (Rom. 8:18). Therefore, in the one made vile to himself, in the other made strong; concerning one humbled, concerning the other strengthened, he gladly bent the shoulder of his strength to all sorts of labor, and in acquiring divine glory, not his own, he truly paid worthy tribute to the King. Do you wish to hear that another was vile to himself for a similar reason and nonetheless grew strong for all sorts of labor: "So that I have been made a beast of burden in your presence" (Ps. 72:22)? And elsewhere: "For your sake we are killed all the day" (Ps. 43:22). Behold how vile; behold how strong: vile like a beast of burden; strong for mortifying himself. Issachar, a strong ass, living between boundaries, saw rest, that it was good, and the land, that it was best. Therefore, he who lived between the boundaries almost but not completely abandoned this land of the dying. Almost but not completely he grasped that land of the living. Because he had been content with the vilest, the smallest goods of this life, he possessed the outermost edges of this wretched land. Because through frequent ecstasy of mind he tasted beforehand the goods of everlasting life, he touched the beginning of that blessed land. Issachar, a strong ass, living between the boundaries. Because he did not cast off the goods of this life that are necessary, he did not abandon completely this land. Because he was able to grasp only a kind of extremity of future life, he did not grasp that land at all. And for that reason he lived between the boundaries. This land he tolerated for necessity. That land he craved for enjoyment. And for that reason he lived between the boundaries. He did much to abandon totally this land, but he could not. He sought to enter totally into that land, but he was not able. Therefore he did what he could: He lived between the boundaries. Daily he pressed forward to that land. Daily he slid back to this land. And in this way he remained between the boundaries. Issachar a strong ass, living between the boundaries; he saw rest that it was good, and the land that it was best. Therefore why marvel that he who lived at the boundary of it, saw it? I say, why marvel that he saw, that he knew what he saw, that he craved what he knew? And for this reason he set his shoulder to bearing and became one serving for tribute. It says, he saw rest that it was good. Therefore rest is there, and rest is good. For if it were not there he certainly would not have seen it there. And if it were not good he certainly would not have set his shoulder to bearing on account of it: "The gentle," said the Prophet, "shall inherit the land, and they shall be delighted by the abundance of peace" (Ps. 36:11). Behold what kind of a land it is. Peace is there, rest is there. Full peace, good rest; quiet peace, peaceful quiet. He saw rest that it was good, and the land that it was best. There is no labor in that land, but he cannot reach that land without labor. He labors on account of it, but he does not labor in it. Outside of this land true rest is not found. No labor at all is found in this land. There are two: land and rest. Two against two. Two goods against two evils. There are two great evils: misery and craving, that is punishment and guilt. There are two great goods: tranquillity and stability. Against misery, tranquillity of mind; against craving, stability of heart. To feel no vexation is to rest well. To be disturbed by no tempests of craving is without doubt already to remain in the land. In such a land there is such rest. The mind that is not yet totally gathered to inner joy in no way experiences what true rest is. O, I pity myself, I who until today live a wanderer and a fugitive upon the earth: a wanderer when following craving; a fugitive when avoiding misery. That which I crave is always lacking. That which I flee, I find everywhere. Craving makes me a wanderer. Misery makes me a fugitive. Certainly it is an evil land, a land of misery, such a land in which I live in such a manner: a land of misery and of darkness, where the shadow of death is, where there is no order at all. Without doubt such a land is not stability of heart but hardness and insensibility of mind. But, "Your good spirit, Lord, shall lead me into the right land" (Ps. 142:10). And finally Issachar saw such and craved it because rest was good, and the land itself, best. O happy one, who was able, even for an hour, to forget all evils and to possess that interior peace and rest, at least to a slight degree! No less happy is he to whom it has been given to gather the dispersions of the heart into a unity and to fix desire on that fountain of true happiness. Certainly the former is good, but yet the latter is best. According to that, Issachar saw rest, that it was good, and the land, that it was best. Because it is indeed good to be a long way off from all evils, it is so much better—no, even best—to have adhered to the highest good. Issachar knew this, and for that reason he was unwilling to go far away from such a land, but while living between the boundaries remained in the vicinity of it, while desiring and seeking to touch it at least hurriedly and furtively by means of rare excursions and also to eat frequently of the fruits of that land. For, as you are able to know, the fruit of that land is sublime—a marvelous fruit, a singular fruit. If indeed the mind of man is more often satiated by the fruits of that land and to a certain degree is made fat, suddenly it receives a marvelous fortitude against all perils. It grows strong in the hatred of all vices to such an extent that now it is not enough for him not to consent to receive any vices in himself unless he is also zealous to pursue them manfully in others and to strike them with strong chastisement.

Chapter XL

How and in what order hatred of the vices is born in us

Therefore he soon becomes as strong against all peril as he is a spirited enemy of all vices. This is the reason that Zabulon, who is interpreted "dwelling place of fortitude," is born after Issachar. For what do we understand by Zabulon, except hatred of vices? This hatred of vices is a good hatred, an ordered hatred. Without doubt the Prophet desired to order this affection in us when he said: "Be angry and do not sin" (Ps. 4:5). For what is it not to sin when angry, and to be angry without sinning, except when loving men benefically and not for display, to be indignant with their vices? The Prophet also signified that he himself had this son, when he said elsewhere: "I have hated them with a perfect hate" (Ps. 138:22). And elsewhere: "I have hated every unjust way" (Ps. 118:128). This is that extraordinary soldier of God who does not cease to fight the wars of the Lord, and whom sacred Scripture calls in its usual vocabulary "zeal of the Lord" or "zeal of uprightness." "The zeal of your house," Lord, "has devoured me, and the reproaches of those reproaching you have fallen upon me" (Ps. 68:10). And again, "My zeal makes me waste away, because my enemies have forgotten your words" (Ps. 118:139). And Elijah: "With zeal I am zealous on account of the Lord" (3 Kings 19:10). Phinehas was zealous for the zeal of the Lord, and he received an eternal priesthood. (Cf. Num. 25:11ff.) But from where do you think you have advanced by means of so much fortitude, by means of so much wonderful constancy? Elijah rose up alone against one hundred and fifty prophets of Baal. When he invaded the camp of the Midianites, Phinehas alone pierced through the adulterers with a sword. Behold how much strength they receive; behold how strong they become, who eat of the fruits of that land mentioned above, who refresh themselves with inner pleasantness. Therefore after Issachar, who is interpreted "reward," Zabulon, that is "dwelling place of fortitude," rightly is born since after tasting the sweetness of eternal reward the soul is marvelously strengthened against the arguments of temptations, and suddenly esteeming lightly its own perils it forcefully avenges injuries to the Lord. It is for this reason that Moses, the mildest one of all those who remained in the land, after a forty-day fast when he was refreshed by a marvelous abundance of spiritual delights, suddenly was inflamed with so much zeal against the fabricators and worshipers of the idol, so that after having joined to himself those who were of the Lord immediately he went through the middle of the camps, from gate to gate, killing, and he threw to the ground in death three thousand men of prevarication (Cf. Exod. 32). So Zabulon is born after Issachar because by means of the taste of inner sweetness, hatred of vices is produced, and strength of true fortitude is acquired. The latter is Zabulon, who by being angered is accustomed to placate the anger of God and who by dutifully raging while he slays the vices of men spares them best, as it were, by not sparing them. Without doubt, nothing so reconciles to God, nothing so placates God as zeal of souls.

CHAPTER XLI

How rare it is to have zeal for uprightness arising from a true hatred of vices

O, how many people by the grace of God conceive in the mind and give birth from themselves to many offspring of other virtues, yet they are not able to have this son! How many paupers in spirit do we see today: rejoicing in hope, fervent in charity, abstaining very much, being fully patient—but so excessively tepid and very torpid for the zeal of souls? Some, as if from the constraint of humility, do not dare to rebuke delinquent persons. Others, in order not to seem to disturb brotherly love, fear to denounce sinners. And so others, in other ways, because they are unwilling to be zealous for the Lord, suppose this is virtuous, or they believe it is a virtue. But on the contrary, many persons, because without doubt they are acting in a spirit of fury, think that they act with zeal of uprightness, and the things they enforce in truth from hatred of men, they think or pretend that they practice because of hatred of vices. But, I ask, should they not ask who such persons are who believe that they have already given birth to Zabulon? I ask, should they not ask whether in truth they love those whom they punish so severely, as it were at the instigation of Zabulon? Perhaps they have been completely unable to know by experience those spiritual delights, to which they wish, by means of their whips or even rebukes, to seem to invite those whom they accuse or whip. For those who have known by means of experience those inner joys to which they invite them by so many griefs ought to trust pursuing delinquent persons with compassion, not cruelty. We read that Leah gave birth to Judah and Issachar before Zabulon. And we have already said that charity is signified by Judah and the experience of spiritual joys by Issachar. It is necessary that Judah and Issachar be born first, since the mind that is without charity and interior pleasantness is completely unable to keep the norm of uprightness in its zeal. For charity teaches how one ought to treat those whom Zabulon punishes. Familiarity with spiritual things teaches what that pleasantness is to which they are invited or even are compelled, because of which exterior enjoyment is forbidden (viz., pleasure of the flesh), and for which they are harshly denounced often at the urging of Zabulon. And so Judah ought to teach the manner; Issachar, the cause of reproof; so that with the moderation of Judah it is done in a spirit of leniency, and at the suggestion of Issachar it is done nonetheless for reason of benefit. Nevertheless Zabulon seeks their benefit and not his own so that insofar as he strikes delinquent persons, it is for benefit and not for revenge.

CHAPTER XLII

What is the office of a true zealot

However Zabulon ought not only to reproach delinquent persons but also to defend them from pursuers in a time of tribulation, otherwise it is not true zeal. Nor is he able to be called Zabulon in truth if he is more prepared to strike than to protect. For not in vain is this sixth and last of the sons of Leah called "dwelling place of fortitude": for as has been said above, Zabulon is interpreted "dwelling place of fortitude." See how a house covers over above and surrounds on all sides those who inhabit it, yet nevertheless, unless it is strong and firmly fortified, it is not a dwelling place of fortitude. So do not marvel that perfect zeal, in order that it may be called Zabulon—nay may be Zabulon—ought by doctrine and preaching to protect weaker persons against powers of the air, to defend them on all sides against worldly perils, and to persevere in both not only without fatigue but also invincibly. Thus, he ought to watch here against devices of the devil, there against oppressions of the world. Without doubt, whenever whenever you are strong in both you are a dwelling place of fortitude and you worthily deserve to be called Zabulon. Zabulon ought to be more prompt, and assuredly always more ready to bear evils than to move against evils. And because he has, of necessity, to be angry at subject persons at one time or another on account of guilt, so he grieves when he is compelled to strike them for guilt, more than when he is compelled to be punished on account of their defense. Thus he gladly throws himself against the attacks of perils and willingly sets himself against the hurricanes of raging weather. Otherwise he lives on the shore of the sea in vain, he makes ready in vain a dwelling place in the harbor of the ships if he trembles against the marine danger of earthly oppression, unless he rescues cheerfully and assists generously those worn out daily by storms and cast at last upon the shores.

Chapter XLIII

That it is the task of the true zealot to watch not only against violence but also against fraud

"Zabulon shall live on the shore of the sea and in the harbor of the ships, stretching as far as Sidon" (Gen. 49:13). What then do you think is the reason why he lives on the shore, except that he may defend the extremities of the land and, inasmuch as he is a dwelling place of virtue, may protect the weaker members of the Church? Therefore he sets himself against the perils of those whom he perceives to be fatigued by constant storms of persecution. So that he may always be prepared for bringing aid to the shipwrecked he remains, as has been written of him, in the harbor of the ships. For he knows how to encourage with cheerful consolation, both to lift up to a place of security and to call back to a kind of port of tranquillity, as it were, those oppressed for a long time by temptations, who endure as it were a kind of shipwreck and already are almost broken in pieces. And so in this way Zabulon shall live on the shore of the sea, in the harbor of the ships, stretching as far as Sidon. He spreads himself out broadly along the shore of the sea, running here and there. While he watches all around about the protection of his people, while he prepares himself on all sides against the attack of enemies, he stretches as far as Sidon. Sidon is interpreted "hunting," by which rightly enough fraud of deceptions is understood. Accordingly, Zabulon has his hands full not only to encourage weak ones against the fury of persecutors but also to snatch any simple ones whomever from the snares of the hunters. Therefore, he stretches as far as Sidon as often as he discovers the ambushes of a clever enemy, as often as he detects the fraudulent counsel of false brothers. "A word of such a kind," testifies the Apostle, "spreads slowly like a cancer" (2 Tim. 2:17). For this is that snare of the hunters and as it were a kind of net of malignant spirits hunting simple souls, viz., the tongue of flatterers, the tongue of detractors, of those sowing discord between brothers, of those rousing angers and quarrels. Thus Zabulon stretches as far as Sidon, as often as he prevents deceitful clever devices whether of malignant spirits or faithless men. For we know that such a hunt of souls happens, sometimes by the hidden suggestion of demons and at other times by the open persuasion of men. Nevertheless, Zabulon knows how to detect both carefully and to expose them with caution. Therefore he fixes his dwelling place of fortitude in the region of the sea, in the limits of Sidon, so that he may watch here against the violence of the persecutors and there against the fraud of clever ones, and he fulfills what is read to have been written concerning him: "Zabulon shall live on the shore of the sea, in the harbor of the ships, stretching as far as Sidon."

Chapter XLIV

Of what kind and how great it is to have perfect zeal of souls

He who is able should consider thoroughly of what sort this son should be, and how great should be his virtue by whose office everyone not only defends himself against vices, but also exerts himself to rescue others from the snares of sins. And he labors at least to restrain by resistance the badness of those he is not able to change into better. I do not know if a man is able to receive in this life anything greater from God. I do not know whether God is able meanwhile to bestow upon a man anything greater than this grace, than that by his work perverse men might be changed into better, and that sons of God might be made from sons of the devil. Or perhaps it will seem greater to some that the dead be awakened. Therefore, will it be greater to awaken dead flesh that will die again, than a soul that will live to eternity? Will it be greater to recall the flesh to the joys of the world than to restore to a soul the joys of heaven? Will it be greater to restore to the flesh transient goods that will perish again than to restore to the soul the eternal goods that will last to eternity? O what kind of dowry! How great a distinction to receive such a grace from God! The bride of God ought not to receive any other dowry from her Bridegroom. It is not fitting that the celestial Bridegroom give any other gift to His bride, than that by means of the grace of adoption she might be able to give birth to many sons for God, and from the sons of anger and the sons of Gehenna to add to heirs of the celestial kingdom. Thus at the birth of Zabulon his mother Leah deservedly exclaims: "God has enriched me with a good dowry" (Gen. 30:20). Do you not see of what kind and how great it is to possess zeal of justice and to bring forth from the heart hatred of vices and to practice it in truth? Whoever bears such a son confidently sings with the Prophet: "I have hated every unjust way" (Ps. 118:128).

CHAPTER XLV

How and from whence ordered shame is born

But after these six offspring of the virtues will anyone be permitted to live without sin so that at least after hatred of vices it will be possible to be without vice? Who presumes this? Who dares to hope for this in this life, since an Apostle says: "If we say that we have no sin, we deceive ourselves, and the truth is not in us" (I John 1:8). Is there anyone—I am silent about other things—who is able

at last to abandon completely or to shun perfectly his own sins of
ignorance in this life? Do those who reproach the faults of others
strip themselves thoroughly of the contamination of every sin? Indeed, by a dispensation of great kindness, God often allows those
through whom He arranges to correct the errors of others to fall
unpleasantly, so that from their own fault they may learn how
merciful they ought to be in the reproach of others. But how much
do you think they feel ashamed when they deprive themselves of so
much humility, when they who ought to show to others an appearance in a state of uprightness observe themselves in that on account
of which they reprove others, or perhaps in another more unpleas-
ant fall? Who do you think would suffice to think worthily how
great a confusion pierces their hearts when they see in their life
what is able justly to be censured, even by those whom they often
remember in themselves for their fault, and to be reproved more
harshly and to be punished more sharply? This is the reason why
Dina is born after Zabulon, since often without doubt when a fault
is found shamefacedness follows after too much zeal. For we understand nothing other by Dina except shamefacedness—ordered
shamefacedness. To feel ashamed of a single sin is to have good and
ordered shamefacedness. But he who does not deserve to give birth
to Zabulon believes in vain that he is able to give birth to Dina.

Chapter XLVI

What and of what kind ordered shame is

Learn first to hate sin, and then you will begin truly to feel
ashamed of it. If you truly hate, you quickly feel ashamed of it.
That shame is known to be true when hatred of vices precedes and
accompanies it. Otherwise, if you are caught in sin and confounded
with shame when you are caught, I do not believe that you feel
ashamed of the fault, but of the infamy. For such shamefacedness
descends not so much from sin itself as from the damage to our
reputation. Thus it is not a reason for you to boast as if you have
given birth to Dina. Even perverse men have shame, but if only it
were good, if only it were ordered! For if they had good shame,

perhaps they would not be perverse. For indeed, if they felt perfectly ashamed, they would not commit sin so easily. What kind of shame do you think it is to feel ashamed of poverty, to feel ashamed of lowliness? They are not ashamed to feel shame for that which the heavenly teacher was not ashamed to descend from heaven to teach. "Learn from me," He says, "because I am gentle and lowly in heart" (Matt. 11:29). But on the contrary, those who despise more than follow lowness, feel much more ashamed to have filthy clothing than a filthy mind. How many there are today who would be more ashamed to make in a speech a barbarism against the rule of Priscian than to reveal in their discourse a lie against the rule of Christ? But why do we say this about those who often even boast of their crimes since even those who seem spiritual by no means rise easily above this shame? Often while they serve the advantage of neighbors in the office of preaching, while they dispute strongly against pride, it comes to pass that often they are proud, from which it is evident that they argue tenuously against pride. And if perhaps in the course of speaking they should produce a short syllable (which is accustomed to happen), they probably are more ashamed concerning a vice of speaking than concerning the vice of self-esteem. Believe me, it ought not to be believed that this is that shamefacedness which we ought to understand through Dina.

CHAPTER XLVII

How rare it is to have true shame

Would you like to know better how rare it is perfectly to trample underfoot human shamefacedness and to have this true and ordered shamefacedness that means that Dina has been born? Notice, I say nothing about carnal things, since the discourse seems to me now to concern only spiritual things. Behold, whoever you are who believe yourselves already to have given birth to Dina: If you should be compelled to pass before a multitude with a nude body would you be able not to feel shame? Think, then, if you would be so confounded when you were defiled in the mind by an impure thought. Why do you boast any longer that you have given birth to Dina and have ordered shamefacedness if you feel less shame for the heart than for the body, if you have more fear of the face of men than of the presence of angels? So, should you feel more ashamed of what God made well, than of what you have done evilly? Certainly God made even those parts of the body that we call shameful. However, no one other than you made the shameful things of the heart. Therefore, having carefully considered and duly discerned how rare it is, and how few fully vanquish human shamefacedness and possess only that which is ordered, I think there will no longer be a reason for anyone to be amazed why Leah conceived and brought forth such an offspring so late.

Chapter XLVIII

What the nature of shame is

But lest we seem to have passed over in silence the reason for the name, Dina is interpreted "that judgment." And so she is that judgment by which everyone is by his own conscience addressed, convicted, condemned and punished with a punishment worthy of the disorder. For if he were not conscious of it, there would be no reason at all that he ought to feel ashamed. And certainly, if there were no punishment for disorder, there would be no reason why anyone ought to curse it or shun it so much. And so in a marvelous way, when convicted from its own conscience and deservedly cast down by disorder, the mind of everyone at one and the same time delivers a judgment against itself and exacts satisfaction from itself. This is that judgment in which the person who judges and the person who is judged are one and the same: the same, he who condemns and he who is condemned; one and the same, he who punishes and he who is punished. It was not without cause that sacred Scripture did not wish that such a thing be called judgment without a demonstration. For it always shows a demonstration, and why else this addition except to arouse the soul of the hearer to wonder? True judgment is marvelous and worthy of wonder and worthily proclaimed with a demonstration; in which judgment the more ardently each person loves himself, the more bitterly he rages against himself. For which reason the more eagerly he desires to spare himself, the less he spares himself; since because the more he fears his disorder, the result is that his disorder troubles everyone more severely. But does it perhaps seem surprising to anyone why, if this is worthily counted among the other virtues, it is portrayed by a person of the female sex rather than the male? But we all know that however much the form of beauty may be greater in women than in men, nevertheless constancy of fortitude in works of the virtues is much less. Who does not know that shamefacedness, however honest, softens strength of heart so much, and how it often hinders brave works, when the soul of man shuns to be confounded beyond measure? And so Dina is not a man but a woman, not a son but a daughter.

Chapter XLIX

Concerning the usefulness and loveliness of shamefacedness

And perhaps it was not without cause that after the birth of Zabulon God determined to give Leah not a son, but a daughter who might gently make mild the audacity of the brother and might soften by gentleness the soul of the raging brother. For Zabulon, as it appears from the aforesaid, has an enormous fury, and he shows a very great wrath. But they know, as we all know, that women are better able than men to address swollen souls more gently and to soothe enraged persons more sweetly. Therefore it seems fit that Dina is born after Zabulon, so that the ferocity of the brother might be moderated by the softness of the sister. For she moderates the fury of a zealous soul much in every way, when the soul discovers in itself something by reason of which it should feel ashamed. Assuredly this is the reason, if I am not mistaken, why Dina is born after Zabulon, that her modesty might moderate the fury of her brother. But because Dina endeavors to do nothing bold, nothing magnificent, she does not deserve to produce a tribe among the people Israel. Indeed, often, as has been said, when she more than justly fears to be confounded, she not only does not gather strength for brave and bold things, but she even is accustomed to hinder them. But however much she, since she is a woman, is found fearful with regard to works of fortitude, nevertheless she is provident and circumspect with regard to guarding of honor. And however much she does not know to please by fortitude, nevertheless she does know to please by beauty of form. For it is Dina of admirable beauty and singular form who easily draws the eyes of those who look in admiration of her and quickly attracts by love of her the souls of those who admire. For who does not know how the modesty of shamefacedness renders men commendable and makes them lovable to all? For what is the reason that we nearly always embrace more affectionately shamefaced men rather than others, except that, when we marvel at the modesty of shamefacedness and the grace of modesty in them, we are attracted in a certain measure by Dina's beauty and captivated with love of her by the greatness of her beauty? O how singular is the beauty of this Dina! How famous is her love! Almost no person fails to marvel at her beauty. Almost no person fails to be delighted by love of her. Sichem, that son of Emor, ought to bear witness to this. He adhered to her with such ardent love that he preferred against custom to circumcise all his males rather than not have her.

CHAPTER L

How a shamefaced mind steps over the boundaries of modesty when it is corrupted by pride and vainglory

O how many there are even today who often do not delay in accomplishing for the love of Dina what they have not wished to do for God! And when an occasion of disorder arises, for the sake of avoiding the damage of shamefacedness they do not hesitate to cut off the superfluity of shameful deeds that they ought to amputate for God. They also prefer to undergo the annoyance of circumcision in cutting off the superfluities of their life rather than to seem shameless and to be without shamefacedness. But who is Sichem, and who is his father? Why do they want such names for themselves: Sichem, which is interpreted "shoulder" or "labor," and

Emor, which means "ass"? But if we reflect on their deeds we will quickly find out who they are. For they are those who are accustomed to circumcise their private parts not so much for God as for Dina, not so much on account of conscience as on account of shamefacedness. I say, who are they other than love of one's own excellence and love of vainglory? Such a son from such a father; love of vainglory from love of one's own excellence. Now notice how foolish this Emor is, and you will see how rightly he is called an ass. Let us see for what reason he is exalted, for what reason he boasts. If it is because of that which he does not have but believes himself to have, I ask what will he be able to think up that is more foolish than this foolishness? If, however, he does have it, let him hear what the Apostle says to him: "What do you have that you have not received? If however you have received it, why do you boast as if you did not receive it?" (1 Cor. 4:7). And certainly, to be receiving is actually an honor to the giver, not to the receiver. For what does a man have that is his own, except sin? And of what sort will it be to boast about one's own evil, or about the good of another? And so, the more truly such a braggart is foolish, the more rightly he is called an ass. But in that Sichem is called "shoulder" and "labor," it seems to pertain to the same thing. For we carry burdens with the shoulder, and when we do this certainly we labor. And so Sichem puts his shoulder under for carrying and sweats freely but only to make a name for himself. Let us merely recall what we read concerning Issachar: "Issachar," it says, "a strong ass, saw rest, that it was good, and the land, that it was best, and he set his shoulder to bearing" (Gen. 49:15). There Issachar considers himself an ass and sets his shoulder to bearing. Here Emor is called an ass, and Sichem is shown to have a laborious shoulder. Because, you see, whatever is done for the sake of true delight, all of it can be carried out for the sake of vain delight. Issachar labors for the rest that he sees. Sichem labors for the emptiness of the praise that he craves. Nevertheless, he is rightly called not laborious but labor because by his labor he is not brought to true rest. In what manner he is rightly called labor is proved by the labor of hypocrites, who labor so much for the sake of acquiring the vain favor of men.

RICHARD OF ST. VICTOR

Chapter LI

How the mind that feels shamefacedness is diverted from the uprightness of its intention

This is that Sichem who runs to meet Dina when she goes out, and after overwhelming her, ruins her. Therefore after going out she loses the integrity that she could possibly have conserved by staying within. For since the beauty of shamefacedness is commended, praised and loved by nearly everyone, when Dina goes out, deserts her innermost dwelling, and quickly forgets the memory of her infirmities which was accustomed to make her humble, suddenly the praises of men embrace her and ruin her while they charm her with favors. For when she is delighted by the praise that is offered, what is it other than that she is ruined by Sichem (viz., love of vainglory)? Nevertheless, at that time Dina suffers the damage of her ruin more by violence than by a willful act, since she struggles as much as she can against the perverse delight that flatters her. As often as Sichem overwhelms one who is, as it were, unwilling, then so often the mind feels shame for the disorder of its ruin, and for that reason struggles more strongly, even as he draws her unwilling to the scandalous delight. But what do you think is the reason that compels her to forsake her innermost dwelling and to wander about on the outside, except that often when we feel much shame because of our infirmities we begin to wonder if others feel these infirmities in themselves, and it seems that a certain kind of consolation comes to us if we discover in our degradation at least that we have companions? Thus it happens that we begin to search out the pursuits of others more inquisitively, frequently surveying now a face, now a gesture and the deportment of the whole body, and we begin gladly to learn more about their secrets from the reports of others. Therefore when Dina labors to discover from exterior signs the state of souls in others, what is it other than that after having abandoned herself she goes out to see the women and wanders about outside? Thus when Dina looks around inquisitively at the forms of the women, she doubtless finds some more beautiful, others less. And when by herself she often silently considers how she far surpasses many other women in the greatness of her beauty, why wonder if the appetite of vainglory disturbs her more vehemently? When resistance is not adequate to repel its attack, what is this other than that she surrenders after being conquered by Sichem's strength?

CHAPTER LII

How at one and the same time, while one virtue is being ruined, other virtues are nourished from the same source

It ought to be noted clearly that at one and the same time Dina is ruined, and her brothers are occupied in feeding their cattle. In fact, just as the mind that flourishes with charity and the other virtues is accustomed to grieve over its own evils, so also it is accustomed to rejoice over the goods of neighbors. Therefore while it examines the life of neighbors when surveying their goods and compares its goods with theirs, just as it is often unable to avoid applauding its own favorable things, so it will be necessary that it give thanks for the goods of other people. Certainly, while it considers more diligently the successes of some and the failures of others, the infirmity of the latter and the perfection of the former, the pious mind is surely touched by various affections in turn— now this one, now that. Thus it begins to fear for some, to grieve for others, and to hope for good things for the one and better things for the other. It sees in others those things it ought to love and for which it should rejoice. It sees in certain persons those things it ought justly to abhor, and for which it ought justly to grieve. And so in this way when good affections sport with simple thoughts that run forth here and there out of the examined and self-pleased discipline of neighbors—what is this, other than that the brothers of Dina, the sons of Leah, feed their cattle? Do you see how at one and the same time true love of neighbor produces one thing and vain love of self produces the other? True love of neighbor is responsible for the pastures of the brothers for feeding their cattle. Vain love of self serves as the occasion for the ruin of Dina. Because the deed is not unknown to the father, even before a report of it comes to the brothers, what else does it teach to us except that the idea of corruption disturbs the soul first by means of thought, then by means of affection? But when a thing is pondered for a longer time in the heart, it is turned over and over often by thinking, and sometimes it penetrates to the innermost part of the heart and wounds the affection of the heart. Therefore when the soul is affected by anxiety for things and is touched in turn by various affections, it is not to be doubted that a report has already come to the sons of Leah, the brothers of Dina.

Chapter LIII

With how much insistence and caution a perverted intention ought to be corrected

But how do you think they rage when they are no longer able to ignore the ruin of their sister, or at least are not able to dissimulate any more? What does Scripture say concerning them, except that they are angry; and again, that they are furious because of the defilement of their sister? (Cf. Gen: 34). Certainly, this anger or rather rage of the brothers teaches us how much each person ought to be angry with himself, in what way to be indignant with himself, how to accuse himself, how harshly to rebuke, when he recognizes that he has defiled his conscience with empty boasting. Therefore, with a view toward healing swelling of the mind he ought, whoever he is, to place his infirmities before his eyes and to recall to memory his faults, without which no one passes through this life. He ought also to consider carefully how often he remains dishonest in work, unworthy in speech and impure in thinking so that he may clearly gather how many things in his conduct he should find that rightly ought to be cut off if he wishes to boast truly and not shamelessly. Therefore when such reconsideration of a work is turned over and over in the mind, what is it other than when the pact of circumcision is established with the son of Emor? For what is it to say: "Cut off the shameful parts of your customs," other than "Circumcise the foreskins of your masculine parts"? And what is it to say, "Otherwise you will not be able to boast without shamelessness," other than "Otherwise you will not be able to unite with Dina"? For if

Sichem is boasting, if Dina is shamefacedness, what will shameless boasting, boasting without shamefacedness, be other than Sichem without Dina? Deep-rooted customs that are overcome with difficulty are rightly designated by the masculine sex. These are the men whom the brothers of Dina wished to be circumcised. Nevertheless, Scripture says that they proposed this condition of circumcision to Sichem in deceit. Behold, as we can easily perceive, in no way did they arrange to give their sister to such a husband, and however much he might have been able to fulfill the arrangement of the proposed condition, nevertheless they in no way judged him worthy of such a marriage. And certainly even if we were able to cut off thoroughly all our dishonest deeds from our lives and to be utterly cleansed of all of them, yet nonetheless we ought to boast not about our own merits, but in only the Lord. And perhaps for that reason the brothers of Dina proposed hard things to him, in order that they might make him despair completely of a union with their sister. But Sichem is more ready to bear any things or any cruelties whatever rather than to endure a divorce from eagerly-loved Dina. Certainly it is often as we said above: that those things which we were not able to wrest out of our soul when we arranged to do them for God, the same things are easily accomplished when we fear to incur the disgrace of shamefacedness.

CHAPTER LIV

In what manner and how cautiously one ought to change an intention and ought not to abandon integrity of conduct

What are we to say to this? Perhaps it will be better to sigh silently rather than to respond at all, since we cannot deny this. I shall certainly say this, that deservedly he was displeasing to the brothers of Dina. Circumcision, which was done not so much for God as for Dina and not so much for divine custom as for human shame, deservedly was not able to placate them. Nevertheless it was evil in them to exceed the measure of severe justice and not even to observe a measure of equity in avenging the injury. Therefore Jacob deservedly refutes their indiscreet presumption and justly blames them for so much indiscriminate severity. O how much better it would have been to lead the men who had been circumcised—although not so much for God as for Dina—little by little to the true worship of God rather than to strike them with unexpected and sudden death! And so from this let him gather, let him carefully note how each one ought to spare those who have circumcised themselves, notwithstanding that he remembers that they were not circumcised because of God. Who are those circumcised in this way except conduct not corrected by good intention? Nevertheless in such matters we ought never to destroy integrity of conduct but to change intention. Therefore they err, they err especially who condemn good works although perhaps they were undertaken with an evil intention. Such avengers of their own errors—what else do they do, other than after rushing in with Simeon and Levi upon the circumcised, violently kill them?

Chapter LV

With what consideration we especially ought to correct perversion of intention

It is worthwhile to note carefully in what way so few were able to accomplish so great a massacre. But doubtless an opportune time helped them, when the severity of pain had overwhelmed the very ones who had been circumcised and were to be killed by them. The third day of circumcision, on which Scripture says the pain is accustomed to be the most severe, was chosen for this. But what are these days and why are they said to be only three? If by night ignorance is understood, by day knowledge is rightly understood. And so the first day is knowledge of those things that are outside of us; the second day, knowledge of those things that are within us; the third day, knowledge of those things that are above us. Outside of us, corporeal things; within us, spiritual things; above us, divine things. And so, the first consideration of those who circumcise themselves—but yet they do not do this because of God—ought to be, or rather is accustomed to be, that they consider diligently what harshness they have borne from external sources. The second consideration ought to be what they have acquired within by so much punishment of the body, or rather how much they truly have destroyed within by means of the fault of perverse intention. The third consideration will be what retribution they ought to expect from the God whom they do not doubt that they have not so much placated as exasperated by the observance of simulated servitude. And so on the first day of the first consideration the amputated freedom of beloved custom returns to memory and without doubt pain is caused, certainly grave pain because what was possessed with love is not relinquished without pain. On the second day of the second consideration the soul finds itself to have arrived at injury of the mind by means of damages to the body, and the more just the pain is perhaps the more severe it is. On the third day of the third consideration he perceives that he has endured severe things from his own judgment but he ought to expect more severe things from divine judgment. It is the third day on which, Scripture says, the pain is accustomed to be the most severe. For how much pain do you think pierces through the mind when it carefully considers the evil that it endured, the evil in which it engaged, the evil that it deserved, the evil that it endured externally in punishment of the body, the evil that it incurred interiorly in the guilt of crime, the evil that it deserved from heaven in the presence of the Creator? Certainly, whoever of those uselessly circumcised was able to come to this day suffered not only severely but even most severely.

Chapter LVI

That the mind in all its corruption ought to grieve patiently and ought not to give up hope for its improvement

Nevertheless the mind, aware of its crimes and brought into disorder by its weakness, ought to grieve patiently and not to give up hope for its improvement. It is clearly necessary that it should grieve concerning corruption and that nonetheless it should hope concerning improvement, so that when afflicted by moderate grief and encouraged by the assurance of hope, it may give satisfaction for the past and make provision for the future. We have already said above how we ought to understand grief and hope by Simeon and

Levi. They are those two brothers of Dina, Simeon and Levi, fierce avengers of their injuries. If only they had been as discreet as they were strong! To Simeon it pertains to give satisfaction for that which is wrong; to Levi it pertains to encourage the soul to that which it must provide for the future. Therefore, if you grieve concerning corruption and give up hope concerning improvement, Simeon is there, but alone. If you neglect concerning satisfaction for the past and yet hope concerning security in the future, Levi is there, but alone. For such a task it is necessary that both come together, and each bring aid to the other.

CHAPTER LVII

In what manner and how cautiously a corrupted mind ought to be punished by means of reproach for sin and exaction of debt

But it ought to be considered again that often in that which they do bravely, they go beyond the bounds of proper balance. This we can easily prove from this deed of theirs that we have in our hands. For when they had drawn their swords they violently killed persons joined to them in a pact of alliance, and on account of the violated chastity of one they brought about the sudden massacre of so many men. The sword of Simeon is reproach. The sword of Levi is exaction. For Simeon is accustomed to reproach vehemently in a corrupted mind the evil that it has done, while Levi is accustomed to demand vehemently the good that should be done. Therefore, what does it mean that they fight with these swords, other than that they punish the mind with the goads of reproach and exaction? The mind of certain persons when vehemently inflamed by these goads often laments inconsolably even over the things that it cannot avoid in any way. When disturbed by these goads, often it even ventures to begin those things which it in no way has the strength to complete. From this comes that immoderate sadness of certain persons and also that indiscriminate abstinence which in truth destroys not only the powers of the body but even the strength of the mind. In fact, when Simeon rages, we see that some people are so swallowed up by irrational sadness that they cannot be relieved even a little by any consolations. We have known others who have collapsed so completely by means of immoderate abstinence that afterward no abundance of delicacies, no diligence of cooks, was able to bring them satisfaction. Behold these warriors (I speak of Simeon and Levi), how they fight, in what manner they avenge themselves. What does it mean that they, drawing swords, kill the lovers of Dina other than to weaken by reproach for inevitable things and exaction of impossible things not only the powers of the body but also the strength of the mind to such a degree that in any event the mind cannot restrain itself from its own excesses even for the sake of human shamefacedness? For this reason it is said rightly to them by Jacob: "Simeon and Levi, brothers, are instruments of iniquity, waging war; my soul, come not into their council; my glory be not in their assembly" (Gen. 49:5, 6). O what kind of warriors are these who, when they want to seem to act bravely, kill cruelly and violently their allies in peace? Instruments of iniquity, waging war; my soul come not into their council. O ill-advised men, who, when they venture what they are not able to accomplish, also lose what they had been able to accomplish! Thus, my soul, come not into their council; my glory, be not in their assembly. It is not good boasting to walk about among important things and among marvels above yourself where it might be possible as it were to boast concerning your own virtue. I say, this sort of boasting is not good. Therefore, my glory be not in their assembly: "Because in their fury they killed a man, and in their willfulness they undermined a wall" (ibid.).

CHAPTER LVIII

How by excessive affliction the mind sometimes becomes ungoverned up to the point of shamelessness

What is meant by "man" except vigor of mind? What is meant by "wall," except discipline of body? And so then, that man, the lover of Dina, truly is killed when after vigor of mind has been exhausted by excessive affliction, the soul becomes ungoverned up to the point of open shamelessness. The lover of Dina doubtless perishes by the sword at the time when, by the excessiveness of affliction, vigor of mind fails to such an extent that, as has been said, the mind cannot govern its own excesses, even at the least for the sake of human shamefacedness. The wall is destroyed when by immoderate abstinence the rigor of earlier discipline is thoroughly dissipated. But in such warriors this is admirable above all, nay rather detestable above all that at no time whatever are they satisfied with the counsel of a prudent man. Nor do they at the very least yield to their own experience, certainly not at the time when they begin to fail in body or waste away in heart. The stubbornness of these is pierced through by an arrow of condemnation when it is said to them by Jacob: "Cursed be their fury, because stubborn, and their indignation, because hard" (Gen. 49:7). It is a marvelous stubbornness, but no less mad that a person can be restrained only by the bridle of impossibility from the ardor of his course, from his foolish waywardness. See how these warring instruments of iniquity know how to fight. See how much they do; see how much they do for the sake of Dina. For the sake of Dina, masculine parts are circumcised. For the sake of Dina those circumcised are killed. All this is for the sake of Dina, all for the sake of human shamefacedness.

Chapter LIX

That ordered shamefacedness is not good unless it is also moderate

But since we have just reproved human shamefacedness, perhaps you wonder why we teach that it pertains to Dina in any way, since by Dina we ought to understand only ordered shamefacedness. It is one thing that people feel shame on account of God, and another that they feel shame on account of themselves: "Let your light so shine," says Scripture, "that they may see your good works and glorify your Father who is in heaven" (Matt. 5:16). Thus it is good to feel shame because of disgrace, not so much for our boasting as for divine glory. This perhaps is the meaning of Dina's going out: to feel shame for disgrace before people on account of God. No doubt Dina is found within when our conscience is ashamed before God even on account of its hidden things. That people feel shame on account of God is to have good shamefacedness that is such that undoubtedly pertains to Dina. And so, such shamefacedness is ordered and can in some sense rightly be called human. Nevertheless this kind of shamefacedness is good, if it is not excessive. Certainly if Dina were yet a small girl or had kept herself within the privacy of her bedroom she would not have incurred the stain of corruption and would not have become the cause of so great evils.

Chapter LX

A brief recapitulation concerning the number of principal affections and the way of ordering them

This is Dina who is born after Issachar and Zabulon because after a taste of the joy of internal sweetness and after true hatred of the vices, each person is more truly and also more vehemently ashamed of his weakness. Truly, by Issachar we understand joy of a good conscience; by Zabulon, hatred of sinfulness; by Dina, charm of shamefacedness. And indeed, these are the youngest three of the children of Leah. If we count them with the four mentioned above, we find without doubt that there are seven. For we have already said above that the principal affections are seven: When we set them in order within ourselves we place them in the numerical sequence of the virtues. And so fear is set in order first; next, grief; after these, hope and love. After these four, joy and anger are set in order; and last of all, shamefacedness. Such children born to Jacob from Leah are nothing other than the soul's having begotten from itself worthy children of the virtues by setting in order the impulse of its affections. Therefore by Ruben, the firstborn of Jacob, we understand ordered fear; by Simeon, ordered grief; by Levi and Judah, ordered hope and ordered love. By Issachar, however, ordered joy is understood; by Zabulon, ordered anger; by Dina, ordered shamefacedness.

RICHARD OF ST. VICTOR

CHAPTER LXI

That ordered affections are truly good, if they are also moderated

It ought to be known, however, that these affections are believed to be truly good when they are not only ordered but are also
moderated. For indeed, often when they exceed the control of discretion they lose the name of virtue. But perhaps we can show this
better by an example if we take examples concerning the firstborn
son himself. Certainly if immoderate fear were not perilous, Jacob
would never have said to Ruben: "You are poured out like water;
you shall not increase because you went up to the couch of your
father, and you defiled its covering" (Gen. 49:4). If by Ruben we
ought to understand ordered fear, why, I ask, does Jacob command
him not to increase except that it is evil to exceed the measure of
equity in any ordered fear whatsoever?

CHAPTER LXII

In what way fear goes beyond the limit of equity

However, this son often exceeds the limit of equity in two
ways: either because he is increased excessively concerning some
one thing or because he is enlarged without order to innumerable or
even useless things. Who would deny that Ruben ought justly to
fear after the crime of betraying? But who does not see that that
which was detestable above all else in him was that while he neither
wished nor knew how to keep a proper measure in his fear, by
giving up hope that he himself might be able to correct the evil he
finished with an end more detestable than the beginning? But that
excess of fear which spreads itself without order to various things
easily deceives. As a matter of fact it sometimes steals into perfect
men. For indeed, who of the prelates, however perfect, while he
provides the necessary things of life for his subjects, governs the
care of his anxiety so that he never again dreads more than is right
on account of the adverse misfortunes of things? However, such a
fear then pertains only to Ruben, when it arises not from love of the

118

world but on account of love of neighbor. But who suffices to enumerate all the dangerous misfortunes of troublesome things that rise up here and there, on account of which the infirmity of his subjects—if not his own infirmity—causes him to be alarmed? And who does not see how difficult, or rather how thoroughly impossible, it is never to exceed the limit of proper dread? For this reason it often happens that the more prudent a person is the more anxious he is found to be. And the more each sharper-sighted person knows how to foresee the dangerous misfortunes of surrounding perils, the more he is forced many times to relax the control of his timid anxiety. From one thing and the other we can fitly understand that it is said to Ruben by Jacob: "You are poured out like water; you shall not increase" (Gen. 49:4). For inasmuch as prudence of the flesh is accustomed to be understood by water, so spiritual understanding is often understood by wine. This water is turned into wine by each person when, after being inspired by God, he is raised up by means of the ladder of exterior knowledge to the understanding of invisible things, when "the invisible things of God from the creation of the world are seen, being understood by means of those things which have been made" (Rom. 1:20). Such water abounds all the more for each person, the more copiously his soul enlarges itself in the knowledge of exterior things. Certainly, the more abundant this water grows when the soul surveys all things cautiously, without doubt the more dense is the forest of dreadful anxiety that it produces and the more widely it expands. For such reason, this is rightly said: "You are poured out like water; you shall not increase." And so it is necessary to be on guard with extreme diligence when the water of earthly knowledge abounds so that the fear of many-sided anxiety does not grow beyond measure.

CHAPTER LXIII

To what shameless wandering an excess of fear prostitutes the mind

Certainly when Ruben was still a small child and was in the years of boyhood, he did not venture to defile the couch of his father, either because he was not able or because he lacked the boldness. Nevertheless, when he became an adult, he rushed forth, as it is read of him, with so much audacity that he ruined his father's concubine Bala, the handmaid of Rachel. But if by Bala is understood imagination, how do we reckon that such a handmaid is ruined? But what is the corruption of Bala except the unordered and shameless wandering of thought and imagination? For sometimes an overabundance of fear so greatly prostitutes (I do not say ruins) the imagination that in fact in a time of prayer it is scarcely or not at all able to restrain itself from its fornications. For when even in the midst of praying the mind often receives through the imagination phantasies of worldly cares because of excessive anxiety, what is this except that Bala opens her bosom for fornication with Ruben? Now think how improper it is that at the very time when you ought to pray humbly to the Lord for the removal of eternal evils you begin to have so many temporal perils before the eyes and to turn over in the heart only those things, forgetting the things on account of which you had come and remembering only the things that you ought to have forgotten. This is the reason that often the mind that first was accustomed at all times to place before itself through imagination only goods and evils of the future, later, after being overcome by overabundant fear, is not able to exclude from the secret place of the heart even a slight incursion of the cares of the world. Therefore because imagination often is led by overabundant fear to such shameless wandering of thoughts, Ruben's father rightly says to him, reproaching him for the ruin of Bala: "You are poured out like water; you shall not increase, because you went up to the couch of your father, and you defiled its covering."

CHAPTER LXIV

Concerning the force and efficacy of fear, without which we neither abandon evil nor begin good

In order that we may say something more openly concerning this affection, it seems to have a greater efficacy than the others for either good or evil. Indeed the mind frequently is thrown down from its state of uprightness by that affection, yet having been cast down by whatever way it is never restored without it. For without fear, who is liberated from any sin however small? Without fear we can never leave our evils. Without fear we can never ever begin to be engaged in goods. Are not those words of Jacob obviously said concerning it if we rightly understand where it is said: "Ruben my firstborn, you are my fortitude, the beginning of my grief, first in gifts, greater in authority" (Gen. 49:3)? In which place that also follows, concerning which we have spoken elsewhere: "You are poured out like water, you shall not increase." How this Ruben is firstborn and how he is the beginning of grief is sufficiently obvious, I think, from what has been said above. However, it is easy to show how he is his fortitude and other things that are said of him: "You," he says, "are my fortitude." For who emerged as victor at any time in that battle where spirit strives against flesh and flesh against spirit? Who, I say, has fought against so large an army of his cravings, unless he has fought from fear? Therefore he is rightly called firstborn because all good is begun from fear of the Lord. He is rightly called fortitude, because by fear of the Lord the heart is strengthened against its cravings. He is rightly called beginning of his grief, because useful grief accompanies fear of the Lord. For, in order that each man have his own grief of soul and it be useful to him, it is necessary that fear of the Lord lead the way.

CHAPTER LXV

Concerning the superiority of fear and concerning the other affections, which are ruled by which

"First in gifts, greater in authority." Among all the gifts of God that seem to relate to a person's salvation, a good will is known to be the first and foremost gift by which the image of the divine similitude is restored in us. Whatever a person does cannot be good unless it proceeds from a good will. Whatever is from a good will cannot be evil. Without a good will you cannot be saved at all. With a good will you cannot perish at all. O marvelous gift! O singular gift! This is that first and foremost gift which Ruben the firstborn is given since without doubt an evil will is changed into a good will through fear of the Lord. Why should he not be "first in gifts" who receives the first and foremost gift? First, because all good begins from a good will; foremost, because nothing more useful than a good will is given to people. "First in gifts, greater in authority." Who would deny that this Ruben is greater than the others in authority since he is accustomed frequently to command all his other brothers? In his presence Levi withdraws because when fear comes, hope falls down. Often Judah withdraws in view of his authority, and Zabulon yields because when forced by fear, charity often grows cold and hatred rises up. At his nod Issachar goes out and Simeon comes in because when fear enters by stealth, often joy is excluded and grief is admitted. We have seen how at one time or another Ruben is accustomed to command even his brothers. Now let us see how his authority extends more widely in comparison with the others. Certainly there are some things that we love, and there are other things that we hate, but we are accustomed to fear on account of both when often we dread losing one and meeting with the other. And so Judah and Zabulon divide kingship between themselves, but Ruben extends himself to all of it—because true love pours out itself to good alone; true hatred, to evil alone; but fear, to both good and evil. Zabulon admits his brother Simeon into part of his part. Indeed we grieve for adversities, but not for all because we do not suffer all. Levi is less in authority than Judah and much greater than Issachar. For there are many more things that we ought to love than things that we dare to hope for. But nevertheless it remains that there is much more material for hoping than for rejoicing, since the things that we possess, on account of which we rejoice, are few compared to those we hope that we shall possess. And so Judah and Zabulon surpass the other brothers in the magnitude of their authority. Nevertheless they are completely unable to extend themselves to the measure of Ruben. And so Ruben, who leading the way leaves the others far behind himself, surpasses all. For all things that it is agreed people love, hope, hate and for which they are accustomed to grieve or rejoice are able from themselves to give birth to causes of varied fear. For indeed, the more we love concerning one thing, the more causes of fearing we find inasmuch as it is possible to have as many occasions of fear as there are ways of losing something. And so this Ruben greatly enlarges his kingship, yet not only the multitude of hidden things but also the change of appearances gives powers to him. Concerning what am I able to be secure since I have nothing that I am not able to lose? When do I attain certitude of knowledge here since I do not know countless more things than I know? Therefore, because fear is poured out more widely than the other affections, Ruben rightly is said to be greater in authority when compared to the brothers. And he is forbidden by his father to increase, but clearly he was poured out like water at that time when he went up to the couch of his father and defiled its covering: "Ruben," he said, "my firstborn, you are my fortitude, the beginning of my grief, first in gifts, greater in authority; you are poured out like water, you shall not increase, because you went up to the couch of your father and defiled its covering." Behold Ruben. He chances much evil, because he increases beyond the limit. Great danger is quickly encountered if our fear is not moderated by discretion.

CHAPTER LXVI

How virtues are turned into vices, unless they are moderated by discretion

We ought also to believe concerning the other affections, that they are certainly dangerous unless we restrain them within the limits of equity. Certainly we can easily note from the previously mentioned deed of Simeon and Levi how evil it is for grief and hope to exceed the limit. Concerning them it is said by Jacob: "Cursed be their fury, because stubborn, and their indignation, because hard" (Gen. 49:7). Thus one ought to keep cautious watch over all the virtues so that they are not only ordered but also moderated. For excessive fear often falls into despair; excessive grief, into bitterness; immoderate hope, into presumption; overabundant love, into flattery; unnecessary joy, into dissolution; intemperate anger, into fury. And so in this way virtues are turned into vices if they are not moderated by discretion. Do you not see in what manner all the others need the virtue of discretion if they are not to lose the name of virtue?

Chapter LXVII

How and how late discretion is born, since it is the first offspring of reason

This is that Joseph who, although he is born late, is loved more than the others by his father. For who does not know that the true good of the soul can be neither acquired nor preserved without discretion? Thus that virtue is deservedly loved exceedingly without which nothing is sought for, nothing completed, nothing preserved. But we only deserve to receive such a son late since we are not educated to the perfection of discretion without a great deal of practice nor except by a great deal of experience. We must be practiced in individual virtues and what we are able to undertake in each one of them before we are able to comprehend full knowledge concerning all of them and to judge sufficiently concerning individual ones. Certainly we learn many things concerning discretion by reading, many things by listening, and many things from the innate judgment of our reason, yet we are never educated to the full concerning this without the teaching of experience. He who ought to judge concerning all the others must come after all of them. Therefore, first of all we should strive to apply ourselves to the pursuit of individual virtues, although when we do this it is necessary that we often fall. Consequently we must often rise again and through frequent falling learn what vigilance, what caution is necessary to acquire and keep the good things of virtue. So, when discipline of virtue is learned by long use, the mind, after having been trained for a long time, is at some time brought to full discretion of behavior and rightly rejoices, as it were, concerning the birth of Joseph. Before his birth, when his brothers still did all things without discretion, the more they ventured many things beyond their powers, the more often they were ruined in a worse and more deformed way. This is the reason, as I have already said, that Dina is born after these since disgrace of shame frequently accompanies an ugly fall. But after Dina's birth her brothers discover, as it were, by the ignominy of disgrace and learn by experience that nothing is better to a king than counsel: "Because a prudent man is better than a strong man" (Wisd. 6:1; cf. Prov. 16:32). "For the prudent man speaks of victories, and when he does everything with complete counsel he will not regret it for eternity." Therefore, when the necessary usefulness of counsel is learned by experience and is sought and found by more attentive pursuit, then in a certain manner Joseph is born, by whom the virtue of discretion is understood. However, the reason is evident why neither of the handmaids, why certainly not Leah herself but Rachel alone can bear such a son since it belongs not to sense nor to imagination nor lastly to affection itself but to reason alone to discern and to understand. Therefore, if we understand reason by Rachel, we quickly discover why Joseph can be born from Rachel only since in no way do we doubt that discretion is born from reason alone. Such an offspring from such a mother; Joseph from Rachel; discretion from reason.

CHAPTER LXVIII

Concerning the utility of discretion and its proper nature

This is that Joseph who alone among the brothers is clothed in a tunic reaching to the ankles because only that action which is moderated by the prudence of discretion is brought to such a limit of consummation and of its necessary end. This is that Joseph who is loved more than all the brothers by his father because the virtue that is protector of the others is justly preferred. This is that Joseph, a dreamer and an interpreter of dreams; because in the very moment of temptation, true discretion discerns future dangers from their nature within the very phantasms of suggestions; also, for any other persons whomsoever, it detects the ambush of imminent evils according to the confession of their own thoughts and delivers warnings concerning future perils. This is Joseph whom his brothers emulate and aliens venerate; whom Hebrews sold and Egyptians bought, because the latter more quickly are satisfied with the counsel and more easily yield to the prudence of another, recognizing the darkness of their error rather than presuming concerning their justice and prudence. This is that Joseph, husband of a virgin; lover not violator of chastity, since discretion is accustomed to be the guardian, not the destroyer, of inner purity. This is that boy and messenger who alone remains with blessed Job in all of his punishment, who is eager to announce immediately the hurtful things perpetrated upon him because except by discretion the soul neither comprehends nor corrects the hurtful deeds of the virtues. That boy does not know to die with the dying; discretion does not know how to fail through the loss of things or through the increase of temptations—rather it makes progress. For the more we are pressed upon by painful temptations and the more we are exercised by frequent dangers, the more perfectly we are educated for discretion. Moreover, the losses of other virtues are often the profits of discretion. For Joseph knows to increase not only with those increasing, to make progress not only with those making progress, but truly to go from failure of the brothers to success and to acquire the profits of prudence from the losses of others. Such a son is deservedly named Joseph, since Joseph is interpreted "increase." For this reason it is rightly said of him by his father: "Joseph is a growing son, a growing son and beautiful when seen" (Gen. 49:22). And so, he is rightly called "increase," he is rightly called "growing son" who is always increasing, whose growth is not finished right up to the end.

CHAPTER LXIX

How useful it is, and also how difficult, to conform perfectly to discretion

The very dreams of Joseph bear witness to how great the excellence of this virtue is. The words of his father bear witness, where it is read: "But why shall your mother, your brothers, and I adore you on the earth?" (Gen. 37:10). Father, mother and brothers adore this Joseph since by either spontaneous will or the necessity of constraint they at one time or another conform to discretion inasmuch as the interior sun of the intellectual world, the eye of the heart—viz., the intention of the mind—is guided by discretion; keenness of reason is sharpened by discretion from which it arises; the whole fraternal union of virtues has bounds set by discretion; and any virtues that are not satisfied with his counsel or do not submit themselves to discretion himself quickly lose the name of virtue. It is he who does not neglect the things neglected by his brothers; it is he who censures their excesses. When he is present they are not permitted to venture anything beyond their powers; when he is present they omit nothing by negligence. In his presence they are not permitted to turn aside to either the right or the left nor to act either sluggishly or precipitously nor to venture before the time or delay beyond the suitable time. For this reason there is that severe discord and almost implacable anger between him and the brothers, concerning which Scripture is not silent since it clearly reports that his brothers hate him and cannot say anything peaceable to him. For the admonitions of Joseph seem to them excessively severe, the instructions hard and the counsels unbearable. For what is harder, what more difficult, than never to neglect what ought to be done and in all that one does never to disturb the manner, never to ruin order, and never to exceed proper measure? Believe me, the soul demands nothing more difficult from itself than that it preserve proper measure in all its affection. Indeed, often the brothers of Joseph, when attempting something great while "well done, well done" is shouted on every side, are accustomed to extend their hands not only to useless but also to impossible efforts. Indeed, frequently affection of the soul is unbridled because of such shouting by flatterers, resulting in an immoderate audacity of presumption. Or rather, many times it is led by depraved intention of the mind to the crime of hypocrisy and is cast down. This is that crime, most evil and before others abominable because before all others it is hateful to God, of which Joseph accuses his brothers in the presence of their father, just as Scripture itself clearly declares when it says: "In the presence of the father, Joseph accused his brothers of a most evil crime" (Gen. 37:2). The vice that God hates exceedingly is understood more rightly as none other than hypocrisy. Indeed, as Augustine bears witness, a pretended equity is not equity but a double inequity. This vice is uncovered by Joseph when ambushing evil is discovered and censured by discretion. At one time this vice ruins the sons; at another time the father corrects this vice. When in touching the affections he strikes too harshly and seizes for too long, however, he does not incline the soul to harmony.

Chapter LXX

Concerning the manifold function of true discretion

And so it pertains to Joseph to consider with foresight, to foresee cautiously, to seize skillfully, to reveal quickly, and to censure sharply not only this vice but any ambushing and hidden evil. To the function of Joseph pertains the care and keeping of all his brothers; to it pertains the discipline of each one; to it, the arrangement of things to be done; to it, the foresight of future things. It pertains to his function to give heed carefully and to discuss frequently how much progress the soul makes daily—or perhaps how much it fails—by what thoughts it is attacked more, by what affections it is more frequently touched. Joseph himself ought to know perfectly not only the vices of the heart but also the infirmities of the body according to which he requires that everyone seek health-giving remedies and apply what is found. He must know not only his vices but also the gifts of grace and the merits of virtues. He must distinguish diligently and consider skillfully those things which are goods of nature and those things which are gifts of grace. He ought to have at hand by what plan of temptations the evil spirit fights him; with what consolations of spiritual joys he abounds; how frequently the divine spirit visits him; how by it, although it is one, he is nevertheless not always touched in a uniform and similar manner, but he is filled now with the spirit of wisdom, now with the spirit of understanding, now with the spirit of counsel, or any other of its affections. And so that I may briefly conclude all, this Joseph of ours ought to know fully—insofar as it is possible—the total state and quality of the inner and outer person and to seek out skillfully and to investigate carefully not only what sort he is but also even what sort he ought to be.

Chapter LXXI

Concerning the two offspring of reason, viz., grace of discretion and grace of contemplation

By this Joseph the soul is continually instructed and at times is led to full knowledge of itself, just as by his uterine brother Benjamin it is at times lifted up to the contemplation of God. For just as we understand grace of discretion by Joseph, so we understand grace of contemplation by Benjamin. Both are born from this same mother because knowledge of God and of self are learned from reason. Benjamin is born long after Joseph because the soul that has not been practiced over a long time and educated fully in knowledge of self is not raised up to knowledge of God. In vain he raises the eye of the heart to see God when he is not yet prepared to see himself. Let a person first learn to know his own invisible things before he presumes that he is able to grasp at invisible divine things. You must know the invisible things of your own spirit before you can be capable of knowing the invisible things of God. If you are not able to know yourself, how do you have the boldness to grasp at those things which are above you?

Chapter LXXII

How the soul is lifted up to contemplation of God by means of full knowledge of self

The rational soul discovers without doubt that it is the foremost and principal mirror for seeing God. For if the invisible things of God are seen, being understood by the intellect by means of those things which have been made (cf. Rom. 1:20), where, I ask, have the traces of knowledge been found more clearly imprinted than in His image? We read and we believe that regarding the soul, humans have been made in the likeness of God (cf. Gen. 1:26) and therefore as long as we walk by faith and not by sight (cf. 2 Cor. 5:7), as long as we still see by a mirror and in an enigma (cf. 1 Cor. 13:12), we cannot find, as I have said, a mirror more apt for imaginative vision of Him than the rational spirit. Whoever thirsts to see his God—let him wipe his mirror, let him cleanse his spirit. And so the true Joseph does not cease to hold, wipe and gaze into this mirror incessantly: to hold it so that it does not adhere to the earth, after it has fallen down by means of love; to wipe it so that it does not become dirty from the dust of useless thoughts; to gaze into it so that the eye of his intention does not turn toward empty pursuits. When the mirror has been wiped and gazed into for a long time, a kind of splendor of divine light begins to shine in it and a great beam of unexpected vision appears to his eyes. This light illumined the eyes of him who said: "The light of your face has been sealed upon us, Lord; you have put joy in my heart" (Ps. 4:7). Therefore, from the vision of this light that it wonders at within itself, the soul is kindled from above in a marvelous way and is animated to see the living light that is above it. I say, from this vision the soul conceives the flame of longing for the sight of God, and it lays hold of a pledge. And so the mind that now burns with longing for this vision should know that if it already hopes for what it longs for, it already has conceived Benjamin himself. By hoping the mind conceives; by longing it goes into labor; and the more longing increases, the closer it comes to giving birth.

CHAPTER LXXIII

How arduous and difficult it is to acquire the grace of contemplation

But nevertheless we know (for we have learned this, as Scripture teaches): "Because the hope that is delayed afflicts the soul" (Prov. 13:12). For nothing so affects the soul in the same manner as impatient longing. What is sought more beneficially than the sweetness of this vision? What is sensed more pleasantly? What does the soul experience more joyfully? Rachel knows this, for it is impossible for reason not to know this since every other sweetness is bitter when compared to this pleasure. This is the reason that she is able neither to relax her effort nor to temper her longing. For this reason she has so much anxiety at giving birth and such immensity of grief. And for what reason do you think there is such greatness of grief except from endless effort and impatient longing? Daily it increases: labor from desire, and grief from labor. It is increased continually: longing from effort and effort from longing. Nevertheless, Rachel knows that this matter is beyond her powers, and yet she is able to temper neither her effort nor her longing. For indeed, the mind by its own activity can never attain to such grace. This gift is from God; it is not a reward to man. But without doubt no person receives such and so much grace without a mighty effort and burning longing. Rachel knew this, and for that reason she multiplies effort and more passionately inflames her desire with daily increases. Indeed, in such anxiety of daily exertion, in such immensity of grief Benjamin is born and Rachel dies, because when the human mind is carried above itself it passes beyond all narrowness of human reasoning. All human reason succumbs to that which the mind catches sight of from the light of divinity when it has been raised above itself and snatched up in ecstasy. For what is the death of Rachel, except the failure of reason?

CHAPTER LXXIV

Concerning that kind of contemplation which is above reason

And so when Benjamin is born, Rachel dies, because the mind, having been carried away to contemplation, experiences how great the failure of human reason is. Did not Rachel die and did not the sense of all human reason fail in the Apostle when he said: "Whether in the body or outside the body, I do not know; God knows" (2 Cor. 12:2)? Therefore, let no person suppose that he is able to penetrate to the splendor of that divine light by argumentation; let no person believe that he is able to comprehend it by human reasoning. For if it were possible to approach that divine light by some argument or other then it would not be inaccessible. And thereupon the Apostle indeed boasts not that he went to that but that without doubt he was snatched up: "I know," he says, "a man, whether in the body or outside the body I do not know; God knows; such a one was snatched up to the third heaven" (2 Cor. 12:2). But what is this third heaven? That difference which is between earth and heaven is between body and spirit. Now the worth of human spirit is one thing, that of angelic spirit is another, and the excellence of divine spirit is far different. Indeed, the worth of human spirit that endures punishment and guilt is far surpassed by the excellence of angelic nature, which is free from both. But that spirit which made angel and man precedes both of them incomparably. Any soul is truly raised up to any of these heavens when, as it abandons the lowest things of earthly thoughts, it is transfixed in contemplation of these heavens. And so knowledge of self pertains to the first heaven; contemplation of God pertains to the third. And who do you think ascends to this third heaven, except he who also descends—the Son of man who is in heaven? And so, if there are those who ascend to the heavens and descend into the depths, nevertheless they do not ascend except perhaps to the first and second for they are not able to ascend to the third. Certainly men can be snatched up to this heaven, but they are not at all able to ascend by themselves. Nevertheless we are able to separate into three stages that knowledge of God which one is able to possess in this life, and according to the triple difference of stages we are able to divide the heavens by three inasmuch as God is seen one way by faith, is known another way by reason, and is discerned another way by means of contemplation. Thus the first vision pertains to the first heaven; the second, to the second heaven; the third, to the third heaven. The first is below reason; the second, with reason; the third, above reason. So people can surely ascend to the first and second heaven of contemplation; but none reach to that which is above reason except those snatched up above themselves by means of ecstasy. Moreover, we can conclude suitably enough from the death of his mother that we ought to understand by Benjamin that kind of contemplation which is above reason.

Chapter LXXV

Concerning the supereminence of spiritual contemplations

Compared to the height of such contemplation, any knowledge possessed by creatures is limited and lies in the depths and scarcely occupies the space of a point, as does the quality of the earth with respect to heaven. Compared to knowledge possessed by the Creator, what is any knowledge however great possessed by creatures except that it is like earth in relation to heaven and the center of a circle in relation to the whole circumference? Nevertheless the earth, this lower knowledge of lower things, has these things: mountains and hills, fields and valleys. According to the difference of creatures there will be a difference of knowledges. In order that we may begin from the lowest, the difference between body and body is great since indeed there are celestial bodies, and there are also terrestrial bodies. Nevertheless, the difference between a body of any sort and a spirit is greater than that between any sort of bodies, however dissimilar. But of spirits themselves, some are irrational, others are rational. Thus those who still marvel only at corporeal things seem to have fixed their eyes, as it were, on the lowest things. But those who turn themselves to the investigation of spiritual things already, as it were, ascend to high things. The first and principle thing for the soul that strives to ascend to the height of knowledge must be the effort to know itself. The great height of knowledge is to know the self perfectly. The full knowledge of a rational spirit is a mountain great and high. This mountain transcends the highest point of all mundane knowledges; from the height it looks down upon all philosophy, all knowledge of the world. What so excellent did Aristotle or Plato discover; what so excellent was such a crowd of philosophers able to discover? Truly, without doubt, if they had been able by the keenness of their natural ability to ascend this mountain, if their efforts had sufficed for them to discover themselves, if they had known themselves fully, they would never worship idols, never bow the neck to a creature, never raise up the neck against the Creator. Here those searching failed in the search. Here, I say, they failed and were not able at all to ascend the mountain. "Let man ascend to a high heart, and God shall be exalted" (Ps. 63:7, 8). O man, learn to know; learn to think about yourself and you have ascended to a high heart. The more you advance daily in the knowledge of yourself, the more you always tend to higher things. He who arrives at perfect knowledge of himself already takes possession of the summit of the mountain.

Chapter LXXVI

How rare and how delightful it is to bring spiritual contemplations into use and to turn them into pleasure

O how few are those who ascend this far, either because they do not know or because they are not able. It is very rare to ascend this mountain but much rarer to stand on its summit and to stay there for a while. However it is rarest of all to live there and rest in the mind: "Who," he says, "shall ascend the mountain of the Lord, and who shall stand in His holy place?" (Ps. 23:3). The first thing is to ascend; afterward, to stand. Certainly there is labor in standing, but there is much more in ascending. Certainly many have failed in this ascent because of the excessive labor of ascending; many have descended quickly from its steep summit because of the labor of standing. Perhaps it seemed intolerable to them that not only can one not ascend this mountain except with great labor, but also in truth it is not given to one to stay there without great difficulty. But perhaps you already have ascended, and you already have learned to stand there—yet this ought not to suffice for you. Learn to live there, to make a dwelling place, and to return above to that place after being drawn away by whatever sort of wandering of the mind. Without doubt, by much use it will at times be turned for you into pleasure, into so much that without any difficulty of labor you can exist there continually; indeed it would be greater pain for you elsewhere than to stay longer there. It is a wonderful joy to be able to remain on this mountain without labor. Let Peter, who has been admitted to so great and so uncommon a pleasure, bear witness. He exclaims, "It is good for us to be here" (Matt. 17:4). O happy is he who is able to ascend this mountain and to rest in the mind. O how great! O how rare! "Lord who shall dwell in your tabernacle? And who shall rest on your holy mountain?" (Ps. 14:1). Certainly it is great to be able to ascend and to stand; nevertheless it is greater to be able to dwell and to rest. To ascend and stand belongs to virtue; to dwell and rest belongs to happiness. Each is great and is worthy of admiration. The Prophet marvels at each, the one for greatness of difficulty, the other for greatness of joy. Admiration of difficulty is that exclamation: "Who shall ascend the mountain of the Lord, and who shall stand in His holy place?" (Ps. 23:3). Admiration of joy is that exclamation: "Lord, who shall dwell in your tabernacle, and who shall rest on your holy mountain?" (Ps. 14:1). O how great and what kind of fortitude, to ascend and stand; O how much and what kind of beatitude, to dwell and rest! Who is fit for this work, who is worthy to receive it? "Lord, who shall ascend; Lord, who shall stand on your holy mountain? Send forth your light and your truth; they have led me and brought me to your sacred mountain and into your tabernacle" (Ps. 42:3).

Chapter LXXVII

That without prevenient grace we strive in vain for the summit

Do you see that only Truth leads and brings one to this mountain? Truth leads; Truth is that which guides. I gladly follow Truth; I do not hold suspect such a guide. Truth knows to lead; Truth does not know how to mislead. But what is Truth? What do you say, good Teacher, teacher Christ, what is Truth? "I am," he says, "the Way, the Truth, and the Life" (John 14:6). Therefore let one who wishes to ascend the mountain follow Truth. Follow Christ, whoever you are who wish to ascend this mountain. We have learned from the teaching of the Evangelist: "Then Jesus took his disciples, viz., Peter, James and John, and led them into a high mountain apart" (Matt. 17:1). Thus the disciples of Jesus are led above and apart, that they may take possession of this high mountain. It is a steep way, a secret way unknown to many, which leads to the summit of this mountain. I think only those run without error, only those arrive without impediment, who follow Christ, who are led by Truth. Whoever hastens to high things, you go in security if Truth goes before you. Without it you labor in vain. As Truth does not wish to deceive, so it is not able to be deceived. If you do not wish to err, follow Christ.

Chapter LXXVIII

How much full knowledge of self is effective

Lest the labor of the journey and the difficulties of the ascent terrify you and draw you back, hear and give attention to what the result of arrival is. On the peak of this mountain Jesus is transfigured; on it Moses is seen with Elijah and each is recognized without a sign; on it the voice of the Father to the Son is heard. Which of these is not marvelous? Which of these is not desirable? Do you wish to see Christ transfigured? Ascend this mountain; learn to know yourself. Do you wish to see Moses and Elijah and recognize them without any sign?. Do you wish to understand the law and the prophets without a teacher, without an interpreter? Ascend this mountain; learn to know yourself. Do you wish to hear the mystery of the Father's secrets? Ascend this mountain; learn to know yourself. For he descended from heaven when he said: γνῶτι σεαυτὸν; that is, "Know yourself." Do you now see how much the ascent of this mountain is effective, how useful full knowledge of self is?

Chapter LXXIX

In what ways we reach to the height of knowledge

But what do we say about the fact that Christ did not wish to ascend this mountain without three disciples, nor did he seek to take more than three with him? Perhaps in this work we are taught that without a threefold effort we are not brought to the height of this knowledge. Through the effort of work, through the effort of meditation and through the effort of prayer we are advanced little by little, and finally we are brought to perfection of knowledge. For we experience many things by working; we discover many things by investigation; we obtain many things by prayer. Since there are many things that we are not able to discover either through the experience of work or through the investigation of reason, we deserve through the importunity of prayer to be taught them from the showing of divine inspiration. When it joins these three companions to itself, truth advances in us, raises itself up on high, and exalts itself up to that point by daily increments until at last it touches the summit of the above-mentioned mountain. O how many persons we see today, studious in reading, slothful in work, tepid in prayer, who nevertheless take it for granted that they are able to take possession of the peak of this mountain. But I ask, when will those who do not have Christ as leader take possession of it? For Christ who does not wish to ascend except with three disciples does not lead them. Therefore let one who seeks to have Christ as guide of the journey and leader of the ascent join the effort of work and prayer to the effort of reading. No doubt the mind is not lifted up to the complete height of knowledge without much exercise, without constant effort, without burning longing. This is because one who does not follow the footsteps of Christ perfectly does not enter the way of truth rightly.

Chapter LXXX

How the divine showing happens at the highest point of our effort

But it ought not to be passed over in silence that many persons believe that they have already taken possession of the highest point of this mountain when it is evident that they have scarcely touched the lowest portions of it. It should be a sure sign to you that you have in no way taken possession of the top of this mountain if you have not yet deserved to see Christ glorified. As soon as Christ your leader has established you on the highest point, He appears to you in another condition. In your presence He puts on light as clothing, and just as the Evangelist bears witness, afterwards His garments become as white as snow and of such a sort as no fuller on the earth is able to make, since that splendor of divine wisdom which is seen from afar off from the high peak of speculation is not able to be defined at all by the prudence of human sense. Notice that Christ has one garment in the valley and another garment on the mountain. In the valley He surely has a seamless garment, but He has a glorious garment only on the mountain. Simple truth knows nothing of the divisions of schismatics, and therefore Christ is clothed with only seamless garments, whether in the valley or on the mountain. But there is a great difference between a seamless garment and a glorious garment. Do you wish to come to know the difference of His garments and to receive an open distinction between garment and garment? "If," He said, "I have told you earthly things, and you have not believed, how will you believe if I tell you celestial things?" (John 3:12). Distinguish between teaching and teaching, and you will discover the difference of garments. O how great is the difference between teaching in which earthly things are taught and teaching in which heavenly things are taught—and certainly not without Christ since without Truth neither the one nor the other is understood. For what is truly known where Truth does not speak? Thus it is Christ who teaches both—but earthly truth in the valley, heavenly truth on the mountain. Whenever you continue to remain in the valley, whenever you do not ascend to higher things, Christ does not teach you except concerning earthly and lowest things.

Chapter LXXXI

How every showing that is not accompanied by the witness of Scripture ought to be suspect

But if you already think that you have ascended to a high heart and have taken possession of that high and great mountain, if you already believe that you see Christ transfigured, you should not easily believe whatever you see on it or whatever you hear from Him—unless Moses and Elijah appear with Him. For we know that every testimony stands firm on the word of two or three. Every truth that the authority of Scripture does not confirm is suspect to me, nor do I accept Christ in His glorification if Moses and Elijah do not stand beside Him. I often accept Christ without a witness, both in the valley and in the ascent of the mountain, but never on the summit of the mountain nor in His glorification. If Christ teaches me concerning exterior things or concerning my innermost self I easily accept Him just as in those things which I can prove by my own experience. But truly where the mind is led to a high place, when a question concerning celestial things is discussed, where a question concerning profound things is deliberated, on a peak of such sublimity I do not accept Christ without a witness nor can any probable showing be confirmed without the witness of Moses and Elijah, without the authority of Scripture. Therefore let Christ summon two witnesses to Himself in His transfiguration if He wishes that the light of His splendor, which is so great and so unusual, not be suspect to me. So that His testimony may be confirmed on the word of two or three, according to the evidence of this, He must present the authority of Scripture not only figuratively but also openly to confirm the truth of His showing. It is a beautiful and very joyful spectacle in a showing of truth when manifest reason goes forth on one side, and on the other an expression as open as it is figurative appears for confirmation of the showing. Otherwise I will fear at the height of the day, being afraid lest perhaps I be seduced by the mid-day demon. For whence come so many heresies, whence come so many errors, except that the spirit of error transfigures himself into an angel of light? Certainly you see that each transfigures himself, viz., Christ and the devil, but Christ confirms the truth of His light by two witnesses. And so Moses and Elijah appear with the Lord on this mountain. They appear, however, in majesty, not in the obscurity of the letter but in the splendor of spiritual understanding.

Chapter LXXXII

How there are incomprehensible things that the mind sees by ecstasy from a divine showing

Behold how great those things are which are done on this mountain. But greater yet than all these are those which follow. For the disciples see all this while they are standing; they do not yet fall on their faces. The voice of the Father is not yet heard; the hearer is not yet thrown down. Rachel is not yet dead; Benjamin is not yet born. For later, when the voice of the Father thundered forth, it threw down the disciples. And so the hearer falls down at the thunder of the divine voice because the capacity of human sense succumbs to that which is divinely inspired, and unless it abandons the limitations of human reasoning it does not expand the bosom of the understanding in order to hold the secret of divine inspiration. And so there the hearer falls, where human reason fails. There Rachel dies, that Benjamin may be born. And so, unless I am mistaken, by the death of Rachel and by the fall of the disciples the same thing is indicated figuratively, except that in the three disciples the threefold failure of sense, memory and reason is shown. For then bodily sense, then memory of external things, and then human reason are interrupted, when the mind is raised above itself, being snatched up into supernal things. Let us notice how incomprehensible that is which the voice of the Father uttered, and we shall understand how rightly the hearer succumbed: "This is my beloved son in whom I am pleasing to myself" (Matt. 3:17). It is one thing to say "I am pleasing" and another to say "he is pleasing." Yet nevertheless, one Evangelist has the one; another Evangelist, the other. It follows that if in one it has been said truly, "I am pleased," the sense that is placed by the other Evangelist can be accurately understood, but it cannot be interchanged. We may say truly and without contradiction, "He is pleasing to me in himself, in whom I myself am pleasing to myself," but never, "In whomsoever he is pleasing to me, in that one I myself am pleasing to myself." Therefore, if "I am pleasing" had not been said there, the Evangelist would in no way dare to say this: "This is my Son in whom I am pleasing to myself." Certainly if the Son were other than the Father it would be possible for the Father to be pleased in the Son, but the Father Himself would not be able to be pleasing to Himself in the Son. What does it mean to say "I am pleasing," except as "I am pleasing to myself in myself" and so, "I am pleasing to myself in the Son." Or perhaps does what He says in that place—"I am pleasing to myself"—show that He has a companion in His good pleasure? Because as the Father is pleased in the Son, so is He pleased in the Son and the Holy Spirit. Or perhaps "I am pleasing" is said so that it might be permitted to be understood from this that as the Father is pleasing to Himself in the Son, so certainly He is pleasing to Himself in the Holy Spirit. Which of these is said more rightly? Or rather is this to be understood as a whole rather than one or the other of them separately? Yet these words can be distinguished from each other, even if they do not suffice for making known the depth of the mystery. It is certain, however, that whichever of these is chosen, it declares unity of substance in diversity of persons if it is understood rightly. For that which is said, "This is my Son," shows a diversity of persons; for one and the same person cannot be both Father and Son to Himself. But who grasps the meaning, how one is in relation to the other: different in person, the same in essence? If you seek an example you can discover nothing among creatures that can satisfy you; if you consult reason all human reason cries out. For this assertion is above all human assessment and against all human reason to such an extent that reason would never have given assent to it unless faith had lifted it up to the certitude of these things. Therefore the hearer deservedly falls down in the showing of this mystery; sense fails; human reason succumbs.

CHAPTER LXXXIII

That the mind that is accustomed to remain in the innermost parts perceives divine showings

Such a showing deservedly is not made except on the mountain, nor should such profound sublimity and such sublime profundity of this mystery be manifested in the valley. For those who by life and thought still are in the lowest land show that they are unworthy of the honor of this gift. Therefore let a person ascend to a high heart, let him ascend this mountain if he wishes to receive those things, if he wishes to know those things which are above human sense. Let him ascend above himself through himself; to knowledge of God, through knowledge of himself. Let a person first learn in the image of God, let him learn in His similitude what he ought to think about God. The ascent of the mountain, as has been said, pertains to knowledge of self. The things that happen upon the mountain lead on to the knowledge of God. The former pertains without doubt to Joseph; the latter, to Benjamin. It is necessary that Joseph be born before Benjamin. When can the mind that does not raise itself up to consideration of itself fly up on the wings of contemplation to those things that are above it? The Lord descends on this mountain; Moses ascends. On this mountain the Lord taught and Moses learned about the construction of the tabernacle. What is understood by the tabernacle of the covenant except the state of perfection? Therefore he who ascends the mountain, who gives heed diligently, who seeks for a very long time, who discovers at last what sort he is—it remains that he learn from divine showing what sort he ought to be, what sort of edifice of the mind he ought to prepare for God, and by what obediences he ought to appease God. Therefore, when do you think a mind that still is spread out through various desires, that is dragged this way and that by various thoughts, will be worthy to receive this grace? If it is unable to gather itself into a unity, if it does not know how to enter into itself, when will it be able to ascend by contemplation to those things that are above itself?

CHAPTER LXXXIV

How the mind that eagerly strives for contemplation of celestial things ought to gather itself within

Let one who eagerly strives for contemplation of celestial things, who sighs for knowledge of divine things, learn to assemble the dispersed Israelites; let him endeavor to restrain the wanderings of the mind; let him be accustomed to remain in the innermost part of himself and to forget everything exterior. Let him make a church, not only of desires but also of thoughts, in order that he may learn to love only true good and to think unceasingly of it alone: "In the churches bless God" (Ps. 67:27). For in this twofold church, namely of thoughts and of desires, in this twofold concord of efforts and wills, Benjamin is carried away into the height, and the divinely inspired mind is raised to supernal things: "There is Benjamin a youth in ecstasy of mind" (Ps. 67:28). Where, do you think, except in the churches? "In the churches bless God, the Lord of the fountains of Israel. There is Benjamin a youth in ecstasy of mind" (Ps. 67:27–28). Nevertheless each one must first make of his thoughts and desires a synagogue rather than a church. You know well that synagogue means "congregation." Church means "convocation." It is one thing to drive some things together in one place without the will or against the will; it is another to run together spontaneously by themselves at the nod of the one who commands. Insensible and brute beings can be congregated but they cannot be convoked. Yet even a concourse of rational things themselves must occur spontaneously at a nod in order rightly to be called a convocation. Thus you see how much difference there is between a convocation and a congregation, between church and synagogue. Therefore if you perceive beforehand that your desires are becoming devoted to exterior delights and that your thoughts are being occupied with them incessantly, then you ought with great care to compel them to go within so that for a while you may at least make of them a synagogue. As often as we gather the wanderings of the mind into a unity and fix all the impulses of the heart in one desire of eternity, what are we doing other than making a synagogue from that internal household? But when that throng of our desires and thoughts, after being attracted by a taste of that internal sweetness, has already learned to run together spontaneously at the nod of reason and to remain fixed in the innermost depths, then it can certainly be judged worthy of the name of church. Therefore let us learn to love only interior goods, let us learn to think often about them only, and without doubt we make churches such as we know that Benjamin loves.

Chapter LXXXV

How joyful and sweet it is to have the grace of contemplation habitually

Certainly Benjamin freely lingers in such churches and is wonderfully delighted. When he is no longer able to contain himself because of joy he is led above himself and by ecstasy of mind is raised to the summit. Unless our Benjamin rests delightfully in the contemplation of inner things, without doubt it would not have been written of him by Moses: "Benjamin, the most beloved of the Lord, shall live in him fearlessly, shall dwell the whole day as if in a bridal chamber, and shall rest in his arms" (Deut. 33:12). What do you think is the reason that Benjamin lingers all day in the bridal chamber, that he rests there unceasingly so much that he does not wish to go out even for an hour? We know this, that the bridegroom and the bride are accustomed to remain together in the bridal chamber, yielding in love, holding each other in mutual embraces, and cherishing with alternating love. Therefore whoever that one beloved of our Benjamin may be, unless I am mistaken she flourishes with the privilege of wonderful beauty and singular form. Her intimate company he is never able to dislike and from her embraces he will not wish to be absent for an hour. But if now we come to know the voice of this Benjamin, we cannot doubt at all that his beloved is of so much beauty: "I said to wisdom, you are my sister, and I called prudence my friend" (Prov. 7:4). Do you wish to hear how he cannot dislike the beauty of his beloved whom he calls sister and friend on account of a spotless and most burning love? "Entering into my dwelling, I shall rest with her. For association with her has no bitterness, her company has no tediousness but rather joy and delight, and in her friendship there is good pleasure" (Wisd. 8:16, 18). Let each person say what he feels. I find no other reason that would keep him held so fast within that he is not able to go out even for a short time. However, I know one thing, that whoever is inflamed with longing for such a friend, the more intimately he knows her, the greater he loves; and the more frequently he enjoys her embraces, the more vehemently he burns with longing for her. Indeed her regular company certainly is accustomed not to diminish but to increase desire and to kindle more sharply the flame of love. Therefore it is no wonder that Benjamin himself, who enjoys the sweetness of such a bride, dwells the whole day as if in a bridal chamber and, resting within her arms, is delighted continually by her love. How often do you think he experiences ecstasy of mind; how often, being snatched up in ecstasy, is he led above himself when after being stunned by the greatness of her beauty he is suspended in admiration of it? Without doubt what is written of him is fulfilled: "Benjamin a youth in ecstasy of mind."

It certainly should be noted how the testimonies of Scripture come together. For what the Prophet expresses by the death of Rachel, the Evangelist designates by the falling down of the disciples, and the Psalmist expresses in Benjamin by ecstasy of mind.

Chapter LXXXVI

Concerning two kinds of contemplation

Nevertheless we are able fittingly to understand different kinds of contemplation by the death of Rachel and the ecstasy of Benjamin since it is agreed that there are two kinds of contemplation above reason and both pertain to Benjamin. Indeed, the first is above reason, but not beyond reason; however, the second is both above reason and beyond reason. Surely those things are above reason but not beyond reason which cannot be investigated or refuted by reason although reason experiences their existence. Now we call those things both above reason and beyond reason, the existence of which seems to contradict all human reason. They are such things as what we believe concerning the unity of the Trinity and many things concerning the body of Christ that we hold on the indubitable authority of the faith. For no human reason experiences that three persons are in one simple essence, or that one and the same body is able to be in various places at one time. Without doubt all reasoning seems to cry out against such assertions. These are those two kinds of contemplation, one of which pertains to the death of Rachel, the other to the ecstasy of Benjamin. In the first, Benjamin kills his mother when he goes above all reason. However, in the second he goes beyond even himself when he transcends the mode of human understanding in that which he comes to know from divine showing. It is necessary to consider this not only in Benjamin but also in all his brothers and by all means to observe carefully in numerous places in Scripture how divine Scripture is accustomed concerning the same thing now to extend the signification, now to restrain the mode, or even to alter it. However, it is accustomed to determine in many ways these modes of alternating significations and to make known the sense of it now by place, at another time by action, or by any other circumstances whatever. It is determined by place, as when Benjamin is read to have descended into Egypt; by act, as when Joseph and Benjamin rush into a mutual embrace and join in alternating kisses.

Chapter LXXXVII

How contemplation ends in meditation and how meditation rises up into contemplation

What does it mean that Benjamin descends into Egypt except that the mind's consideration is called back from contemplation of eternal things to contemplating temporal things, and the rays of understanding are brought down from the light of eternity, from the peak of heaven, as it were, to the darkness of mutable things, and in such a confusion of alternating things they carefully weigh the reason of divine judgments and penetrate them in great part? And what does it mean that Joseph and Benjamin come together and join in kisses except that meditation and contemplation often run to meet each other with the witness of reason? For as much as it pertains to general consideration, just as the grace of contemplation is understood by Benjamin, so the grace of meditation is understood by Joseph. But properly and more clearly, pure understanding is designated by Benjamin; true prudence, by Joseph. By Benjamin, of course, that kind of contemplation which concerns invisible things is meant; by Joseph, that kind of meditation which is concerned with morals. Since indeed comprehension of invisible things pertains to pure understanding, foresight concerning morals truly pertains to true prudence. We call pure understanding that which is without admixture of imagination; moreover true prudence differs from that which is called prudence of the flesh. True prudence concerns acquiring, increasing and preserving true goods; prudence of the flesh concerns transitory goods, according to which the children of this world are called more prudent than the sons of light. (Cf. Luke 16:8.) As often as Joseph falls upon the neck of Benjamin, so often meditation ends in contemplation. Benjamin receives his brother falling upon himself when the mind rises up from the effort of meditation to contemplation. Benjamin and Joseph join in kisses when divine showing and human reason unite in one witness to truth. Do you see how divine Scripture changes the mode of signification concerning one and the same thing? Yet everywhere it adds something, for which reason it does not let its sense lie totally hidden. In the death of Rachel contemplation ascends above reason; in the entry of Benjamin into Egypt contemplation descends to the imagination; in the affectionate kissing of Benjamin and Joseph human reason gives applause to divine showing.

THE MYSTICAL ARK

BENJAMIN MAJOR

BOOK I

CHAPTER I

Concerning contemplation and its excellence

If the One with the key of knowledge allows, I wish through a gift of His inspiration to unlock somewhat the mystical ark of Moses, by presenting the results of our nightly work. And if in this hidden place of divine secrets and distant storehouse of knowledge there is something hidden, which our humble self can draw out for the benefit of others, we will hesitate neither to explain it publicly nor to offer it for common use. While much has been profitably said on this topic, much still remains. The mystical meaning of the ark in the allegorical sense, that is, as it represents Christ, has been articulated by learned persons and investigated by more penetrating minds before. Despite this, we do not presume to be guilty of carelessness by now saying something about it in the moral sense. However, so that our zealous concern for it be made sweeter, and our sense of wonder at it be made stronger, let us consider the opinion of that finest Prophet, who calls it the ark of sanctification. He says, "Rise up Lord to your resting place; you and the ark of your sanctification" (Ps. 131:8). "Ark of sanctification": Do we think that which is called the ark of sanctification received its name from its reality? Let us pay careful attention and profoundly recall that, whatever it is, it is called an ark of sanctification for *you*, whom our learned teacher taught saying: "You will be holy just as I also am holy" (Lev. 11:44). Therefore, you being sanctified today, tomorrow and on the third day, do not fail to pay attention to what it means for *you*, that it is called the ark of sanctification. If Moses is correctly to be believed, we know that whoever touches it is

sanctified (Exod. 29:37). If the power of sanctification does go forth
from it, then all worthy people will seek to touch it. Would that
someone be found among you, a man such as the one from
Ramathaim, who having put on vestments of glory befitting a high
priest, would thus be worthy to enter into the Holy of Holies and
be cleansed from his impurities not only by seeing but by touching
this thing called the ark of sanctification. But what will I say about
that one if perchance he was given the key of knowledge by Him
who opens and no man closes, thus enabling him to see what this
ark of sanctification contains? Indeed, I think something precious
was placed in this ark. I very much wish to know what this ark is,
which can sanctify those who approach it, and thus which can
worthily be called an ark of sanctification. However, concerning
Wisdom, I do not doubt that it is Wisdom herself who conquers
malice (Wisd. 7:30). No less do I know that from the beginning
whoever was restored to health was restored to it by Wisdom
(Wisd. 9:19). But it also is sufficiently certain that no person can
please God unless Wisdom is with him. Does anyone doubt that it
pertains to sanctification for a person to be cleansed of all his impurities, and for the mind of anyone to be purified of all malice and
wickedness? These are the things that pollute a person. However,
he is purified by Wisdom when She, attacking more bravely, conquers malice, that is, reaching powerfully from one end of the earth
to the other and setting all things in order pleasantly (Wisd. 8:1).
And I think to be purified in this way is to be sanctified. When the
Lord began to teach Moses about the construction of the tabernacle,
He first instructed him about building the ark, in order to indicate
from this that all other things were to be constructed for the benefit
of the ark. I think no one doubts that the ark is first and foremost
among the holy places within the tabernacle of the covenant.
Therefore, a seeker, except one who doubts that Mary chose the
better part, easily recognizes that this sacred structure signifies
grace. But what is that best part which Mary chose (Luke 10:42)
except to be free from preoccupations and to see how sweet the
Lord is? (Cf. Ps. 33:9.) For as Scripture says, while Martha was
solicitous, Mary, sitting at the feet of the Lord, heard His word.
And so by hearing she understood and by understanding she saw
the highest Wisdom of God, which, since hidden in the flesh,

cannot be seen by eyes of the flesh; and while sitting and listening in this manner, she was free from preoccupations for contemplation of highest truth. This is the part that the elect and the perfect will never have taken from them. This is surely an activity without limits. For contemplation of truth begins in this life but is celebrated forever in the next. Surely by contemplation of truth a person is educated for justice and perfected for glory. Thus you correctly see that by this sacred structure, preferred above everything else because of its dignity, is meant the grace of contemplation. O how singular a grace! O so singularly preferred, for we are sanctified by it in this life and made happy by it in the next. Therefore, if the ark of sanctification means the grace of contemplation, then this grace is justly coveted, for whoever receives it is not only purified by it but sanctified too. Doubtless nothing else either so purifies the heart of all its worldly love, or so kindles the soul for the love of heavenly things. Certainly constant contemplation of truth purifies and sanctifies, contempt of the world cleanses and love of God makes us holy.

CHAPTER II

How beneficial and pleasing this grace is for those making progress in it

But the same thing, which is called by David the ark of sanctification, is called by Moses the ark of the covenant. But why ark? Why ark of the covenant? And not of any person whatsoever, but of the Lord? We know that every precious thing—gold, silver and precious stones—is usually placed in an ark. Therefore, if we consider the treasures of wisdom and knowledge, we shall quickly discover what the storehouse of such treasures is. What ark will be suitable for this activity, except the human understanding? However, this ark is built and gilded according to divine teaching, when human understanding is moved forward toward the grace of contemplation by divine inspiration and showing. But when we make progress toward this grace in this life, what do we receive other than some pledges of that future fullness when we shall engage forever in eternal contemplation? And so we receive this grace, as if it were a pledge of divine promise and a token of divine love, even as a kind of bond of covenant and memorial of mutual charity. Do you not see how rightly the ark of the covenant, in and by which such grace is symbolically expressed, is said to be "of the Lord"? Because he who desires or believes that he receives such a token of so much love ought willingly to gird himself for every labor, I doubt not that each one among you would willingly serve like a Hebrew slave six years for such grace so that in the seventh year he might go forth a free man, gratuitously, and thereafter be pleased to be free of preoccupation for the contemplation of truth. Truly if anyone is found among you who is Jacob—or who may be thought worthy of such a name because he is a strong and powerful man in combat, a nimble wrestler and such an overthrower of vices that he rises above some by fortitude and overthrows others by discretion; surely whoever is such a person would gladly serve seven years, and seven more, for such grace, to such an extent that the days seem few to him because of the greatness of love, provided that he can come, even late in time, to the embrace of Rachel. For it is necessary that a person wishing to attain Rachel's embrace serve seven years, and seven more for her, in order that he may learn to rest not only from evil works but also from useless thoughts. Many, even if they know how to be free of activity in the body, are nevertheless completely unable to be free from preoccupations in the heart. They do not know how to make a Sabbath on the Sabbath and for that reason are not capable of fulfilling what is written in the Psalm: "Be free from preoccupations and see that I am God" (Ps. 45:11). Indeed, being free from activity in body but wandering everywhere in heart, they are by no means entitled to see how sweet the Lord is, how good the God of Israel is to those who are right in heart (Ps. 72:1). And this is the reason that enemies laugh at their Sabbaths (Lam. 1:7). But the true Jacob does not cease to labor until he comes to the goal of longing—serving in the household of the true Laban, who is truly dazzling white because glorified. The Father glorified the true Laban with the brightness that He had with the Father before the creation of the world (John 17:5). It was necessary for Him to suffer and so enter into His glory (Luke 24:26) that He might add the dazzling whiteness of glory to the form of a servant and be truly dazzling white (Phil. 2:7–9). Having been made whiter than snow (Ps. 50.9) and crowned with glory and honor, He became beautiful not only among the sons of men but also among the spirits of angels and He was such a man as the angels long to look upon (1 Pet. 1:12). Do you not see how great is this grace for which one labors so willingly with so much long-suffering and which is acquired with so much labor and possessed with so much joy? Certainly Moses spoke of this grace in many places in his writings in language which has a deeper sense, but here in a mystical description he separates it more fully when he divides it according to kinds.

CHAPTER III

*Concerning the particular nature of contemplation
and in what it differs from meditation and thinking*

However, so that we may be able to comprehend more fitly and distinguish more correctly those things which must be said about contemplation, we first ought to inquire by determining and defining what it is in itself and how it differs from thinking and meditation. It ought to be known that we regard one and the same object in one way by means of thinking, we examine it in another way by means of meditation and we marvel at it in another way by means of contemplation. These three differ very much from each other in mode, even though at some times they come together with respect to an object, since concerning one and the same object, thinking proceeds in one way, meditation in another way, and contemplation in a quite different way. By means of inconstant and slow feet, thinking wanders here and there in all directions without any regard for arriving. Meditation presses forward with great activity of soul, often through arduous and rough places, to the end of the way it is going. Contemplation, in free flight, circles around with marvelous quickness wherever impulse moves it. Thinking crawls; meditation marches and often runs; contemplation flies around everywhere and when it wishes suspends itself in the heights. Thinking is without labor and fruit; in meditation there is labor with fruit; contemplation continues without labor but with fruit. In thinking there is wandering; in meditation, investigation; in contemplation, wonder. Thinking is from imagination; meditation, from reason; contemplation, from understanding. Behold, these three: imagination, reason, understanding. Understanding occupies the highest place; imagination, the lowest; reason, the middle. Everything that is subject to the lower sense is also necessarily subject to the higher sense. Thus, it is evident that all things that are grasped by the imagination, as well as many other things that are above it, are grasped by reason. Similarly, those things which imagination and reason grasp, as well as things which they are not able to grasp, are perceived by the understanding. Thus, see how widely a ray of contemplation that illuminates everything expands itself. It often happens that with regard to a single thing, one person may be engaged with it by means of thinking; another, by means of meditation; and a third, by means of contemplation. Although they do not go by a different route, nevertheless they go by a different motion. Thinking always passes from one thing to another by a wandering motion; meditation endeavors perseveringly with regard to some one thing; contemplation diffuses itself to innumerable things under one ray of vision. For through understanding, the chamber of the mind is enlarged to a measureless size so that it is suitable for grasping many things, and the fine point of the soul of the contemplative is sharpened so that it is sharp-sighted for penetrating subtle things. For contemplation cannot exist at all without a certain liveliness of understanding. Just as it is by means of the understanding that the eye of the mind is fixed on corporeal things, so also it is agreed that it is enlarged by the same power in order to grasp such an infinity of things under one vision of corporeal things. And then as often as the soul of the contemplative is enlarged with a view toward lower things, as often as it is raised up with a view toward highest things, as often as it is sharpened with respect to inscrutable things, as often as it is carried away with marvelous quickness and almost without delay by innumerable things, it ought not to be doubted that this happens by means of a certain power of the understanding. These things have been said for the sake of those people who consider these inferior things unworthy either to be perceived by the understanding or to pertain everywhere to contemplation. Nevertheless, that which considers lofty matters where the soul makes use of the pure understanding is especially called contemplation. However, contemplation is always concerned with things, whether manifest in their nature, known intimately by means of study, or perceived from a divine showing.

CHAPTER IV

The definition, individually, of contemplation, meditation and thinking

And so it seems that it can be defined thus: Contemplation is the free, more penetrating gaze of a mind, suspended with wonder concerning manifestations of wisdom; or certainly as it was determined by a distinguished theologian of our time who defined it in these words: Contemplation is a penetrating and free gaze of a soul extended everywhere in perceiving things; but meditation is a zealous attention of the mind, earnestly pursuing an investigation concerning something. Or thus: Meditation is the careful gaze of the soul employed ardently in a search for truth; thinking, however, is the careless looking about of a soul inclined to wandering. And so it seems that it is a shared characteristic of the essence of these three, as it were, that they are a kind of sight of the soul. For when nothing is observed by the mind, not one of these can be named or said to exist. However, it is a shared characteristic of contemplation and meditation to be employed concerning beneficial things, and to be engaged principally—nay continually—in the pursuit of wisdom and knowledge. But certainly in this they usually differ greatly from thinking, which is accustomed to relax at almost every moment in improper and frivolous things, and without any restraint of discretion to rush or to go headlong into everything. In truth it is a shared characteristic of contemplation and thinking that they move about here and there by a certain kind of free motion and according to a spontaneous command and are not impeded from the impulse of their going about by any difficult hindrance. However, in this they differ greatly from meditation, the pursuit of which is always, with whatever labor of activity and difficulty of soul, to grasp any lofty things whatsoever, to break through obstructions, to penetrate into hidden things. Nevertheless, it often happens that in its wandering thoughts the soul may encounter something that it strives strongly to know and pursues that vigorously. But when the mind for the satisfaction of its own desire begins to pursue such inquiry, already, by thinking it goes beyond the mode of thinking, and thinking passes over into meditation. Certainly, it is usual that something similar occurs concerning meditation. For after a certain truth has been sought for a long while and is found at last, the mind usually receives it with strong desire, marvels at it with exultation, and for a long time clings to the wonder of it. Already, this is to go beyond meditation by meditating, and meditation passes over into contemplation. And so, it is the property of contemplation to cling with wonder to the manifestation of its joy. And in this, assuredly, it seems to differ as much from meditation as from thinking. For thinking, as has already been said, always turns aside here and there with a rambling walk, while meditation always aims, with fixed advancement, toward further things.

CHAPTER V

That the mode of contemplation operates in many ways

But although that penetrating ray of contemplation is always suspended near something because of greatness of wonder, yet it operates neither always nor uniformly in the same mode. For that vitality of understanding in the soul of a contemplative at one time goes out and comes back with marvelous quickness, at another time bends itself, as it were, into a circle, and yet at another time gathers itself together, as it were, in one place and fixes itself, as it were, motionless. Certainly if we consider this rightly, we see the form of this thing daily in the birds of the sky. Now you may see some raising themselves up on high; now others plunging themselves into lower regions and often repeating the same manner of their ascent and descent. You may see some turning to the side, now to the right, now to the left, and while coming down a little ahead now in this part, now in that, or advancing themselves almost not at all, repeating many times with great constancy the same changes of their movements. You may see others thrust themselves forward in great haste. But next, with the same rapidity, they return to the rear, and moving themselves often they continue and prolong, with long-lasting repetition, the same going forth and returning. You may see how others turn themselves in a circle, and how suddenly and how often they repeat the same or a similar path—one time a little wider, another time slightly smaller, yet always returning to the same place. You may see how others suspend themselves for a long time in one and the same place with beating and rapidly vibrating wings and fix themselves motionless by means of agitated motion, as it were. And they do not depart at all from the place where they are suspended, clinging closely for a long time, as if by the performance of the work and of their constancy they might seem, by all means, to exclaim and say: "It is good for us to be here" (Matt. 17:4). According to this pattern of proposed similitudes, the flight of our contemplation is varied in many ways and is formed in a varying mode according to the variety of persons and activities. At one time it rises from the lower to the higher; at another it falls from the higher to the lower. By the quickness of its consideration it moves at one time from the part to the whole; at another time from the whole to the part. And at one time it draws the argument for that which it ought to know from a major premise; at another from a minor. At one moment it turns aside into this part, at another moment into the opposite part; it elicits an idea of contraries from knowledge of contraries, and usually varies the performance of its reasoning according to the differing mode of opposites. At some time it runs forward and quickly runs back when it discerns the quality or mode of anything whatsoever, either from the effects or from the causes and whatever has preceded or followed. But sometimes our speculation is led as it were in a circle, when some things are considered that are in common with many things or when, for the determination of any one thing whatsoever, a reason is drawn and assigned now to similar things, now to things having similar essences or accidents. However, the fixed focus of our consideration is placed in one and the same place, immobile, when the attention of the contemplative gladly remains with the being of any thing whatsoever, in order to observe and marvel at its proper nature. But lest our words seem to have the odor of human philosophy or to fall away from the even tenor of Catholic doctrine and simple style, perhaps we shall more fitly say that to rise and fall, to go and return, to turn aside now here, now there, to continue at one time in a circle, and finally to cling together in unity: This is nothing other than by means of the greatest quickness to pass, in the mind, now from the lowest things to the highest, or from the highest to the lowest; now from the oldest things to the newest or from the newest to the oldest; at one time from unequal to equal kinds of merits and rewards; at another time, to consider with diligent examination the circumstance and connection of everything whatsoever; and finally, at some time, satisfying the soul with the rareness of some speculation and wonder at the rareness. See, as we have said above, how the activity of our contemplation is always suspended and is drawn forth according to some thing, while the soul of the contemplative gladly remains in the manifestation of its joy and is always eager either to return into itself frequently or to continue immobile in the same place for a long time. Listen—concerning that mode of contemplation which is accustomed to go forward and back in a certain manner: "The living creatures will go and return in the likeness of flashing lightning" (Ezech. 1:14). Learn also about that by which the soul is carried away into different things and is driven in opposite directions, running to and fro, now into this part, now into that. "The just shall shine and shall run to and fro, like sparks in a thicket of reeds" (Wisd. 3:7). The one who moves upward and downward, as it were, is described by the Psalmist in a few words: "They rise all the way to the heavens and they fall all the way into the abyss" (Ps. 106:26). With respect to that mode of contemplation which, for instance, is led in a circle, you are admonished by the prophetic voice where it is said: "Lift up your eyes in a circle and see" (Isa. 60:4). The ray of contemplation is fixed motionless in one place, for example, when anyone experiences in himself Habacuc in that place: "Sun and moon stood still in their dwelling place" (Hab. 3:11). Notice—we have already taught what contemplation is, by determining and defining. It remains for us to divide it according to species, and to see how many kinds of contemplations there are.

Chapter VI

How many and what the kinds of contemplation are

There are six kinds of contemplations in themselves, and within each there are many divisions. The first is in imagination and according to imagination only. The second is in imagination and according to reason. The third is in reason and according to imagination. The fourth is in reason and according to reason. The fifth is above but not beyond reason. The sixth is above reason and seems to be beyond reason. And so, there are two in imagination, two in reason and two in understanding.

Without doubt, our contemplation is engaged in imagination when the form and image of those visible things are brought into consideration and we, being amazed, give attention, and in giving attention are amazed how many, how great, how diverse, how beautiful and joyful are these corporeal things that we imbibe by means of corporeal sense. Marveling we venerate and venerating we marvel at the power, wisdom and generosity of that superessential creatrix. However our contemplation is engaged in imagination and is formed according to imagination only when we seek nothing by means of argumentation and investigate nothing by means of reasoning, but rather our mind runs freely here and there, wherever wonder carries it away in this kind of manifestation.

The second kind of contemplation is that which is in imagination, but yet is formed by and proceeds according to reason, since it comes about when we seek and find a rational principle for those things which we engage in imagination and which belong, as we have already said, to the first kind of contemplation. Indeed, with wonder we bring discovery and knowledge into consideration. In the first kind of contemplation we look at, examine and marvel at things themselves; in the second kind we do the same with the reason, order and disposition of these things, and the cause, mode and benefit of any one thing. And so this contemplation is in imagination but according to reason, because it proceeds by means of reasoning about those things which are engaged in the imagination. And although this contemplation in which the rational principle of visible things is sought seems to be in reason according to something, nevertheless it is rightly said to be in the imagination because whatever we seek or find in it by means of reasoning, we undoubtedly accommodate to those things which we engage in imagination when we apply ourselves to those things by reasoning about them.

We have said that the third kind of contemplation is that which is formed in reason according to imagination. We truly use this kind of contemplation when by means of the similitude of visible things we are raised up to speculation of invisible things. This speculation is in reason, because it applies only to those things which go beyond imagination by means of attention and investigation, since it directs attention toward invisible things only, toward those only which it grasps by reason. But it is said to be formed according to imagination because in this speculation a similitude is drawn from an image of visible things, and the soul is assisted by this similitude in the investigation of invisible things. And indeed, although it is advanced by reasoning, this contemplation is rightly said to be in reason but according to imagination, because all its reasoning and argumentation begin with a foundation and acquire support in imagination, and it draws the reason for its investigation and assertion from the particular nature of things that are imaginable.

The fourth kind of contemplation is that which is formed in reason and according to reason: because it is when, far removed from every function of imagination, the rational soul directs its attention toward only those things which the imagination does not know but which the mind gathers from reasoning or understands by means of reason. We apply ourselves to speculation of this kind when we bring into consideration the invisible things of ourselves which we know through experience and acquire from understanding; and we rise up from consideration of these things to contemplation of celestial souls and highest goods. However, this contemplation is in reason because it gives its attention only to things of the understanding that are far removed from things of sense. And indeed, this contemplation seems to take a beginning and to acquire a foundation especially from those invisible things of ourselves which it is agreed that the human soul knows by experience and understands by means of common understanding. But in this case alone, this contemplation is also rightly said to be in reason, because these invisible things of ourselves are understood by reason, and in this,

the mode of reasoning is not surpassed in the least. This contemplation, therefore, advances according to reason alone because it
gathers some things from invisible things that are known by experience, and other things that it does not know from experience it
gathers by reasoning. In this contemplation the human soul makes
use for the first time of pure understanding, and since it is far
removed from every function of imagination, our understanding
itself seems in this activity to understand itself by means of itself for
the first time. Although the understanding seems not to be absent
in those previous kinds of contemplation, yet it is almost nowhere
present, except where reason or even imagination meditates. In the
previous kinds of contemplation reason uses, as it were, an instrument and gazes, for example, into a mirror. In the present kind of
contemplation it operates by means of itself and gazes, as it were,
by means of sight. Accordingly, here it inclines itself to the lowest
part, as it were, since it does not have anything by which it might
descend lower by itself.

We have said that the fifth kind of contemplation is that which
is above reason yet not beyond reason. However, we rise up into
this watchtower of contemplation by the raising up of the mind,
when by means of a divine showing we know things that we are not
capable of sufficiently grasping fully by any human reason or investigating fully by any of our reasoning. Such things are those which
we believe and prove by the authority of divine Scripture concerning the nature of Divinity and that simple essence. Thus our contemplation truly rises above reason when, by means of the raising
up of the mind, the rational soul perceives that which transcends
the limits of human capacity. It ought to be held to be above reason
yet not beyond reason, when human reason is not able to oppose
that which is perceived by the fine point of the understanding, but
rather, it more easily gives assent and alludes to the attestation of
such.

The sixth kind of contemplation is that which is engaged with
those things which are above reason and seem to be beyond or even
against reason. In this highest and most worthy watchtower of all
contemplations, the rational soul especially rejoices and dances
when from the irradiation of divine light it learns and considers
those things against which all human reason cries out. Such things

are almost all the things that we are told to believe concerning the Trinity of persons. When human reason is consulted concerning these, it seems to do nothing other than to oppose them.

Chapter VII

What things are common to them

And so two of these are in the imagination, because they direct attention toward sensible things only. Two are in reason, because they apply themselves to intelligible things only. Two subsist in understanding, because they direct attention toward intellectible things only. I call "sensible" whatever is visible and perceptible by corporeal sense. However, I call "intelligible" those invisible things which can nevertheless be understood by reason. In this place, I call "intellectible" those invisible things which cannot be understood by human reason. Thus, among these six kinds of contemplation, the lower four are engaged especially with created things while the two highest are engaged with uncreated and divine things. Again: Among the first four, the two higher are engaged concerning invisible things; the two lower, concerning visible and corporeal things. Without doubt the lowest two are engaged with visible and created things. However, the highest two are especially engaged with invisible and uncreated things. The middle two are engaged especially with invisible and created things. I have said "especially" for the reason that there are some things concerning invisible and created things that cannot be grasped in any way by human reason. According to this they go with the number of intellectible things and show themselves to pertain more to the two highest kinds of contemplations. Similarly, concerning the highest and uncreated things, it seems that some are accessible to human reason, and according to this ought to be counted among intelligible things and to be adapted especially to those two middle kinds of contemplations. And so it seems that the first two have this in common, that both are engaged about visible things. Yet they seem to differ especially in this, that the first, being impelled by wonder, is accustomed to run here and there without any function of reason. However, in the second, a rational principle is sought and assigned to those things which are engaged in the mind by imagination, and that which is already known to us in a familiar way is led into wonder. The second and third have this in common but uniquely so in comparison with the others: that equally in both, imagination seems to be mixed with reason and reason with imagination. However, they differ in this: that in the second a rational principle is sought for and adapted to visible things, as has been said; while in the third, a rational principle is drawn from visible things for the investigation of invisible things, and in the latter we are often instructed concerning invisible things by visible things and we are clearly shown some things by other things. In this we advance from the examination of visible things to knowledge of invisible things. The third and fourth have in common that they direct attention, as is agreed, toward invisible and intelligible things, but they especially differ in this, that in the third, reason is mixed with imagination, while in the fourth pure understanding is mixed with reason. In the fourth and fifth, reason and understanding come together in unity, and in this they especially agree in harmony. But in the fourth, understanding advances by means of reason. But in the fifth, reason does not go before understanding at all, but it follows or at the most accompanies it. For what is first recognized by means of divine inspiration is afterward affirmed by the testimony of reason. It happens jointly in the fifth and sixth that both of them pursue intellectible things. In the fifth, human reason seems sufficiently to concur. But in the sixth, all human reason seems to be contrary, unless it is supported by a mixture of faith.

Chapter VIII

What the character of each is, individually

It is characteristic of the first contemplation to cling to the wonder of visible things simply and without any reasoning. It is characteristic of the second to pursue the rational principle of visible things by reasoning. It is characteristic of the third, by reasoning, to rise by visible things to invisible things. It is characteristic of the fourth to gather invisible things from visible things by reasoning and to advance to the knowledge of unknown things by the understanding of things experienced. It is characteristic of the fifth to allow reason admission into the understanding of intellectible things. It is characteristic of the sixth to transcend and tread under foot, as it were, all human reasoning in the understanding of intellectible things.

Although contemplation cannot exist without imagination in the first three kinds taken together, in the first, imagination subsists below reason, as it were; in the second, imagination receives reason; in the third, imagination rises to reason.

Again: Although the three highest taken together cannot exist without pure understanding, in the first of these (that is, in the fourth) understanding inclines itself to reason; in the fifth, understanding raises reason to itself; in the sixth, understanding transcends reason and, as it were, abandons everything below itself.

Again: Although in the middle there are four taken together that cannot exist without reasoning, in the second kind of contemplation, reason stoops to imagination, as it were to the lowest things; in the third, it draws imagination with it, as it were, to higher things; in the fourth it receives and conducts understanding, which descends, as it were, below itself; in the fifth, reason rises above itself, as it were, to understanding and alludes to it in its sublime things.

In the first kind of contemplation, imagination rests in itself. In the sixth, understanding gathers itself to itself and subsists in itself. In the second, reason descends below itself. In the fifth, reason rises above itself. In the third, imagination rises above itself. In the fourth, understanding descends below itself.

In the first kind of contemplation, imagination occupies the lowest and solitary place. In the second, reason descends to the lowest place it can. In the third, imagination rises to the highest place it can. In the fourth, understanding descends to the lowest place it can. In the fifth, reason rises to the highest place it can. In the sixth, understanding occupies the highest and solitary place.

CHAPTER IX

In what proportion they relate to each other and are accustomed to mix together by turns

Indeed, it should be noted that just as the last two kinds of contemplation rise above reason, so the middle two rise above imagination. As the higher of the last two usually admits no human reason at all, so the higher of the middle two ought to exclude all imagination from itself. As the lower of the last and supreme two is above reason yet not beyond reason, so the lower of the middle two rises above imagination, although it is not yet beyond imagination. As the two middle ones descend below pure and simple understanding, so the first and lowest two descend below reasoning. I call "simple understanding" that which exists without the function of reason, while "pure understanding" is that which exists without imagination's coming into view. But, as the higher of the two middle ones descends below simple understanding, yet it docs not subsist below simple understanding because of those things in which it is engaged; some it comprehends by simple understanding while it gathers others by reasoning; so also the higher of the two lowest seems to descend below thinking, yet it does not subsist below that because it usually represents some things by means of imagination and gathers other things by reasoning. And again: As the lower of the two middle ones usually descends and subsists below simple understanding, so the lower of the two lowest usually exists near to reason. For the former one also directs attention toward only those things which the mind has gathered from the imagination by means of reasoning, and the latter one directs attention toward only those things which the mind impresses on the imagination by means of the senses. Although this first and lowest kind of contemplation is said because of that to subsist below reason—or rather below reasoning—surely it should not seem irrational, as it were, and wholly contrary to reason, since an agreement with reason through attention and even through disposition can easily be shown. But as has been said, in as far as it concerns its proper nature, nothing is gathered by reasoning. Nevertheless, these kinds of contemplations that we have separated are accustomed sometimes to be mixed together, and this mode of proper natures that we have assigned is accustomed to be mingled by being mixed one with the other. However, our purpose in this place was to teach the characteristic of each individually according to the evidence of doctrine, and no less to show what they might have in common and in similarity.

Chapter X

That even perfect persons scarcely advance to all six kinds of contemplations

Everyone who desires to arrive at the peak of knowledge must know these six kinds of contemplation familiarly. Certainly we are suspended above the earth and raised to the heavens by these six wings of contemplations. Even if you lack some of them now, you should not doubt that you are near perfection. Certainly with me, and with persons similar to me, it goes well if only one—or if one of these three pairs of wings—is given. "Who will give me wings like those of a dove, and I will fly away and rest?" (Ps. 54:7). Nevertheless, I know that on the first pair of such wings, one is not permitted to fly upward from earthly things to heavenly things and to seek and penetrate the lofty places of the heavens. For as it was said above, in those six kinds of contemplations, the whole consideration of the first two is taken up with earthly and corporeal things; nothing in them treats of invisible things. Thus, however sublime, however very subtle the flights we may have around these earthly things on these first two wings of contemplations, it should not be enough for us if we suffice only for that, in which we see that the philosophers of this world are distinguished. You clearly show that you are an earthly animal and in no way a heavenly one as long as you are content with only two wings. How are you able to cover your body, how are you able to fly? Certainly, if until now you are an earthly animal, if until today you continue to live in an earthly body, and thereupon a body of such a kind as the Apostle describes and admonishes you to mortify, it will certainly be good to have in readiness that with which you may, when you wish, cover such a body and hide it from the eyes of your memory. He says: "Mortify your members which are upon the earth, fornication and impurity" (Col. 3:5). However, what is it to cover such a body under the designated wings of contemplation except to temper the craving for earthly things by consideration of earthly mutability—nay rather to lead it into oblivion? You carefully consider, I think, how much such a veiling and obscuring by wings you should be capable of. Again: You have in these wings that with which you may be able to fly, when you wish. Surely it is good to fly well and to go as far away from the love of the world as you can. In any case, they fly well on these wings who daily consider the deceitful nature of earthly mutability and, by continual reconsideration, separate themselves from the vain desire for it. Thus, although you may not be able to fly up as far as heavenly things on these two wings, nevertheless perhaps by flapping them you will be able to find a safe and tranquil haven. Press forward in these things as much as you can; grasp at least the edge of the sea: "If I use my wings at daybreak and dwell in the farthest limits of the sea" (Ps. 138:9). The farthest limits of the sea: the end of the world and the end of one's own life. And so, to dwell in the farthest limits of the sea is to look forward with longing to the end of the world and to the end of life. I think by flying he already grasped the farthest limit of the sea who could truly say: "I desire to die and be with Christ" (Phil. 1:23). I think that you have not received these two wings of contemplations in vain if you have flown to such an extent. Yet it should be too little for you that you receive these two wings; but to prove that you are a celestial animal, be zealous and be busy about having at least two pairs, and then you will certainly have those with which you can fly up to heavenly things. The four animals that the prophet Ezechiel saw, and having seen, described, certainly had four wings. By this they showed that they were celestial, not terrestrial. Ezechiel says: "Four faces for each one, and four wings for each one" (Ezech. 1:6). However, as we read there, they cover their body with two; for without doubt they fly with the other two. And so, when you begin to have four wings, when you think that you are now a heavenly animal and have put on a heavenly body, yet nonetheless be zealous to cover that body under the aforementioned wings. For there are heavenly bodies and there are terrestrial bodies; and the glory of heavenly things is one thing, and the glory of terrestrial things is another. The brightness of the sun is one thing, and the brightness of the moon another, and star differs from star in brightness (1 Cor. 15:40–41). Thus, if your whole body is full of light, not having any darkness in it, it will be good to hide that from the eyes of human arrogance and to temper the brightness of its own sense of worth in light of the uncertainty of human mutability. "A person knows not his hour, but just as fish are taken by a hook, and birds are seized by a snare, so people are overtaken by misfortune suddenly falling on them." (Eccles. 9:12.) And for that reason it is good for a person to hide his good things, not take his merits entirely for granted, and keep himself always in humility. Thus, with the first pair of wings a person covers his body; with the second he flies to heaven. Why do those two middle kinds of contemplations, which, as has been said, have to do with invisible things only, not raise a person to heavenly and invisible things? Any spiritual person has enough to do always to be in heavenly things by zeal and desire so that he can say with the Apostle: "Our conversation is in heaven" (Phil. 3:20). Nevertheless, if with the same Apostle you prepare to penetrate as far as the third heaven, you ought never to take it for granted that you can do it on two pairs of wings. Without doubt, it is fitting that he who desires and strives to fly up to the secrets of the third heaven and the hidden things of Divinity have all those six wings of contemplations which have been indicated above. Certainly, in this case, even perfect persons are scarcely able to have these six wings of contemplations in this life. All of the elect among humans and also among angels shall have all these in the future life, so that concerning either nature it can be said truly that there are six wings for one and six wings for the other.

Chapter XI

How the first four kinds of contemplations are described mystically

It seems to me that Moses speaks of these six kinds of contemplations under a mystical description when he resolves to make that material but mystical ark according to the Lord's command. The first kind is indicated in the construction of the ark; the second, in the gilding of it; the third, in the crown of the ark; the fourth we understand by means of the propitiatory; by the two cherubim, the fifth and sixth. However, if we are mindful of the shape and the material product of those six works made by hand, only the first is built from wood. All the others are made up of gold. So, surely, when we wish, we imbibe by corporeal sense and represent by imagination all those things of which the first kind of contemplation consists. For all the other things from which the other contemplations begin we either gather by means of reasoning or understand with the simple understanding. Thus, think what sort of difference there is between wood and gold, and perhaps you will discover how appropriately the former things are indicated in the wood while the latter are represented in the gold. Those which are subject to imagination are represented in wood; however, those which are subject to understanding only are represented in gold. In itself, gold glitters with a great brightness; in itself, wood has nothing of brightness, except it kindles fire and nourishes a ministering flame of light. So, surely, imagination in itself has neither the light nor the brightness of prudence—except that it is accustomed to arouse reason to discretion and direct it to the investigation of knowledge. However, that second kind of contemplation, in which the rational principle of visible things is sought, is rightly represented in the gilding of wood. For what is assigning the rational principle of visible things and things that can be imagined other than a kind of gilding of wood, so to speak. No less rightly is the crown of the ark able to represent by mystical indication the third kind of contemplation, in which we are accustomed to rise by means of visible things to invisible things, and to rise up to knowledge of them by means of the guiding hand of imagination. For although the crown was attached to pieces of wood at the upper part of the ark, nevertheless it was surpassed by some other higher extension of pieces of wood. So, that kind of contemplation which is engaged in reason according to imagination certainly is supported by imagination when it draws a reason from the similitude of imaginable things and erects a ladder, as it were, by which it may be able to rise to the speculation of invisible things. However, in every part and everywhere, the propitiatory is placed over wood, and on that account with sufficient suitability there is represented in it the kind of contemplation that, when going beyond all imagination, is engaged in reason according to reason. And as the propitiatory (inasmuch as it is the cover of the ark) nowhere descends below wood, nor is permitted to be attached to wood, so when this contemplation surpasses all imagination and does not agree to let itself be mixed with anything, it is mindful of invisible things only and directs attention toward invisible things only.

Chapter XII

How the last two kinds of contemplations are indicated mystically

The last two kinds of contemplations are expressed by an angelic figure. Indeed, that material product rightly had not a human but an angelic form, which was necessary for representing by a similitude those kinds of contemplations whose object goes beyond all human reason.

Certainly it ought to be noted that those four previously mentioned contemplations are, in a certain manner, joined together into one. However, these two last ones are separate and are set apart. And indeed in those first four kinds of contemplations we grow daily from our own activity, yet with divine assistance. But in these two final ones everything depends on grace. They are wholly far removed and exceedingly remote from all human activity, except to the degree that each person receives the clothing of angelic similitude from heaven and by divine providence puts it on himself. And perhaps not without cause did this last material product and angelic figure receive the name "cherubim"; perhaps for the reason that without the addition of this highest grace no one would be able to attain to fullness of knowledge. But one of the two cherubim was said to stand on one side and the other on the other side, so that one is understood to stand on the right while the other stands on the left. Consider, I ask you, how aptly they are set over against each other and are placed in opposition as a representation of those things, the former of which seem to agree with reason, the latter, to go against reason. But perhaps someone will hasten to seek what it would be especially fitting to understand in this. See, therefore, it is not by chance that by that cherub who stood on the right, the kind of contemplation should be understood that is above reason yet not beyond reason. However, by that one which was on the left, the contemplation should be understood that is above reason and seems to be beyond reason. However, we know that the left hand is often held under the clothing, and we know how it is kept hidden while the right hand is openly extended more often. For this reason, more secret things rightly are understood by the left hand; more open things, by the right hand. Now the more open things are consistent with reason, while the more hidden things are opposed to reason. Thus, we rightly understand the fifth kind of contemplation by the right-hand cherub. No less properly is the sixth kind of contemplation able to be understood by the left-hand cherub. With respect to those things which should be said concerning the ark of Moses and the grace of contemplation, these things can probably suffice for more learned souls. But because we are at leisure and speak to people at leisure we ought not, on account of people who are more sluggish, to be sluggish in repeating these things with a beneficial and, for some perhaps, a necessary supplement. Being more free from preoccupations, we ought to treat the same material more broadly. And so, after the manner of a contemplative, according to the style of contemplation, let us explain concerning contemplation. Nor should we observe merely in passing the pursuit of so much joy and the manifestation of so much wonder. We have furnished this brief compendium for persons who are busy, while we explain the same things, repeating them more broadly, for persons at leisure—both together on guard to hold back hasty travelers who violate the pattern and to urge on the unwilling curious explorers of innovation. Thus let us now return to the individual kinds of contemplation and speak first of all concerning the first.

BOOK II

CHAPTER I

The first kind of contemplation consists of consideration of and wonder at visible things

The first kind of contemplation is in consideration of and wonder at corporeal things with respect to all those things which enter into the soul by means of the five bodily senses. Indeed this is the lowest of all contemplations and ought to be the beginning. For those who are unlettered until now ought to begin with this, so that they may gradually rise to higher things, as it were by means of certain stages of advancement. And so, to this kind of contemplation pertains all wonder at the Creator, wonder that rises up from consideration of corporeal things and is indicated in this description of the ark by the joining together of pieces of wood. And by a sufficiently suitable distinction, those things which pertain to imagination are indicated by pieces of wood, just as those things which seem to pertain to reason are indicated no less by gold. However, it is not permissible for this ark to be made of pieces of just any wood, but only of pieces of Setim wood, which are very incorruptible. Now, any honest and truthful investigations of things pertain to pieces of incorruptible wood. Pieces of incorruptible wood are any considerations whatsoever of things and any reconsiderations whatsoever of works that do not lead to corruption of mind and that watch over the integrity of sincerity and truth. And so in such an abundance of visible things, among so many kinds of manifestations, everyone ought to see that he chooses and takes care not to bring before the eyes of the mind anything by which he might

174

pollute the purity of his heart. Therefore, he who desires to rejoice perpetually concerning internal incorruption ought to remove incitements to pleasures from the view of his consideration. He should separate from that multitude of his recollections whatever arouses avarice, whatever incites gluttony, whatever inflames luxury. Surely that one who comes to despise things of the world by means of a regard for things of the world is drawn to the world and those things in the world that are profitable in contemplation. Hence, that great contemplator of worldly things sought and found the fruit of such contemplation, and he left a book: "Vanity of vanities," said Ecclesiastes, "vanity of vanities, and all is vanity" (Eccles. 1:1). That one does not take up contemplation of vanity in vain who rises up into praise of the Creator from that which he has a regard for in the lowest things and discovers in all His works something marvelous, laudable and lovable. "Lord, our Lord, how wonderful is your name in the whole earth" (Ps. 8:2). Behold, marvelous. "From the rising to the setting of the sun, laudable is the name of the Lord" (Ps. 112:3). Behold, laudable. "The Lord is just in all of his ways, and holy in all of his works" (Ps. 144:13). Behold, lovable. Thus rigid pieces of wood, strong pieces of wood, hard pieces of wood are any considerations whatsoever that restore the vigor of the mind, strengthen it with respect to constancy, and establish it in steadfastness. Finally, pieces of wood that produce neither a stain of filthiness nor a fault of falsity are free from every corruption. And so, in like manner, any true assertion, any firm declaration whatsoever concerning corporeal things pertains to pieces of Setim wood, to pieces of incorruptible wood. And so this ark of wisdom ought to be made from pieces of incorruptible wood, from irrefutable declarations, so that we may think about all these things that, made by one God and created from nothing, are seen in the world, while with respect to all these things we define nothing that disagrees with truth.

CHAPTER II

That the material of this contemplation is abundant,
and how the philosophers occupy themselves in it

As has already been said, this contemplation has for its material all that which bodily sense is able to touch. Certainly, the material is abundant and the forest is not small. All may run; all may enter individually; no one is held back; each one may choose what he marvels at more greatly. Sufficient material superabounds for each one to make an ark for himself. Nevertheless, each person should learn to choose pieces of incorruptible wood, so that he may think nothing contrary to the true tradition. The philosophers of the gentiles strove zealously, desiring to choose for themselves from this same forest the material for their construction and to construct for themselves an ark of wisdom. Therefore they began to cut down, shape and put together pieces of wood and by defining, dividing and arguing, to discover, hold and teach many things. Holding various opinions and founding many sects, they made many arks. As they entered into that shady and thick grove, they engaged in an infinite number of questions. God handed over the world to their disputation (Eccles. 3:11), but they vanished in their thoughts (Rom. 1:21), and those who were searching failed in this search (Ps. 63:7) because no person was able to discover a work in which God was active from the beginning until the end (Eccles. 3:11). By His Spirit, God revealed to whom He wished, when He wished, as much as it was necessary to know concerning these things. What wonder if those who have been taught by the Spirit of God were able to execute a work worthy of wonder, since they were willing neither to follow their own spirit nor to advance behind the thoughts of their own inventions? Furthermore, in our time there have arisen certain pseudo-philosophers, fabricators of untruth. Wanting to make a name for themselves, they are eager to discover new things. Nor was it a concern of theirs so much that they might affirm truth, as that they might think that they had discovered a new thing. Taking it for granted concerning their mental ability, they thought that they were able to make an ark of wisdom for themselves, and being caught up in their own inventions, they handed on new opinions, thinking wisdom was born and would die with them. Behold: The arks of all these very wise persons have rotted, because they were not made of pieces of Setim wood, that is of pieces of incorruptible wood. Behold: All the princes of Thaneos have been made fools, because God makes foolish the wisdom of this world. For that hitherto vainglorious worldly philosophy has been made foolish to such a degree that from among its professors innumerable persons daily become its mockers; from among its defenders, they become its attackers; and cursing it, they profess that they know nothing other than Jesus Christ and Him crucified. Behold: how many who earlier were making things in the workshop of Aristotle learn at last with wiser counsel to forge things in the workshop of the Saviour. Those who formerly were making vessels of reproach are now taught to make vessels of glory, daily confessing the Lord in vessels of psalms because they are ashamed to have made a work worthy of confusion and to have been fabricators of untruth often. Where now, I ask, are the sects of the academics, stoics, peripatetics? Where are their arks? Behold, all of these have already slept their sleep. All these men of riches have found nothing in their hands (Ps. 75:6) and have left their riches to strangers and their sepulchers, houses into eternity (Ps. 48:11–12). Behold, they all rotted with their arks, perishing together with their teachings and traditions. But the ark of Moses remains up to the present day, never more stable, never more strong than today, inasmuch as it has been established by the authority of Catholic truth, since it is made of pieces of Setim wood, that is of pieces of incorruptible and unspoiled wood, and all of its narrative of history and doctrine has been interwoven with true declarations and extraordinary assertions. Behold, we have seen of what material it ought to be made; it follows that we must learn the dimensions and the manner of construction, so that according to the example of Moses we may follow not our own mind but the pattern of divine instruction in all of this. Now let us return to that kind of contemplation which is agreed to be the lowest of all and first, and for that reason is the beginning. We have said that it is represented in this description of the ark by the joining of pieces of wood only.

Chapter III

Concerning the threefold distinction of the first speculation

This speculation is considered in a threefold way. The first is with regard to things; the second, with regard to works; the third, with regard to morals. That which is with regard to things pertains to the length of the ark. That which is with regard to works pertains to the width. That which is with regard to morals pertains to the height. For we know that length is naturally prior to width. Similarly, we know that width holds a prior place with respect to height. For length can be understood without width, and width, without height, although they cannot be separated at all from each other in the essential nature of things. But height without width, or width without length, is not able to exist nor is it possible to understand it. For simple length is understood when a quantity is extended from point to point into a line running through individual points, at least by means of thought only. We speak of simple width when mentally we stretch out a quantity from line to line and by means of individual lines spread it out into a surface. For, just as a line is length without width, so a surface is width without height. However, height is when a quantity thickens from surface into surface and produces a solid body, which receives three dimensions. Thus I think it is sufficiently evident to a person who considers these things rightly, that length is naturally prior to width, and width to height. So, certainly, that consideration which is with regard to things is naturally prior to that consideration which is with regard to works and to that which is with regard to morals. For who does not know that things themselves are always naturally prior to their workings at any time? In other words, who does not know that no workings can exist in any way other than from or in things? Similarly, morals themselves, whether good or bad, are accustomed to be and ought to be considered with respect to works. For the greater part, the works of men, insofar as they are ordered and moderated, pertain to good morals, while insofar as they are disordered and immoderate, pertain no less to bad morals. For this reason, it is sufficiently established that just as consideration of things is prior to that of works, so consideration of works is naturally prior to that of morals. And so it is rightly said that consideration of things pertains to the length of our ark; consideration of works, to the width; and consideration of morals, to its height.

CHAPTER IV

That the first stage of this speculation is considered in matter, form and nature

However, the first consideration of these three is tripartite. The first consideration of this subdivision is with respect to matter; the second, with respect to form; the third, with respect to nature. We easily grasp matter and form by means of bodily vision. For we distinguish without error between a rock and wood, a triangle and a square. However, that which pertains to nature is now partly accessible to sense but partly lies hidden more deeply, being set aside for reason. Nature is considered as an intrinsic quality of things, just as form consists of an extrinsic quality. Now the exterior quality of things is perceived for the great part by bodily sense, as flavors by taste, odors by smell. However, even if a man had not sinned in the least, he would never be able to approach with the sense of the flesh that power of nature which lies hidden within since it has been imprinted most deeply on the innermost part of things. But yet he might have seen it easily by means of the acuteness of his natural capacity, if the eye of reason had not been blinded under a fog of error since it had been surrounded by a cloud of sin. Now when we, enveloped by the darkness of ignorance, daily seek something concerning this, we touch it by means of argument from experience, rather than see it. And so the reason is well known why the length of our ark, according to the Lord's pattern, ought not—or, better, is not able—to be other than two and one-half cubits. For human knowledge has a full cubit, where it has certitude and is capable of understanding by some mental ability those things which ought to be known. Thus, corporeal sense has one cubit with regard to viewing matter, another cubit with regard to consideration of form, and a half cubit with regard to

179

perception of nature, which it penetrates only in part. For indeed, as has been said, nature is partly accessible to sense and is partly set aside for reason. And so these three—matter, form and nature—because they are together in corporeal substance and are not able to be divided mutually from themselves, extend themselves in a line, as it were, and show themselves to pertain to the length of the ark.

CHAPTER V

That the second stage is considered with regard to the working of nature and of human activity

And so when the mind has been exercised according to this triple consideration that is with respect to speculation of things, it ought to transfer itself subsequently to speculation of works, so that when it has been taught to extend its consideration to both natural and artificial works, the width of our ark can receive a measure of predetermined size. For the working of nature is one thing, and the working of human activity is another. We are easily able to grasp a working of nature, as in grasses, in trees and in animals: in grasses, how they grow and mature; similarly in trees, how they leaf out, blossom and bear fruit; in animals, how they conceive and give birth, how some grow and others die. While we daily direct attention to how all things that have been born, die, and how those that have grown, grow old, we exercise our mind in the investigation of natural workings. An artificial work is considered a work of human activity, as in engraving, in painting, in writing, in agriculture and in other artificial works, in all of which we find many things for which we ought worthily to venerate and marvel at the dignity of a divine gift. And so, because they cooperate mutually with each other, natural work and artificial work are joined to each other on the sides, as it were from the side, and are united together in themselves by mutual contemplation. For indeed it is certain that a work of activity takes a beginning, continues and gains strength from a natural working; and a natural working makes progress from activity, so that it is better. In an artificial work, human knowledge has one cubit because if it were not capable of understanding that work, it would certainly not have discovered it at all. But in a natural work human knowledge cannot have a full cubit, because it comprehends it only in part. It easily judges what is accustomed to be born from which things, for fruit is not sought on a grapevine, nor a cluster of grapes on standing grain, nor grain on a tree. But yet, when would human knowledge suffice to explicate which of these or why any one thing is accustomed to be born from another? Thus, when the acuteness of our natural ability spreads itself out on every side in this twofold consideration of nature and artifice and runs here and there in manifold ways with marvelous liveliness of understanding, our ark receives a suitable measure for itself, according to the mode of divine instruction.

CHAPTER VI

That the third stage of this speculation consists as much in human regulations as it does in divine ones

After the first consideration, which is with regard to things, and the second, which is with regard to works, there follows the third, which consists in morals and pertains, as we have already said, to the height of our ark. The discipline of morals comes partly from divine instruction and partly from human instruction. To divine instruction pertain the divine services and all the sacraments of the Church. To human instruction pertain human laws, customs, courtesies, parish laws, civil laws and many other such things. Human instruction is for the lower life; divine instruction is for the higher life. The former is for gaining prosperity and tranquillity of temporal life; the latter, for seizing salvation and the fullness of eternal beatitude. In human instruction, human knowledge is able to have a cubit because it is probably able to understand what it is able to find there. We do not doubt that there are two cubits in the divine sacraments. For it is one thing that we see externally with regard to the thing or the work of a sacrament; the spiritual power that lies hidden within a scarament is quite another. And so, you are able to believe the thing of the sacrament that lies hidden within, but you are utterly unable to see it, and for this reason you are not able to extend your knowledge in this part up to a full cubit. However, this last speculation, which is in morals, pertains, just as we have already said, to the height of our ark. Since, in fact, when human teaching is subject to divine teaching, the soul advances from both and tends toward the height. For without doubt, the soul that clings to those things which pertain to the first or second consideration still lingers in lowest things. But the more perfectly it clings to these things that belong to the third consideration, the more assuredly it always rises to higher things.

It surely ought to be noted that natural working and divine instruction have a full cubit with regard to a thing, but they are only able to have a half cubit in our knowing. On the contrary, however, artificial working and human instruction are scarcely able to have a half cubit with regard to a thing, but they are able to have a full cubit in our knowing. Therefore, when the rational soul has been fully exercised in this threefold speculation, the measure of our ark receives on all sides a length suitable for itself. The Prophet showed himself to be in this kind of contemplation when he said: "I have been meditating on all your works" (Ps. 142:5). And elsewhere he says: "Because you have delighted me, O Lord, in your making" (Ps. 91:5). And elsewhere he exclaims in wonder at these things: "How glorious are your works, O Lord! You have made all things in wisdom" (Ps. 103:24). And in the same Psalm he mentions many things concerning these same works by explaining them. And so we are able rightly to separate into seven stages the whole of this first kind of contemplation.

The first consists of that admiration of things which rises up from the consideration of matter.

The second stage consists of that wonder at things which rises up from the consideration of form.

The third consists of that wonder at things which consideration of nature brings to birth.

The fourth stage of this contemplation is engaged in consideration of and wonder at works connected with the working of nature.

The fifth is engaged in consideration of and wonder at works, but according to the working of activity.

The sixth stage consists of considering and wondering at human instructions.

Finally, the seventh subsists in considering and wondering at divine instructions.

These seven stages of ascent happen first to those who strive zealously to climb up the mountain of God and to enter the temple of Ezechiel. One enters by seven steps, to the exterior doorway that leads into the outer atrium. "And the ascent of it," he says, "is in seven steps" (Ezech. 40:26). Thus you are now acquainted with the stages of beginning that should be pursued by anyone who desires to understand the art of contemplation. How this kind of contemplation begins in the imagination and runs to and fro according to the imagination was taught in the previous book and it will not be necessary to repeat it here.

CHAPTER VII

That the second kind of contemplation consists of considering and wondering at the rational principle of visible things

Now since we have already said as best we could the things that seemed to need saying again concerning the first kind of contemplation, let us pass on to the second, which is indicated by the gilding of the ark, as has already been said. Therefore, if the first kind of contemplation is rightly understood to take place by considering the actual appearance of corporeal things, it follows, I think, that the second kind of contemplation ought to be understood to take place by examining the rational principle of these same things. Therefore, we are occupied in the gilding of our ark as often as we examine thoroughly the rational principle of visible things and are suspended with wonder at the discovery and examination of these same things. As often as we understand by directing our attention and direct our attention in understanding to this earthly machine, we see how marvelously all things are made, how fitly ordered, how wisely disposed. We gild our ark when we consider the cause, mode and effect, the benefit and rational principle of each thing. O how much it abounded in the gold of knowledge! How it was able to suffice for him to gild his whole ark, who truly said: "Now God gave me to speak from the heart. For he gave me true knowledge of these things which exist, so that I might know the disposition of the world and the powers of the elements; the beginning, end, and mid-point of times; the alterations, changes, and divisions of seasons; the course of the year and the dispositions of the stars; the natures of living creatures and the angers of beasts; the force of winds and thoughts of persons, and the differences of bushes and the powers of roots" (Wisd. 7:17–20). Finally, hear what he brings forth at the end, so that you may understand more fully how great an abundance of such gifts abounded for him in the work of his gilding. He says: "And whatever things are hidden and unforeseen, I have learned" (Wisd. 7:21). Thus the gilding of our ark consists of contemplating the rational principle of divine works, judgments and sacraments, and no less the rational principle of human actions and instructions. Finally, let us be prepared, according to the witness of Peter, to give at every request an account concerning that faith and hope which are in us (I Pet. 3:15). And we who know how to commend by an exposition the rational principle of divine sacraments and also divine judgments have already gilded the highest or extreme point of our ark.

CHAPTER VIII

That the material of this contemplation is abundant

He who has already advanced to the second species of this contemplation finds in such a prolixity of material a sufficient abundance where he may spread out the sails of his speculation and practice the navigation of this disputation. For who does not see how widely a sea of such consideration may extend, and how this great and broad sea may spread itself out abundantly in many ways? In admiration at such immensity the Prophet exclaims: "Your judgments are a great abyss" (Ps. 35:7). The hidden judgments of God certainly are a large and great abyss: large in number; great in depth; wholly infinite and wholly inscrutable. Here are those marvelous manifestations of the people who see marvelous things in the depth. For how many marvelous things do you think they see in this depth—those who go down to the sea in ships in order to carry out a working in deep waters? Many there are indeed, who come together to the great, broad sea, some for crossing the sea, others for fishing. Certainly, those who desire to pass from people to people or from a kingdom to another people come in order to cross. But those among them who are fishers of men surely come in order to fish by spreading out their net for a catch. Thus, sending the net of the ship now to the left, now to the right according to the command of the Lord, they often catch an abundant multitude of fish, namely catching the wandering senses and the slippery affections of men and drawing them out onto dry land. But they do not always cast out the same net, just as they do not always send it for the same catch. Now they spread out the net of argumentation, now that of exhortation; sometimes in order to show something true, sometimes in order to condemn falsehood; sometimes in order to elicit something hidden, sometimes in order to convince of justice, sometimes in order to advise against some injustice. Surely those who know how to carry out such an undertaking work in deep waters; these, I say, are those who see marvelous things in the depth. Truly wisdom concerning a hidden thing is drawn out by these persons. Hear what that great contemplator of wisdom says: "How glorious are your works, O Lord! You have made all things in wisdom" (Ps. 103:24). "You have made," he says, "all things in wisdom." Without doubt, he who thus exclaimed saw marvelous things. Surely he saw marvelous things in the depth and drew wisdom from a hidden thing, who grasped that all things were made in wisdom and without doubt knew well that wisdom reaches powerfully from one end to the other and sets all things in order pleasantly (cf. Wisd. 8:1). Behold, how this gold of wisdom appeared in all the divine works, how the gold of wisdom shone, how the brilliance of divine wisdom obscured everything else in his eye. Assuredly, he had known this well; he was easily able to gild his ark—in fact, it is well known that he who was constrained by the greatness of his wonder to exclaim "You have made all things in wisdom" had already covered his ark with gold on all sides. Let us also try as much as we are able and exert ourselves greatly in gilding our ark so that all the divine works made in wisdom may also appear to us—so that insofar as it is possible we may understand, and what it is impossible to understand we may at least believe without hesitation that everything has been made in wisdom, not only those things which He made, but also whatever He permits to be made, never permitting anything to happen without a rational cause nor to be acting without divine justice, however hidden.

CHAPTER IX

How the philosophers exercise themselves in the matter of this contemplation

But I do not think that it ought to be passed over in silence how the wise persons of this world have striven to gild their arks, so that we will be ashamed not to labor in the gilding of our ark. The philosophers of the gentiles endeavored when examining the hidden causes of things to draw wisdom from a hidden thing; and they drew out gold from the depth, penetrating as far as the hidden bosom of nature by the acuteness of their natural capacity. They began to investigate, discover and make known publicly the hidden causes of things, and to prove all doubtful things by means of nondoubtful conclusions. And so by much profound investigation and worthy wonder they discovered from whence comes the earthquake by which the deep seas swell up in power. And discovering many other things in this way and committing them to writing they took care to transmit them to posterity. And so, in great part they were able to gild their ark—but only externally. For them it was a small concern, and no possibility, that they might gild it internally. Since their riches were quickly used up, they did not have a sufficient abundance of gold with which they might be able to gild it internally, for in fact their riches were used up in gilding it externally in full. For it was not given to the same faculty to discover the physical principles of things and determine the hidden causes of justice in those things which happen. It is quite one thing to investigate and to show the hidden causes of things according to physical principles, while quite another not to be ignorant of the rational principle of divine judgments. The investigation of nature pertains to the external gilding of our ark; the conclusions of divine justice, to the internal gilding. In any case, those who thought things happened by chance more than by divine command lacked this gilding inwardly, and those who held as sacred the alter of fortune believed that the goddess gave no attention to human affairs in view of the fact that they perceived that good and evil happen alike to a good person and an evil person, a just person and an unjust person, a person sacrificing victims and a person despising them. But He himself, whose eyes examine the sons of men (Ps. 10:5), makes His sun rise upon good and evil persons, and causes rain to fall equally on the just and the unjust (Matt. 5:45). Now we, for whom gold already abounds as much from the profit of our labors as from the spoils of the Egyptians, should take care to clothe our ark with gold—not only exteriorly but also interiorly. Let us pay attention to how He made all these things in His wisdom, how He founded the earth by means of His wisdom and stabilized the heavens by means of prudence; how the abysses of the heavens burst forth and clouds increase from dew by means of His wisdom—and we shall have gilded our ark, but only exteriorly. Let us consider no less that the universal ways of the Lord are truth and mercy; let us also consider how the Lord is just in all His ways and holy in all His works—and we shall have gilded our ark internally. How, do you think, had he covered over all the beauty of the pieces of wood in his ark with gold who had clearly grasped and constantly affirmed concerning the Lord that His mercies were over all His works (Ps. 144:9)? Let us also strive, according to the example of the Prophet, to cover all things of this kind with gold and to conceal the morning star under such glittering, although to our eyes it appears small or nothing in comparison to the divine reason and disposition by which the beauty of all exterior things has been created and disposed.

CHAPTER X

Concerning the division of the second contemplation

When we spoke above concerning the first kind of contemplation, we divided it into seven stages. It would be too lengthy just now to mention each one in series and to show how the ark ought to be gilded along every cubit, in length as much as in width or height.

So, in order that we may not go on at too great a length, we have judged it best to refrain from these things at this time. However, if anyone should undertake to gird himself for this work and should strive to cover over his ark with gold, nothing prevents him from borrowing the gold of knowledge from external knowledge and secular disciplines, provided that he knows how to cleanse himself from all the dross of falsity or vanity and to purify himself in the innermost part to a full and perfect purity, such as the dignity of these works requires. However, we have said that the gilding of our ark consists of assigning the rational principle of visible things. Now who does not know how almost all earthly philosophy labors especially in this, so that by means of its sagacious investigation, it may discover and bring forth in public the hidden causes of visible things? See how great, how many riches of doctrine and treasures of knowledge these excellent geniuses among the philosophers collected, preserved and bequeathed to you for uses of this sort. Nevertheless, as has been said, all these things are insufficient even for the external gilding of the ark. However, if you desire to gild it internally as well, it is better for you in such an undertaking to seek material from Christian theologians rather than philosophers of the world. Just as the treasures of the latter are insufficient for the external gilding of the ark, so those of the former are insufficient for the internal gilding of the ark. For neither are the latter able to perceive fully the hidden nature of things, nor are the former able to penetrate perfectly the hidden justice of God. But behold: Now we show you one treasure chest that we know is superabundant and inexhaustible for this kind of activity. Certainly where it lacks the gold of understanding, it will not be wanting in the pure gold of faith. Surely if you were able to examine thoroughly and to commit to memory all the words of the philosophers and all the investigations of the Catholic religion, nevertheless you would find countless things in the hidden territory of nature and in the hidden things of divine judgments, the rational principle of which you would be unable to penetrate. But what you cannot understand, you can believe. Notwithstanding that you are unable to perceive the rational principle of these, nevertheless you should not doubt that, according to the rule of faith, they are just and ordered. For this reason, it is said to you in this manner: "If you do not believe, you shall not understand" (Isa. 7:9). Therefore, believe with the blessed Job that nothing is done on the earth without a cause (Job. 5:6). Believe that the judgments of the Lord are judged true in themselves (Ps. 18:10), and you have gilded your ark inside and out.

CHAPTER XI

Concerning the particular nature of the second contemplation

It has been said that the second kind of contemplation has this in common with the previously discussed kind—that is, it is engaged with imagination and employed in consideration of visible and imaginable things. Nevertheless, they differ especially in this—that in the former one nothing is sought by reasoning, but it is led wholly by imagination. The present one, however, is woven together by reasoning and formed according to reason. The former one is in imagination according to imagination, while the present one is in imagination according to reason.

It ought to be noted that in the part that is supported by faith more than woven together by understanding—in that part, I say, it nowhere goes beyond the limits of its particular nature. For when it examines the innumerable separate and ordered works of God and His innumerable just and true judgments by means of the liveliness of its understanding, it understands from these which things are right, and it judges those things also are right whose rational principle it does not suffice to penetrate. You see, therefore, that where it follows the traces of faith, this speculation certainly is not led wholly away from the path of its reasoning. This speculation about which we are now speaking is moved according to reason to such an extent that in it even imagination itself seems to be disposed and ordered according to reason. For certainly in the first speculation, the thought by which wonder leads it follows imagination alone; in this present speculation, however, imagination is formed, disposed and moderated by reason. For while a person seeks the rational principle of invisible things by means of silent investigation, not only does he conceive them in another order than if he discovers them by means of the senses, but he also often depicts them under another form. Hence he discovers more quickly the reason why they ought to be done and ordered in this manner, since he sees the evil that would follow if they were otherwise. And so, just as in the first, imagination draws thought after it, so in this, reason surrounds and disposes imagination. However, for that reason, both are said to be in imagination because both are certainly occupied by intention and investigation with that which we represent by means of imagination as often as we wish. For by whatever the rational soul is snatched through diverse watchtowers in this twofold speculation, the eye of speculation is always fixed in imagination by the plan of its intention or by zeal.

CHAPTER XII

Concerning the third kind of contemplation

Now let us see about the third kind of contemplation. It pertains to this kind whenever we grasp the quality of invisible things by means of the similitude of visible things, and whenever we know the invisible things of God by means of visible things of the world. So it is agreed as it is found written, that "the invisible things of God from the creation of the world have been seen, being understood by means of those things which have been made" (Rom. 1:20). Rightly, however, this contemplation that, in order that it may rise to invisible things, supports itself with the staff of a corporeal similitude and lifts itself up to high things by means of a ladder, so to speak, of the particular natures of corporeal things—rightly, I say, such a speculation is indicated by the crown of the ark that is fastened in the lower part to pieces of wood but in the upper part rises above the extent of the wood. And so the crown encircles the upper part of the ark and descends in part below the wood, although for the greater part it goes beyond the extent of the wood. So it is no wonder that this speculation spontaneously inclines itself to investigating the particular natures of corporeal things, so that it may have something from which it may draw a similitude from one thing to another. However, spreading itself more widely, it includes the narrowness of lower things within itself. Not being satisfied with the things it gathers from likeness, but proving different things by different arguments and gathering others by means of reasoning, it leaves all corporeal likeness far behind itself by a discussion of a chain of reasoning and goes beyond the supreme height of our ark by means of consideration. In this way the crown of the ark is supported when it is raised to the height, because in understanding invisible things the soul of the contemplative is assisted not a little by means of the likeness of visible things. The crown, as much as the ark itself, both expands wider and rises higher when by means of visible things a keen contemplator clearly perceives invisible goods of a greater number and a more excellent worth than those visible things. For the great number of invisible goods is far too abundant for such a number of corporeal similitudes to be able to represent it. Nevertheless, all corporeal things have some similitude to invisible goods. Some have a kind of slight similitude, exceedingly far away and almost foreign, while others have a nearer and more evident similitude. The nearer they are, the more evident they are. Above these are others, exceedingly near and related, and, if I may say so, completely expressed to such a degree that they seem no longer to approach by means of visible things but seem to cling and to be ingrafted much more than merely to come near to. Thus, from these things that come near to those things and show a more evident image of invisible things, we ought in any case to draw a similitude, so that our understanding can rise by means of those things which we know well to those things which we do not know through experience. So it is that the crown of the ark does not go down to the lower part of the ark. Nevertheless, it joins itself to the ark in its upper part.

CHAPTER XIII

How in this kind of contemplation a person begins to become spiritual

In this first state a person begins to exist as a living creature, and he learns to be made a spiritual being, because now he should begin to bring together spiritual things and to be formed in the novitiate of his senses, as he endeavors more and more each day to taste those things which are above, not those which are upon the earth. It is great labor to abandon accustomed things, to leave behind in the lowest place the lowest of ingrained thought, and to fly from earthly things to heavenly things by means of a higher investigation.

Here, first, that one who teaches a person knowledge, the wisdom of God, that light "which illumines all persons coming into this world" (John 1:9), begins to pour out itself: at one time to pour the ray of its light on the eyes of the mind, and at another time to hide itself by withdrawing. And so it frequently visits the soul. At one time it lifts it to a high place and at another time presses it down to a low place and abandons it to itself. But it returns again unexpectedly, and when it was not hoped for, it appears and shows itself merry. Here finally it begins to form a kind of prelude of a marvelous vision that precedes the sight of intuition, and just as the eagle begins to thrust himself into diverse places by his own flying back and forth when inciting his young to flight, so it first begins to kindle the soul of the contemplative with longing for flying and at some time to instruct it perfectly for full flight. Here, first of all, the soul recovers its ancient dignity and claims for itself the inborn honor of its own freedom. For what is more alien to the rational spirit, what is more guilty of ignoble slavery, than that the truly spiritual creature should ignore spiritual things and the creature that has been made for invisible and highest goods should not be able at the least to rise up to the contemplation of invisible things, not to mention to stand in such contemplation. Here, I think it is sufficiently clear how rightly the intimate continuing presence and continual intimacy of this speculation that takes third place is indicated by the crown; how fitly that is called "crown," by which the victorious soul is crowned. Hence, in any case, he who has been able by means of contemplation of the mind to pass over from the hardships of this place of exile to the liberty of invisible joys receives the crown of spiritual knowledge. Then at last that rational spirit, who has sat for a long time in the darkness and the shadow of death while chained in poverty and iron, violently breaks through the mid-point of an infinite number of the lowest longings and carnal thoughts that are attacking on all sides and resisting everywhere—while at last the darkness of ignorance is dispersed and the chains of concupiscence are broken by the power of Him who leads forth in fortitude those who have been chained, smashing to pieces bronze gates and shattering iron bars, rising above the constrictions of deep-seated custom and obduracy of mind. Finally, with difficulty, he returns to the palace of his justice, when he wholly gathers himself on the throne of the heavenly dwelling place, so that as for the rest he may be able to sing confidently with his fellow-soldiers and similar triumphant ones: "Our conversation is in heaven" (Phil. 3:20).

CHAPTER XIV

Concerning the distinction of those things that pertain to this speculation

It ought to be known that no measure is prescribed for our crown, but the measure of it is determined in great part by the crown itself, since it is called "crown." For it would not be called crown if it did not encircle and crown the higher part of the ark on all sides. Therefore, it is necessary to extend and enlarge the crown according to the length and width of the ark, so that it can encircle and crown it. So it is evident that, in accord with the dimensions of the ark, the crown is two and one-half cubits long and one and one-half cubits wide. However, we are not able to determine the height with a similar reasoning nor are we able to compare it with the height of the ark. For it would never be called the crown if it covered the whole ark rather than ornamenting only the highest part of it. So as we have already said above, it is the property of this speculation to draw a similitude from visible to invisible things and to rise from the consideration of the former to knowledge of the latter by the assignment of a proposed similitude. Thus, if there were one measurement for both, and if this ark and that crown have precisely the same measurement in length as well as in width, what else ought to be understood in these than that we ought to learn to draw the rational principle of similitudes for the investigation of invisible things from all those things—from all those things, I say, that we have said pertain to the length or the width of our ark? Now in the speculation of things, as has been said, consideration of matter, form and nature pertains to the length of the ark. But the working of nature and of activity pertain to the width of it. And so by means of all these things we ought to and can draw out suitable rational principles of similitudes for the investigation of invisible things. When we have the use of such activity at hand, we have enclosed our ark with a crown as is necessary and proper. Now, it has been said that instruction—human as well as divine—in the consideration of morals pertains to the height of the ark, so that the ark of our understanding seems to have a full cubit from human instruction and one-half a cubit from divine instruction. But why is it that the previously mentioned crown seems to touch only the upper portion of the ark, except that it is evident that human instructions have a very distant and completely foreign similitude to invisible and spiritual things? Who does not know that these things are found in the use of temporal things and not in the figure of eternal things? However any visible works of the Creator have been created and disposed for this, that they may both serve the needs of the present life and also exhibit a shadow of future goods. Whence it is that the working of activity, insofar as it imitates nature, exhibits in itself a shadow of invisible or future things. However, concerning the remainder, the more human instructions are distant from a similitude of invisible things, the more those discovering them thought no such thing in their instruction. Nevertheless, as often as we discover in the former a kind of similitude to the latter things, we should see that perhaps it may not agree with another consideration of those things which we assigned above to the length and width of the ark. However, concerning divine instructions, it should be noted that we ought to understand some things simply and seek nothing in them according to the mystical sense, while some things ought to be employed according to the literal sense, and yet are capable of representing something according to the mystical sense. Thus, because a mystical understanding is sought for in the most sublime commands and according to the most profound understanding, that one-half cubit, which is ascribed to the height of our ark with respect to divine instructions, is adorned in its upper parts by the golden crown. But the adaptation of the similitude in this part does not wholly withdraw from the particular nature of those five considerations mentioned above. For this reason, the crown extends itself there according to the length and width of the ark, so that it can encircle it on all sides.

CHAPTER XV

That this kind of contemplation is rightly divided into five stages

This third kind of contemplation is rightly separated into five stages according to those five modes of consideration mentioned above on the basis of which the rational principle of similitudes is sought and assigned in the investigation of invisible things. For when a similitude from one thing to another is adopted, it is formed by a varying order according to these same modes. And so, the first mode is when a similitude is taken from that of which something is constituted, or better from that which it is itself. The second and third modes take their similitude from that which something is in itself. The fourth and fifth take their similitude from that which something is through itself. And the second, certainly, is taken from that which it is in itself, but externally; the third, from that which it is in itself, but internally; the fourth, from that which it does through itself, by some impulse of necessity; the fifth, from that which it does through itself, but by means of the purpose of will. So the first mode of such reasoning in this speculation is drawn from the particular nature of matter. The second and third are drawn from the quality of the thing itself; but the second is from the external quality that we have called form, while the third is from the internal quality that we earlier called nature. However, the fourth mode is gathered from that which is done in the thing itself or from itself according to a natural motion. Finally, the fifth is gathered from that which is done according to artificial motion. A similitude is drawn from the particular nature of matter when it is said: "His legs are marble columns, which have been set upon golden bases" (Song of Songs 5:15). Extrinsic quality consists of color and figure. A similitude is assigned from color in that which is read: "My beloved is dazzling white and ruddy" (Song of Songs 5:10). A similitude is taken from the quality of a figure when a quality is commended by a mystical description in sacred

Scripture: "The appearance of wheels, and their workmanship, is as if it were a wheel in the midst of a wheel" (Ezech. 1:16).

Note that extrinsic quality pertains to sight only, just as intrinsic quality pertains to any of the other senses. To hearing pertains that assignment of a similitude, where you hear: "And the sound which I heard was, as it were, the sound of harpers harping on their harps" (Rev. 14:2). However that passage in which Wisdom speaks of herself seems to have a view to smelling: "I gave off an odor, smelling like cinnamon and balsam; I gave pleasantness of odor, like choice myrrh" (Ecclus. 24:20). A similitude is adopted from the delights of taste when Wisdom acknowledges concerning herself: "My spirit is sweet above honey and my inheritance, above honey and the honeycomb" (Ecclus. 24:27). That which you have elsewhere is full of the pleasures of touch: "Like the ointment on the head which flows down into the beard, the beard of Aaron" (Ps. 132:2). Let so much be said concerning intrinsic quality, certainly as regards that part which the senses of the body are able to touch. With regard to the grace of similitude, a natural working is drawn into consideration when it is promised by the voice of a Prophet from the Lord: "Even as rain and snow fall from heaven and do not return there above but saturate the earth and spread over it and make it to sprout forth and give seed to the one sowing and bread to the one eating; so shall my word be that goes forth from my mouth" (Isa. 55:10). The adaptation of a similitude is from an artificial working when you hear from the Apostle: "Built upon the foundation of the apostles and prophets, with Jesus Christ Himself the chief cornerstone" (Eph. 2:20). We have striven zealously to report these things to you concerning the rational principle of similitudes in the construction of our crown like a kind of seed of doctrine (just as above, in the gilding of the ark) so that you might have that by which you may be able, when you wish, to gather an abundant crop of knowledge. But to explain this topic fully and sufficiently would require a tract of its own. The more the reason of this speculation pays attention to this reasoning, the more this topic needs a more careful and greater inquiry. However, it is evident that in our times the greatest and almost the chief consolation of spiritual men is in this and subsequent speculations. For there are very few who are able to rise up to the two highest kinds of contemplation. However, those who wish to examine these present things fully ought to be mindful that, according to the manner of the ark, its crown has four sides.

Chapter XVI

That those things which pertain to this speculation are still able to be distinguished in another manner

However there is yet another thing that we can note rightly with respect to this crown, if by it we ought to understand a plenitude of invisible goods, since the crown encircled the propitiatory on all sides and enclosed all of it within itself. For as far as pertains to the arrangement of the ark, it ought to be understood that there is no other propitiatory than the cover of the ark itself: namely, a kind of golden panel, completely made of the purest gold, which was drawn out from the lower part at the summit of the ark and was encircled on all sides by the golden crown, as has been said already. And so by these two things (that is, the crown and the propitiatory) we understand two kinds of contemplations, one concerning invisible goods, the other concerning invisible substances; as for example in angelic or human spirits. What does it mean that the crown encloses the whole propitiatory within itself except that the beatitude of the just includes all their longings within itself? As long as we live subject to the beggarly elements of this world, we extend our longings beyond our joys, because the things that we crave are infinitely more than those we are able to possess in this life. But blessed is the multitude of supernal spirits; it does not extend its desires beyond the plenitude of its joys, because it is wholly unable to lay hold of the immensity and infinity of its happiness that the crown of its blessedness encircles on every side and always encloses in the bosom of its greatness. The joy of these is not only from contemplation of the Creator, but even in contemplating His creatures. For while they now discover a marvelous God in all His works, why marvel if everywhere they venerate by marveling and marvel by venerating the mighty deeds of Him whom they love? And so they discover not only in incorporeal creatures but even in corporeal creatures that at which they marvel, that in which they worthily venerate their Creator. Thus there are some things that are above them, others that they see within themselves, and others they see beneath themselves. All these things they continually contemplate; contemplating, they marvel; marveling, they rejoice. They rejoice concerning divine contemplation; they give thanks concerning mutual vision; they delight in the speculation of corporeal things. The lowest part of the crown, which goes down below the propitiatory and is fixed to the wood, indicates that delightful manifestation that they have in the lower creatures. The middle part of the crown, which is joined to the propitiatory, represents that most ardent longing of charity which they produce from the delightfulness of mutual vision. The highest part of the crown, which is raised up above the propitiatory, expresses that ineffable joy that they imbibe from continual contemplation of their Creator. Let us learn when contemplating to marvel and when marveling to contemplate in what way citizens of that supernal beatitude indefinitely behold all things that are beneath them and understand the rational principle and the order of everything they see from on high; how they continually rejoice concerning mutual community and indestructible charity; how they burn insatiably in that vision of divine brilliance—let us learn these things, and we have crowned our ark. Let us think how they go out and go in and discover pastures—and we shall have completed the crown of our ark according to a manner suitable for it. You certainly see that they discover spiritual pastures not only in interior things, but even in exterior and corporeal things. Without doubt corporeal goods, in so much as they have a similarity to invisible and incorporeal goods, are able to provide spiritual pastures for spiritual persons, and no wonder. For if visible goods were to have no similitude at all to invisible things for the investigation of invisible things, by no means would they be able to assist us, nor would what is read concerning them be evident, namely, that the invisible things of God from the creation of the world have been seen, being understood by means of those things which have been made (Rom. 1:20). Again, if these things did not disagree with those by many dissimilitudes, without doubt they would not be perishable, transitory and insufficient. Nevertheless, the dissimilitude of these to those is incomparably richer than the similitude. Certainly the surpassing greatness of future fullness is limitless in comparison with these. For this reason, the highest parts of the ark scarcely touch the crown and are joined to the lower parts of it, because the highest things of the ark are the lowest things of the crown, and they speak only in part by so many signs of their similitudes.

CHAPTER XVII

That in this speculation we make use of the leading hand of corporeal similitudes

Between the second kind of contemplation and this third kind of which we are now speaking, the difference seems to be this: that the former of which we spoke above is engaged in imagination and is governed according to reason; however the latter is in reason, but follows imagination. In this speculation he turns to invisible things by means of everything that the soul investigates in many ways, and he presses forward to grasp them. And so, for that reason this speculation is in reason, because it pursues the investigation of those things only which bodily sense is wholly unable to grasp. But since the investigation of this speculation cannot be led to the knowledge of invisible things without the assistance of corporeal similitudes, reason seems to be following the leading hand of imagination in this part and is shown clearly to hold on to it, the leader of the journey as it were, in the course of its search. For while imagination presents forms of visible things to reason and instructs itself from the similitude of the same things for the investigation of invisible things, in a certain manner it brings reason to that place to which it did not know how to go by means of itself. For reason would never rise up to the contemplation of invisible things unless the imagination, by means of representing the forms of visible things, were to show from what it should draw a similitude to those things and form the mode of its investigation. For this reason our inner person calls the outer person his leader when he says: "Truly, you are a person of one mind, my leader and my friend" (Ps. 54:14). For it is certain that the soul is not able to come to an exterior idea except by means of bodily sense. Thus the inner person rightly calls the outer person his leader, without whose service—or better without whose teaching—he does not attain to knowledge of visible things. But he does not attain to knowledge of invisible things either since he is not able to rise up to knowing them without an idea of visible things. Thus, as often as he is urged to grasp by means of bodily sense the experience of knowing things, so often, to be sure, does our inner person seem to follow his leader. Without doubt, the sense of the flesh precedes the sense of the heart in knowing things, because, unless the soul first were to grasp sensible things by means of bodily sense, it would completely fail to discover what it should at the least be able to think concerning them. But perhaps it is not marvelous if the sense of the body leads the sense of the heart to that place where it is able to go itself. But it is truly marvelous how the sense of the body leads that of the heart to that place where the former is not able to rise by itself. Certainly, bodily sense does not grasp incorporeal things; nevertheless reason does not rise to the latter without the guiding hand of the former just as reason already has taught. Certainly, even if man had not sinned at all, the exterior sense would aid the interior in the knowledge of things; for who does not know that Adam received his Eve for assistance? Truly, it is one thing to have a partner on his way; it is another thing to seek a leader on his journey. But because Eve once drew her husband after her against the counsel and command of God, and he inclined to consent to her counsel, Adam, having been weakened by punishment for his lying, already had necessarily to follow her and up to this present day he is in need of her daily teaching. Nevertheless, now concerning the guidance of her assistance, he not only is not confused, but he also glories, with her office mediating, when he is led by the stony path of corporeal similitudes to contemplation of invisible things: "You are a person of one mind, my leader and my friend" (Ps. 54:14). However, I think it is evident and does not require lengthy exposition, how his leader may be of one mind or, better, a friend to the inner person. Think now, how the motion of the body actually reaches to the motion of the heart, and you will discover very quickly how it may be of one mind with him. The foot or hand is moved immediately, as the soul wills. At its command, the eye is moved about. According to its decision the tongue is moved and the lips or any other members whatsoever of the body are moved. What, I ask, are more dissimilar in the nature of things than spirit and body? Yet where, I beg you, do we find so much unanimity of such perfect concord, so that almost—nay, completely at the same time—to will to become is also to become and to will to move is also to move. There is only one member of the body, in that part in which the sexual desire rules, that does not comply with the command of the inner person.

Truly, since the inner person would be able, from divine assistance, to stop this contradiction of his by means of moderate bodily affliction, he already dares to call the outer person "of one mind" and to name him a man of his peace in succession. He says, "A man of my peace" (Ps. 40:10). Behold, how he is "of one mind." But how is he "a friend"? Certainly it is sufficiently evident that whatever happens in any part of the body, wherever it is injured, wherever it is favored with any delight whatsoever, this comes immediately to the notice of the soul, with the result that since it is completely unable to remain hidden, every pain or delight affects bodily sense; and just as the inclination of the heart goes out immediately, without any opposition, by means of the motion of the body, so every sense of the body enters without delay into the soul. And as in all its action the motion of the body complies with the decision of the heart, so every corporeal feeling enters into the soul without being resisted. Such a sudden speed of sympathy or thanksgiving demonstrates how no harm or delight of the body can truly be hidden from the soul. As it is possible at one and the same time to will to move and to move, so it is possible at one and the same moment for the body to feel and for the heart to feel with it; to be delighted without, to give thanks within. Choose what you shall marvel at more greatly: either such quick obedience of the body to the soul or such intimate knowledge of the soul for the body. Marvelous obedience, when the motion of the body almost anticipates every longing of the soul. Marvelous intimacy of knowledge, when whatever the body feels, the soul almost feels beforehand. And the inner person of ours certainly has knowledge concerning this servant of his household. He has, I say, that at which he may marvel; not however, that of which he may boast. There is no greater glory than for the soul to have known those things which are accustomed to de-

light or to injure his body. But without doubt it will be a great thing
when the inner person has begun to know, through many instances
of experience, in what way he ought to comply with the desire of
the flesh in necessary things and to oppose it in unnecessary things,
lest, if he should assist less, he might stir up an enemy for himself
and nurture rebellious ones. On the other hand, if he attacks too
much, he may kill a citizen and overwhelm a helper. Surely the soul
scarcely attains to such a kind of perfection of knowledge by means
of many arguments or after many experiences. But once it does
acquire this, without doubt it advances not a little bit on account of
it. Without this, Adam would never have been able to make good
use of her assistance. By means of this our outer person is gradually
taught to despise the delights of Egypt and finally to forget them;
and no less is he accustomed to take delight in spiritual nourish-
ments. This will seem a marvelous thing—perhaps unbelievable to
some. But if it is not believable from me, then let it be believed by
means of one who has experienced it. Let us hear that one whom
this experience has taught, and let us give attention to what he says:
"A man of my peace, in whom I hope, who ate my bread" (Ps.
40:10). And again in this place: "Who together with me took sweet
foods; we walked in the house of God in harmony" (Ps. 54:15).
Scripture shows what that bread is which our inner person lays
before the outer person and with what food he refreshes him, when
it says: "My tears have been my bread day and night, while it is said
to me daily: where is your God?" (Ps. 41:4). And elsewhere it says
again concerning such bread: "Rise up, after you sit, you who eat
the bread of grief" (Ps. 126:2). And so at one time the inner person
alone eats such bread, while at another time, with scarcely any
great struggle, he compels his household to eat with him. The spirit
alone eats its bread, when the soul grieves for its sins, yet it is not
able to force out tears for any reason. Both eat the bread of grief and
choose one food as if of one mind, when the inner person groans
deeply and the outer person sheds tears abundantly on account of
his groaning. First a person is pricked with compunction on account of fear, while afterward he is pricked with compunction on
account of love. The compunction of fear causes bitterness; the
compunction of love causes sweetness. Therefore, whoever is
pricked until now by fear only is certainly fed with foods that are

spiritual but not yet sweet at all. Whoever already sheds tears because of longing for eternal joys refreshes himself with foods that are both spiritual and sweet. Thus, when that inner person begins to refresh his household with such foods, he is truly able to sing about it: "Who together with me took sweet foods." Thus the more both persons advance toward purity with such zealous effort, the more rapidly they run. Truly, that an attack of malignant spirits should throw the peace of their flesh and spirit into confusion after the perfection of such concord appears clearly to one who understands rightly about that which is added on to the Scripture passage. For what does it mean that the inner person who has been created according to God laments concerning a person of his peace and a person of one mind, and then hurls the javelin of a curse not into that person but into others—what does it mean except that by means of a rebuke he rages in those whose rage has lost the quiet of his peace? He says: "You truly are a person of one mind, my leader and my friend, who together with me took sweet foods; we walked in the house of God in harmony" (Ps. 54:14–15). And he adds immediately, "Let death come upon them" (Ps. 54:16). It does not say "upon you," but "upon them." Thus, he avenges himself concerning those by whose deceit he lost the partner of his peace. For often malignant spirits, envying the peace of the spirit, disturb the peace of the spirit when they weary the flesh with unexpected and violent temptation, and they make an enemy for the spirit from one of one mind, a seducer from a leader, and they make a stranger from a friend and an enemy from the household. Now, behold, when we wish to examine one place in Scripture more fully, we are compelled to survey adjacent passages. For when the order of reason demands, that we say something concerning the guidance of the outer person, the obscurity of the adjacent words constrains us to extend our exposition a little further.

Chapter XVIII

That this kind of contemplation is in reason according to imagination

Let us now return to that from which we have been digressing, namely how, by the imagination of visible things, we are assisted to the investigation of invisible things. Truly, in this the outer person assists the inner person in the course of his investigation. For that purpose he represents to him an image of invisible things by means of the imagination of visible things. And while he completes the duty of his leadership, he leads the inner person by means of the stony path of similitudes to that place which he dares not enter. So servants often go before their lords in the way as far as the royal palace gates, and yet while the lords hasten within to the interior of the palace, the servants remain outside. Thus I think it is evident, as we have already said above, how we ought to understand that this kind of contemplation exists in reason and according to imagination, because there are invisible things that we perceive mentally and yet we form them in us out of a similitude of visible things. For what shall I call the form of visible things except a kind of picture of invisible things, as it were? Should there be anyone who says that he has never seen a lion and yet longs to see one, if the image of a lion, portrayed suitable in some picture, is shown to him, certainly the sort of thing he ought to conceive in the mind is suggested immediately from that which he sees. Thereupon, he considers according to the features that have been portrayed on a surface, and he forms in the mind the solid members and the living animal itself. Now think how much difference there is between that which we see externally and this which it shapes internally for him in his thinking. So certainly in this kind of contemplation the invisible things that we engage in the mind differ greatly from those things which we perceive by means of imagination, and yet we draw upon the similitude of the latter, in order to portray the former. We have now declared how we were able to give a reason why this kind of contemplation seems to be in reason and according to imagination.

Chapter XIX

How whatever a ray of contemplation illumines pertains to the permission or working of God

The order of reason requires that some things be said briefly in this place concerning the rings and the poles, so that the same order may be followed in exposition as the author wished to follow in description. First we must consider what the sides of the ark represent, so that in a suitable manner we may know which circles we ought to place on which side. As we have already said above, by the ark we understand the grace of contemplation. Therefore, since the ray of contemplation already radiates from on high and enlarges itself in every direction because of the elevated capacity of the mind, all things that are able to be subject to contemplation clearly show themselves to pertain to this ark. It is one consideration when we pay attention daily to which of the things are either just or unjust. It is quite another consideration when we perceive in human custom that one thing is proper while another is improper. Thus in our ark they build two sides mutually opposite to each other, the one being "fairness," the other, "iniquity." No less do they make two other sides, mutually facing each other in direct opposition, one being "success," the other, "misfortune." However, it ought greatly to be wondered at and is worthy of great wonder how, when God moderates and disposes all things justly, either a good will or a bad will of whatever sort is now driven away by adversity on this side, now bound by prosperity on that side, so that neither the one nor the other increases continually nor exceeds the manner of divine disposition. Think now, in what manner the walls in our ark, while they extend themselves along the length and measure the width, cut off two other walls running transversely and limit them to a specified length. In any case, according to this similitude, at one time divine dispensation serves diverse wills as it wishes, so that they may discover how they may extend themselves; at another time it opposes them so that they may not exceed the manner of the previously established design. For, lest we escape, we are bound in the one by the chains of cupidity and impeded in the other by the restraint of necessity. Often we let go of many things lest we lose what we long for; no less often do we let go of many things lest we run upon what we hate. Thus where adversity and perversity come into mutual contact they form, in a certain manner, a corner in our ark. Where prosperity and perversity mutually meet, they make another corner. The meeting of fairness and prosperity constitutes the third. The striking together of fairness and adversity constitutes the fourth. At the first corner evil persons are reproved; at the fourth, good persons are reformed.

Again: At the second corner evil persons are abandoned; at the third, good persons are defended. Reprobates certainly are reproved by adversity; they are not reformed, however. Indeed if they reformed themselves, they clearly would not be reprobates. But by means of adversity good persons are reformed from their evils and are even advanced to better things. Again: By prosperity evil persons are released in themselves and are abandoned by God. However, by prosperity good persons are both assisted with respect to good things and defended from evil things. The first corner is for reproving; the second, for abandoning; the third, for defending; the fourth, for reforming. Then it is clear that those walls which extend the length of the ark are called by Moses the sides of the ark. Just as in the arrangement of the ark the length of these two walls is greater than that of the other walls, so the dignity of these also is more sublime in the signification of things and the contemplation of truth. For who does not know how incomparably greater that separation is, which is between just and unjust, than that which is between proper and improper? The first pertains to the walls that extend the length of the ark. On the other hand, that which is proper and improper pertains to those walls which extend the width of the ark. And so the consideration of any things whatsoever, according to which they are done justly or even unjustly, pertains to two sides of the ark. Who does not know that those things are done justly that are done by the working of God; those things that are done unjustly are done by his permission only?

Chapter XX

That the wisdom of God, since it is simple and one, is drawn into contemplation by means of different considerations, and it is called now knowledge, now foreknowledge, now disposition or predestination

Since we are already acquainted with those things which the sides of the ark represent and already comprehend by means of an exposition the four corners of it, let us now seek what those four rings of gold are that we are commanded to place individually at individual corners. Concerning gold, it is sufficiently evident that it surpasses all other metals by the greatness of its brilliance. But what is brighter, what more luminous than divine wisdom? We find nothing comparable to it. Concerning this gold, we use the material for diverse workings, as it were, when we consider by means of a different mode that which in itself is simple and one. Although the wisdom of God certainly is simple and one, as has been said it is sometimes called foreknowledge, sometimes called knowledge; now we call it predestination, now we call it disposition. So one thing is separated by us into different modes, so that it is grasped in some sort of mode, or partially, because of our limitations. It is knowledge by which it knows all things. It is foreknowledge by which it sees all things beforehand from eternity. It is predestination by which from all eternity it ordains all people beforehand either to life or to death. It is disposition by which it leaves nothing disordered, by continually disposing all things everywhere. We bend these modes of our consideration in a circle, as it were, when we see that in every ordering of divine wisdom the beginning agrees with the end. Divine foreknowledge never errs in its foresight; nor is divine predestination deceived in its purpose; nowhere does its knowledge err in its judgment; nor does its disposition waver in its purpose. For when a circle is bent back upon itself in every part, without doubt just as a beginning is not found in it, so an end is not found. Nonetheless, both those considerations pertain to these circles, in that our mind is able to discover in every contemplation of divine comprehension neither beginning, nor end, nor middle. The circumference of these circles is drawn in every part equally distant from one middle point, since in one thing as well as in another every divine examination nowhere strays very far from a definition of the one and simple truth. These circles comprehend everything within themselves, and they enclose the universe within their embrace. These are, I think, those four rings that were commanded to be arranged by Moses at the four corners of the ark.

CHAPTER XXI

That according to diverse modes of contemplation, divine wisdom seems more marvelous in some, more delightful in others

Two of these rings have a place on one side, the remaining two on the other side. And so individual rings are allotted to specific places, although all work together equally for transporting the whole ark. For any one of such circles ought to have a position there, in the place where each one appears to our consideration to be more marvelous or more delightful than the rest. For each one withdraws farther, as it were, from that place where it excites to a lesser degree the wonder of the person contemplating and generates less delight in the soul of the one wondering at it. Thus, two receive a position on one side, and two others receive a position on the other side. However, it has been mentioned above how those things which are done by the permission of God pertain to one side and how, in like manner, those things which are done by the working of God seem to pertain to the other side. The ring of foreknowledge and the ring of knowledge are arranged on the side of permission. Similarly, the ring of predestination and the ring of disposition are arranged on the side of divine working. Do you wish to know how rightly, with how much order the rings which are called "of knowledge" and "of foreknowledge" direct especially those things which are done by the permission of God? Consider, if you are able, how wonderful it is that He is able to know beforehand from eternity all these things, the multitude of which is so innumerable and the variation so manifold. Although this foreknowledge of His is marvelous when it is with respect to both, nevertheless it appears more marvelous with respect to evil things than with respect to good ones. For we know that those things which are evil, since they are done unjustly only, are done by His permission, but never by His working. Furthermore, consider, if you are able, of how much wonder it is worthy that He was also able to know beforehand those things which He leaves to the will of another, and indeed to a will which did not yet exist and had not as much as been made. For He never makes an evil will, although He permits it to exist. Certainly we marvel less that He Himself is able to know beforehand from eternity those things which were to be done by Him, although they are so many and almost innumerable, than that He knows beforehand those things which He placed under an alien power and an opposing will. However, what are we going to say concerning His knowledge, which we know comprehends with one ray of simple vision the quality, mode, order and place, and number of all things that are? O truly marvelous! O truly awesome! If you seek where that which is truly marvelous everywhere might appear more marvelous for our consideration, who does not see that it is more marvelous in the hidden things of God than in the manifest ones? What is it like to see incessantly the hidden things of men, namely the secrets of thoughts, affections, wills and intentions, and not to be able to hide any inclination of the heart in the presence of the gaze of divine knowledge? As often as He directs attention to the good thoughts of men, what does He see according to all these in the secret place of hearts, other than what He Himself has placed there? Indeed, without opposition He Himself causes any good inclinations of hearts, and He works with these very things. It is truly marvelous above all else that He cannot be ignorant of all those things which He Himself does not inspire in human hearts. This is that supreme and singular wonder in the sharp-sightedness of divine knowledge: that nothing can be hidden from Him in so deep and so dark an abyss of evil hearts. Behold why the rings of providence and knowledge receive a place on the side of permission, where, as reason teaches plainly, the most marvelous things suggest themselves for our consideration. However, the other rings of divine predestination and disposition ought to have the other side. Why this should be, does not, I think, require much exposition. For as we pass over in silence the things in this part that appear more marvelous, who would deny that among these things those appear more joyful which serve the salvation of the elect and look to this side only? Since indeed we embrace more affectionately, venerate more joyfully, love more ardently and praise more honorably the rational principle of divine predestination and disposition in the restoration, advancement and glorification of those being saved rather than in the just condemnation, casting down and damnation of evil persons. Now predestination seems especially and properly to pertain so much to this side that it is usually spoken of almost entirely with respect only to foreordination to life and refers to the other part only in an improper use and improperly. Although divine disposition may pertain to either of the two because it never allows anything to remain disordered, nevertheless all its ordering serves only the welfare of the elect. Behold, now we have said which rings we ought to arrange on which side.

CHAPTER XXII

In what speculation does divine foreknowledge or knowledge appear more marvelous

Perhaps this question still occurs to the soul: In which corner ought each ring to be placed? Pay attention. Perhaps they pertain more especially by some singularity of supereminence: the ring of foreknowledge to the first corner; the ring of knowledge to the second corner; the ring of predestination to the third corner; the ring of disposition to the fourth corner. We have already said above that the striking together of adversity and iniquity makes the first corner, and we have taught that it pertains to the reproof but not to the reformation of evil persons. Therefore, if you are mindful of the foreknowledge of God, what will you find that you ought to marvel at more in it? If He knows beforehand that they never wish to come to their senses from their evils, why, I ask, does He reprove reprobate persons by lashes of evil adversities? Why does He bring words of fatherly care, as it were, to them, constrain them with words of guidance and terrify with threats those whom He foresees to be sentenced to eternal evils? Therefore, if you do not find in divine foreknowledge something to marvel at more, there is no reason to marvel that it is attached to this angle most tightly. Again, it has been shown above that the meeting of prosperity and perversity makes the second corner and that it pertains to the abandoning of evil persons and not at all to their delight. Now I ask you, turn back the eyes of the understanding to consideration of divine knowledge; regard it carefully, marvel, and be awed. It is very astounding how God continually looks at the evil things of men, which He detests and hates so much. I ask, is the omnipotence of

God not able to restrain so many and so great evils that omnipotent wisdom is nowhere able to ignore and omnipotent goodness is never able to love? This approaches a highpoint of such wonder: that He even gives evil persons temporal goods, by which in a certain manner it seems that these evils that He detests before and above all things multiply in them. For, as has been said above, by temporal goods evil persons are released in themselves and are abandoned by God. But does that clear-sightedness of divine knowledge not consider how evil persons abound in His gifts? Is He perchance in any way ignorant in what spirit they do things? But who would dare to say this? Therefore, pay attention to how difficult it is to venerate with proper wonder the hidden meaning of this perplexity, and you will discover how rightly such a ring of divine knowledge ought to be joined most closely and attached most firmly to this corner.

Chapter XXIII

In what speculation does divine predestination appear more delightful

Again, the third corner, as presented above, is formed by the meeting of honesty and prosperity and is acknowledged to pertain to the consolation and protection of good persons. Here, now, I ask you, look from this corner to the corner opposite to it and pay careful attention now to the one, now to the other, so that you can discover more quickly and penetrate more sharp-sightedly the reason that you seek for the position. In this corner, good persons are supported by the prosperity of this world; in the opposite corner, evil persons are lashed by worldly adversity. Let us pay more careful attention, let us examine more often—in the former the affection of God, in the latter His severity: affection with regard to good people, severity with regard to evil people. How severe do we think it is that in the present He does not spare those whom He leads to eternal punishment, and that He does not allow them to pass through temporal life without punishment? How kindly will that One be who does not cease to support with temporal goods, as much as it may be expedient for them, the good persons whom He has, nevertheless, preordained to true and eternal good things?

Discuss, if you can, of what kind, how great, how kindly He can be gratuitously, in that He predestined the latter to eternal goods (while the former were rejected) and nevertheless does not deny temporal goods for use—nay, for benefit. What can be discovered in the predestination of God that is sweeter and more joyful than this consideration? Rightly, therefore, divine predestination is described to be preeminently in that corner, where the temporal prosperity of the elect serves for benefit. That gold ring rightly has a fixed place there, where the brighter it is, the more joyful it undoubtedly appears.

CHAPTER XXIV

In which speculation of things does divine disposition usually appear more joyful

In order that we might come at last to that fourth corner, we have set forth at length above that it is where adversity, running from the opposite direction, exercises uprightness. For it pertains, as was said there, to the reformation of good persons. Since good persons do not pass through this life without stain, and however perfect, they discover how they can advance by increasing and have in this corner that by which they may be purged and equally that whereby they may be exercised. The last of our rings watches most fittingly over this corner, because it does not have another place in which it receives an individual position. Here again, if we compare this corner with the corner opposite to it, we shall discover more quickly the reason we seek. In the opposite corner evil persons prosper; in this corner good persons are lashed. In the former, evil persons become more and more lukewarm in their feelings toward God on account of those goods which they receive, because of which they ought to burn more passionately in love of Him. In the latter, on the contrary, in good persons, having been disposed by God, it happens that that whereby it seemed the ardor of love ought to be extinguished in them is that whereby it is kindled more strongly in them. The more sharply they are beset with the evils of the world, and the more they are weakened by severer lashing, the more strongly they are kindled to the love of God. Marvel, I beg you, marvel and be greatly awed—either how in evil persons the love of God disappears on account of a benefaction, or in what way in good persons divine longing grows on account of a lashing. Without doubt, love of God gained more strength in Lawrence from burning than in Nero from imperial power. Nay, in Lawrence it became hot by burning; in Nero, it was completely lacking because of the imperium of power granted. And what is still greater and more marvelous, the flame of love probably gained more strength from so sharp a pain than it could have from whatever or however much temporal glory.

Whence, I ask you, comes such counsel, and such a marvelous work of art? You see how the supreme Artisan, who gives birth, assists and nourishes opposites from opposites, shows the skill of His art. It is helpful both to compare this corner with others and to commend the order of divine disposition by means of a comparison with the other corners. In the first corner, as has been said, evil persons are punished but they are not purified. In this corner good persons are lashed and reformed. Why is it, I ask, that the same lashes correct the same faults in the good but are utterly unable to correct them in the evil—nay I should rather say, almost a small temporal flame boils out fully the rust of a similar corruption in the elect, while in the reprobates, such bitterness of so many torments and that cruel fire of Gehenna cannot suffice to boil the rust out for eternity? Why, I ask, does a dissimilar effect not have a dissimilar cause, unless because the rational principle of the divine ordering of things, while it is marvelous on both sides, appears more just than kindly in the reprobate, while in the elect it is kindly but much more than severe? Behold we have already compared the fourth corner concerning which we have been speaking, first with the second corner, and second with the first corner; now in the third place, it is compared with the third corner. And so in the third corner good persons receive a benefit for consolation. In the fourth corner, of which we now treat, they feel themselves to be wearied by lashings. In the former they are assisted; in the latter they are exercised. In the former they pause pleasantly; in the latter they fight bravely. In the former as they are about to undertake military service they take possession of the payment from their king; in the latter by fighting they obtain the victory and by conquering they

213

acquire the palm of eternal reward. In the former corner it happens in them that they are God's debtors in the faith on account of having received divine favor, while in the latter corner on account of the merit of their patience and fortitude it is accomplished in them that they become, if it is proper to say so, God's just creditors. "As for the rest," said the Apostle, "there is laid up for me a crown of justice which the Lord, the just judge, will return to me on that day" (2 Tim. 4:8). "He will return," He says, not "He will give," and "just judge," not "kindly judge." But so that he might become a just debtor of so great a reward he first must voluntarily become a liberal giver of such a benefit. Consider, therefore, what sort of thing it is when God contrives some great effort, when He busies Himself with much exercising, when at some time He completes in the elect a certain marvelous work of art, in order that from being accused defendants they become just; from slaves, free persons; from miserable debtors, persons rich in benefits and heirs of the kingdom of heaven. This is, I think, a sufficient reason why that golden ring of divine disposition watches over this corner in a singular manner, where by means of a struggle of modest labor, it lifts a man to eternal rewards. This is that place in which such a golden ring shines more and glows with a more ruddy brilliance. This is, I say, that place in which divine disposition appears more glorious and delightful while they rejoice in tribulation and are pleased with insults. And so from the things that we have already said concerning the corners or sides of the ark, we have shown with sufficient clarity, I think, how on one side the rings of foreknowledge and knowledge should appear more marvelous and how on the other side the rings of predestination and disposition should appear more delightful.

CHAPTER XXV

That great wonder and remarkable exultation always ought to accompany the manifestation of contemplation

I think that it will not be laborious to discover what sort of poles such rings ought to have or which pole we ought to place on which side. Indeed, in the things that ought to be marveled at more, there is undoubted need for great wonder; however, in those which seem to be more delightful, it will be beneficial to employ great exultation. Therefore, our wonder ought to be great and our exultation strong, both being of the sort the contemplation of divine works requires. Let each be great; let each be strong; let both be solid after the manner of poles that are sufficient for carrying so great a load. Therefore, concerning both, let us make a wooden pole, not a reed staff. However, it ought not to be made of just any wood, but of Setim wood, namely a wood strong and incorruptible so that they may be unbendable on account of fortitude and incorruptible on account of long-suffering. Such good poles have both great and lasting wonder and extraordinary and continuing exultation. So that they may have a form after the manner of poles and may fulfill the function of poles, let both be solid and gilded. Therefore, let both be made of hard firm oak, set in order according to the pattern of justice, and covered over with the gold of wisdom, so that both may be strong by fortitude, set in order by equity and shining by discretion. This sort of gilding on these poles pleases very much in every way, because prudent and careful discretion fares well in everything. Therefore, let our admiration be discreet, so that we wonder at nothing that is false in God's foreknowledge or knowledge. Let our thanksgiving be no less discreet, so that we venerate nothing that is in divine predestination or disposition. In any case, He knows that both of these are marvelous without the patronage of falsity. He knows that both of these are sweet without the seasoning of vanity. Therefore, we marvel at nothing that is false in the foreknowledge of God or in His knowledge; we venerate nothing that is vain in God's predestination or disposition when we cover our poles with the gold of wisdom in the manner we ought. Therefore poles of this sort are inserted through the rings of gold, and according to the Lord's example and order they are never taken out. Your wonder ought always to be with respect to the manifestation of divine foreknowledge or divine knowledge. Your delight ought always to be with respect to the consideration of divine predestination and disposition. In the former you will always find what you can marvel at; in the latter you will find that in which you can delight. Why will it be necessary to seek some things in behalf of other things, and to run here and there through empty things with wandering of thoughts? Nowhere is there more abundant matter for admiring; nowhere is there a more beneficial cause for showing joy. Surely in the former and the latter you will find that at which you can marvel and in which you can delight. For although each pole clings more closely to one side, neither distances itself very much from the other. Therefore, your admiration always ought to be of the former things and your delight always in the latter things. Let poles of this sort always be inserted in this way through golden rings, and you will rejoice that you have fulfilled the Lord's command.

Chapter XXVI

That the mode of contemplation is varied according to the mode of wonder and exultation

By these poles our ark is carried here and there; by these poles it is lifted up on high; by them it is set down in a low place again. Assuredly with regard to the rational principle of divine works and the contemplation of them, the more fully you delight by wondering and wonder by delighting, the more willingly you remain, the more carefully you examine and the more deeply you are illumined. As often as your soul is snatched away by various things on account of your admiration and is fixed delightfully on individual things, so often is your ark carried about because your contemplation is enlarged. If your wonder snatches you up to higher and more profound things and suspends you delightfully in the investigation of these things, no doubt your ark rises up on high because your understanding grasps more subtle things. When the wonder of speculation and the delight of wonder decrease or even cease, your ark is set down in a low place because the divine showing comes to an end. And so, in this way, according to the quality and quantity of our wonder and exultation the ark now is turned in a circle, now is lifted up to the heights, and now is set down in a low place because according to the longing of a soul burning with desire, a showing is formed and the understanding is illumined in many ways.

Chapter XXVII

That in every contemplation of mutable things it is necessary to cling to consideration of divine wisdom

Now, it seems worthy to consider how suitably Moses adds something concerning the rings and poles immediately after he expounds by a mystical description the three kinds of contemplation that arise from visible things as has been shown above. For who does not know that so great a changing multiplicity and so great a manifold variety of this visible machine of the world are subject to such great confusion, since all things happen equally to the just and the wicked, the good and the evil, the clean and the unclean, those offering sacrificial victims and those condemning sacrifices; as the good person, so also the sinner; the liar and also the one who told the truth. What, I ask, does this order of things mean? Nay rather how great a confusion is it that all things happen to all persons equally; that by an equal allotment both good and evil happen to good persons, and evil and good happen to evil persons? For the fog of this confusion overclouds the sight of an inexperienced person so greatly that he doubts or thoroughly distrusts that God has a care for human things. Hence, in any case, who would deny that it is a fact that in ancient times people erected a shrine and consecrated an altar to Fortune? Certainly, if good things and evil things were perceived to strike only good persons and evil persons respectively, an inexperienced person would not deny that it happens rightly and justly. If good things happened only to good persons and evil things only to evil persons, they would perhaps labor less in assigning the reason for such a disposition. Perhaps it seems suitable to divine justice that except by many labors upright persons do not advance to eternal rewards. Now, however, when the common lot universally involves all, how much do you think human consideration fluctuates in so great an abyss of divine judgments? For if divine justice does not ignore so great a diversity of moral character, why, I ask, does it not regulate the differences in such diverse moral characters? If God foresees the end of all evil persons and has preordained certain persons to life, why is it, I ask, that He generously gives the gifts of wisdom and other spiritual charisms even to some reprobate persons and, having deprived many of His elect of the riches of these virtues, allows them to lie for a long time in vices? But if we tightly grasp the above-mentioned rings of divine wisdom with the hand of faith in every fluctuation of such a sort, we shall quickly raise ourselves to a firm condition of certitude. If we cling bravely to these rings, if we believe firmly that God not only knows all things and disposes all things but that He has foreknown and foreordained everything from eternity, then we will easily be able to foresee how He commends the skill of His wisdom in all these things—because in such a dark fog of so much confusion nothing is able to be hidden in the presence of the sight of His foreknowledge or knowledge; because at no time in so great a forest of so many disturbances does any obstacle of stumbling of any size whatever impede the course of His predestination and disposition; because in the midst of such a tortuous winding path of mutability He runs to the designated place by the narrow paths of equity and kindness without any turning aside in wandering.

BOOK III

Chapter I

Concerning the matter of the fourth contemplation and its particular nature

After we have said those things which seemed to need saying concerning the rings and poles, the order of exposition demands that we ought to say some things concerning the fourth kind of contemplation. This kind of contemplation, as we have already said above, is with respect to incorporeal and invisible essences, namely angelic spirits and human spirits. The material is surely worthy; knowledge of these things is quite worthy. For this is that noble— nay that most noble—creature created according to the image of God, exalted above all creatures, made for the highest good, and deserving to be blessed by the Creator of all goods Himself. The knowledge of all other creatures certainly looks at the knowledge of these from the lowest place, as it were, and however much it may increase, even though it may raise itself up very much, it cannot reach to the peak of this height. Pay attention to how rightly it is indicated by the propitiatory because it was not gilded at all but was solid gold, being made of only clean and purest gold. The propitiatory is commanded to be made of pure and clean gold; from it you will learn that in this consideration you ought to use an intellect that is subtle and pure. How does the imagination—the creator, moderator and restorer of corporeal phantasies—do this? The imagination, maker of so many phantasies—which continually creates so many new forms of corporeal things, restores ancient forms and skillfully disposes and orders many and varied modes as it wills—withdraws far from this activity. So abundant a multitude of its representations are of no advantage here; indeed, they are greatly at a disadvantage. Why do you rush yourself shamelessly to this work? Why do you force yourself with such rudeness into the workshop of this contemplation? Why are you in this workshop? What have you to do with pure understanding? You do not know how to work in gold; you have nothing in such a craft. You who always disturb the pure intellect do not know how to purify gold. Your gold has been mixed with dross; indeed, you have no abundance of gold at all. Our propitiatory ought to be made from the cleanest gold; there is nothing for you to offer; there is nothing at all for you to do for or in such an activity. In this work we have no need of your poor and undisciplined works. You have no gold; nor do you know the art of goldsmithing. Whatever it is other than gold that you prepare to offer, we have no need for it. Take what is yours and go. In this work we have no need for the hairs of she-goats, the skins of rams or even any pieces of wood whatsoever. Although you are very rich and even if you have these or something more than these, nevertheless, you cannot have gold, nor do you have anything by which you may assist the goldsmiths. The hairs of she-goats—the filth of concupiscences from the delight of foul flesh—when reconsidered often with careful examination, are able to assist persons being pricked by compunction in prayer. Examples of suffering—any skins of rams that have been made red with their own blood—are able to assist those afflicted with any tribulation. Workings of kindness—any trees of this sort, when cut down from the forest of the world and hewn according to the standard of justice—are able to be useful by the work of fruitful mercy to those assiduous in ministering. But the memory of every one of these and of any such things whatsoever can disturb rather than assist souls that are suspended in the watchtower of this contemplation. For the more perfectly we forget the phantasies of corporeal things, the more deeply and freely we examine the hidden things of super-mundane essences. Therefore he who strives eagerly to be making a propitiatory for himself should cleanse his gold and strive zealously to purify his intellect of every incursion of phantasies. Who would grant me to find a man of riches, a man fully learned, and finally such a man who lacks neither an abundance of gold nor the activity of the art for making the propitiatory by which the ark is covered? Who is that one who knows how to clean his gold from all dross, who knows how to purify his heart of every phantasy, as much as the dignity of the work demands or the authority of the instructor urges? Who is that one who knows how to enlarge such a work according to the manner defined by divine example and to restrict it to the established measurement? Who is that one who knows how to turn his heart only toward the view of supermundane manifestations while leaving behind in the lowest place thoughts of lowest things and also knows how to spread out on every side the rays of his understanding as much as the greatness of this speculation demands? Who, I say, is that one who discovers such an abundance of gold in his possession; who flourishes with such a lively understanding that he has sufficiently and at hand both material and method whereby he can extend his propitiatory to such a length and expand it to such a width that he can cover the whole ark; who reaches out to such an extent to the concord of celestial souls and the harmony of spiritual joys that he both presses down all earthly glory and all human prudence by means of despising and meanwhile conceals them from himself by means of forgetfulness? The best cleanser of gold is the skilled maker of the propitiatory who knows how to cling to celestial things with so much intention, seeking to taste only those things which are above so that he may not be mindful by longing nor turn by thought to any things of the lowest kinds. Clear reason does not permit it to be hidden, from one who views more carefully and understands more rightly, how much this kind of contemplation goes beyond the aforementioned three by the marvelous excellence of its worth.

CHAPTER II

How this kind of contemplation differs from the first and second, and how much it stands out

Do you wish to know how much the difference is between the first contemplation and this fourth one of which we speak? Discuss, if you are able, how much gold and wood differ from each other. For the first work is made out of wood; the fourth, out of gold. And the first species of consideration is represented by the first work;

the second, by the second work. By how much do we think that spirit and body differ from each other? If body and body differ from each other by so much, how much greater will be the difference between body and spirit? Compare, if you will, the sun with a rock, and you can easily observe what the difference is between highest and lowest bodies. Yet the difference between a body and any spirit whatever is believed to be much greater than the difference between any bodies whatever, however dissimilar. I think that there will also be a difference of knowledges according to the difference of essences. The instrument of each of the speculations can at least instruct you how great the difference is between these things that we bring together in turns. The first contemplation is supported by imagination; the fourth one, by reason. But how great do we think the difference is between imagination and reason, except that it is as great as that between lady and handmaid, between fame and disgrace, erudition and foolishness?

You have seen how much this kind of contemplation rises above the first; pay attention now to how much it differs from the second. Compare in turn the representation of both. Think what difference there is between the gilding of the ark and the gold of the propitiatory, namely between the second work and the fourth. Pay attention to the location and place of both. The former adheres to wood while the latter is placed over wood. The former rises up from below; the latter surely lies at the summit; yet both works are made out of gold. For in both of these speculations the rational principle of existing things is sought. But in the former the rational principle of visible things; in the latter, the dignity of invisible essences we either investigate thoroughly if hidden or marvel at if manifest. Therefore we ornament certain woods with the gleam of gold when we discuss the cause, mode and disposition of things according to the direction of reason. But that artful work of our propitiatory is rightly put over all woods, since when treading underfoot everywhere the incursion of phantasies of corporeal bodies, the soul is raised to high places by the force of this sublime investigation and is suspended in wonder at them. Certainly, there the gilding of our ark rises up little by little from below, and while it gradually advances toward the higher part, at some time it lays hold of the highest point of our ark. So no wonder that the soul itself, on account of knowledge of visible things and consideration of vain and mutable things, compels itself to flee the things that it marvels at less and escape from a kind of flood of an immense storm, as it were, into a breeze of true liberty, and when the peril has been escaped completely to tread underfoot all inferior things by means of despising, and to rest in true goods by means of longing. Nothing is more true, nothing more certain, assuredly and without any doubt whatsoever, than that the more carefully the mutability of earthly things is observed, the better and the more clearly it is understood that they must be fled from by means of fear and trod underfoot by means of despising. For although innumerable things ought to be marveled at in themselves on account of divine disposition, nevertheless these very same things ought to be despised on account of their mutability and fled from for our benefit. Why is it that the propitiatory is not joined directly to the pieces of wood but is separated by the interposition of the gilding except that on account of knowledge of mutable things and contemplation of mutability we are driven away from them? Therefore let each one of us pay attention to such a propitiatory and then return to himself. Behold our propitiatory: It rises above so that it may direct; it lies so that it may be quiet. Therefore ascend to a high heart, fix your longing in the height, and you will find a couch as delightful as it is tranquil.

CHAPTER III

Again: How it differs from and rises above the second

We can now show the particular and special difference between these contemplations if we are willing to turn our attention more carefully to the representation of them. It is necessary that the propitiatory, as the covering of the ark, have some density, while gilding often—nay always—seems to have no solidity, not to mention thickness. For what can I more rightly call gilding, other than a kind of deception of the exterior sense? When gilding is placed over that ark it falsely declares to external sight that it is solid gold. So without doubt gilding is that knowledge which flows into the deep places of some wise persons but deceives the eyes of carnally foolish persons much more than it illumines them. For what does knowledge of exterior things mean to you unless perhaps it leads you to knowledge of interior things? Yet your wisdom is foolishness in the presence of God. Of what benefit is it for you to have known all other things and not to know yourself and to be ignorant of your Creator? Why do you boast of the world so much, O philosopher? If it is necessary to glory, do not glory in yourself, but in the Lord (2 Cor. 10:17). Certainly if this foolish wisdom and untaught teaching of yours advanced you to knowledge of yourself or even to knowledge of God, it would make you not so much tumid as timid. If you are rightly wise, if you are truly wise, do not have conceited wisdom but have fear. "What do you have that you have not received?" (1 Cor. 4:7). You ought to glory in the one from whom you have received and glorify the one from whom you have received. "Why do you glory as if you have not received?" (1 Cor. 4:7). "If I want to glory, I will not be foolish, for I will speak the truth" (2 Cor. 12:6). You surely see that I have the name from the thing: I am called a philosopher, a lover of wisdom: "I have said to wisdom, you are my sister, and I have called prudence my friend." (Prov. 7:4). You are deceived, deceived, O philosopher; the appearance of things deceives you and concupiscence overturns your heart. This which you reckon as wisdom and call wisdom is foolishness in the presence of God. Therefore you say, what place does it have in the ark of wisdom, or why is such a work in need of such gilding? If it shines on the surface, if it has no solidity, why does it have any place in such a work? Hear, if you will, what is acceptable in our work and what is unacceptable to us in your work. Your ark does not have a covering; you do not know how to make a propitiatory. But content with gilding alone, you glory concerning the completion of the work you do, and you do not know how to continue the work. This is clearly worthy of mockery by all because you have begun to build and you have not been able to complete. Foolish and unwise, you do not know, or else you pretend not to know, that a vessel that does not have a cover ought according to divine command to be broken to pieces at the first opportunity. It is right that the vessel should be broken to pieces since always and everywhere it lies open for all sorts of impurities. O impure philosopher, you clean your vase externally, but internally it is full of all kinds of filth. Content with outward reputation alone, you show no zeal in purifying your conscience. Your ark shines outwardly; it is inwardly filthy inasmuch as it does not have a covering. Striver for outward reputation; neglector of conscience: Do you not pay attention to something because it was necessary to do this and not necessary to omit that? Let your ark shine outwardly and let it shine no less inwardly. Let it shine outwardly on account of this statement: "So let your light shine before men that they may see your good works" (Matt. 5:16). And no less let it also shine inwardly on account of this: "O blind Pharisee, first make clean the inside of the cup and the dish so that the outside may be made clean" (Matt. 23:26). Thus our ark has need of gilding, but it is not fitting for it to be content with gilding only. For without a covering it cannot maintain internal purity. Therefore strive according to the divine example to make the propitiatory; receive a cover of the sort that is suitable for the ark of wisdom. O unclean philosopher, if you wish to have an ark of wisdom clean within, if you crave to maintain purity of heart, ascend to this fourth stage of contemplation that is indicated by the propitiatory of the ark. We have already said above that this is that speculation that is concerned with invisible substances, namely human and even angelic spirits. Therefore the first thing in this consideration is that you should return to yourself, enter into your heart, and learn to estimate the worth of your spirit. Investigate what you are; what you have been; what you ought to be; what you are able to be—what you have been by nature; what you are now by sin; what you ought to be by activity; what you are yet able to be by grace. From your spirit learn to know how you ought to estimate the worth of other spirits. This is the gate. This is the ladder. This is the entrance. This is the ascent. By this we enter the innermost parts. By this we are raised up to the highest. This is the way to the summit of this speculation. This is the artful skill of making the propitiatory. This, without doubt, is the art by means of which purity of heart is recovered and, when recovered, is preserved. You certainly see how rightly we call this work the covering of the ark. By it we protect the purity of the innermost parts. Assuredly, if your ark with its gilding were under such a cover, namely a propitiatory of such sort; if your philosophy served such a philosophy it would also be acceptable to us. But our theologians know better than worldly philosophers how to use these things. Finally, hear what is acceptable to us in our work and what ought justly to be acceptable to you in the gilding of our ark. First: that it is placed upon wood; second: that it is placed underneath the propitiatory; third: that it is placed between the two. It is placed over wood so that it may stand out in relief and hide for you the concupiscence of the eyes, and you may have a covering for your eyes lest perchance your eyes may be uncovered and see vanity. It is placed underneath the propitiatory so that it may be lifted up to higher things and so that knowledge of lower things may serve higher things and sharpen by means of much exercise the eye of the mind for comprehending higher things. It is placed between the propitiatory and the wood so that it may separate them and stop the human soul from love of lower things lest perchance after being cast down from sublime things, drawn away by its own concupiscence from the place of pleasures and enticed after its own concupiscence, the soul should go and become a wanderer and a fugitive upon the earth.

CHAPTER IV

How it differs from and how much it rises above the third

We have just compared the fourth stage of contemplation with the first and second stages; now if it seems right, it should be compared with the third stage. We can probably do this better if we turn our attention to the representation of each of these. And so, turning attention to the representation of both, namely the golden propitiatory and the golden crown, I discover many differences between them. I pass over in silence the fact that the crown is fastened to wood, for the third stage of contemplation is supported by imagination, as has been shown above, while the fourth stage (the one about which we speak here) strives zealously to tread underfoot all imagination by the loftiness of its investigation. For this reason, according to the expression of similitude, our propitiatory ought neither to adhere to wood nor to be attached to wood. I also pass over the fact that the crown, which stands, rises up into the heights, while the propitiatory, which lies down, expands itself round about in greater amplitude because through pleasure in the sweetness of this contemplation and sweetness in the pleasure, the soul finds for the first time a place of great security and a solitary place of marvelous tranquillity for itself. Such unaccustomed and unexperienced delight gathers the longing of the heart to quiet and sets it in order for peace. Now, however, I direct your attention to the size of both, and in this respect I do not pass over the difference between them without careful consideration. For behold what I am unable to deny: They do not differ at all in the quality of the material, but there is much in every way in which they differ from each other in the quantity of the material. Each is made out of gold, because each is engaged in reasoning. But the small amount of gold from which the crown is made is exceedingly small if it is compared with the size of the propitiatory. In fact the measurement of the propitiatory in length as well as in width is defined with great care by divine teaching. Divine teaching is completely silent, however, concerning the size of the crown. No measurement of it is given, as if the divine word were to hint silently concerning the making of the crown, that he who is able to understand will understand and any person will make as much as he is able to make. I think that if its height could have extended itself up to a half cubit, the divine word would not have passed by this in complete silence. But the Lord who teaches a person knowledge knew His creation and could not completely conceal from him how much a lack of gold supports error in this human work and how the limitation of human mental sense constricts him in the watchtower of this contemplation. For now one abounds with the gold of wisdom in this place where he lacks every instrument with which these things ought to be understood—or if he possesses an instrument it is dull. What sort of instrument, I ask, will a person find in order to comprehend that peace which surpasses all sense? By which sense, I ask, does he comprehend what eye has not seen, nor ear heard, nor has arisen in the heart of man? (1 Cor. 2:9; Isa. 64:4). For when Paul, or a person similar to Paul, is raised up above himself and snatched up to the third heaven, certainly he does not investigate by his own spirit those hidden things about which no person is allowed to speak, but

God reveals them to him through His own Spirit. But whatever human understanding attains according to this mode by a sort of ecstasy of mind, the watchtower of the third consideration does not grasp it because of the immeasurable constriction of its limitation. In fact, whatever human experience sees when snatched away by means of ecstasy of mind pertains to another kind of contemplation and not to this kind. Therefore, why marvel if the limitation of its knowledge constricts the human mind especially in that consideration where the mind labors with great helplessness of sense with respect to those things which ought to be investigated? For whatever it gathers by means of thinking or discovers by means of the similitude of visible things concerning knowledge of invisible things, this is found to be almost nothing in comparison with truth. Why is it that no measure at all is prescribed for the crown, while a measure is portrayed so carefully in the description of the propitiatory? I think that it is clearly meant to be understood from this why there should be so much lack of gold in this present work.

CHAPTER V

How strongly the mind is able to pursue this contemplation and how it advances to it by much consideration and knowledge of itself

He who seeks to abound in the gold of wisdom ought to pursue this fourth contemplation according to his strength and to exert himself vigorously in constructing the propitiatory. For a work of this sort is very pleasing in every way, and in this work every person offers of his own accord almost always more than is necessary—not to say as much as suffices. An abundance of gold will never be lacking for the one who pursues this work vigorously. If you seek a reason, accept a reason. When you begin to pursue spiritual contemplations and to rise up through consideration of your spirit to contemplation of spirits and to make spiritual things from spiritual things in this way, you also begin in a like manner to be spiritual. In this contemplation you will undoubtedly complete what you began to be in the preceding contemplation, namely spiritual. Do you know sufficiently that the spiritual person judges all things, of what sort this knowledge will be, and how great will be the abundance of this gold that is able to judge all things? Do you still wish it to be shown openly to you from what source you can provide this abundance of gold for yourself? Does it go beyond comprehension that the kingdom of God is within us? Behold, you say, the kingdom of heaven is within us but is gold within us in a similar way? Why not, I say. So! Have you forgotten that the kingdom of heaven is like a treasure hidden in a field? Behold, from what source an abundance of gold abounds abundantly to you. You have it at hand. Dig it up, if you will. Go quickly, sell what you have, purchase this field, and seek the hidden treasure. Whatever in the world you crave, whatever in the world you hesitate to part with, expend it freely for freedom of the heart. After purchasing the field, dig in the depths of it, exulting no doubt like persons who dig up a treasure and rejoice greatly when they have discovered a sepulcher. It is necessary to seek this treasure in the depths because wisdom is drawn from a hidden place.

But wretched me; from what source does gold come to me for the gilding, the crown, and the propitiatory? I do not have silver and gold, and from what and how can these things be made? By what art, I ask, can I procure this gold for myself? I am not able to dig; I blush to beg. I know what I shall do. I shall go quickly to my Father, the Father of mercies from whom comes every good gift and every perfect gift, because He who gives copiously to everyone and does not reproach them is rich toward all. And so I pour out my prayer in His presence; I announce before Him my poverty and lack of gold; and I shall say to Him: Lord, you know my lack of wisdom; my property is like as nothing before you; give me understanding, Lord, and I have gold and am rich. Since I am weak, guard my soul and I shall have a propitiatory of the sort I crave. O how great an abundance of gold existed for him who was able to sing in truth: "I have understood more than all who teach me. I have understood more than the elders because I have sought your commandments" (Ps. 118:99–100). O what kind of propitiatory he had who sang confidently before the Lord: "You have protected me from the assembly of the wicked, from the multitude of those working iniquity" (Ps. 63:3). Late but at last Paul made a propitiatory for himself when he declared openly, "I am aware of nothing against myself" (1 Cor. 4:4). Without great counsel he would not have known how to cleanse the ark of his conscience and without a golden propitiatory he would not have been able to keep clean the secret places of the heart. But up to this time, when he had been persecuting the Church of God, I think that he did not have a propitiatory. However, since he did this unknowingly and did not have the gold from which he might make himself a propitiatory it was reckoned to him for an indulgence. In what way was he able to make the propitiatory when he saw nothing with open eyes? But after he received the light of his eyes (Acts 9:17–18) he became a man who sees his poverty and henceforth takes more attentive care of himself; and he returned into himself and learned by experience that the kingdom of heaven is undoubtedly within us. For after finding the treasure hidden in a field he was enriched very much; and after being made famous he began to possess much property, beyond measure, more than thousands of pieces of gold and silver. Finally listen to someone glorying not so much about the gold as about the treasure: "However, we have this treasure in earthen vessels" (2 Cor. 4:7). O man of riches; O man truly made famous! Was not that man who spoke of wisdom among the perfect the richest among all the Easterners? But what are we to say concerning that person who not lately like Paul but from the beginning of life has made for himself a propitiatory by which he also has preserved the purity of his heart? For this reason he also said: "For my heart does not reproach me with regard to all my days" (Job 27:6). Finally if you also desire to fulfill the Lord's command, guard your heart with all care and you have begun to make the sort of propitiatory the Lord requires from you. Learn by an example what it is advantageous to do; hear how David points himself out to you as an example: "I was meditating in the night with my heart; I was busily engaged and I searched my spirit" (Ps. 76:7). He was meditating with his heart; you also meditate with your heart. He searched his own spirit; you also search your own spirit. Occupy yourself with the field; pay attention to yourself. While pursuing this exercise you will undoubtedly discover the treasure hidden in a field.

CHAPTER VI

*How from speculation of one's self an understanding of spiritual things is
secured or is restored after being lost*

On account of this exercise the abundance of gold increases,
knowledge is multiplied, and wisdom is increased. On account of
this exercise the eye of the heart is cleansed, natural capacity is
sharpened, and understanding is enlarged. He who does not know
himself cannot rightly estimate the value of anything. He who does
not consider the worth of his original condition does not know how
all earthly pride should lie under his feet. He who does not first
reflect upon his spirit knows nothing; he does not know what he
ought to think concerning the angelic spirit or the divine Spirit. If
you are not able to enter into yourself, how will you be capable of
examining those things which are within or above you? If you are
not worthy to enter into the first tabernacle, with what impudence
do you dare to enter into the second tabernacle, that is, into the
Holy of Holies? If you are not able to struggle along the high paths
so that with the Lord Jesus or at least with Moses you can ascend
into a high mountain, with what impudence do you come forth to
fly to the heavens? First return to yourself; then you may dare to
examine those things which are above you. First the sun illumines
the boundaries of its rising, then it mounts up to higher places. For
this reason, it is said by Solomon: "The sun rises and sets, and it
returns to its place, where rising again it wheels round to the south,
and is turned to the north" (Eccles. 1:5–6). Therefore the sun
returns to its place so that it may rise again there; and rising again
little by little from that place, it raises itself up to higher places so
that later it touches the peak of heaven. "The sun rises and sets, and
it returns to its place" (Eccles. 1:5). The sun rises when understanding of truth is inspired in the heart. The sun sets when the ray of
understanding is withdrawn. But after setting, the sun returns to its
place in order that it may rise again. The very place of this sort of
sun is the soul. Understanding is born from the soul itself when it is
visited by divine grace. What does it mean that the sun returns to
its place except that the sight of the mind turns back to consideration of itself? Therefore, after setting, the sun returns to its place

because by the withdrawal of grace, the eye of the mind is caused to rebound to the consideration of its defects. When divine grace withdraws itself for the moment, a man is compelled to learn that he is nothing and that he is able to do nothing by himself. But the sun rises again after returning to its place because by consideration of his own weakness, lost understanding is restored.

CHAPTER VII

How understanding that has been received from speculation of one's self is enlarged to all things

In its place the sun, rising again little by little, ascends to higher places since by knowledge of himself a man rises up into contemplation of heavenly things. But when he is led all the way to the highest point, there he gladly remains since he is refreshed there by a marvelous delight of supercelestial manifestations. Zealously the sun contrives delays in this place where it bends its course into a circle. On that account it wheels round to the south, but it is not carried there by means of desire, but rather it is turned to the north. (Cf. Eccles. 1:6.) The southern region is very pleasant from the excess of light and the heat of the day because it is a very delightful and delectable sight to contemplate the orders of blessed spirits making merry in the splendor and charity of God. Undoubtedly the region of the north has nothing of such a sort, for it has been given over to perpetual darkness and condemned to continual cold because the hearts of the reprobates—being cold by malice and blind by ignorance—are deservedly tormented in such regions. Therefore the sun does not pass completely to that place but is only turned around, for I think it is not drawn by any longing to such an unlovable region. Nevertheless, it is turned so that it may look, as if from afar, at those things that are there and may know with what precaution it ought to seek to escape those evil things. In the east we receive knowledge of our moral character and the discretion between virtues and vices. In the south we contemplate the rewards of good merits, the joys of supernal citizens, and the secret things of divine mysteries. In the west we come to know the retributions of evil merits and the end of evil spirits and reprobate men. Do you see how much the full knowledge of himself can do for a man? For indeed, from this he advances to knowledge of everything celestial, terrestrial and infernal.

CHAPTER VIII

Concerning the triple sense by means of which consideration of self is able to run here and there

Therefore if you desire to fly up to the second or even the third heaven, you must pass through the first. For indeed, the spirit examines everything thoroughly, even the depths of God (1 Cor. 2:10). Therefore if you prepare to examine thoroughly the depths of God, examine first of all the depths of your own spirit. For indeed, the heart of man is deep—nay, rather it is perverse and inscrutable (Jer. 17:9). Inscrutable, yes, except perhaps to one who is spiritual. For the spiritual person judges all things and is judged himself by no one because only spiritual persons have been found worthy to see the works of God and his marvelous things in the depths. Certainly in the depths you will find many things worthily awesome and wonderful; there it is possible to find another kind of orb, wide and full indeed, another kind of fullness from the orb of the earth. There the spiritual person has his own kind of earth; there he has his own heaven; not just one but a second after the first and a third after the first and second. And in order to separate this triple heaven by a suitable distinction let the first be called the imaginative, the second the rational and the third the intellectual. And so imagination takes a place in the first heaven, reason in the second, and understanding in the third. And of these, the first is gross and fleshly in comparison with the others, and in its own certain way it is touchable and corporeal since it is imaginary and phantastical, drawing after itself and retaining in itself forms and similitudes of corporeal things. But the remaining two are very subtle by comparison with something wholly corporeal and are very far from the denseness of that. So surely, without any doubt, it is evident that this exterior heaven that we call the firmament is visible and corporeal; and indeed, it is itself the first and lowest of all the heavens. What the earth is to this visible heaven, so bodily sense is to that internal, phantastical and imaginative heaven. For just as this visible heaven contains within the expanse of its vault the multitude of everything earth bears and nourishes, so imagination encloses within its bosom the similitudes of everything the senses touch and the faculty of desire brings to mind. And so similitudes and images of all visible things are contained in the first heaven. Meanwhile the rational principles, definitions and investigations of all things visible and invisible pertain to the second heaven. However, contemplations and understandings of spiritual things themselves and also divine things pertain to the third heaven.

CHAPTER IX

Concerning the intellectual sense by which alone invisible things are able to be seen

The eye of the understanding is that sense with which we see invisible things—not as with the eye of reason with which we seek and find hidden and absent things by means of investigation or as we often understand causes by effects or effects by causes, and now one set, now another set of things by every possible mode of reasoning. But just as we are accustomed to see corporeal things visibly, presently and corporeally by means of bodily sense, so the intellectual sense grasps invisible things invisibly, to be sure, but presently and essentially. However, this intellectual eye has before it a great spread-out veil that has been darkened on account of the delight of sin and intertwined with the changing multiplicity of so many fleshly desires. This keeps the sight of the contemplative from the secrets of divine mysteries, except insofar as divine esteem has admitted anyone for his own benefit or the benefit of another. The Prophet, who said to the Lord "Unveil my eyes," bears witness to this (Ps. 118:18). Certainly he who asks that they be unveiled by the Lord shows that he has veiled eyes. Nevertheless by means of this very eye, the soul sees those things which are on this side of the veil, that is the invisible things of itself, namely those things which are in itself. Yet it does not see all things because not all things are on this side of the veil. Also, by means of the eye with which it sees certain things of itself, it is not able to see itself, i.e., the essence of the soul itself. But there is doubt whether we are going to see those things which we have shown are beyond the veil by this same eye of the understanding or if there is one sense that we use in order to see invisible divine things and in the same way we use other senses in order to see the invisible things of ourselves. But those who assert that one sense has a sight of higher things and another has a sight of lower things should look from whence this can be proved. I believe that it is here that they completely confuse the signification of this word "understanding." For they restrict its signification, now concerning only the superior, now only the inferior speculation, and at another time they comprehend both senses under one signification of the word. Notwithstanding, are we to call this twin sight of superior and inferior things "twin" in the sense of "from one head," or are we to call it "twofold"? Instrument of the same sense, or twin effect of the same instrument: Whichever of these we wish to choose, nothing prevents us from saying that both of these pertain to the intellectual heaven. Why, is this heaven not said to have two great lights? Just as it is necessary to believe concerning other heavens, so it is that the more sublime and subtle speculation is the greater light in this highest heaven, and the lower and more obscure speculation is the lesser light.

CHAPTER X

Concerning the intellectual watchtower and its superior height

This ultimate and highest heaven has its day. Without doubt it also has its night, and as long as we are in this life, if we direct our attention to this heaven what other than night do we have or are we able to have until night completes its course again, and the light of dawn, casting a reddish glow, drives away the darkness of night? Nevertheless, this night will be illumined like day because any day of this lowest heaven is surpassed by the brilliance of this night. Indeed, God placed the moon and stars in the power of the night and for that reason this night is my illumination in my delights. For it has its moon, that lesser light which we have indicated above, and it has stars, which expand their light everywhere and are assuredly the multiform modes of divine showings. But those who sleep, sleep at night. They cannot see the lights of this heaven nor sing with the Prophet before the Lord: "Because I shall see your heavens, the work of your fingers, the moon and stars which you have created" (Ps. 8:4). Likewise they cannot sing: "In the middle of the night I will rise up to praise you" (Ps. 118:62). What am I to say concerning such a man, since in vain he expects day and sees neither it nor the light of the rising dawn? Certainly those who are such "are taken away like wax that runs down; the fire has fallen upon them and they have not seen the sun" (Ps. 57:9). Happy are those who venture to sing confidently concerning the morning of this day: "In the morning I shall stand before you and see, for you are not a God who wills iniquity" (Ps. 5:5). I think that he signified the middle of the day who said concerning his beloved: "Show me where you, whom my soul loves, pasture, where you lie down in the middle of the day" (Cant. 1:6). I think that he wanted to signify the morning of this day and that he was warmed for a long time by desire for it, who said: "I hoped until the morning" (Isa. 38:13). Who among you rejoiced greatly that he might see this day, and then saw it and was happy? Certainly that one is great, whoever he is. Nevertheless, I believe that no one can reach the mid-point of this day, at least in this corruptible flesh, although I dare not deny this concerning the morning. Surely whoever among you can come to the brightness of this day when the sun has risen in heaven will see the truth of the judgment that the light seems softer and the sun more delightful to the eye. The sun of this day has its rising; but it knows no setting, just as the day itself does not have an evening although it begins from dawn. He knew that heaven of heavens for one day only. But one day in its courts is better than a thousand days in a lower heaven. For surely the second heaven has many days and also innumerable nights, according to which its sun rises and sets and returns to its place. So the first heaven received a moon in time, and its sun knew its own setting. But the sun and moon of the highest heaven remained in their dwelling place. For when the lights of this heaven have come to the summit they fix their course, and in the future they are never ever inclined to set. If entirely and without doubt the kingdom of heaven is within us, if it can be found within us, where, I ask, other than in this highest of heavens, is it sought more rightly, found more quickly and possessed more securely? I think that all the regions of that kingdom abound in gold because the kingdom of heaven is like a treasure hidden in a field. For if you seek and love the gold of knowledge and the treasure of wisdom where, I ask, will you be able to find more abundant riches than in this highest of heavens? Where, I beg you, will the brightness of the highest wisdom be able to shine forth better for you, other than in the express image of that One and in His most excellent work, namely in the creation, restoration and glorification of the soul? Surely from this watchtower, from a nearby point as it were, he is able and is accustomed to see what that loftiness of the angelic spirit is, what that supereminent magnitude of the divine Spirit is. In no place is it seen more nearly, is it discerned more clearly, than from the summit of this lofty seat which is that highest and sempiternal beatitude of supernal citizens. In no place other than from this most excellent of the heavens does that spirit who examines thoroughly all things, even the depths of God, contemplate more serenely those invisible things of God which are perceived by the intellect through those things which have been made. Nowhere in all His works, other than in the creation, restoration and glorification of the soul, does His power appear more sublime, His wisdom more marvelous, His mercy more delightful. I think you surely see from whence comes to you that abundance of gold that I promised to you earlier; namely how from much consideration and knowledge of your spirit you will be raised up to the knowledge and contemplation of the angelic spirit and the divine Spirit.

Chapter XI

The triple distinction of the fourth speculation

But, since we already know through exposition from whence we abound with gold for such and so great a work, let us see what the Lord commands concerning the length and width of our propitiatory and why he is completely silent concerning its height. If we reflect on the nature of things, we shall be able to learn with regard to bodies themselves how we ought to proceed with an investigation into spiritual contemplations. We see in exterior things that every bodily thickness begins with length, increases with width, and ends with height. And so, the length of the propitiatory, if I am not mistaken, indicates those things which are in spiritual nature at the beginning; the width indicates those things which are for advancement; and the height indicates those things which seem to be for consummation. According to these three things we have mentioned we make a triple distinction of divine gifts in spiritual essences. First, the spiritual nature is created in order that it may exist. Second, it is made just so that it is good. Third, it is glorified so that it is blessed. And so by creation it starts toward good; by being made just it is enlarged in good; by glorification it is consummated in good. The goods of creation are for the beginning; the goods of justification are for advancement; the goods of glorification are for consummation. The first goods are gifts of the Creator; the second goods are both gifts of the Creator and merits of the creature; the third goods are gifts of the Creator and rewards of the creature, the consummation of gifts and the recompense of merits. And so, the first goods pertain to the length; the second, to the width; the last to the height. For in the first, as has been said, the rational creature starts toward the perfection of future fullness. On account of the second, it makes progress, increases and is enlarged. In the last it is raised to glory and is consummated in glory.

CHAPTER XII

Concerning the subdivision of the first stage of this contemplation

Therefore first let us see concerning the length of our propitiatory, which we are commanded to extend to two and one-half cubits. As often as we consider in the heart, investigate carefully, distinguish suitably and discuss sufficiently those spiritual goods of our creation which we have designated above, so often do we draw out the work of our propitiatory in length and extend it to a certain measure. And so in this drawing out of the construction of the propitiatory a threefold distinction of divine gifts suggests itself to us, concerning which alone, or most of all, the frequent and careful reexamination of our consideration ought to be engaged. From the very condition of its creation it is natural for every rational creature to exist, to know and to will. Think how necessary, how just, and how fitting it is for divine goodness to give discretion of good and evil to so worthy a creature and so excellent a nature, and at the same time to allow freedom of will so that its good might be both received and willed, both a gift and freely done. As long as you exert yourself in such a discussion, you labor in drawing out your propitiatory. Examine carefully, contemplate, and wonder at freedom of the will, discretion of judgment and sublimity of essence: With this you make your propitiatory according to the harmony of order and you draw out the due measure of quantity in length. I would be surprised if by yourself you did not pay attention to how useful or how necessary continual consideration of all these things is. For from this the mind is illumined, inflamed and confirmed in the good.

CHAPTER XIII

How in the first stage of this contemplation the mind ought to exercise itself, and how much such exercise is effective

Therefore, think about continually, consider earnestly, investigate carefully the will—not only your own, but also that of another, whether good or evil. Know your own will, so that you may know what to correct, and also for what you ought to give thanks. Also, think about the souls of the perfect, and even of the perverse; the souls of good spirits and of malignant spirits, so that from the consideration of opposites there may shine forth what it is expedient to imitate and what to avoid. Pay attention to what you know; pay attention to how much you do not know. Come to know how much you are set above brute spirits according to natural ability; come to know how much you are below angelic spirits according to intellect. If you pay attention to how much you surpass a brute spirit by means of mental sense you will sing heartily, "I will bless the Lord who gave me understanding" (Ps. 15:7). If you think about angelic understanding you will surely declare: "God, you know my lack of wisdom" (Ps. 68:6). Therefore it is very beneficial and necessary for me to examine my ignorance in order that I may know what I lack and may say with the blessed Job: "If I have not known anything, my ignorance is my own" (Job 19:4). But, as often as I direct attention into myself, how or how often has He shown me uncertain and hidden things of His wisdom? Surely my soul magnifies the Lord who teaches us more than the knowledge possessed by birds and draft-cattle because it is He who illumines all men who come into this world. (Cf. John 1:9.) You see how great the benefit of this twin consideration is: namely to direct attention to the affection of the rational will and also to the sense of reason. But what should I say concerning the third of the designated considerations: Do we contemplate in wondering and marvel in contemplating the essence of the soul, the nature of the essence and the excellence of the nature? I think one's own experience can easily teach each one how much this speculation is able to encourage the soul against vices and to stir it up toward good. Come to know your worth, O man, I beseech you; think about the excellent nature of your soul, how God made her according to His image and similitude, how He elevated her above every corporeal creature, and immediately you will begin to marvel how a famous virgin daughter of Zion has been expelled from heaven to earth, and in like manner you will begin to cry out to the Lord: "What do I have in heaven and what have I wished for upon the earth besides you?" (Ps. 72:25). What is marvelous, I ask you, if in remembrance of my original condition, if because of the glance of my soul, the disorder of my external appearance overwhelmed me suddenly and without delay? For who does not feel shame to have given over the mistress of the world, the citizen of heaven, the beloved of God, to servitude to the body; to have prostituted her to unclean spirits; to have held her for a long time under the yoke of servitude in order to take care of the flesh in its longings? Surely anyone will marvel, when he comes to know his soul, when he directs his attention correctly to what the soul is or ought to be. I say, he will marvel from what and to what she has been expelled: How a mistress of nations has been made a widow; how a princess of provinces has been placed under tribute. I think that he wished to recall us to this consideration who said: "How is it, Israel, that you are in the land of enemies; you grow old in an alien land; you have been wholly defiled with dead persons; you have been counted with those who are in hell" (Bar. 3:11). And so, in this triple consideration we ought, as we have already said, to bring to completion the length of our propitiatory.

CHAPTER XIV

The designation of those things which cannot be comprehended in this stage of speculation

Now in the first and second consideration you can extend your knowledge as far as a cubit, but in the third you cannot do this at all. For where you have an instrument apt for that which one ought to know, there you undoubtedly possess a cubit of extraordinary certitude, as it were, because you are able to grasp by experience an idea of the thing being known. For your knowledge increases to a full cubit, as it were, when you reach firmness of certitude by means of experience. But for whom I ask, has not his own experience taught what it is to will or to know? Does not each one gather this, as often as he wills in his own heart? Do you not know how limitless are the things you will; how limitless, those you do not will; how innumerable, those you know; how innumerable, those you do not know? But how do you see your will, how do you come to know your thought? In like manner, how are you able to see or know the substance of your soul? Who, I say, in this present fleshly condition now sees or even has been able to see his soul or any spiritual substance whatsoever in its purity? Undoubtedly, in this respect the human intellect has been blind from birth and must of necessity cry daily to the Lord: "Illumine my eyes" (Ps. 12:4). Surely, if anyone in this corruptible flesh has been able to see what things of this sort are, he has been led above himself by ecstasy of mind. In that which he sees he passes beyond the limits of the human intellect, not by his own activity but on account of a divine showing. But whatever human experience has been able to reach in this way, it is undoubtedly evident that it does not pertain to this kind of contemplation but to another kind. Therefore, however much you exercise your natural ability in this consideration, however much you continue your effort without interruption, however much you enlarge your sense in this respect, you will not be able to extend your knowledge to a full cubit.

Chapter XV

That we ought not to neglect those things which we comprehend only in part

Nevertheless, there are many things—and they ought not to be despised in the least—concerning the particular nature of spiritual essence that we are able either to gather from the authority of divine Scripture or to prove by the testimony of reason. Therefore let us strive to know in whatever way and as much as we are able, although we cannot extend it as far as a cubit by experience. Modest it is, but there is much that can be known in this consideration. Certainly, it is modest with regard to fullness, but much in every way with regard to benefit. Therefore, do not neglect what you can know concerning this cubit, even though you cannot complete it at all. That I may not be silent about the rest of the things that seem to pertain to this speculation, how much loss do we think you incur if you are ignorant concerning the immortality of the soul and do not believe it at all? For if it were not established concerning the immortality of the soul, who, I ask, would prepare himself for future retribution? Who, I beg you, would restrain his life so that he would not go after his passionate cravings? Who would make satisfaction for evils that have been committed? Who would gird himself for brave works? Who would have patience in the midst of so much bitterness of divine lashings if he utterly despaired of a future life? Everything that is affirmed concerning the redemption of the human race, everything that is believed concerning the divine sacraments, whatever is taught concerning divine instructions, whatever is hoped for concerning divine promises, is utterly destroyed if there is no hope for perpetual life for the soul. If we are persons who have hope in Christ in this life only, we are the most miserable of all people. See, we have left everything behind and have followed after Him. What, therefore, will we have if the dead do not rise again? Why do we die the whole day long on account of Him if no crown of justice is to be hoped for from Him, if the death of human beings and beasts is completely the same, and likewise the original condition of both? What advantage will it be for me if I do a great work of wisdom and justice? Do not they who eat and drink and pass their days in the good life and who feast ostentatiously daily do much better than those who are dying the whole day? Will it not be much better to go to the house of entertainment than to the house of mourning if after this life a person has no more than a beast has? (cf. Eccles. 7:3). If the dead do not rise again, why should I not rush and overflow with delights and enjoy the good things that exist? Why should we not willingly hear that voice which is saying: "Let us eat and drink, for tomorrow we die"? (1 Cor. 15:32; cf. Wisd. 2:6; Isa. 22:13, 56:12). You certainly see how many evils would follow if there were doubt concerning the immortality of the soul. We ought not to disdain in the least what we are able to accomplish with respect to this cubit, although we do not suffice for its completion. Therefore, the work of our propitiatory is begun with this triple consideration of essence (spiritual, that is) and of its discretion and will, and our work is drawn out to a definite measure. He who has exercised his soul fully in speculation of these things has finished the length of his propitiatory. Now that we have said these things concerning the length of the propitiatory, we now turn the hand of investigation to its width.

CHAPTER XVI

Concerning the subdivision of the second stage of contemplation

As we have said, those things which are at the beginning pertain to the width. However, justification enlarges our good that begins with the work of creation and on account of this shows that it pertains to the width. Yet without two things this, work cannot be consummated. For it is never accomplished if the Creator does not cooperate with His creature. Indeed, if He willed, the Creator could complete everything by Himself without the work of the creature, just as when He willed, He was able to create so many and such great things from nothing. If we presume to push forward with our own strength without His aid, we labor in vain. He bears witness to this who says in His Gospel: "Without me you can do nothing" (John 15:5), because it is He "who works in us to will and to accomplish according to a good will" (Phil. 2:13). For it is "not of the one willing nor of the one running, but it is of God who shows mercy" (Rom. 9:16). For without Him, what will I be able to do by myself, who cannot even say "Jesus is Lord" except in the Holy Spirit (1 Cor. 12:3)? Certainly it is He who works all things in all persons, apportioning to each one as He wills (1 Cor. 12:11). Nevertheless, in the work of our justification voluntary consent is required by Him who says: "If you are willing and listen to me, you shall eat the good things of the land" (Isa. 1:19). He ascribes free will to persons when this work is hindered, where it is said: "If my people had listened to me, if Israel had walked in my ways, I would perhaps have humiliated their enemies for nothing and laid my hand upon those troubling them" (Ps. 80:14–15). If we do nothing at all in such a work, we appeal in vain for His aid, and falsely call Him helper. For it is one thing to do; it is another to give aid. For what does it mean to give aid except to cooperate with one who is working? That one understood that he had His aid and cooperation with regard to good who said, "Lord you are my helper and my deliverer; do not delay" (Ps. 69:6). We seek His aid daily when we cry out to Him in daily prayers: "Help us, O God our salvation" (Ps. 78:9). Therefore it is obvious that this work in which the Creator cooperates with His creature is accomplished by two. In this work, there is need for one's own activity and for divine grace. For anyone depends in vain upon free will unless he is supported by divine assistance. Our justification is accomplished by our own deliberation and divine inspiration. For to will only just things is already to be just. Indeed we are rightly said to be just or unjust from the will alone although we are judged in both cases from what we do. God cooperates with us in two modes, namely inwardly and outwardly: inwardly by secret aspiration; outwardly by the open aid of His works. But that cooperation which is exterior has nothing to do with this kind of contemplation, since our propitiatory must be made of pure gold, and this speculation ought to subsist in pure understanding. And so our own deliberation and divine inspiration are the two things by which the width of our propitiatory is brought to completion.

Chapter XVII

That, similarly, there are some things in the second stage of this contemplation that cannot be comprehended

We learn by daily use what this deliberation is and after so much experience we cannot hesitate concerning certitude of it. For this reason we are able to extend our knowledge in this respect as far as a full cubit. But I ask, who in this life, at least, suffices to comprehend in what manner divine grace is accustomed to visit the heart and by its inspiration to incline everything to its will? However much we labor in this consideration we do not extend our work in this respect to a full cubit. For how can human understanding comprehend the manner of divine inspiration since in His Gospel the Lord reminds us of the incomprehensibility of the same thing: "The Spirit blows where it wills and you hear its voice, and you do not know whence it comes or whither it goes" (John 3:8). And so we are taught by the authority of Scripture about the assistance of divine grace, a thing we prove by the daily failure due to our infirmity and the clear effect of the cooperation of grace. Indeed with regard to this, His grace is often withdrawn from us so that human infirmity may be taught by its own failure how it cannot do anything good by itself. Again with regard to this, the same grace that earlier had been removed is restored again so that by its effect we may experience what we are as the result of a gift from God. Why is it that in one and the same thing now we are able, now we are not able, except that now we have helping grace, now we do not have it? And so it is clear that we are allowed to doubt very little concerning the assistance of divine grace, although we are able to comprehend very little about the modes of its cooperation. We are not able to complete a cubit in the work of this consideration of ours because we do not extend our natural ability as far as the limit of comprehension in the width of this investigation. The reason is clear why the width of our propitiatory cannot extend itself as far as two cubits and why, according to the divine example, it properly has one and one-half cubits. Therefore if you exercise your soul to the fullest in this twofold consideration, you complete the width of your propitiatoɪ y according to a suitable manner.

CHAPTER XVIII

Concerning the first and second distinctions of this contemplation and the difference between them

Let no one think that the consideration of will that we proposed above is the same as this consideration of deliberation we now have assigned to the width. To the former pertains that which is done in the mind from the operation of nature only; to the latter, that which is done frequently in the mind from the work of activity. To the former pertains any power of the soul implanted in it naturally; to the latter, any virtue of the soul joined with it by activity. Finally, to the former pertains any motion of the soul that is moved by some natural force; to the latter, any motion of the soul that is produced by some guidance of rational disposition. We are accustomed to call "will" that power of the soul which is able and accustomed to form itself into so many affections and to change in manifold ways through the soul. I say, we are accustomed to call this power of the soul "will." In a similar way, if I may say so, we call the motion and the act of such an instrument "will," and we say that the will itself wills. We call "will" not only the act of willing that which is brought about by natural motion only but also that act of willing which any consent of the soul accompanies on account of deliberation. But in any case the lack of words compels us at one time to extend the signification of words, at another to restrict it, and to vary it suitably under the pressure of necessity. But in order that we may sufficiently distinguish what we ought to ascribe to this consideration, it seems that every consent of the soul and everything that is done in the soul from consent pertains to this consideration. In a similar manner, any sense or motion whatsoever of the soul that is done against consent or beyond consent is ascribed rightly to consideration of the length. For, as has already been said above, the goods of creation ought to be assigned to the length of our propitiatory while the goods of justification ought to be ascribed to its width. And we know that everything in the soul that is beyond consent is certainly not able to make a person just. And so to the first consideration pertains careful direction of our attention to those goods which the mind may naturally possess in abundance or be in want of. But to the second pertains knowledge of which goods the mind may already possess on account of virtue and which it may not yet be capable of possessing. It is easy, I think, to see or to have known how it is necessary or beneficial to possess both of these considerations intimately and to draw them into contemplation frequently. For from the first consideration a person discerns to which goods he is naturally more inclined, to which evils he is more liable; which endeavors he ought to pursue more vigorously, which evils he ought to guard against more earnestly; by which exercises he is able better to advance, by which vices he can more easily be corrupted. However, from the second consideration one discerns to which sins he is subject or by which merits he stands out, and what punishment or reward he is to expect for these; how much he advances or falls behind each day; with how much activity of soul he is to busy himself in order to blot out past evils, avoid present ones, and prevent future ones; with how much constancy of soul he is to strive in order to recover lost goods and keep or increase goods in his possession. What a pleasing, what a suitable, and how delightful a manifestation to draw into speculation according to the first consideration so many qualities of the soul, so many of its thoughts, and so many of its affections, and to suspend the soul in wonder at them. O how marvelous a speculation! O how amazing a pleasure of delight to have before the eyes according to the second consideration so many virtues of the soul, so many of its exercises, so many of its efforts and merits, and to cling for a long time in contemplation of that sort.

CHAPTER XIX

That the things pertaining to the third distinction can be comprehended by none of our senses

But now it surely seems worthy to consider why he who has carefully described the length as well as the width has been completely silent concerning the height of our propitiatory. It has been shown above that those things which are for glorification undoubtedly pertain to this third consideration, just as those things which are for justification pertain to the width of the propitiatory. But what human sense is able to grasp the mode of our glorification? What reason is able to comprehend it? Who has seen the witness of such evidence in another or has deserved to be undergoing the experience of this thing in himself? Surely in this life a man neither has sufficient proof of this thing nor is capable of understanding any experience of it. Rightly, therefore, no measure for the altitude of the aforementioned work is commanded since the manner of our glorification, as has been said, can be comprehended by no sense of ours. And, indeed, the propitiatory is believed to have some thickness, but this is not reckoned in comparison to the dimension of the others. So in any case we hold by the witness of faith to the certitude of our glorification although we are not yet able to grasp by means of the understanding the mode of its quality or its extent. But human eagerness reckons for very little or almost for nothing everything that it cannot test by means of experience. However we know that after a full cleansing of conscience, after much practice of justice, the human mind at long last begins at some time to hope for that which earlier it had scarcely been able to believe in. In this way the measure of our propitiatory rises in height and grows in solidity. I believe that it pertains to the solidity of this propitiatory when the mind begins to glory in the Lord and give no small thanks for good testimony of conscience, so much so that it truly dares to make confession, since "our glory is this: the testimony of conscience" (2 Cor. 1:12). But if you want your propitiatory to increase in height and to receive a suitable solidity in the proportion that it is capable of becoming in this life, you must never cease, never be inactive until, as I have said, you possess some betrothal gifts of that future fullness, and receive the first fruits, however small, of eternal happiness, and begin to have a foretaste of the sweetness of divine pleasantness. Surely he wished to animate us to a longing for this who said: "Taste and see that the Lord is sweet" (Ps. 33:9). Therefore we believe that your propitiatory already has something of thickness if you have already tasted that the Lord is sweet. But however much you grow with respect to this grace, however much you advance in it, you ought always to reckon this to be very little and to consider it as nothing with regard to the greatness of future felicity. Surely this is what sacred Scripture means by remaining silent, for it said nothing at all concerning the height of our propitiatory. It is as if it might cry out more loudly and penetrate farther and better by keeping silent itself because everything the human mind is capable of grasping thus far in this life concerning the abundance of internal pleasantness ought to be reckoned as if it were nothing. By remaining silent it cries out that it considers itself wholly unworthy to instruct us concerning the measure of this work; in this life human infirmity is scarcely able to rise up to the beginning of the work.

CHAPTER XX

How this kind of contemplation can be divided into five stages, and what things pertain to the first stage

But since we have divided into three portions the first consideration, which pertains to length, and also have divided into two portions that second one, which pertains to width, we can now cut this entire kind of contemplation into five portions and divide it into just as many stages. In the first stage of this contemplation we consider those things which pertain to the quality of the soul or the particular nature of its essence: that the soul is a kind of perpetual life that cannot be extinguished at any time by any pains or torments; that it is not only able itself to live in perpetuity but is able to animate the body to life and sense; that it needs no support; that it subsists eternally without assistance. Furthermore we consider how it has been diffused through so many members of the body since it is simple in itself and lacks individual essence in the parts; how in its whole body, in a kind of world of its own, as it were, it is certainly completely everywhere, just as God is found completely everywhere in all creatures of His; how in that world of its own it moves and disposes all things by the will alone just as in this world God, who created everything by the command of the will, rules all things by the same command of the will alone. In this manifestation and in others you will discover other things worthy of much consideration, which you cannot see without wonder and cannot wonder at without delight. Yet, what wonder is this if we discover many marvelous and awesome things in the rational spirit since it is the especial creature of God and has been made according to His image and similitude? For although God is marvelous in His works and very great and laudable in all His mighty deeds, nevertheless, I beg you, where will the more extraordinary marvels of His powers appear other than in His image, in His similitude? Without doubt the activity of the omnipotent Artisan, which appears marvelous everywhere, stands out singularly in such a work.

Chapter XXI

Concerning the consideration of those things pertaining to the second stage

In the second stage of this contemplation those things are considered which are for knowing or can be devoted to the pursuit of truth, and whatsoever things come together and lead to an increase of knowledge. Surely in this consideration we rightly marvel with worthy awe and wonder at the fluency of thinking, the agility of imagination, the sharpness of natural ability, the examination of discretion, the capacity of memory, the liveliness of understanding and any other things whatever concerning this. For who is capable of thinking worthily; who is capable of estimating the value sufficiently; who is not terrified in the wonder of his consideration if he pays careful attention to that fluency of human thinking which is so manifold; the speed of it that is so restless and indefatigable, that runs through so many, such varied and such an infinite number of things; that keeps quiet for neither an hour nor a moment of time;

that passes through so great an expanse of space or so great a duration of time in so much haste? Furthermore we ought to pay attention to how easy a passage, how agile a running through, lies open everywhere from highest to lowest, from lowest to highest; from oldest to newest, from newest to oldest. But concerning the agility of the imagination and the skill of that faculty, what are we going to say or what are we able to say worthily about that which portrays with such great speed the image of all those things which the soul supplies? Whatever the soul takes in from outside by means of hearing, whatever it conceives from within from thinking alone, the imagination forms the whole by means of a representation, without delay and laying aside all difficulty, and it represents the forms of any things whatsoever with marvelous haste. What is it, I ask, to execute pictures of so many things and of so much in a moment, in a blink of the eye, and again to remove the same things with the same ease, or to change in many ways in one and then another manner? When it wishes, does the soul not create daily by means of the imagination a new heaven and a new earth and in that world of phantasms as it were every hour another kind of creator causes and forms according to his will creatures of that sort as large as you like? Nevertheless, if we pay attention to the sharpness of natural ability, we more quickly discover what we ought to marvel at in that. See how many—no, almost how infinite—are the things that are accessible to human natural ability that cannot be reached at any time by bodily sense. See how that sharpness of human natural ability is accustomed to investigate deep things, to penetrate whatever things are innermost, hidden within, perplexing, obscure and placed in darkness—and to unfold, disentangle, make clear and bring them out into the light. With subtlety, so to speak, it daily approaches, bursts into and passes through the innermost bosom of hidden nature and the secret recesses of its liveliness, making haste and always striving with eagerness to penetrate into farther places and to mount up to higher things. Pay attention to how many disciplines of knowledge it discovers, how many arts it hammers out. Then you will begin to be struck with amazement and to faint from excessive wonder. So if you pay attention to the capacity of memory and its breadth, undoubtedly you will discover what you ought to marvel at worthily. How great, I ask, is that inner chamber of such immense breadth, that comprehends, conceals and preserves so many substances of things, so many forms of substances, so many kinds of things, so many species of kinds, so many individuals of species—indeed so many particular natures, so many qualities, so many quantities, actions and passions, conditions, positions and places of individuals during the revolution of its extent of time, and after having preserved them for a long time, it brings them forth in the midst of all? Think, if you are able, how great, how wide, how large, how deep, how high, those treasuries are that are able to collect from all sides and to preserve without confusion so many treasures of knowledge and jewels of wisdom. Without doubt the capacity of memory is marvelous but the liveliness of the understanding is no less marvelous. It is easy to ponder and gather how great and marvelous it is from the things already said. For whatever sense touches, thought produces; whatever imagination forms, natural ability investigates and memory conserves. The understanding grasps knowledge of these things, and when it pleases it admits them to consideration and draws them into contemplation.

Chapter XXII

Concerning the consideration of those things pertaining to the third stage

In the third stage of this contemplation we consider the will of the rational soul and its manifold affection. For who is able to explicate worthily all the modes of change it assumes in a momentary disturbance; how it accustoms itself to change in many ways with the impulse of alternating changes? Let each one think by what disturbances his soul is daily affected. From that let him gather how the soul is changed in many ways. Now it raises itself up into confidence, at another time it falls into a lack of confidence; now it is fixed by steadiness, at another time it is shaken to the foundations by sudden fear. Now anger disturbs it, at another time a great anger stirs it up. It is not so great a marvel that it is affected at single moments by various qualities and diverse disturbances. But it is extraordinarily awesome that it is often touched at almost the same moment by contrary affections. Now it is led by hatred, now by love; now it is distracted by rejoicing, now by lamentation. How often in the midst of the marvelous dancings of our thanksgiving do we see how a cause of sadness, suddenly coming on and rising up, shakes the soul violently and throws it down. Suddenly all the celebration of the exulting soul is turned into lamentation. It is not so great a marvel that the soul itself often and suddenly assumes contrary qualities with respect to different things. But it is very marvelous that with respect to one and the same thing it leads over from one kind of affection to an opposite kind of affection. For afterward we often pursue with hatred things once loved very much and for a long time, and we suddenly detest violently things formerly regarded as good and longed for. But so that we may yet marvel more amply, if you wish to pay careful attention to one and the same affection of man, you will see that concerning one and the same thing, the affection changes in many ways. For now from great it becomes small; at another time it becomes great from small. At some time, from great it becomes greater; at some time, from a moderate size it becomes smaller. And so, again, the same affection of the soul increases and decreases about the same thing; now it swells up violently and now almost, now completely fails and often after full failure it revives completely. Pay attention to this in human affection: how great it is in great things, how sublime in sublime things; how small it is in small things, and worthless in worthless things; how, I say, it is great and sublime when it raises itself up into the height; how it is small and worthless when it throws itself down into the lowest parts. When it raises itself up in daring, you will often see that it even despises death and in the midst of the greatest perils it has no trepidation. However, afterwards in the silence of the night you will see the same soul suddenly frightened and losing steadiness of soul on account of a slight breath, the motion of one leaf, or even the falling of leaves. But who would suffice to enumerate all the qualities of human affection? Who would suffice to explicate all the modes of its changes? There are almost as many varieties of affections as there are differences of things. For just as we feel differently about different things in the approval of things, so we are affected in differing ways about different things in the affection for things. For the longing of affection is accustomed to be varied according to the judgment of approval.

CHAPTER XXIII

Concerning the consideration of those things belonging to the fourth stage

In the fourth stage of this contemplation, in like manner we contemplate and wonder at the power of deliberation: how it daily makes so many affections of the soul into virtues, in so much as it both sets them in order by means of discretion and fixes them in a good intention. For since a virtue is nothing other than an ordered and moderated affection, as a result of good intention it is brought to be an ordered affection, and by means of discretion it is brought about that it becomes a moderated affection. However we always ought to devote vigorously all the effort of our deliberation to this task and to pursue this exercise both strongly and frequently, so that all our affection runs about, passing from illicit things to licit things and so that even in licit longings it everywhere preserves the moderation of equity. Is it not brought about daily by the power of deliberation that evil affections are restrained, lessened and destroyed? Is it not brought about continually by the power of deliberation that good virtues are nurtured, advanced and strengthened? See how it condemns certain affections forever but exalts others everlastingly according as its function is to put down the mighty from their seat and exalt the humble. (Cf. Luke 1:52.) And so it humbles the one and exalts the other, raising a poor man from the dust and lifting up a pauper from the dung. Is it not the function of the power of deliberation to put in order as it wishes that whole tumult of the internal family of so many thoughts and affections, and in the manner of one who commands to make them subject to its laws, to make judgments and to do justice daily, to be ruling from sea to sea and from the river to the limits of the orb of the earth? Is it not the function of this very thing to strike carnal longings with strong punishment, to restrain forcefully the tumult of fluctuating thoughts, and to gird itself daily for spiritual battle in order to carry out revenge among the nations and rebukes among the peoples? Is it not the function of this very thing to suppress strongly all the soul's rebellious impulses and haughtinesses of pride and to crush courageously the hostile army of vices in order to fetter their kings in foot shackles and their noblemen in iron manacles? However the power of deliberation ought not only to restrain vices but even in fact to improve virtues. It ought to strike the household of Nebuchadnezzar with strong punishment but to put in order wisely and nourish carefully the house of David. And that power will judge among the nations, fill up ruins, and severely shake the heads of many in the land. And that power "will sit upon the throne of David and be set over his kingdom that it may establish and strengthen it in judgment and justice" (Isa. 9:7). However, who can worthily describe what or how great that terrible tumult of virtues is that orders the battle array of the soldiers' encampment, provides discipline of this and arranges the ordering of it? Of what sort, I ask, and how much to be trusted are those phalanxes of virtues that overturned the chariots of Pharoah and his army and still fortify and surround the chariot of our Solomon? The chariots of God are multiplied by ten thousands; thousands of those rejoicing, the Lord is among them, in Sinai, in a holy place. But if any perfect soul flourishes with such great virtues in this life, how great, I ask, will be that consummation of virtues which he will have in that supreme glory of future plenitude? Think, if you are able, how great will be that abundance of future goods, both bodily and spiritual. What and how multiple are the differences between these? Certainly there will be a difference of affections according to the difference of goods. For we will not be affected in the same way about smaller or greater goods, where every affection of ours will be just as ordered in everything as it will also undoubtedly in like manner be moderated in everything. What, I ask, will be for you that number of virtues in so many ordered and moderated affections of the soul? If you are able to raise yourself up into the watchtower of this consideration I marvel if you do not believe that a thousand thousand serve Him and ten thousand times a hundred thousand assist Him. Consider carefully, therefore, what sort of manifestation it is or how delightful the virtues of so many holy souls are by which they prevail for the moment or possess in order to prevail in the future and to lead the soul into contemplation and suspend it in such wonder.

CHAPTER XXIV

Concerning the consideration of those things pertaining to the fifth stage

In the fifth stage of this contemplation, just as we have already said above, we marvel with fixed attention and direct our attention with wonder at the quality and modes of aspired grace. Without doubt whatever good is done in the hearts of good persons, that sevenfold Spirit works it in them by inspired grace. Behold one and the same Spirit always and everywhere has the care of so many minds, and it devotes the service of its grace in many ways. See, it instructs the minds of so many persons in so many ways and inclines the wills of all of them to the judgment of its own will without any compulsion. When it reveals itself, truth is understood; when it inspires itself, good is loved. For without cooperating grace we do not suffice either for knowledge of truth or for love of virtue. Nevertheless, how great, how marvelous that one is believed to be, since whatever virtue it works in us, it is attributed to us for merit. And in a certain marvelous and incomprehensible manner, He inspires the good pleasure of His will in us in such a way that whatever goodness of His grace imprints or reforms in us ought justly to be reckoned to us for merit. For by the sound judgment of human will and wholly without any compulsion, every good will is stirred up by inspired grace to the good pleasure of divine goodness, and for that reason whatever is done in him by divine influence, out of a free concord of the mind, is reckoned to a person for the glory of retributions. However that grace which cooperates with good efforts works some things in us that are for the enlarging of debt; some things that are for the increase of merit; and some things that seem to be for the beginning of reward. As often as the gift of knowledge and wisdom grows larger in us so often does divine favor increase the debt of our servitude and make us more obligated to Him. And so these things and any such things whatsoever have more to do with the enlarging of debt than of merit. But whatever virtue divine goodness inspires in us accumulates for the merits of retributions. In fact, whatever intimate pleasantness, whatever divine sweetness, is imparted to our minds by divine influence seems in a certain manner to look toward the beginning of reward. One and the same Spirit works all these things. For His unction teaches us concerning all things, and the charity of God has been diffused in our hearts by the Holy Spirit who has been given to us. It is no less evident that any joy whatsoever from Him is in the Holy Spirit. However, do you wish to know more openly for what fruit this Spirit is accustomed to make our spirit fruitful? The Apostle says, "The fruits of the Spirit are charity, joy, peace, patience, long-suffering, and goodness" (Gal. 5:22). O how many, O how great are those things which this Spirit works in us, apportioning to individuals as He wills! For "there are diverse kinds of graces, but the same Spirit. Indeed, to one a word of wisdom is given through the Spirit, to another a word of knowledge, to another faith, to another the grace of healing, to another the working of miracles, to another prophecy, to another discretion of spirits" (1 Cor. 12:4, 8–10) and other innumerable things in this manner. Consider, I beg you, how remarkable and wholesome it is that these workings of such a divine Spirit lead into speculation and strengthen one's soul for humility and charity in the contemplation of these things. For the soul advances much in every way, both to love of God and to despising of itself, when it frequently pays attention and fully recognizes how it is able to do nothing by itself. O how much we ought to admire and embrace the grace of that one by whom He works all our works in us in such a way that they are as much His as ours: His gifts and our merits. We have already indicated above how manifold and diverse the affections of the human heart are. Yet the Spirit of the Lord daily combines them little by little in His elect and skillfully forms them into one harmony and by the plucking instrument of His graces fits them together in a certain harmonious consonance like a learned harp player who stretches these and loosens those, until a certain melody, mellifluous and sweet beyond measure, resounds from them into the ears of the Lord Sabaoth as if from the playing of many harpers upon their harps (cf. Rev. 14:2). But if so marvelous a harmony and so manifold a consonance arises from one heart in so great a plurality of so many affections, what, I ask, or how much will be that consonant concord and concordant consonance of supercelestial souls in so great a multitude of so many thousands of angels and so many holy souls exulting and praising Him who lives world without end? That multiform grace of the divine Spirit does and sets in order all these things. This is the Spirit that, as has already been said above, works all things in everyone. Therefore, if we have exercised our sense in the five stages of this contemplation, if we are ready and inclined for such speculation, surely we have completed our propitiatory according to the manner set forth in the divine example.

BOOK IV

CHAPTER I

Concerning the fifth and sixth kinds of contemplation

It still remains for us to treat of the fifth and sixth kinds of contemplation, which Moses seems to indicate by a mystical description in these words: "You ought also to make two cherubim of gold and of beaten work for both sides of the oracle. Let one cherubim be on one side and the other on the other side. Let them, spreading their wings and covering the oracle, cover both sides of the propitiatory. And let them look at each other with their faces turned toward the propitiatory" (Exod. 25:18–20). It gives us pleasure to turn our attention eagerly to this description, both to affirm the rule of our teaching from the similitude that is set forth and in accord with the formula of this description to forge the form and manner of our work. For I think that something great, something excellent, is proposed to us in this work since it is represented to us under such a form, since it is assigned such a name and it seeks to imitate the form of angels: "You ought to make two cherubim of gold and beaten work." That which it is necessary to represent to us under angelic form must be something truly great, excellent, even above the earthly, and completely other than human. Certainly the word "cherub" means "fullness of knowledge," and under the indication of this word it seems that a kind of great thing of hidden knowledge is being proposed and promised. But still we ought also to observe this, that we are accustomed to call not just any angels "cherubim," but only those who are supreme and united immediately to God. And so the form of this sort of work challenges us to supermundane—no, to supercelestial—things, and under this demand it invites our understanding to the speculation of supreme and divine things.

It is evident that things that seem to pertain to these two last kinds of contemplation are above a person and go beyond the mode and capacity of human reason. For this reason it is necessary to represent these things according to the expression of a similitude by means of a figure that is angelic rather than human. For unless the matter of these speculations goes beyond the limitation of human thinking, it is necessary that the model for forming our work have a form of human rather than angelic similitude. Therefore, it is necessary for us to raise ourselves above ourselves and to rise up by means of contemplation to those things which are above reason if we desire to form the flight of our understanding according to the manner of the angelic similitude. And so let us seek what those things are which are above reason, which transcend the power of human reason and the mode of our thinking.

CHAPTER II

That the things pertaining to these last speculations go beyond human reason

Just as it is evident that there are certain things that are below reason, so without doubt it is evident that there are certain things that are above reason. And between these there are certain other middle things, which are at least accessible to reason although they are below reason; these things we perceive by means of corporeal sense. Those things which we investigate by reason are according to reason only. Those things are above reason which we learn by a showing or prove by authority only. White and black, hot and cold, sweet and sour, we learn by corporeal sense; we do not prove them by reasoning. True and false, just and unjust, beneficial and unbeneficial, we discern by reasoning and not by any corporeal sense. However, no corporeal sense teaches, nor does any human reason fully convince us, that God is three in person in one substance and one in substance in three persons. But yet some learn this by a showing while others believe and prove it incontestably by authority only. And so corporeal things are below reason, but divine things are above reason. That certainly is above reason which no corporeal sense is able to reach nor any human reason to penetrate. We call "above reason" what we truly believe exists although we are able neither to comprehend it by the intellect nor to prove it by a proof from experience. And indeed, there are many things among such divine things to which human reason easily gives assent and does not wish to contradict but receives as true and agrees to be certain although it is able neither to prove them by a proof from experience nor to comprehend them fully by the intellect. Therefore everything of that sort which transcends the smallness of our capacity by the greatness of its incomprehensibility ought rightly to be said to be above reason. Nevertheless in these things that our smallness is not able to comprehend, the angelic highness practices free flights of contemplation. Therefore so that we may be able in whatever kind of way to hammer out the form of angelic similitude in ourselves, it is necessary to suspend our soul with continual quickness in wonder at such things and to accustom the wings of our contemplation to sublime and angelic flights.

CHAPTER III

That those things which are beyond reason can be distinguished by a twofold division, and what kind of things belong to which division

We are divinely commanded to make two cherubim. By this we are advised to seek two kinds of contemplation in the things that are above reason. And so let us direct our attention toward the things that are above reason, and we shall discover that they can be distinguished by a twofold division. For some of these things are above reason but not beyond reason; others, however, are both above reason and beyond reason. At the outset we wish to forewarn that in supreme and divine things when we assert that something goes beyond or is contrary to reason, we wish this to be understood with respect to human reason, not divine reason. For everything that is agreed to exist in that supreme and divine Being subsists in the supreme and unchangeable reason. Nevertheless, we believe with certainty many things with respect to the divine nature concerning which, if we consult reason, all our reasoning resists and all human reason protests. For what human reason holds the Son to be coeternal with the Father and equal in all things to Him from whom He has being, life and understanding? Therefore in these things that are above reason, many things like this can be discovered, which seem to be completely against reason if they are considered by human judgment. We say that those things are above reason which we suffice neither to prove by any proof from experience nor to investigate fully by any reasoning. However, those things seem to be beyond reason which customarily oppose examples and contradict arguments. In things above reason proofs from experience are lacking and arguments fail. But things beyond reason contradict both examples and arguments. The former we often prove by authority, confirm by arguments and establish by similitudes. Nevertheless, we do not fully comprehend by our understanding any of these things that have been proved and established since, as has been said, we are not sufficiently able to prove them by any proof from experience or any clear example drawn from those things which we know by experience. However, the latter things are established now by miracles, now by authorities; at another time they are learned by showings. For infidels they have often been established by a multitude of miracles; for the faithful they are established daily by the authorities of the Scripture' yet to prophetic men they have often been made manifest by a great variety of divine showings. Nevertheless, these are of such a sort that unless faith mediates they cannot be proved at all to other persons even by those who have learned them through a showing. And so for attesting these things there is more need for miracles than examples, more authorities than arguments, more showing than reasoning. However those loftier things are of such a sort that no human reason can suffice for investigating them unless it is aided by divine showings or authentic witnesses. But when it is supported by such assistance many reasons come together from all sides for the faithful mind and then many arguments come forth that aid it in its investigation, establish it in its discovery and defend the conclusion produced in its assertion. And so I think such things have rightly been said to be above reason, not however to go beyond reason. But these latter things are such that when they are proved and believed by miracles or authorities, if we consult human reason concerning these things and intend to give assent to its counsels, reason begins at once to weaken whatever in these things it earlier held certain by faith. And human reason does nothing at all in the investigation, discussion and assertion of these things unless it is supported with a mixture of faith. Therefore, since we speak according to human understanding, those things which are of such a sort are said to be not only above reason but even beyond reason. However, the former things are rightly ascribed to the fifth kind of contemplation; the latter things seem to pertain to the sixth kind of contemplation.

CHAPTER IV

That those things pertaining to these kinds of contemplations are alien from all imagination

I think that already in our exposition it should not be lacking why the angelic creature of this work ought to be golden. If those things are declared golden which are considered in reason and are comprehended by reason, how much greater are those things which surpass reason? If things that exceed imagination are golden, how much greater are the things that exceed reason? In this twin speculation nothing from imagination, nothing from phantasy ought to suggest itself; for whatever manifestation this twin watchtower of the last work sets forth, it far exceeds every property of corporeal similitude. For if any corporeal phantasies are always accustomed to obscure rather than aid that fourth kind of contemplation, how much farther ought they to be from these more worthy and much more sublime things and how much more ought they not to appear with them? And so let imagination withdraw for a time; let it withdraw and completely vanish. There is nothing in which it is able to assist this work. For where reason fails, what can imagination do? What would imagination do there, where there is no changing and no shadow of vicissitude; where the part is not less than its whole, nor the whole is more universal than its individual parts; indeed, where the part is not lessening the whole, and the whole is not made up from parts, since that is simple which is set forth universally, and that is universal which is brought forth in the particular as it were; where the whole is single; where all is one and one is all? Certainly without doubt human reason fails in these things. And what can imagination do there? Without doubt in such a kind of manifestation imagination can hinder it and is completely unable to assist.

CHAPTER V

What the supereminence of these last contemplations is

How great the supereminence of these last speculations is can be gathered easily from this: that every consideration and examination carried out by these is continually engaged with supreme and divine things. Therefore let anyone who is able think how much human knowledge has ascended when it has merited to be raised up to these stages of contemplation. For that which is laid as a foundation for perfection in the first stages of contemplation is consummated in fullness in these last two stages. For in the first two stages we are instructed with regard to awareness of exterior and corporeal things. In the two middle stages of contemplation we are advanced with regard to knowledge of invisible things and spiritual creatures. In the last two stages of contemplation we are raised up to the understanding of supercelestial and divine things. Therefore we should begin with the lowest and best known, in order to raise up the advancement of our knowledge little by little and to ascend by means of the awareness of exterior things to knowledge of invisible things. For when you have grasped knowledge of exterior things and have senses that have been exercised in teaching concerning them, you ought to ascend to higher things and obtain knowledge of spiritual creatures. But when you have been fully exercised in accordance with your ability in such a mode of knowing you still have something by which you may be able to ascend higher. Now those supreme and divine things still exist far above; strive as much as you are able and attempt to reach them. Surely if you have been raised up to the speculation of these things you will not be able to discover beyond these any other things to which you still have to ascend. Certainly there is nothing beyond God, and for that reason knowledge is unable to ascend higher or farther. Therefore if "cherubim" means "fullness of knowledge," see how rightly the last product of our work, in which the supreme stages of all knowledge are expressed in a symbolic figure, is named "cherubim." Certainly you are able to grow daily in awareness of God, and each day you are able to be lifted up higher and higher in this lofty flight. But above this watchtower of contemplation you are now completely unable to find another that is higher. For it is one thing to run about here and there in this kind of manifestation and to enlarge one's knowledge in knowing God; it is another thing to want to seek above these things for other and higher things that you cannot find in any way. There is nothing above God—nothing that exists, that might be able to exist, or that can be thought to exist. There is nothing higher to which knowledge might ascend, nor is it capable of ascending higher. And so, the fullness of knowledge is to know God. However the fullness of this knowledge is the fullness of glory, the consummation of grace, perpetuity of life: "This is eternal life: that they may know you, the true God, and Jesus Christ, whom you have sent" (John 17:3). And so, to know Him who is the true God is the conclusion of all consummation. These last speculations advance us to the fullness of this knowledge little by little and whenever they are able to guide. The perfection of this fullness is begun in this life, but it is consummated in future life. Therefore, the symbolic expression of this work in which we are initiated to the fullness of all knowledge is rightly called "cherub."

CHAPTER VI

That it is arduous and difficult to obtain grace for oneself in these last kinds of contemplation

But now let us consider what it means that we are commanded to make these last works of beaten work. Surely beaten work is produced by striking, and little by little it is brought closer to the intended form by means of frequent blows and much hammering.

Therefore I think that there is need in this work more for inner compunction than profound investigation; more for sighs than arguments; more for frequent lamentations than an abundance of argumentations. However, we know that nothing so purifies the innermost places of the heart and nothing so renews the purity of the mind; nothing so drives away the clouds of ambiguity; nothing leads better or more quickly to serenity of heart than true contrition of soul, than deep and innermost compunction of soul. But what does Scripture say? "Blessed are the pure in heart, for they themselves shall see God" (Matt. 5:8). Therefore, let him who desires to see God and hurries to rise up in contemplation of divine things strive for purity of heart. O how much urgency, O how much carefulness is needed in such skillful zeal and zealous skill before the soul thoroughly cleans away the dross of earthly love and consumes it with the fire of true love; before the soul melts down the gold of its understanding to that purity in order that the soul may produce aptness and worth according to the dignity of this work. Without doubt and without any contradiction it is neither a light nor an easy thing for the human soul to assume angelic form and go beyond a certain earthly state to a truly more-than-human one, to receive spiritual wings, and to raise itself to the heights. O how often it is necessary to place one's gold in the fire and draw it out again, to turn it now on this side, now on that, and hammer it with frequent blows on all sides before one forges the angelic form and produces the cherubim. O how much prudence, O how much foresight there must be in forming the material of our work. Hence, one ought to be tempered by regard for love and fear of the Divine, lest the soul that has been relaxed because of excessive regard for divine mercy should become soft on account of excessive confidence in Him or the soul that has been hardened with immoderate regard for divine severity should little by little become tepid because of hopelessness and should despair completely concerning the consummation of the work it has undertaken. O with how much prudent caution, O with how much frequent reproof it is necessary to watch and press forward, lest any deviation of the mind or wandering of thought be hidden from the sharp-sightedness of discretion or pass through without reproof and strong criticism. But who can worthily describe what skill and care are needed while the human soul transforms itself into the figure of heavenly and winged animals and transfigures itself into an image of them? Certainly it is first necessary that one be accustomed to walking in heavenly places with dwellers in heaven and never again descend to earthly undertakings and the care of external things (except for the duty of obedience or the office of charity only) before he dares to attempt those angelic ecstasies into the lofty secret places of divine incomprehensibility.

CHAPTER VII

That a man strives in vain for these contemplative ecstasies unless he is aided by divine showings

Hence I think it is easily considered how much the superior dignity of this last, superexcellent work goes beyond the other things mentioned above. By a certain emulation of its activity this work imitates the archangelic sublimity of that supreme hierarchy in the angels. Think, I beg you, how excellent this is, that it draws into itself by means of imitation a similitude of that order of spiritual beings which adheres without mediation to the supreme light and sees face to face, without a mirror and without an enigma. I ask, of what sort is that human understanding which strives daily for those contemplative ecstasies of supercelestial souls and on account of the good pleasure of divine esteem is raised up at some time for contemplating the mighty works of the supreme majesty? Who is suited for this? Who is found to be a worthy artisan for this work unless divine grace precedes and follows him? In short, it is one thing to make the ark; it is another thing to form the cherubim. We can know and prove daily by proofs from experience, nor is it foreign to our senses, what it is to put the ark together, cover it with gold, surround it with the crown, and add the cover. But who has seen or might be able to see cherubim? But how shall I represent that form which I am not capable of seeing? I think that Moses would not have been capable of representing that unless he had learned it earlier by means of a showing. For this reason it was said to him: "Observe, so that you may make everything just as it has been shown to you on the mountain" (Exod. 25:9). And so, first

Moses is led up on the mountain and it is made manifest to him by means of a showing; afterward he should be able to come to know what he ought to perceive concerning such a working. And so it is necessary to ascend to a high heart and by ecstasy of mind learn further from a showing from the Lord, what that is for which one must sigh and strive and to what condition of sublimity one ought to accustom and arrange his soul. For if he has once been allowed to enter into that light-streaming glory of angelic sublimity and if he has been worthy to enter into that manifestation of divine rays—by what secret longings, by what deep sighs, by what indescribable lamentations do we think that he who is such a person presses onward? With what continual recollection, with what pleasant wonder do we believe that he reexamines the brilliance he has seen and turns it over in the mind by longing for it, sighing for it and contemplating it until, at last, at some time he is transformed "in the same image from light to light, as by the Spirit of the Lord" (2 Cor. 3:18). He says "by the Spirit of the Lord," not by his own. If one wishes to make beaten work and to form the cherubim, in this business the best kind of skill presses on by sighs and lamentations, as we have already said above. For what does it mean to produce our work by means of striking other than by means of great contrition of heart to obtain from the kindness of the Lord that for which no one can suffice by himself? Yet on that account let no one consider these things of which we now speak to be equal with the works mentioned earlier, or believe that they differ very little from each other because they have a common material and are both made from gold. Surely if any metal more precious than gold could have been discovered, doubtless from it this angelic form would have been made. And so the supereminence of its worth is commended much more on account of form than material. And so we are commanded to make the cherubim and to form images not of human beings nor even any angels whatsoever but of superexcellent spirits so that the worth of these last speculations might shine forth better out of such a figurative adumbration.

CHAPTER VIII

That the fifth kind of contemplation permits the rational principle of similitudes; but the sixth completely exceeds the particular nature of all similitude

I think that it ought neither to be neglected nor to be passed over without careful consideration that one is advised by the voice of the Lord concerning these two cherubim, when it is said: "Let one cherub be on one side, and the other on the other" (Exod. 25:19). And so they should be set up on both sides of the oracle, covering both sides of the propitiatory. Of course, we understand the same thing by the oracle as we do by the propitiatory.

Therefore let us inquire what these two sides of our propitiatory are, so that as a consequence we may discover why one of the cherubim must stand on one side, and the other on the other. As we have already shown satisfactorily above, we understand by the propitiatory that kind of contemplation which is concerned with rational spirits. However, we believe that the rational creatures — both angelic and human — have been created according to the image and similitude of God. It has been written about humans: "God created a human according to His image and similitude, according to the image of God He created him" (Gen. 1:27). Concerning angelic nature, we think of a passage that we read elsewhere: "You were a seal of similitude, full of wisdom and elegant in the delights of the paradise of God" (Ezech. 28:12–13). Behold, the angelic nature has been called a seal of similitude, even for that part which stood not in truth. On the other hand, the prophet David openly proclaims and says: "There is none similar to you among the gods, O Lord" (Ps. 85:8), and Isaiah clearly declares: "Whereas all peoples are before him as if they do not exist, and they are counted as if nothing and worthless" (Isa. 40:17). How are they "as if nothing and worthless" if they have some similarity to the divine? Perhaps what one says, the other contradicts? Absolutely not! For behold, I read in the writings of David: "God, who will be similar to you?" (Ps. 82:2). But again, I find in the writings of the same person: "Lord, the light of your face has been sealed upon us" (Ps. 4:7). Therefore, what else can we gather from such diverse statements except that truly and without doubt on account of one thing we manifest similiarities to our Creator and on account of another thing, dissimiliarities. Indeed, how is a person not dissimilar to Him in many ways, for concerning him it has been truly written: "Whereas every person living is totally vanity" (Ps. 38:6). Behold how dissimilar. "And yet a person passes through in an image" (Ps. 38:7). Behold how similar. For what is a person that he can conform to the King his Maker? But in any case an angel in heaven does not emulate perfectly that similitude of its Creator. "Who is like you among the strong O Lord; who is like you, magnificent in holiness, terrible and praiseworthy, and doing marvelous things?" (Exod. 15:11). See, therefore: Is it not probable that those things in which we are similar pertain to one side and those things in which we are dissimilar pertain equally to the other side? And so, if you will, let one side of our propitiatory be called "divine similitude in rational substances," and let the other be called "many-sided dissimilitude with the same essences of supreme Divinity." Therefore, let us see how one of the cherubim stands on one side and the other on the other side, and which ought to stand on which side. We have already said above that the contemplation of those things which are above reason but not beyond reason pertains to one cherub. To the other cherub pertains the contemplation of those things which are above reason and seem to go beyond reason. However, it is evident that the first one mentioned is much easier than the second. For this reason it ought to be and is accustomed to be first in our use. The more difficult the other is, the later it ought to be. And so let the first of these contemplations be called the first cherub. Let the second of them be called the second cherub. Therefore, a cherub of one sort ought to stand on one side, and of another on the other. Surely a cherub seems to stand on one side when the ray of contemplation is fixed on those things, for the investigation and confirmation of which any adaptation of a similitude is easily accommodated. A cherub stands on the other side, as it were, when human understanding raises itself to that contemplation to which no adumbration of similitude fully joins itself. For consideration of similitude pertains to one side, as has been said, just as consideration of dissimilitude pertains to the other. However, it is evident that those things which allow themselves to be joined to some similitude can more easily be comprehended and are nearer to and much closer and more proper for reason. Indeed, the farther the others recede from human reason, the more they transcend the rational principle of any similitude applied to them. And so the first cherub stands on the side of similitude; but the second stands on the side of dissimilitude so that those things which are not beyond reason and which allow some similitude may touch the side of similitude as if from nearby and cling to it by means of consideration. In a similar manner those things which seem to be beyond or against reason and to go beyond every particular nature of a similitude applied to them have the side of dissimilitude next to themselves and look at it from nearby. However, if you wish to refer what is being called "one side and the other" to the right and left sides, certainly the similitude of such a consideration leads us to the same judgment. For our right hand is more often accustomed to be extended for the sake of working, and for this reason it is evident that it is seen more frequently. Indeed, the left is concealed under our clothing more often than the right, and for this reason it is seen more rarely. Therefore, the more hidden things are correctly designated by the left hand, just as the more manifest are designated suitably enough by the right. And so the first cherub stands at the right, as it were, since it fixes the eye of contemplation on those things which are not totally alien to reason. However, the second cherub is set up on the left because it particularly contemplates only those things which all human reason seems to oppose.

Chapter IX

How love of everything and approval of self are moderated by these two kinds of contemplation

Very much in every way do these two kinds of contemplation either strengthen us against evil or assist us to virtue. Hence it is added concerning them: "Spreading wings and covering the oracle, let them cover both sides of the propitiatory" (Exod. 25:20). When we cover something we usually do it in two ways: now for hiding, now for protection. Often when we place an umbrella between ourselves and the sun we moderate the heat of the sun as well as its brightness. If by divine providence we receive grace for these two kinds of contemplation and if we press forward carefully in them according to the grace that is received, I believe that they will serve us for an umbrella from the heat of the day, and for security and hiding from the wind and rain (cf. Isa. 4:5–6). I wish that we might be carried away with so much zeal and longing for the viewing of these and led above ourselves for wondering at these with so much alienation of soul that for a while our mind might know nothing of itself while it is astounded as it is suspended in the viewing of such cherubim, so much so that it might dare to say with the Apostle: "Whether in the body or out of the body, I do not know; God knows" (2 Cor. 12:2). See how deeply under the wings of the just-mentioned cherubim he hides who knows nothing of himself for a while. But if the shadow of these wings is unable to alienate the attention of the mind in such ecstasy, nevertheless it ought to obscure that golden gleam of the propitiatory and to moderate it for our viewings, because it is accustomed always to do this. The gleam of our propitiatory is obscured without doubt by a shadow's being brought over it, when everything that seems to shine in us is despised in comparison to a greater and more supereminent brightness. The brightness of our propitiatory indicates the worth of the spiritual nature, while the spreading of the wings that are placed over it indicates the loftiness of divine supereminence. Why wonder, therefore, if both sides of our propitiatory are covered over by such a shadow? For, as has already been said, everything that is perceived in us as similar or dissimilar to divine things is dark in comparison to divine things. However, that which covers over usually, as we said, moderates not only the brightness, but even the heat as well, and renders both more tolerable. As we all know, it often happens that we do not know how to keep ourselves from self-esteem in our grace and to be moderate in our love. Assuredly by continual contemplation of and deep wonder at divine things, it happens that an excess and superfluity of both are curbed in us. I believe that no one at all—I say not one of all the rational spirits— is able to restrain that private love and opinion of personal excellence to a true and proper measure of equity, unless he truly knows how to despise himself in comparison to those things which we have mentioned. Therefore, the above-mentioned cherubim are rightly said to cover both sides of our propitiatory because nothing at all is found in us that is not either foreign in quality or incomparable in quantity to supreme and divine things.

Note that just as the ark is covered by the propitiatory, so the propitiatory itself is also commanded to be covered by the spreading of the above-mentioned wings. Without doubt, just as love and approval of the world are covered over by contemplation of the spiritual creature and its eminence, so love and approval of self are moderated in everyone by contemplation of the creative essence and its supereminence.

CHAPTER X

With how much eagerness of soul spiritual men ought or should be accustomed to be eager for these last kinds of contemplation

But if the afore-mentioned cherubim continually and sufficiently spread their wings, then certainly they adequately cover the sides of the propitiatory. What does it mean to spread your wings by a continual stretching out except to be eager for divine contemplation in every place, at every time, and to pursue it everywhere with such zeal and longing? When birds want to fly they spread out their wings. So, we surely ought to spread the wings of our heart by longing and wait for the time of divine showing at every hour—nay, rather at every moment, so that at whatever hour the breath of divine inspiration drives away the clouds of our mind and discloses the rays of the true sun after having removed every cloud of darkness, then the mind, immediately shaking the wings of its contemplation, can raise itself to the heights and fly away. Having fixed its eyes on that light of eternity which shines from above, it can fly through all the clouds of earthly changeableness and transcend them with the force of a soaring eagle. I would say that a person fulfills the command and example of the Lord and stands erect with outspread wings, as it were, when, after receiving grace in these last kinds of contemplations, he always strives zealously, as much as he can, to show himself ready and prepared for such a flight. The result is that when the time of divine good pleasure comes and the breath of aspiring grace blows, he is found fit to be admitted to that manifestation of divine secrets. However, we ought to suspend our souls and strive with vigorous longing in such an expectation not only for that which we are able to have in this life but even for that manifestation of divine contemplation which we hope for in the future life. Certainly such a grace is given to us for this; I say, the understanding of eternal things is poured into us for this: that we may know what we ought tirelessly to seek for by means of effort or sigh for by longing. But the richness of divine knowledge increases in us in vain, unless it increases the flame of divine love in us. And so longing always ought to grow in us on account of knowledge and also knowledge on account of longing; and by mutual increases they ought to minister for mutual increases, and by mutual enlargement they are able to grow with mutual enlargement. At every hour the soul that is perfect and continually dedicated to the contemplation of supreme things ought to await with supreme longing the end of its wandering and the exit from this workhouse, in order that it may deserve to see that face to face which it now sees by a mirror and in an enigma. For this reason Abraham sat in the doorway of his tent (Gen. 18:1). For this reason Elijah stood in the entrance of his cave (3 Kings 19:13). Both were prepared to go forth, and both were in suspense at the coming of the Lord. Each one waited: one in a cave, the other in a tent. Nevertheless, both were in a doorway; but one stood, the other sat. You have observed, I think, that one of these considers the trouble of this life a misery; the other thinks it a battle. The same wanderings of time are judged a prison by Elijah and a military expedition by Abraham. There are those who see themselves in a cave, as it were, and consider their flesh to be a workhouse while they endure with difficulty the trouble of this life. Others make a tent, as it were, from their bodies, gird themselves for the warfare of the Lord, and patiently endure their life so that they may be devoted to the Lord's gains. And so one lives impatiently, the other lives patiently; while one is anxious about himself, the other exerts himself for the Lord's gains. One stands and labors very much; the other sits, feels labor scarcely at all, and reckons it as nothing as he waits for the coming of the Lord. Both are found in the doorway and in the exit itself. Let us be silent for now concerning those who live cheerfully and rest while they lie pleasantly in the inner parts of their tent—not to call it a palace. The two persons mentioned above are anxious concerning the coming of the Lord: both he who struggled in suspense for the coming of the Lord, while sitting in the doorway and enduring patiently the trouble of his warfare; and that one who labored almost impatiently in longing for the object of his expectation while standing in the doorway and waiting for the hour of his visitation. Do you wish to hear how unwillingly he lived who stood in the entrance of his cave? "O Lord take my soul from me, for I am no better than my fathers" (3 Kings 19:4). However, I ask, why is it that he who stood thus in suspense in this place covered his face when he experienced the Lord passing by? Perhaps in the presence of the Lord he recognized more perfectly his own imperfection and was ashamed for his imperfection to be seen? You who feared to be seen nevertheless wished to see. O how many there are who already believe that they are prepared and yet tremble with fear at the very moment of His visitation where previously there was no fear. And they now fear to be making the going forth that previously they eagerly sought.

Chapter XI

How, after much weariness of their longing, some are usually, others are not usually lifted up above themselves by visiting grace

Behold one who, standing, waits. It is read that he neither went out the doorway nor ran to meet the Lord. Nevertheless, he looked out from the cave but with a covered face. He heard the voice of one passing by as He passed by. And he who already sighed for rest knew from the showing of the Lord what he now ought to do. However, at the coming of the Lord the other person springs forth from the tent and runs to meet the One who approaches with an uncovered face. He brings Him in, feeds Him, and receives the promise of the Lord according to the wish of his longing. He plies the Lord Sabaoth with questions and enters into that secret place of divine judgments when he receives foreknowledge of future things. However, what does it mean that from his place Elijah pays attention to the Lord's passing by, except that from those things which take place round about us by divine providence, he understands accurately the government of divine ordering and the grace of its cooperation? While a strong wind is followed by an earthquake, earthquake by fire, and fire by a still small voice, the presence of the Lord passing by is perceived. So it is that while the mind often suddenly feels itself completely shaken by certain great and marvelous disturbances, at one time thrown down by great terror, at another time melted by great grief or disordered by shame, and again brought to great tranquillity and even security of soul, beyond hope and expectation, whether it wills it or not—it ponders the operation of visiting grace and recognizes very clearly that these things are brought about by divine power. We have God present and passing by, as it were, when we are not yet capable of cleaving for a long time to the contemplation of that light. To hear the voice of the Lord (or even the voice of His instrument) giving warning is to know from his inspiration what His good, pleasing, and perfect will is. But that one who goes out from a tent, as it were, running to meet the Lord who approaches, sees face to face after having gone out. So he who has been led outside of himself by ecstasy of mind contemplates the light of highest wisdom without any covering or shadow of figures and finally not by a mirror and in an enigma but in simple truth, so to speak. He draws the interior vision outward when by means of great reconsideration and vigorous examination he makes what he saw by ecstasy comprehensible and expressible to himself and now by proof of reason and now again by the application of similitudes he draws it forth for the understanding of all. But the bull-calf from which the Lord is fed is sacrificed when the mind of man, having been strengthened by these levels of advancement, cuts off by the good pleasure of his own will what earlier he willingly cherished and protected; when he puts limits on his own pursuits or uses, so that he can hope to cleave more perfectly to divine contemplation and to be more acceptable to divine mercy. We feed the Lord when by the sacrifices of our virtues and by the enlarged intention of a restricted life we nurture and increase the good pleasure of His charity in us: "Behold," He says, "I knock at the door; if anyone will open to me, I will come in to him, and I will eat with him" (Rev. 3:20). Surely we eat with the Lord in our midst when we gladly devote that to His service and zealously serve at His good pleasure in that by which we might increase His good pleasure toward us and also increase our trust in Him. On account of this accumulation of confidence it happens that the mind is suddenly enlivened beyond hope and above expectation, to long-craved and greatly-longed-for grace. Indeed, we pursue the Lord as He goes forth, when, while pressing foreward carefully to the divinely taught understanding, we marvel at recognizing the light of divinity by which we are raised above ourselves to contemplating higher things. And while clinging to the traces of revealing grace, we accompany the Lord who passes through. However, after we have gone out, to stand with the Lord who stands means to cling for a long time by means of contemplation to the light being shown in that state of loftiness. He who transcends all the unsteadiness of human mutability and the uncertainty of ambiguity by a higher raising up of the mind stands with the Lord who stands. And while fixed intently upon that light of eternity he draws into himself the similitude of that image which has been seen: "All of us," says the Apostle, "looking upon the glory of the Lord with uncovered face are transformed into the same image from splendor to splendor, as if by the Spirit of the Lord" (2 Cor. 3:18). In this raising up of the mind human understanding often enters into that abyss of divine judgments and is even taught the foreknowledge of future things, as has already been said.

Chapter XII

That some of those things which are accustomed to be seen by ecstasy of mind can be brought down for the understanding of all —while others can never be so treated

It ought to be noted that at one time, when placed outside, we draw the vision of the Lord within; at other times, when placed within, we go out with the one who goes out. For this that is known concerning the Lord's brightness by means of ecstasy of mind is comprehended efter a while even by the mind in its ordinary state. And we are often led into alienation of mind because of greatness of wonder on account of that which we examine within ourselves in our ordinary state. Again, it ought to be noted that when placed outside, at one time we bring the vision of the Lord in, while at another time we do not bring it in. For we do not read that Abraham brought back the Lord on the occasion of his second going out. For indeed, there are certain things of a sort that exceed human understanding and cannot be investigated by human reason. Yet, as has been already said above, they are not beyond reason. Therefore, when we learn any things of this sort by means of ecstasy of mind, we bring the vision perceived exteriorly back with us, as it were, if we understand afterwards by means of a suitable reason those things that we learned earlier by means of a showing. But when those things which seem to be above reason and beyond reason are learned in ecstasy by means of a showing, as it were, because we are incapable of assigning or comprehending the rational principle of these things by means of any human estimation after we return, we leave outside, as it were, the perceived vision of which we retain only a sort of memory. For what does Scripture say? It says, "The Lord departed after he finished speaking with Abraham, and the latter returned to his place" (Gen. 18:33). The Lord goes away and Abraham returns when the sense of understanding is recalled to the ordinary state after the grace of a showing has been withdrawn. And so at the first going out, Abraham with great weariness compels that One whom he saw to come into his tent. However, at the second going out, after a lengthy vision and a long discoursing together, he did not bring Him back at all. We bring the exterior vision into ourselves when afterward we bring down a suddenly perceived theophany for the understanding of all by means of reasoning. The exterior vision is not brought in, in any way at all, when the more a contemplative showing is discussed according to human reason, the more it seems to be contrary to all human opinion. For in such a kind of speculation, before the soul returns to its usual state, the Lord departs and goes far away and shows the magnitude of His incomprehensibility by the remoteness of the vision. And so these two kinds of things that are known from the Lord's showing in this twin vision seem to refer to those two cherubim mentioned above. Surely this is that sufficiently worthy material of which the angelic form and winged animals must be forged. We form the cherubim for ourselves from this material when we accustom ourselves to draw into contemplation the secrets of our faith, which we have either learned by a showing or received from theologians, and also when we accustom ourselves to suspend our soul in wonder at them and to feed, humiliate and inflame it greatly with longing for divine things. Following the example of Abraham and Elijah, we ought to await the coming of the Lord at the very exit of our habitation, and in the doorway as it were. According to the divine pattern we ought to spread out the wings of our cherubim and hasten with quick steps of longings to meet the grace of a showing.

CHAPTER XIII

That a holy and contemplative soul ought to be prepared for receiving grace at every hour

The holy soul and friend of the true Bridegroom ought always to thirst with great longing for the coming of her Beloved, being always prepared to run to the One who calls and to open to the One who knocks. I say, the soul ought always to be anxious about this matter and to be found prepared, lest the One who comes suddenly and unexpectedly finds her less adorned and less splendidly dressed and lest He endure any of the trouble of a long period of waiting when shut out for a long time. Troublesome and very burdensome to one burning with desire are these words: "Command, command again; command, command again; wait, wait again; wait, wait again; a little here, a little there" (Isa. 28:10, 13). These surely are words of a lazy soul, a soul that is tepid, less careful and excessively ungrateful. For what can such a soul say when she is found in her sordidness, when she grieves that she has been caught off guard by an unexpected coming of the Lover and is ashamed to be found less adorned and less splendidly dressed? She says, "I certainly ought to have known beforehand about your coming so that I could receive you solemnly and run to meet you with all due swiftness in the way in which I ought. In the future, therefore, announce your coming to me in advance and inform me beforehand of the hour of your coming by means of a messenger who comes in advance. And so, let a messenger run between, to teach me what you wish me to do. I say, let an intermediary messenger run between us, to instruct me concerning individual things and teach me not only about my condition but even about your condition. Let him teach me how it is with you and what from me will be pleasing to you. And so: Command and command again; announce and announce again. It is not fitting for lovers not to know mutual pursuits and mutual longings for one another; nor does it suffice for a soul that is seething with burning desire to hear only once. Therefore I beg you: Command and command again; command and command again." Perhaps He greatly loves and burns greatly with desire for those things which He pursues so and seeks so urgently by an intermediary. Let us see, therefore, what He must do. Behold, according to His word, after messengers have been sent often and have been sent again, finally at last He follows after His messengers so that the soul may enjoy fully the desired embraces and may be caressed with mutual love. Behold now He stands before the door; behold now He knocks at the door. Behold the voice of your Beloved as He knocks: "Open to me my sister, my friend, my dove, my unstained one, for my head is full of dew, and the curls of my hair are full of the drops of the night" (Song of Songs 5:2). What, I beg you; what, I say, does it profit that He sent messengers in advance, if He finds a closed door? But at the very least, why at the voice of the Beloved do you not spring up, open, bring in and fall into an embrace? She says, "I have stripped off my garment; how shall I put it on? I have washed my feet, how shall I stain them?" (Song of Songs 5:3). However, let Him wait a moment if He will, in order that I may receive Him. He knocks and demands to enter; you say: "Wait." Behold, He knocks again; you say: "Wait again." And you say, "Why is it important if He waits a moment?" O how much I fear lest you draw this moment of time into a long time, until He passes by, turns away, and withdraws after He has been long and greatly wearied. Your voice and your too-late complaint show this to Him: "I opened the bolt of my door to my beloved; and He has turned away and passed by" (Song of Songs 5:6). But behold the One who comes again, who does not reckon the injury of the earlier contempt: He stands behind the wall, looking through the windows, gazing through the lattices. Hear Him calling; receive as you wish the One who knocks. Lo, your Beloved is speaking to you: "Arise my friend, my love, my beautiful one; be quick and come" (Song of Songs 2:10). Why do you not immediately spring forth, run, grasp and unite with a kiss? Why do you still say, "Wait"? Behold, He still waits. Behold He calls again: "Arise my friend, my spouse; come into the opening of the rock, into the grotto of the wall" (Song of Songs 2:13–14). Why do you say, "Wait again, yet a little while"? O ungrateful soul, O hard heart! Do you continually cast down your friend? Do you continually weary your Beloved? He knocks, and you do not wish to open. He calls, and you do not wish to go out. He knocks once and then again, and you command Him to wait and to wait again; a moment and a moment. He calls once; He calls again. Nevertheless you force Him to wait and to wait again, a moment and a moment. A moment in one place and a moment in another; a moment here, a moment there. And so, your Beloved is forced very often to do what you say, a moment and a moment. For you draw a moment and a moment into a longer and longer time. In this way you cheat your friend and weary your Beloved. O how much better, O how much more right it would be for you to keep watch before the door, so that with Abraham and Elijah you might await the coming of your Beloved, run to Him when He comes, and receive Him with rejoicing. Surely as the dove of your Beloved, being supported by wings in the opening of a rock, in the grotto of a wall, you ought to have looked outside with an outstretched neck, seeking and awaiting the advent of your only One with the kind of song and sighing that a dove makes. But perhaps our cherubim still do not have wings, or if they have them they have not yet stretched them out. Perhaps we have not yet fully formed our work nor yet completed that angelic form in its wholeness according to the Lord's declaration.

CHAPTER XIV

How few persons there are who have a soul always prepared for the reception of grace

I remain silent about those who are outside, who have never been able to know spiritual delight. They hear the commands of the Lord from the daily lectures or the writings of the doctors, yet they never come to a state of rest. Sinning daily, they demand that a time of penance be given to them daily. While some from among these gladly hear the words of life, what do they say by their effort except, "Command, command again." And while they heap sins upon sins, what else do they shout by their longing except "Wait, wait again." Demanding a daily interval of penance and proposing a daily time for the recovery of one's self, what do they do except prolong it daily? For the carnal mind, certainly the whole span of this life seems very short for satiating his desires. And while a soul of such sort now expends much time in other things and yet reckons it all as but a moment, what else, I ask, resounds in the ear of divine patience except "a moment here, a moment there"? But meanwhile, being silent concerning these persons, what, I beg you, are we to say about ourselves: We who have put on the garb of religious persons; we who have been given over to spiritual practices; we who continually receive, as it were, certain betrothal gifts of divine love? What, I ask, shall we say especially, we who have no enjoined duty other than to read, to chant and to pray; to be meditating, speculating and contemplating; to be free from preoccupations and to see how sweet the Lord is? (Cf. Ps. 33:9.) Who among us will not be ashamed to say these things and weary our Beloved with words of this kind: "Command, command again; command, command again; wait, wait again; wait, wait again; a moment here, a moment there" (Isa. 28:10, 13). If I am not mistaken, you who daily pursue reading and meditation receive His messengers and come to know His commands. From the hidden recesses of Scripture we daily draw out new understandings. What is this other than that we listen to some messengers of our Beloved? Surely all sacred reading and wise meditation serve this undertaking. And so some persons by means of readings, others by means of meditations, run to meet the messengers of divine secrets who present the commands of our Beloved to us and instruct us concerning individual things. It often happens that one and the same passage of Scripture says many things to us in one thing when it is expounded in several ways: Expounded morally it teaches us what our Beloved wishes us to do; taken allegorically, it reminds us what He has done for us through Himself; interpreted anagogically it proposes what He plans to make of us in the future. And so in this way He often commands and commands us again and announces many things to us by one messenger, as it were. One and the same command is often proposed under various enigmas and figures so that it may be impressed more deeply in our minds. And while the same thing is said to us in many ways and at many times, what else is this except that the same thing often seems to be commanded and commanded again and that there are many who daily receive messengers of this kind? Nevertheless, concerning former tepidity or negligence, they wish to correct it very little or not at all. Surely they thirst for the sort of thing about which they can boast but not for that by which that can be built up. Indeed, they strive after knowledge, not sanctity. They long to be pretenders to knowledge much more than to be saints. While they seek new meanings and new understandings by their daily striving, what do they cry out by striving and zeal except "Command and command again; command and command again"? We listen to messengers of this sort daily, and with now some, now others arriving we still daily rudely drive out the ones and the others. Then we cry out loudly in the ears of the Lord Sabaoth: "Command, command again; command, command again." But the more the messengers abound, surely the more sharply, and harshly our own conscience accuses and crucifies us. For this reason it often happens that we arrange to correct our life; yet we always delay. And while we propose that this correction take place in the future, it happens that the future always remains *future*—nay, perhaps it *never* will come. Often, however, some specific future time is set up so that our life may be corrected. Meanwhile to our Beloved we say, "Wait." And when that future time becomes the present time, it is transferred again to another future time. Again we say: "Wait again." How many persons often propose and firmly establish with themselves that if it is once granted that they may be able to free themselves from the alien affections by which they are entangled in the meantime, then they will nevermore wish to fall into these same things. In the meantime they demand that they be waited for, and when perchance they have lost rather than cut off these affections, they are busily occupied with vigorously repairing what they have destroyed, and again they wish and demand that they be waited for, for yet a moment. Surely they say this: "A moment and a moment." For indeed, however great it is, whatever does not satiate a longing seems too little for an affection. And so, those persons who are of such a sort demand that they themselves be waited for and waited for again, a moment and a moment. A moment here and a moment there. A moment and a moment: often in connection with one affection yet at one time and then another. Here and there: in connection with one affection and another, yet at one time. And in all these things we sing a hateful song to our Beloved: "Wait, wait again; wait, wait again; a moment here, a moment there." When do you think such a lazy and tepid soul will be able to form that beaten work and to forge the angelic form? This is especially true since in this work there is need for the spreading out of wings when urged especially by the very command of the Lord, in so much as in such a pursuit we are never permitted to put down the wings of our longings from elevating our intention.

CHAPTER XV

That it is hard and difficult for any perfect soul to gather itself completely within itself and to rest in longing only for the Godhead

A very small, brief delay—I shall not say of a year, nor shall I say of a month or a day—is troublesome enough to the longing of one who is impatient. Indeed, hope which is put off grieves the soul. And so the beloved of a true friend and the friend of a true beloved, as has been said already above, always ought to be prompt and prepared to receive without any insult of a delay the friend who knocks and to run with all due speed to meet the one who calls. However we know that a singular love does not accept a partner nor does it admit a companion. See to it that the very time He begins to knock at the door is not the first time that you begin to want to throw out the crowds of those who make noise. Moreover, when such a crowd is found with you at that time, what will you say? I say, what will you say, except, "Wait and wait again"? Waiting and waiting again for throwing out the crowd of strangers, for throwing out your household. All thoughts, empty as well as noxious, which do not serve for our benefit must be judged to be strangers. In truth, we possess them like domestic servants or slaves, whom we involve for our use or benefit. But because a singular love loves solitude and seeks for a solitary place, it behooves us to throw out the entire crowd of such a sort, not only of thoughts but also even of affections, so that we may be at liberty to cling more freely and more joyfully to the embraces of our beloved one. How great, I ask, is the delay in such waiting? How often must one repeat: "Wait and wait again, a moment here and a moment there"? A moment in one place, a moment in another. A moment in the garden, a moment in the hall, a moment in the chamber until at last finally after much waiting and great weariness He enters the bedchamber and occupies the most intimate and secret place. A moment in the garden while the whole crowd of those making a disturbance is dispersed. A moment in the hall while the chamber is decorated. A moment in the chamber while the bridal bed is prepared. And the Beloved is forced to wait a moment and a moment in all of these places: a moment here and a moment there. He is heard from the garden. He is seen in the hall. He is kissed affectionately in the chamber. He is embraced in the bed-chamber. He is heard by memory; seen by understanding; kissed warmly by affection; embraced by applause. He is heard by recollection; seen by wonder; kissed warmly by love; embraced by delight. Or if this pleases you better, He is heard by a showing; seen by contemplation; kissed warmly by devotion; drawn close for the infusion of His sweetness. He is heard by a showing when the whole tumult of those who make noise is quieted down and His voice only is heard as it grows stronger. At last that whole crowd of those who make a disturbance is dispersed and He alone remains with her alone and she alone looks at Him alone by contemplation. He is seen by contemplation when on account of the sight of an unexpected vision and wonder at the beauty of it, the soul gradually glows, burns more and more, and finally at last catches fire completely until it is thoroughly reformed to true purity and internal beauty. And that chamber of internal habitation is superbly adorned everywhere with purple garments, linen the color of hyacinth, and twice-dyed scarlet, until finally at some time after the chamber has been adorned and the beloved has been led in, when boldness now increases and longing distresses, when she is no longer able to restrain herself, she suddenly rushes into a kiss and with pressing lips fixes a kiss of intimate devotion. By devotion He is kissed often and in many ways while in the meantime the bedchamber is prepared, until the innermost recess of the soul is composed in supreme peace and tranquillity and finally, when the Beloved is brought between the breasts, she melts completely in desire for Him with a kind of ineffable infusion of divine sweetness and that spirit which clings to the Lord is made one spirit. Concerning the things that happen later, I think that after having known by experience so much sweetness and such inward pleasantness, the soul can no longer contrive any delay nor further weary the Beloved with any waiting while He is knocking. In this respect the soul will no longer say, "Wait and wait again," especially when to her every delay is excessively long and waiting seems burdensome. From now on I think she will gladly watch with the patriarch Abraham or even with the prophet Elijah at the entrance of her habitation so that she may always be prepared for receiving her Beloved. At this time, I think, our beaten work begins to make a great deal of progress and to approach consummation since our cherubim now begin to spread out their wings widely and to suspend themselves at every hour for flying, as it were.

CHAPTER XVI

How it is almost impossible for any soul to pour itself completely outside of itself and to go above itself

Although such a soul may be ready at this time to receive the One who comes, I do not know if it is equally prepared and prompt to run forth to meet the One who calls. I fear lest in this respect it will now say to its Beloved: "Wait, wait again; wait, wait again; a moment here, a moment there." For I think that we do not receive the One coming and follow the One calling with the same ease. It is one thing to go in with Him; it is another to go out to Him. In the former the soul returns into itself and with its Beloved enters into the innermost sanctuary of its heart. In the latter it is led out of itself and is raised up to contemplating lofty things. For what does it mean that the soul goes into itself, except that it gathers itself completely within itself? But what does it mean that it goes out from itself, except that it completely pours itself outside of itself? And so when the soul enters with her Beloved into the bed-chamber, she alone delaying and enjoying the sweetness with Him alone, this is nothing other than that she forgets all external things and delights in supreme and intimate love of Him. She sees herself alone with the Beloved, when, after having forgotten all exterior things, she aims her longing away from consideration of herself and toward love of her Beloved. And on account of these things that she considers in her innermost places, she kindles her soul with such affection and rises up with thanksgiving from the consideration of both her goods and her evils. Hence, on account of grace received and forgiveness granted, she renders sacrifices of inner devotion. The Beloved is led into the innermost place and situated in the best place, when He is loved from innermost affection and above all else. Think what it is in your life that you have loved more ardently, craved more anxiously; what affected you more pleasantly and delighted you more deeply than all other things. Consider, therefore, if you feel the same force of affection and abundance of delight when you burn with longing for the supreme Lover and when you rest in His love. Who doubts that He does not yet occupy that innermost recess of your affections if the dart of intimate love pierces your soul less and excites it less fervently in divine affections than it was accustomed to penetrate and excite it sometimes with respect to alien affections? But if straightway you perceive a force of delight, or perhaps a more powerful force of longing, in your innermost parts concerning divine things—something more powerful than you have experienced in other things—see if there is yet perhaps another thing of some sort by which you are able to be consoled or delighted. Certainly, as long as we are able to receive consolation or pleasure from any alien thing whatsoever, I do not yet dare to say that our Beloved possesses the innermost recess of most ardent love. Whatever sort of soul you now may be, take action, hasten now to bring Him into the innermost and most secret sanctuary of your heart. For who would deny that the innermost sanctuary of the human heart has or even can acquire recesses of such a sort that the force of supreme and singular love cannot be torn away by any alien delight whatsoever, when it has been fixed by affection to something? Certainly, if you seek or receive any sort of alien consolation, although you may perhaps love your God supremely, nevertheless you do not love Him singularly. Therefore, He is not yet led into the innermost place; He is not yet situated in the best place. If you do not busy yourself to bring Him into your innermost place, how can I believe that you either wish or are able to follow Him to his sublime place? Whatsoever sort of soul you are, let it be a certain sign to you that you love your Beloved less or you are loved less by Him, if you are not yet worthy to be called to those contemplative ecstasies or to be following the One who calls. For how perfectly do you love or are you loved if in longing for supreme things you are not snatched to supernal places and do not pass over by means of alienation of mind into those anagogic endeavors? Do you wish to know that the loftiness of divine showings may be an open disclosure of divine love? "Now I do not call you servants but friends," He says, "because I have made known to you everything that I have heard from my Father" (John 15:15). Pay attention to this as well: The mode of a divine showing depends upon the magnitude of divine love: "Eat, friends; drink and become inebriated, most beloved" (Song of Songs 5:1). Behold, those who are friends and beloved, eat; but those who are most beloved, drink. Indeed, they not only drink, but they also become inebriated. Certainly those who eat, while they chew choice food, swallow that in which they delight, but not without delay or some sort of labor. But those who drink swallow with the greatest speed and ease that for which they thirst. Therefore, do not those persons seem to you to eat, who with great effort and prolonged meditation can scarcely reach the delights of truth? However, in a certain manner those drink, who with the greatest ease and delight imbibe from divine showings what they ardently crave concerning the intimate pleasantness of truth. Therefore those who are beloved, eat; but those who are most beloved, drink. This is because the mode of manifestation is ordered according to the measure of love. However, inebriation accomplishes alienation of mind and the infusion of a supernal showing carries away into ecstasy of mind only those who are most beloved. The Prophet wanted to indicate such inebriation when he said: "They shall be inebriated by the richness of your house, and you shall cause them to drink from the torrent of your pleasure" (Ps. 35:9). Therefore, if we crave to overflow with this inebriation, and to make frequent use of this contemplative ecstasy of mind, we must endeavor to love our God intimately and supremely and cling at all hours with supreme longing to the joy of divine contemplation. This will mean that our cherubim have spread-out wings. Behold, with how much labor we have already sweated; behold how much circumlocution we have used in the same matter, so that our cherubim might spread out their wings sufficiently and cover over our propitiatory with whatever kind of obscuring is necessary.

CHAPTER XVII

Concerning those things pertaining especially to the fifth kind of contemplation

Now it remains for us to inquire why the aforementioned cherubim ought to look mutually at each other, and in looking turn faces to the propitiatory: "Let them look mutually at each other after turning faces to the propitiatory" (Exod. 25:20). However, we said above that those things which are above reason yet nevertheless not beyond reason pertain to the first cherub; and that those things which are above reason and seem to be beyond reason pertain to the second cherub. And so, according to this distinction, you see that not by chance do those things which are considered concerning the unity of that supreme and simple divine essence pertain especially to the first cherub; to the second cherub, however, pertain those things which are considered concerning the Trinity of persons. For there are many things that are believed, asserted and proved by the authority of Scripture concerning the Trinity of persons that seem wholly opposed to nature and contrary to all human reason. And so all things of the sort that concern the Trinity are rightly said to pertain to the second cherub, by which those things that oppose human reason are led into contemplation. Let us see how those things which are considered concerning the unity of Divinity in one simple nature exceed the mode of human understanding, and yet they are no less fit for reason. For that reason they especially pertain to the first cherub, that is to the first kind of contemplation. Certainly, we believe that the principal and supreme One of all is truly simple and supremely one; and in that one simple good, all good exists. As far as essence is concerned, nothing is more simple than that One. As far as efficacy is concerned nothing is more manifold. As far as essence is concerned, what is more simple than that which is truly and supremely one? As far as efficacy is concerned, what is more manifold than that which is truly and without doubt able to do everything? See how difficult it is to comprehend by means of human reason everything that exists; then you will understand how incomprehensible that good is in which every good exists. It is above reason to comprehend how that good is truly simple and supremely one, and how that good is every good. Nevertheless human reason easily acquiesces in this assertion and refers to it by its testimony, when it considers, affirms and truly bears witness that if in that supreme and sempiternal good anything of good were lacking, it would not be full and perfect and wholly sufficient. Therefore, how can that which is boundless and infinite be comprehended? "Great is the Lord, and praiseworthy beyond measure; and of his greatness there is no end" (Ps. 144:3). But what sense is able to grasp, and what reason is able to comprehend, how at one and the same time He can be both truly simple if He is boundless and supremely one if He is infinite? Nevertheless reason bears witness by reasoning that that which is not truly composite is truly simple, because everything that is composite can be divided naturally, and that which is naturally divisible is also changeable according to something. Therefore reason agrees that He is truly simple, since He must be unchangeable, because He is agreed to be the best of all and supreme: "With him there is no change, nor any shadow of change" (James 1:17). Therefore, if it is good that He is unchangeable, in like manner it will be good that He is a simple being. Therefore, it follows that He is supremely simple because He is supremely good. Therefore, if nothing is more simple than that, then nothing is more subtle than that; and that of which nothing is more subtle, nothing is deeper than that; and nothing is more inscrutable than the deepest thing, and it follows that nothing is more incomprehensible. Yet let us see what may happen as the result of the mutual collocation of simplicity and boundlessness, unity and everything. If every good is there, He is the supreme good and everything is there; therefore He is the supreme power, the supreme wisdom, the supreme goodness, the supreme happiness. But where supreme simplicity is, everything that is there is one and the same thing. And so it is one and the same thing for Him to exist, to live, to understand, and to be able to be good and blessed. See how incomprehensible this is. There is not one who is powerful, another who is wise, another who is good and another who is blessed. Think therefore, what that power is for which it is the same to do as it is to wish to be doing. Pay attention to what that wisdom is for which it is the same to be able to do as to know. Give thought to what that goodness is for which whatever is pleasing to it, for this reason it is fitting that it be pleasing, and whatever is displeasing to it, for this reason it is fitting that it be displeasing. Consider what that life is, for which it is the same to be as to be blessed. Again, pay attention to this: that if He is truly omnipotent, He is also able to be everywhere. Therefore, He is potentially everywhere, both the place where He is and the place where He is not. But if He is there potentially, He is also there essentially, because His power is not one thing and His essence, another. Therefore, essentially He is within all things and outside all things, below all things and above all things. If He is within all things, nothing is more secret than He is. If He is outside all things, nothing is farther away than He is. If He is below all things, nothing is more obscure than He is. If He is above all things, nothing is more sublime than He is. What is more incomprehensible than that than which nothing is more secret, nothing farther away, nothing more obscure, nothing more sublime? Again, if He is in every place, nothing is more present than He is. If He is outside every place, nothing is more absent than He is. But is anything more absent than that very One who is the most present of all, and is anything more present than that very One who is the most absent of all, who does not have to be one thing and another in order to be everything that exists? But if nothing is more present than the most absent and if nothing is more absent than the most present, what is more marvelous than this, what is more incomprehensible? Again, if His power is not one thing and His happiness another, wherever supreme power is, there supreme happiness is also. Therefore, supreme happiness is everywhere. How can there be a place of supreme misery in the inferno or how can any place be miserable in which supreme happiness is nowhere absent or never lacking? All these things are marvelous and truly incomprehensible. Reason approves many things—nay, almost an infinite number of things—concerning the unity of Divinity and the consideration of true unity, and yet it does not comprehend them. And so, all things of this sort are above reason but not beyond reason, and for this very reason, according to the conclusion mentioned above, they show themselves to pertain to the first cherub.

CHAPTER XVIII

Concerning those things which pertain especially to the sixth kind of contemplation

Concerning the Trinity of persons, however, and speculation about the Trinity, how many things are firmly believed and truly asserted that nevertheless seem to be not only above reason but even against reason? We believe in one God—Father, and Son, and Holy Spirit: the Father from nothing, the Son from the Father only, the Holy Spirit from the Father and the Son; the Son by having been begotten, the Holy Spirit by having proceeded. And so we believe in one and the same God, triune in persons and one in substance. For which reason the Father is one person, the Son is another, and the Holy Spirit is another. Nevertheless the Father is not other than the Son, nor are the Father and the Son other than the Spirit of both. For the person of the Father is one; the person of the Son, another; the person of the Holy Spirit, another; yet they all have one substance, the same essence, and a single nature. We believe all these things; we confess all these things openly, and they are agreed truly to be. Yet in all these things if they are considered according to human opinion, human reason seems to oppose them strongly. If the Father is unbegotten and the Son is only-begotten, will not the substance of the Father be unbegotten and that of the Son be begotten? And since both have one and the same substance, will not the same substance be begotten and unbegotten, that is begotten and not begotten? Can the same substance beget itself and be born from itself? Can the same substance be born and not be born; can it experience birth and not experience birth? If we say that the Son is born, what shall we say concerning His birth? Will not His birth be eternal "with whom there is no changing nor any shadow of change" (James 1:17)?

If at some time His birth was not, how is He coeternal and coequal with the Father? And if His birth will cease to exist at some time, how will that nature be unchangeable in which something passes away? If He always was, how does He who never began to be and without whom the Father never would be able to exist as Father receive being from another? And how is His birth complete, if it is still future? Or perhaps it is repeated continually, so that it can exist always? Therefore, in this case will it not be multiple and infinite rather than one, as much as it will be necessary to repeat it into infinity? But whatever is said concerning the birth of the Son, see to it lest perchance we are able to seek out by reasoning the same thing about the procession of the Holy Spirit. Behold these things; if they are considered according to human opinion these things seem to oppose human reason. If the Holy Spirit is of the same power with the Father, does it not have itself the same power that the Father has? Can it beget such a Son as the Father is able to do? Or perhaps it does not have the power to beget the Son—a Son of the sort who is omnipotent? Or perhaps it does not wish to do so, although it is able? Therefore, how will the Spirit possess with the Father similitude of will and fullness of the similitude? Concerning the Trinity of persons, you will find many things of this sort—they are almost innumerable—which you will discover are not only incomprehensible but even discordant to human reason. You will find many such things, I say, concerning the Trinity of persons and many such things concerning the union of substances in the incarnation of the Word.

What, I ask, is it in which humanity and Divinity are united so that they can be one person? Is it something that is of man, something that is of God, or something that is of both? But if it is not of both, how are they able to be united in that which is alien to one or the other of them? If it is something that is of man, therefore it is a creature. If it is something that is of God, it is above a creature, and is no longer a creature. If it is something that is of God and of man, how can it be both and not be both, that is, a creature and not a creature? But this question is very much a secret and to such an extent, as far as I am concerned, it is not debatable and hence may perhaps be more rightly suppressed. But what can we say concerning the soul of Christ inasmuch as we dare not deny that He has received complete fullness of grace? For whatever the Father has from nature, Christ receives from grace. For in Christ complete fullness of Divinity dwells corporeally (Col. 2:9). If He receives complete fullness of grace, therefore He also receives fullness of wisdom, and fullness of power. Therefore, if He possesses equal wisdom and equal power with the Father (which cannot be denied), how can He be equal to the Father and a creature be coequal with the Creator, a thing that is not to be confessed? But if without any doubt He possesses equal power and equal wisdom, how is He not capable of being completely coequal with Him? But why do we say this concerning the soul of Christ, when concerning His body we believe and hold many things according to the affirmation of faith that reason opposes and judges impossible? When Christ distributed His body to His disciples, did he carry Himself in His hands? Again: Was it He Himself who carried and was carried? Again: Was He the same one who was given? When He was taken by the disciples and was ground by their teeth, was He injured? Or perhaps in that which was given, He was incapable of suffering, just as He was also invisible, although according to that which He gave, it was not only visible but also capable of suffering. Therefore, was one and the same body at one and the same time both visible and invisible, capable of suffering and incapable of suffering? See how incomprehensible this is and how impossible it seems to be. See in how many places the same body of Christ is consecrated and held daily. Is it therefore divided into parts, so that it may be held in so many places? How then will it be truly incapable of suffering and truly incorruptible? But when it is dispersed through so many places, where does it remain integral and uncorrupted and completely indivisible? Therefore if you pay attention to how many places it is, in how many places it is able to exist by the same power of sanctification, where, I ask, will your thinking lead you, except that it seems to you that one and the same body is able to exist in an infinite number of places at the same time? But you see how this is not only against the particular nature of bodies but also above every particular nature of spirits. Therefore if those things which we believe with certainty concerning the body of Christ are so incomprehensible and seem so incredible, how much more and far more excellently do those things which are considered concerning the soul of Christ surpass all human reason. Nevertheless, incomparably more sublime are those things which come to mind to be considered concerning the Trinity of persons. And so all such things that seem not only to go beyond the narrowness of human reasoning but also to make it foolish are rightly said to pertain to the second cherub. And so it has been rightly said that those things which are considered concerning the unity of divine substance pertain especially to the first cherub. But those things which are considered concerning the Trinity of persons pertain especially to the second cherub. And so the first consideration pertains to the fifth kind of contemplation, but the second consideration pertains to the sixth and ultimate kind of contemplation.

CHAPTER XIX

Concerning the mutual coming together of the two last speculations

However, with respect to this twin consideration, that is the fifth and the sixth kinds of contemplation, we ought to observe carefully and take careful precautions so that as we affirm things pertaining to one, we do not destroy things pertaining to the other. Thus, let us make the case for the unity of that supreme and divine substance in such a way that we do not empty the Trinity of persons; let us prove the Trinity of persons in such a way that we do not disperse the unity of substance. And so those aforementioned cherubim should mutually look at each other and because of mutual consent in harmony, should not turn the eyes of their speculation in a contrary direction by means of any consideration of the part of their understanding. How many persons, in what they determine concerning the unity of supreme Divinity, strive to empty out the true faith in the Trinity? Again: How many, in what they affirm concerning the Trinity, wish to disperse the unity of the divine essence? Arius said: The Father is one thing; the Son is another; and the Holy Spirit is another. He would have spoken quite rightly if he had said "another person" and not "another thing." In any case, he dissolved the unity of Divinity by what he said. Sabellius said: When God wishes, He is Father; when He wishes, He is Son; when He wishes, He is Holy Spirit; nevertheless He is one. In what he said, he truly undertook to empty out the faith of the Trinity. Surely in matters of this sort our cherubim turn their faces aside from one or the other aspect, because by a contrary assertion they often maintain diverse conclusions and themselves give assent to opposites. According to the first cherub we say that it is the one and only God who created everything from nothing. According to the second cherub we affirm that it is one person who is begotten, and it is another person who proceeds from both. But these two cherubim look at each other mutually, because we say that one and the same God is one according to substance and three according to person. According to the first cherub we say that the Father, and the Son, and the Holy Spirit are united in one substance, in one essence, and in one nature. According to the second cherub we say the Father is one in person, and the Son is another in person, and the Holy Spirit is another in person. Let the cherubim look at each other mutually, and we undoubtedly confess openly that Father, and Son, and Holy Spirit are not one thing and another thing, although they are truly one person and another person. One person is Father; another is Son; and another is Holy Spirit according to the second cherub; yet the Father is not one thing; the Son is not another thing; the Holy Spirit is not another thing according to the first cherub, when we affirm truly that according to mutual regard Father, and Son, and Holy Spirit are not three gods, but one God. According to the second cherub we confess that the substance of the Son has been united with our substance in one person. According to the first cherub we affirm with certainty that the substance of the Father, and of the Son, and of the Holy Spirit is one and indivisible. Then according to mutual regard we confess openly that the Son alone truly was incarnate. And so cherub looks at cherub when what one says, the other does not contradict. Cherub looks at cherub when the fifth kind of contemplation asserts those things which are for its consideration in such a way that it does not wish in any way to empty out those things which belong to the other cherubim. The cherubim look at each other mutually when the last two kinds of contemplation come to meet each other by turns and allude to sharing with each other and to the harmony of truth. Again: One cherub looks at the other when (as usually happens) our speculation begins with the penultimate kind and concludes with the last. Or, on the contrary, it begins from the last and descends to the penultimate.

Chapter XX

Concerning the mutual coming together of the three last speculations

However, the two cherubim not only ought to look at each other; they certainly also ought to turn their faces toward the propitiatory in looking at one another. The designated cherubim turn their faces toward the propitiatory when they draw a similitude of reason from those things which are subject to the fourth kind of contemplation in order to support their assertion in what they jointly agree about with respect to sublime and divine things. For indeed, we understand the fourth kind of contemplation by the propitiatory, just as in the two cherubim we understand the fifth and sixth. Now, just as it has been said above, the fourth kind of contemplation is engaged especially with those things which are usually considered about the rational but created spirit. In contrast, the fifth and sixth are engaged principally with those things which are properly considered about the divine and uncreated Spirit. Therefore, since we know that the rational creature has been made according to the image of the Creator, from that nature we rightly seek in a more familiar manner the rational principle of a similitude and we form the mode of our investigation. From that nature, I say, in whose created condition, we ought not to doubt, traces of the divine image have been impressed more forcefully and expressed most clearly. And so what else does it mean that the cherubim turn their faces toward the propitiatory, other than in the speculation and investigation of divine things to pay attention to the rational creature and to advance higher toward an understanding of Divinity from the examination of a similitude? If you marvel how God the Maker of everything brought into actuality from nothing at the very beginning of the world so much and so many various species of things just as He willed, think how easy it is for the human soul to fashion by means of the imagination any representations of things whatsoever at any hour and to form some unique creatures, as it were, as often as it wishes, without preexisting material and from nothing, as it were. What at first perhaps seemed unbelievable will begin to be a little less marvelous. In the foregoing you will discover a very remarkable thing: that God reserved the truth of things, which is the supreme truth, for Himself; but He conceded to His image the formation of images of things at whatever time. If you marvel how one and the same God is able to exist in all places when He has not been divided into parts but is everywhere complete, pay attention to the fact that one and the same soul is diffused through all members of the body and yet itself is not divided into parts but is whole and undivided in the individual members. Therefore, in this way the soul exists in its own body according to its own measure; that is, it exists in a world of its own control, which it also receives to be ruled. If you marvel how without any opposition and by only the nod of His will God inclines to His good pleasure all things that are done in the world, consider that the soul moves, moderates and sets in order every member of its body by means of only the decision of the will. And so in both as far as similitude is concerned there is one mode of action, although it is diverse in the comparison of equality. In all these things the first cherub directs itself to the propitiatory when it draws a rational principle of similitude from the rational creature for contemplation of the Creator. In this rational creature itself, if we pay careful attention, we can find, we believe, some trace of the supreme Trinity. For there is something there from the mind itself, namely its wisdom; and there is something there from both the mind and its wisdom, namely their love. For every mind loves its wisdom and for that reason love of its wisdom proceeds from both. For wisdom is from the mind alone, but love is from mind and wisdom equally. So the Son (that is, the wisdom of the Father) is from the Father alone; however the Holy Spirit (that is, the love of both) is from the Father and the Son. In this way the second cherub discovers how beneficially it is able to turn the face of its consideration toward the propitiatory, if it seeks the support of a similitude in the speculation of divine things.

Surely it ought to be noted that these three things that come together in the consideration of the soul do not make a Trinity of persons; just as those three in God divide into three persons according to a difference of individual properties. See, therefore, that in these things that have been drawn forth in the soul by means of a similitude, the dissimilarity is greater than the similarity to that supreme Trinity. Do not marvel that the second cherub more nearly touches the side of dissimilitude in our propitiatory. It looks at the side of similitude as if from afar. If it is marvelous to you how the Son (namely, the wisdom of the Father) alone has become incarnate, how He came to us in flesh and nevertheless did not depart from the Father, reflect on the fact that in the image-Trinity of the mind only wisdom is embodied in the human voice and comes forth by means of the bodily voice. After it has come forth it is recognized; when it is recognized it is retained in the mind; yet it is not separated even a little bit from that mind from which it was born. There are many such things in the rational mind according to which the second cherub ought to direct itself toward the propitiatory. Behold, now by means of an exposition we know according to the Lord's testimony how the two cherubim are to look at each other; and no less do we know for what reason and benefit they ought to turn their faces toward the propitiatory.

CHAPTER XXI

*That a multitude of divine showings always accompanies the frequent use of
the three last kinds of speculation*

We also ought neither to neglect nor to pass over without
careful consideration that which is promised by the voice of the
Lord when it said to Moses: "I will speak to you from above the
propitiatory," that is "from between the two cherubim" (Exod.
25:22). Think how great and what sort of a thing it is to consider
God at any hour when there may be a need and in any sort of
necessity to seek and receive divine counsel when it may be necessary. If you do this, then you will be able to notice how necessary
and beneficial it is to possess these last three modes of speculation
familiarly. "Whence I will speak to you." From what place, I ask,
or whence? "From above the propitiatory and from between the
two cherubim." Therefore, if he wishes to possess the divine oracle
familiarly, let a man ascend to a high heart and by means of the
mind's going above that aforementioned propitiatory, let him take a
place between the two cherubim so that by means of the third kind
of contemplation he may ascend to the fifth and sixth. After the
mind has been elevated above the propitiatory it is turned toward
the place between the two cherubim when the contemplative soul,
going beyond not only the corporeal but even the spiritual creation
by means of a sublime consideration, is suspended in wonder at the
supreme Unity and Trinity. We are raised up, as it were, above the
propitiatory to the mirror of this wonder when from investigation
of the rational creature and consideration of the divine image we are
advanced higher toward recognition of Divinity. We run to and fro
in the middle, between the propitiatory and the two cherubim as it
were, when from the mutual combination of the three last speculations we progress more fully toward the perfection of each speculation. And so we ought gladly to run to and fro between these
three kinds of manifestations and by means of the mirror and image
of the supreme Trinity and Unity to penetrate more deeply into the
speculation of the glory of the same Trinity and Unity. If we
willingly reconsider and frequently draw into consideration and
admiration that which we have recognized concerning the worth of

the rational creature and the worth and splendor of the Creator, then we shall be worthy to recognize from divine showings those things concerning the same kinds of manifestations which we were unable to understand previously. This is what is promised to you when it is said: "Whence I will speak to you." Therefore, think how beneficial it is to reconsider often the mysteries of our faith and to have them frequently in memory, since from such effort we shall be able to obtain a multitude of divine showings. Therefore if we can neither see by ecstasy of mind nor comprehend by means of pure and clear understanding those things which we believe concerning the Trinity of persons and the Unity of substance in God, nevertheless, insofar as it is possible for us, let us draw into frequent consideration those things which we receive from the Catholic tradition and hold by faith. The result of this will be that from such effort we can deserve an abundance of divine showings. For indeed, I think that the consolation of divine showings will not be completely foreign to those who both often and willingly behold by the eye of faith the hidden secrets of divine mysteries. How much more familiar will the consolation be expecially to those who, contemplating these things continually by the eye of understanding and seeing them often by means of ecstasy of mind, are not able to satisfy their longing? Therefore, whoever carries out the function of Moses; whoever accepts the pastoral office; upon whom it finally rests according to the Lord's command to lead the people of the Lord out of the house of bondage, through the wilderness and into the promised land—this person certainly ought to move about by means of free flight everywhere among those three kinds of contemplation which have been previously mentioned. This he should do so that he may always be found more worthy, who ought to be instructed worthily from the oracle of the Lord and made certain above any uncertainty as often as may be necessary concerning both his ignorance and the ignorance of his people. Therefore, if you desire to recognize from divine inspiration what is the good and perfect will of God, you must always be ready and disposed toward these last three kinds of manifestations. By the merits of this exercise perhaps you will be worthy to test the truth of that promise: "Whence I will speak to you."

CHAPTER XXII

That in every kind of contemplation it happens that a contemplative person may enter into ecstasy of mind

Although it is usual and seems proper in the two last kinds of contemplations to see by means of ecstasy of mind, however, on the contrary in the first four kinds it is a common thing and almost ordinary to rise up into contemplation without any alienation of the soul. Nevertheless every kind of contemplation can and usually does happen in both modes. Among those things which are subject to the first kinds of contemplation we are able to learn some things from divine showing and also to perceive them with the eye of contemplation by means of ecstasy of mind. Again, we are accustomed, as we have knowledge and the ability, to draw those things which pertain to the two last kinds of contemplation into consideration according to the ordinary state of the soul and to see them also by means of contemplation. But since those things which pertain to the last two always go beyond the discernment of the human mind, when the mind draws them into consideration according to the state of soul usual for all, or, on the contrary, when the human mind itself goes beyond itself and passes into alienation in order to perceive something more penetratingly and more clearly in these things, it is necessary to express this very thing mystically and suitably in an angelic form rather than a human representation. However, we know from the mystical example of Moses that all these kinds of contemplation can be perceived by means of ecstasy. But on the other hand we know from the work of Bezeleel considered as a typological foreshadowing that they can be drawn into contemplation without any ecstasy of mind. In order that Moses might be able to see the ark and both cherubim from a divine showing, he ascended the mountain and entered into the cloud. However, in order that Bezeleel might look at and labor on that mystical work, it is read that he had to seek out and approach neither a mountain nor a cloud. What does it mean to approach a mountain except to rise up to a high heart according to the prophetic statement? But then a cloud covers a mountain of this sort when the memory of everything exterior is forgotten by the mind. Moses remains on this mountain for six days; on the seventh day from the middle of the cloud he is called to a conversation with the Lord. As has been noted, we are occupied with our works for six days; on the seventh day, we rest. Therefore, we spend six days, as it were, on this mountain, when with much labor and great activity of soul we accustom ourselves to remain longer in such a state of sublimity. However, one comes to the seventh day, as it were, when so much lifting up of the mind is changed into pleasure for the mind and is approached without any labor at all. The soul now arrives at the seventh day, as it were, when in that state of sublimity it is finally at some time composed in supreme tranquillity so that it lays aside not only all care and anxiety but almost goes beyond the entire limit of the human ability to suffer. When the Lord calls, the soul is admitted to a conversation with the Lord when on account of divine inspiration and showing it is admitted into that abyss of divine judgments. Moses enters into the middle of the cloud when the human mind, having been engrossed by the boundlessness of divine light, is put into a state of sleep with supreme forgetfulness of self. So you can marvel, and you ought justly to marvel, how there the cloud harmonizes with the fire, and the fire with the cloud: the cloud of ignorance with the fire of illuminated understanding; ignorance and forgetting of things known and experienced with the showing and understanding of things previously unknown and unexperienced up to that point. For at one and the same time human understanding is illumined with respect to divine things and darkened with respect to human things. This peace, darkening and illumining of the uplifted soul are summed up by the Psalmist in a few words when he says: "In peace, in the same, I will sleep and I will rest" (Ps. 4:9). In truth, the soul finds peace when, after it has been led above itself, it in no way feels the vexation of the human ability to suffer. It sleeps in this peace when, after it has been lulled to sleep in supreme tranquillity, whatever it has been accustomed to think about when not intoxicated now comes to it with forgetfulness. For he who sleeps does not know those things which are around him—indeed he does not even know himself. Therefore alienation of mind is rightly expressed by "sleep." By alienation the mind is absent from usual places and while occupied by sleep, as it were, it goes away from human things for contemplation of divine things. And then it falls asleep "in the same" when by means of contemplation and wonder it rests in Him to whom it is one and the same thing to be everything that is, and who alone can truly say, "I am who I am" (Exod. 3:14). Therefore, what Moses indicates by the seventh day, David more openly calls it "peace." And what for the former is "to enter the middle of a cloud," this is for the latter, "to fall asleep." And what one says by "he rests in the same," this is what the other says by "he goes up and remains with the Lord." And so according to the similitude of Moses, as it were, after ascending to the summit of the mountain, he enters into the midst of the cloud, and at that time he sees and contemplates the aforementioned ark and cherubim by means of a showing from the Lord, when after having been snatched away into sublime things by raising up and alienation of mind, the soul is advanced on account of divine inspiration to those six kinds of contemplations which we have already described. It was said to Moses: "See that you make all things just as they have been shown to you on the mountain" (Exod. 25:40). If all things were shown to him on the mountain by the Lord, therefore he was shown not only the cherubim but also the ark. This is what I have already said above, namely that the things pertaining to any kind of contemplation whatsoever are able to seen in ecstasy of mind by means of a showing from the Lord. But nonetheless from the work of Bezeleel it can be concluded that any of these things can be and are accustomed to be drawn into contemplation without any ecstasy of mind. For what, I ask, does it mean to make the ark, to clothe it with gold, to encircle it with a crown, to cover it with the propitiatory, and to add the cherubim, except to acquire the art of the above-mentioned kinds of contemplations, to learn and put into use one contemplation after another by much effort and labor, and, finally, to consummate the work at some time and in the end to be perfect in all things? But in order that I may be silent concerning the ark, what shall I say concerning the cherubim themselves? Do we read that Bezeleel climbed the mountain or entered a cloud in order to form them or see them when they had been formed? From this it is clearly meant to be understood that those two last kinds of contemplation, whose characteristic quality seems to be that they are exercised in ecstasy of mind, are nevertheless accustomed at some time to be confined within the bounds of human comprehension. All kinds of contemplations can be carried out in both modes and are accustomed to be exercised now by ecstasy of mind, now without any ecstasy of mind.

CHAPTER XXIII

That some have the gift of ecstasy fortuitously while others possess it from virtue, as it were

Among those who are led above themselves in their contemplations and are carried up to ecstasy of mind, some await and receive this even now only from the summons of grace. On the other hand, others can acquire this for themselves by great activity of soul, yet with the cooperation of grace. The former have this gift fortuitously, as it were; but the latter already possess it as though from virtue. This experience is fortuitous, as it were, to each one in that he is not able to have it when or as he wishes. Therefore those who are able to do nothing at all in this from their own activity but can only await the hour of the summons of grace have this as though fortuitously. Those who in great measure are already able to have it when they wish are said to have the efficacy of a grace of this sort from virtue. We have the representation of one thing in Moses; the other, in Aaron the priest. For it was only by the grace of a showing from the Lord that Moses deserved to see the ark in the cloud on the mountain. He did not have it in his power at all to see it when he wished. However, Aaron had it in his power in great measure to enter into the Holy of Holies as often as the office of priest itself or reason required and to see within its veil the ark of the Lord. It is certainly sufficiently evident that the Holy of Holies occupied the innermost and most secret place in the tabernacle of the covenant. Therefore, just as we understand the supreme point of the mind by the peak of the mountain, so we understand the innermost part of the human mind by the Holy of Holies. But in the human soul the supreme point is undoubtedly the same as the innermost part, and the innermost part the same as the supreme point. And so we understand the same thing by the peak of the mountain and the oracle of the tabernacle of the covenant.

Therefore, what does it mean to approach the peak of the mountain or the interior tabernacle, other than to ascend to, to take possession of and to occupy the supreme and innermost recess of the mind? Indeed, by that first tabernacle we understand the common state of the soul that we all know; but by the second tabernacle we understand that state of soul which is by ecstasy of mind and which few know as yet. To the former especially pertains the rational sense; but to the latter, the intellectual sense. In the former surely we gaze at the invisible things of ourselves; in the latter we contemplate invisible divine things. But a dense veil of forgetting separates and shuts off these states from each other (that is, the one known to all and the other experienced by few). For when we are carried away either above or within ourselves by ecstasy of mind in contemplation of divine things, we immediately forget all exterior things—nay not only those which are outside us but also those which are in us. And again: When we return to ourselves from that state of sublimity, we are completely unable to recall to our memory, with that truth and clarity we earlier observed, those things which earlier we saw above ourselves. And although we may retain in memory something from that experience and see it through a veil, as it were, and as though in the middle of a cloud, we lack the ability to comprehend or call to mind either the manner of seeing or the quality of the vision. And marvelously, in a way remembering, we do not remember; and not remembering, we remember; while seeing we do not discern; looking at, we do not examine; and as we direct our intention to something, we do not penetrate it. Certainly you see that the human mind—whether it goes into that innermost place of hidden secrets or whether it goes out from there to exterior things—you see, I say, that each of these has a veil of forgetting. And so it means the same thing to enter the cloud and to penetrate within the veil. But although that which Moses accomplished and that in which Aaron was employed often are concerned with the same things, nevertheless they differ especially in that which each of them does, since in this hour the former was mindful only of the good pleasure of another; the latter undertook it as a duty, as it were, and accomplished it in great part as he wished. But so that Aaron might be able to have the proper and ready thing in order to go within the veil when he wished and it was necessary, he had acquired and possessed for himself the pontifical accoutrements and clothing sufficient for that office. What does it mean to have clothing sufficient for that office, except to acquire those merits of virtues by which it is possible to have in use the function of a grace of this sort? However, it is proper for whoever wishes to penetrate to the interior of the veil to move forward not only clothed in the pontifical clothing but also surrounded with a cloud of aromatic smoke, according to the Lord's command; the result will be that at the hour of his entrance he is fervent with so great an exhalation of celestial desires and a boiling over of aromatic smoke, as it were, that he comes to Him in contempt of self and considers everything that might be pleasing among the accoutrements of the inner man to be worth nothing. Perhaps it means the same thing for Moses to leave the crowd behind at the foot of the mountain and for Aaron to take off ordinary clothing before entering into the tabernacle; or again, for Moses to ascend the mountain with the elders of Israel and for Aaron to go into the interior tabernacle with pontifical clothing. Perhaps it is not one thing and then another when Moses reaches the peak of the mountain with only Joshua after having left the elders behind on the ascent of the mountain, and Aaron hastens into the Holy of Holies with aromatic incense. And again: No less does Moses penetrate into a cloud and Aaron penetrate within the veil. The result is that between the two actions there is only this difference as far as concerns the mystical teaching: That one went secretly into that secret conversation of divine showing from only the calling of the Lord; the other went from his own deliberation.

BOOK V

CHAPTER I

That we advance in the grace of contemplation by three modes

We advance in the grace of contemplation by three modes: One from grace alone; another with the addition of human activity; a third from the teaching of another person. We have a type and example of these three in three persons: Moses, Bezeleel, and Aaron, if we reflect upon their deeds. First of all, Moses saw the ark on the mountain and in the cloud without any labor of activity and solely from the showing of the Lord. Bezeleel formed it by his own labor when he had been able to see it. However, Aaron was accustomed to see the ark that already had been formed by the work of another person. After the manner of Moses we see the Ark of the Lord without any human activity when we receive the ray of contemplation solely from a showing from the Lord. But we then advance in this very thing from our own work when we acquire skill in the same grace by means of our effort and labor, according to the example of Bezeleel, as it were. However, we then learn that we can see the Ark of the Lord by reason of the work of another, as it were, when we are accustomed to the use of such grace from the instruction of others. But we do not want what we say concerning the working of our activity to be understood as though we were able to do anything at all without the cooperation of grace, since our activity cannot do anything whatsoever except from grace. But it is one thing to receive the grace of contemplation as divinely given; it is quite another thing to acquire a gift of this sort from God by means of the cooperation of our own effort. And so, we obtain this

308

grace by three modes: Now from divine inspiration, now from our own exertion, and now from the instruction of another.

But in fact, it ought to be noted that some persons are advanced to this grace by their own activity and without the teaching of any doctrine, who nevertheless in their contemplation are never in any way carried away as far as ecstasy of mind. However, some persons advance to the same grace by instruction from another more than by their own keenness of mind, who nevertheless in their contemplations often rise up as far as ecstasy of mind. For this reason it is read that Bezeleel did build the ark, although he never went into it. But in fact, it cannot be doubted that according to custom Aaron entered into the ark that had been built already by the work of another and placed within the veil. Behold: In this work we who take up, as it were, the office of Bezeleel take the trouble to impart instruction to you for the pursuit of contemplation and to sweat greatly in making this ark. Nevertheless, you go before me by a long way in this grace if, after having been assisted by these things you hear, you are better able to go within the interior of the veil and if you are able to perceive by ecstasy of mind and see, as it were, within the veil that at which we labor out in the open, as it were, and comprehend and assign according to ordinary usage.

It should be noted that some persons, when they return to themselves in the ordinary state of the soul, are completely unable to recollect and to grasp those things which they catch sight of in alienation of the mind. So it is that King Nebuchadnezzar saw a dream, but when awakened from sleep, he was not able to recall the dream to memory (Dan. 2:1). Some persons easily reexamine afterward what they considered by ecstasy. Others greatly sweat with much labor in order to do this. So it is that King Pharaoh saw a dream and retained the vision (Gen. 41:1–8). On the other hand, King Nebuchadnezzar recovered the lost dream with much diligent effort. The Ark of the Lord was shown to Moses on the mountain by a showing from the Lord; but afterward in the valley it was known familiarly and seen often. Again, other persons who rarely and as though fortuitously have ecstasy of mind in their contemplations begin at some time to have it familiarly. Hence it is that at long last Moses habitually went within the veil to the Ark of the Lord, which he first learned to see in the cloud only at the calling and showing of the Lord. There are many things in all these mysteries that now neither can be nor ought to be treated individually.

CHAPTER II

By what modes every contemplation is accustomed to happen: that is, by enlarging of the mind, by raising up of the mind, by alienation of the mind

It seems to me that the quality of contemplation is varied according to three modes. For now it happens by enlarging of the mind, now by raising up of the mind and at another time by alienation of the mind. Enlarging of the mind is when the sharp point of the soul is expanded more widely and is sharpened more intensely; yet this in no way goes beyond the mode of human activity. Raising up of the mind is when the vivacity of the understanding, being divinely irradiated, transcends the bounds of human activity; nevertheless it does not pass over into alienation of mind, so that what it sees is above it, and yet it does not withdraw even a little from accustomed things. Alienation of mind is when the memory of present things is forgotten by the mind, and by a transfiguration from divine working the mind goes over to a state of soul both alien and inaccessible to human activity. Those who are worthy to be raised up to the supreme stronghold of such grace experience these three kinds of contemplation. The first rises up from human activity; the third from divine grace alone; the middle one from the combination of both, that is from human activity and divine grace. In the first stage we construct a stronghold, as it were, with our labor when by our effort and activity we acquire the art of contemplating. In the second stage, the ark is raised up on supporting shoulders and follows the traces of the cloud that goes before, as it were, when with busy activity and the cooperating grace of a showing that goes before, as it were, the ray of contemplation is enlarged. In the third stage the ark is carried into the Holy of Holies and is placed within the veil, as it were, when the sharp point of the contemplative soul is gathered to the innermost recess of the mind and is cut off from the memory of exterior things by a veil of forgetting and alienation. And so the first stage pertains to constructing the ark; the second, to carrying forth the ark; the third, to bringing in the same and covering it with a veil. That which is said to Abraham by the Lord is rightly understood concerning the first stage: "Raise your eyes and look from the place in which you now are, to the North and the South, to the East and the West. I shall give you all the land which you see" (Gen. 13:14–15). That which is written concerning Moses is rightly understood concerning the second: "From the plains of Moab, Moses ascended upon Mount Nebo, on the peak of Pisgah opposite Jericho. And the Lord exhibited all the land from Gilead to Dan" (Deut. 34:1). It concerns the third, however, that after the Lord led the witnesses of his transfiguration into a high mountain, he was covered over by a luminous cloud and also, just as has already been said above, that Moses approached the Lord in the middle of a cloud (Matt. 17: 1–8; Exod. 23: 16–18).

In the first Scripture passage Abraham is not commanded to ascend the mountain, nor is it read there that the Lord exhibited anything to him; but from the place in which he was, he was commanded to raise his eyes and to look around at the land that he was to receive. No mention of an ascension or exhibition is read there, in which either the elevation of a raised-up mind or the demonstration of a divine showing might be indicated. We raise our eyes from the place in which we are or are accustomed to be when we do not abandon the common and accustomed state of the soul in the manifestations of our contemplation. The mode of our comprehension is the place in which we are for a time by means of the understanding. We consider the greatness of the inheritance we shall receive when by the eyes of our contemplation we foresee long before how great a width of perfection we shall finally be able to attain at some time by means of the progress of our devotion. In these words of Scripture nothing is intimated that seems to go beyond human activity. For this reason they are suited for that first stage of contemplation. But that Moses is commanded to ascend the mountain and that the Lord is said to have exhibited to him the land of promise—give attention how expressly these seem to indicate the second stage of contemplation. What does that mountainous ascent of Moses mean except a kind of elevation of the human mind above the level of human possibility into supernal things?

Moreover, what does that exhibition from the Lord mean except the infused illumination of inner aspiration? To catch sight of the land of promise on account of a divine demonstration is to come to know the fullness of future retribution from the showing of a divine representation and to pursue contemplation of this sort. It seems to be by human activity that Moses ascends the mountain; by divine grace that the Lord shows him the land of promise. From the foregoing, this witness of Scripture gives evidence that it refers to the second stage of which we have spoken. However, since it is read that when Moses ascended the mountain he approached the Lord in the middle of a cloud, we can gather sufficiently from what has been said above how this can refer to the third stage or mode of contemplating. For what does it mean to go into a cloud on the occasion of the divine calling except to go into ecstasy of mind and to be darkened in the mind concerning the memory of nearby things by a cloud of forgetting, as it were? It concerns the same mode of contemplating that a luminous cloud overshadowed the disciples of Christ. One and the same cloud both overshadowed by shining and illumined by overshadowing, since it both illumined with respect to divine things and overclouded with respect to human things. And so every contemplation is accustomed to happen by these three modes: by enlarging of the mind, by raising up of the mind, by alienation of the mind—"Raise your eyes round about and see" (Gen. 13:14): Behold, this concerns that kind of contemplation which comes by enlarging of the mind. "Who are those who fly like clouds?" (Isa. 60:8): Behold this concerns raising up of the mind. "I said in my ecstasy, every man is a liar" (Ps. 115:11): Behold this concerns alienation of the mind.

CHAPTER III

Concerning enlarging of the mind, by what modes it is accustomed to increase

That mode of contemplation which takes place by enlarging of the mind is accustomed to increase according to three stages: by art, by exercise, and by attention. We truly acquire for ourselves an art for something when we learn by accurate instruction or from wise investigation how something ought to be done. Exercise is when we put into use what we have received by means of the art and make ourselves ready and prepared for carrying out such a function. Attention is when we pursue with zeal what we have accomplished with the greatest care. And so, it is first necessary to acquire the art of any discipline; second, to put it to use; third, to pursue with the greatest liveliness that for which we have been trained and exercised. And so, by these three stages, as it has been said, the inner recess of the mind is enlarged and made more capable for any learning and skill. Certainly, the more fully, the more firmly something is learned, the more richly the mind will be enlarged for holding larger and deeper things. But nevertheless, it seems evident that whatever skill has been obtained by instruction is strengthened, enlarged and perfected by use and exercise. Again: What does it mean that in one and the same effort in which we are instructed and are exercised we see now more subtly, now more clearly, unless it means that enlargement and sharp-sightedness of the mind increase according to the mode of attention? Therefore, the first stage is instruction in the art itself; the second, frequent exercise of the same; the third, careful and zealous exertion in the exercise itself. And so the human mind is reminded of the first stage of its enlarging, when it is said to it by the Prophet: "Set up a watchtower for yourself; lay out bitternesses for yourself; direct your heart in the straight way in which you have walked" (Jer. 31:21). You hear concerning the second, when you read: "I will stand upon my lookout; I will fix my position upon the fortification, and I will contemplate what is said to me" (Hab. 2:1). This concerns the third: " Go across to the islands of Gethim and see; and send into Cedar, and consider vigorously" (Jer. 2:10). What does it mean to stand upon a watchtower, except to acquire knowledge of contemplating? For we raise up a watchtower for this: in order that we may be able to see for a long distance from it and to enlarge our vision in all directions. And so in these words is rightly indicated that enlarging of the mind in which a watchtower of contemplation is raised up and knowledge of such an effort is acquired. However, what does it mean to stand upon a lookout and to fix a position, except to strengthen by use the knowledge of speculating? For what one person calls a watchtower, another calls a lookout. Whether they are public or private lookouts, we are accustomed to raise up watchtowers so that when looking out from them we can see imminent dangers long beforehand. So we raise up as it were a spiritual watchtower, the grace of contemplation, so that we may be able to anticipate the ambush of tempters. However, it is one thing to ascend and set up a watchtower; it is another thing to stand on it and even to fix one's position. The former is by the acquisition of a skill; the latter is by the exercise of a skill. However, in as much as we are commanded "to consider vigorously," who does not see how this pertains to that third mode of our enlarging: "Send into Cedar and consider vigorously." Indeed it is rightly said and taught that the capacity of the mind increases and is enlarged by the vigor of consideration and attention. And so, if you pursue carefully you will be enlarged more and more to a greater perfection of keensightedness by means of these three stages of advancement. There is great enlargement of the mind in these things; but no less is there delight.

CHAPTER IV

Concerning raising up of the mind, by what stages it is accustomed to rise up

No less does that mode of contemplating which occurs by the raising up of the mind increase according to three stages. For when divinely inspired and irradiated by that light of heaven, human understanding is raised up: sometimes above knowledge, sometimes above activity and sometimes even above nature. Raising up of the mind ascends above knowledge when any one of us learns from a divine showing any such thing that goes beyond the mode of our own knowledge and understanding. Raising up of the mind is raised above activity when human understanding is divinely illuminated with respect to that for which none of its own knowledge suffices, neither that knowledge which it has at the present nor that which it is capable of acquiring by any activity of its own. The inner recess of the mind is enlarged above nature when human understanding, being breathed upon by divine inspiration, passes completely beyond the mode of human nature and the bounds of human activity, not only of individuals but generally. The soul of a speculative person is lifted up above knowledge when it experiences what is said: "Let a person ascend to a high heart, and God will be exalted" (Ps. 63:7, 8). God is exalted in the glance of the raised-up soul when, by God's showing, something is manifest to it concerning the loftiness of divine majesty that seems to go so far beyond the mode of knowledge it possesses. For indeed, that loftiness of Divinity which has nothing in itself by which it is capable of increasing or being exalted has the power of increasing daily in our knowing and of appearing more sublime in the viewings of our contemplation. The mind that has been raised up is carried even higher above the activity of the mind when what is said is fulfilled in it: "He spread out his wings and took them and carried them on his shoulders" (Deut. 32:11). Certainly it does not belong to human activity to go on a journey through the air. But although we are not able to fly, we are able to be carried by the wings of those supporting us. And so it seems to be above activity but not above nature to make a journey through the air. And so the contemplative soul ascends above the limits of its own activity when the divine esteem, by the manifestation of His secrets and, as it were, by spreading out and raising up His wings, carries the soul even higher to that summit of supereminent knowledge to which it would not be able to go at all by its own activity. But the Prophet sighed for this raising up of the mind that certainly transcends, so it seems, the mode of human nature, when he said: "Who will give me wings like a dove, and I will fly and be at rest?" (Ps. 54:7). What the Lord foretold by Isaiah has a reference to the same: "Those who trust in the Lord shall renew strength; they shall receive wings like eagles" (Isa. 40:31). Without doubt, it is above human nature to have wings and to fly to the heights whenever one wills. However, what does it mean to receive wings against nature, as it were, unless it means to possess on account of virtue a certain marvelous efficacy of contemplating, by which when you wish you can penetrate, on the wing of your keen-sightedness, into the difficult things of secret knowledge and into places inaccessible to all human activity? And so, we truly begin to be winged creatures when, after having received in this the gift of grace divinely given, we transcend the bounds of the human condition by the flight of our contemplation. Every kind of prophecy, if it happens without alienation of mind, seems to pertain to this third stage of raising up. For is it not above human nature to see concerning past things that do not now exist; to see concerning future things that do not yet exist; to see concerning present things that are absent from the senses; to see concerning the secrets of another's heart that are not subject to any sense whatsoever; to see concerning divine things that are above sense? It still remains for us to seek this: Namely the causes by which ecstasy of the human mind is accustomed to happen and also the stages by which it is accustomed to increase.

CHAPTER V

That ecstasy of the human mind is accustomed to be produced by a threefold cause

It seems to me that we are carried away into alienation of mind by three causes. For it is now according to greatness of devotion, now according to greatness of wonder, now according to greatness of exultation, that the mind is completely unable to restrain itself and, being elevated above itself, goes over into alienation. The human mind is elevated above itself by greatness of devotion when it is kindled from below by so great a fire of longing for heaven that the flame of inner love increases beyond a human mode. When the soul has been liquefied according to the similitude of wax and thinned out to a resemblance with smoke, it is released by this flame from its former state, raised to supernal things and sent forth into the heights. By greatness of wonder the human soul is led above itself when, as it is irradiated by divine light and suspended in wonder at supreme beauty, it is shaken with such overpowering awe that it is utterly driven out of its state. In the manner of flashing lightning, the more deeply the soul is cast down into the depths by despising itself with regard to that invisible beauty, the more sublimely, the more quickly it is elevated to sublime things when it rebounds by means of the desire of highest things and is carried away above itself. By greatness of joy and exultation, the mind of man is alienated from itself when, after drinking of—nay after having become completely inebriated by—that inner abundance of interior sweetness, it completely forgets what it is and what it has been. And it is carried over into an ecstasy of alienation by the excess of its dance and suddenly is transformed into a kind of supermundane affection subject to a kind of state of marvelous happiness. Therefore, as long as we do not feel such ecstasy in ourselves, what ought we to feel about ourselves, other than what we have said above: except because we are loved less, save only that we love less? For whoever you are, if you love fully and perfectly, perhaps the excess of your love and the anxious care of your burning longing might carry you into an ecstasy of that sort which we partially described to you above. Surely if you were wholly worthy for divine longing, if you showed yourself worthy of so much honor, perhaps He would shine on the eyes of your understanding with so much brightness of His light and inebriate the longing of your heart with so much pleasantness of His intimate sweetness that He would snatch you up above yourself and elevate you to supernal things by ecstasy of mind.

I think we shall discover these three anagogic modes of ecstasy described mystically in the Song of Songs, in the same order in which we have placed them here. That is rightly understood with respect to the first in which it is said: "Who is she who comes up from the desert like a column of smoke from the spices of myrrh, incense, and all the powders of the perfumer?" (Song of Songs 3:6). We rightly understand with respect to the second that which we read much later in the same Song: "Who is she who comes forth like the dawn rising?" (Song of Songs 6:9). That which we read in the last part is rightly associated with the third: "Who is she who comes up from the desert, flowing with delights, leaning upon her beloved?" (Song of Songs 8:5).

Chapter VI

That the first mode of ecstasy arises on account of greatness of devotion

Do you wish to know better how suitably we are able to match the first passage from the Song of Songs to the first mode of ecstasy? The first ecstasy of mind, as you have heard above, is by the anxious care of longing and greatness of devotion. Smoke always rises from fire. Who would deny that spiritual love is a fire? And so that elevation of the mind into supernal things which takes its origin from fervor of love, is likened to smoke, if I am not mistaken. However, what do we understand by such smoke except the longing of a devoted mind? Therefore, the soul ascends like smoke into supernal regions when, being impelled to this very thing by a burning love, her longing carries her away above herself. As we all know, a thin column of smoke is both graceful and straight. Therefore, so that your ascent may draw to itself the similitude of smoke, let your longing be anxious and unified, arising from a right intention. Now if by myrrh we understand contrition of the flesh; by incense, devotion of the heart; and by all the powder of the perfumer, the consummation of all the virtues, consider how all these things, which can be understood easily by themselves, come together to the same conclusion. For it is sufficiently evident that anyone who is full of charity cannot be without other signs of the virtues. For if the Apostle is believed, the consummation of virtues is charity.

It surely ought to be noted that the holy soul truly rises up like smoke from the desert when from those things, either good or evil, which she discovers in herself, she kindles her affection in longing for the celestial bridegroom. However, as far as merit is concerned, that elevation of the mind which, when favored by grace, arises from intention, from its own intention, seems to me to be greater than that which arises from a showing alone or from some divine inspiration. Therefore, in order that the soul may be found worthy of other modes it is necessary for her to begin with an ascent of this kind and to rise up first of all from the desert, as it were. Nevertheless, in order that the soul herself may become a thin column of smoke, it is necessary that she rise up above the desert itself, although she must begin to become such in the desert. Yet the mind itself is not carried away into ecstasy of mind unless it is elevated above itself, unless it deserts itself in the lowest place, and makes itself a desert by deserting, so that after having deserted it goes upward in the manner of smoke more and more into sublime places.

CHAPTER VII

That the first mode of ecstasy sometimes comes from only the effervescence of burning desire

Nevertheless this kind of ecstasy of mind is accustomed to come at one time from only the effervescence of burning desire, at another time from both effervescence of this sort and a divine showing added to it. For why should that spiritual and incorporeal fire of divine love not possess the same vigor in spiritual things as corporeal fire itself is accustomed to have in corporeal things? We know sufficiently how corporeal fire itself is accustomed to affect any small amount of liquid poured into a vessel. At first the fire begins to agitate the liquid itself from below; but later it continues to throw it now into this part, now into that, now upward, now downward; after a little while it begins to raise it upward and to fill the entire vase up to the brim from any small amount whatsoever. Finally the fire manages to raise the liquid above itself and to empty it out from the inside of the vessel with a certain kind of violence and to pour it out and to expel it forcefully. So when the human soul has been kindled from below by divine fire, it often burns and rumbles in itself against itself, boils and froths up, is angry with itself, despises itself, is greatly displeased with itself, treats itself with great contempt, gazes at highest things with longing, and eagerly desires supermundane things. When it has been heated for a long time in this sort of boiling and thrown about a great deal, when it has been repelled from the lower part by contempt for inferior things and drawn to the higher part by longing for supernal things, it often happens that by the impulse of the Spirit it is completely carried away into higher things when longing impels it out of itself, since it has been thrown above itself, almost forgetting itself, and has been raised up into ecstasy. In this way the ardor of celestial longing rises above its burning self when it brings the human soul to a vigorous boiling by means of divine love. And just as we can show by the above example, when any aromatic powder of the perfumer is thrown into a fire, insofar as it is not consumed by the voracious flame, it is sent up into supernal places by means of the impetuosity of ardor and by a certain kind of thin smoking exhalation. See, I beg you, how when nature is questioned and Scripture consulted, they speak in one and the same sense with equal agreement. And so ecstasy of the mind divinely inflamed can and is accustomed to come from only the boiling up of burning desire, as we have previously said above.

Chapter VIII

That the first mode of ecstasy sometimes comes from both effervescent devotion and a divine showing added to it

Also, sometimes this kind of alienation of mind comes from the mutual coming together of the longing of a burning soul and some marvelous mirror of divine showing—something we are able to gather from Abraham's first going out, concerning which we have said something above. For what does Scripture say concerning him? "The Lord appeared to him as he sat in the valley of Mamre, as he sat in the doorway of his tent in the heat of the day. And when he raised his eyes, three men appeared standing before him. When he saw them, he ran from the doorway of his tent to meet them" (Gen. 18:1–2). If by the tent we understand the dwelling place of the human mind, what will a going out of this sort be except ecstasy of the human mind? For truly, we are led outside ourselves in two ways: At one time we are outside ourselves, but we descend below ourselves; at another time we are outside ourselves, but we are raised above ourselves. In the former we are taken captive by mundane things; in the latter we are brought back to supermundane things. But just as there is a twofold going out, so there is also a twofold return. From both goings out we return as it were to the dwelling place of our usual life, when after worldly labors or, preferably, after a manifestation of celestial contemplations, we bring the eyes of our mind back to the consideration of our morals, and through investigating our innermost being we examine by studious reconsideration what sort of person we are ourselves. That which is read concerning the prodigal son in the Gospel is rightly understood with regard to the first return since when he returned to himself, he said, "How many of the hired servants in my father's house abound with bread, while I perish with hunger in this place?" (Luke 15:17). But no less rightly do we understand with regard to the second return what we read in another place concerning the Apostle Peter. "When Peter returned to himself he said: Now I know truly that the Lord sent his angel" (Acts 12:11). Behold, in both cases it is read, "When he returned to himself." But why this, unless first of all they were seen to have gone out from themselves? For one is led far from himself into a distant region; the other, by angelic leading, is raised by alienation of mind above the common state of human possibility. And so in the first going out, he descends to the lowest; in the second, he is raised up to the highest. In the first we are removed from the Lord; in the second we approach near to the Lord.

Therefore, what is the meaning of the going out by which Abraham is met by the Lord except the ecstasy of the human mind by which the mind, when carried up above itself, is lifted up into the secrets of divine contemplation? If we seek the cause of his going out we will quickly find it. For the vision that appeared exteriorly undoubtedly drew him to exterior things. However the cause of the divine appearance is hinted at secretly in that the Lord is said to have appeared to him as he was sitting in the door of his tent in the very heat of the day. Certainly you see that the heat of the day was very hot when the Lord appeared to him. What, I ask, is this heat of the day, except the boiling up of ardent longing? And so, that love which loves darkness, the love, I say, which hates light, ought not to be called "heat of the day." However, we know that "He who does evil, hates the light; however he who does the truth comes to the light so that his works may be made manifest, since they have been done in God" (John 3:20–21). And so what else does that heat of the day mean except burning love of truth, longing for truth and the supreme good? At that time the patriarch burned, as it were, with a heat of such a kind that finally it drove him away from his household and forced him to sit in the doorway at leisure, to be unpreoccupied, to see, and without doubt to perceive the sought-for and wished-for breeze of divine aspiration and to moderate his longing by the breath of that one. Consider, I ask you, how that heat from which he then boiled up drew him to that place from which he was able to catch sight of those three persons whom he did not doubt ought to be worshipped by right. Perhaps if he had then directed his attention toward his household and had remained in the inner part of his tent, he might not have seen those persons who were to be worshipped, and if he had not seen them, at that time he probably would not have gone out. Therefore two things that offer the occasion for that going out come together in a unity: excess of heat and novelty of vision. It often happens in the human mind, according to a similitude of these things, that while it is inflamed with an excessive fire of passion of celestial longing, it is deemed worthy to see something from divine showing, whereby ecstasy is sustained in those ecstatic contemplations.

CHAPTER IX

That the second mode of ecstasy is accustomed to come from greatness of wonder

Now that these things have been said concerning that ecstasy of mind which rises up from greatness of devotion, it seems necessary to speak concerning that which is accustomed to rise up from greatness of wonder. Who does not know that wonder takes its beginning when we discern something beyond hope and above expectation? And so when something begins to be seen that it is scarcely possible to believe, the newness of the vision and of a thing that is scarcely believable is accustomed to lead to wonder of mind. Therefore pay attention to how suitably that ecstasy of mind which takes its origin from wonder is indicated in that place where it is said: "Who is she who comes forth like the dawn rising?" (Song of Songs 6:9). What is the dawn except new light mixed with darkness? And, I ask, whence comes wonder, except from an unexpected and incredible manifestation? And so wonder itself has sudden light mixed with darkness, a light of vision together with remnants of incredulity and the darkness of uncertainty, so that in a marvelous manner the mind undoubtedly sees what it is scarcely able to believe. But the more greatly we marvel at the newness of a thing, the more carefully we pay attention to it. The more attentively we look, the more fully we come to know. And so attention increases on account of wonder and knowing increases on account of attention. The mind that, on account of the wonder of a vision, gradually advances to an increase of knowledge rises up like the dawn. Indeed, the dawn arises little by little—and as it is raised it is enlarged, and as it is enlarged it is brightened. But in a marvelous manner when at last the dawn ceases at the day, it comes to a fading away because of the increase of its advance. So that it may be greater, it receives that whereby it comes near to day, and finally fades away so that it is nothing. So, in any event, when the human understanding has been irradiated by divine light, while it is suspended in the contemplation of intellectible things and stretched out in wonder at these things, the more it is always led to higher or more marvelous things; the more widely and fully it is enlarged. The more remote it is from lower things, the purer it is found to be in itself and the more sublime with regard to sublime things. But in a raising up of this sort, while the human mind always makes progress towards higher things and by daily progressing finally goes beyond the bounds of human capacity at some time, at last it happens that it completely fails with respect to itself and, being transformed into a certain kind of supermundane affection, goes completely above itself. Indeed, the morning light ceases while it is increasing (it does not cease to be light, but it does cease to be *morning* light) so that the dawn itself is no longer the dawn. In like manner, human understanding increases from the greatness of its enlarging so that it is no longer itself (not that it is not understanding, but that it is no longer *human*) when in a marvelous manner and by an incomprehensible change it is made more than human, and "beholding the glory of the Lord it is transformed into the same image from splendor to splendor, as by the Spirit of the Lord" (2 Cor. 3:18). Therefore, from these things I think you can ponder how properly that ecstasy of mind which takes its origin from greatness of wonder is indicated by the mystical description in which it is said: "Who is she who comes forth like the dawn rising?" (Song of Songs 6:9).

CHAPTER X

That the second mode of ecstasy sometimes begins from wonder alone and ends in most fervent longing of devotion

Surely it ought to be noted that just as that first mode of ecstasy, concerning which we have spoken above, arises from devotion, so on the contrary the second, concerning which we now speak, does not so much begin from devotion as end in it. In the former mode the soul rises to the contemplation of truth by an excessive longing for truth; in the latter the soul is inflamed to devotion by a showing of truth and contemplation of it. See if perhaps this is not mystically intimated to us by Scripture when it adds the following to the words we set out above. After having said, "Who is she who comes forth like the dawn rising," it immediately adds: "As beautiful as the moon, as bright as the sun" (Song of Songs 6:9). Let no one expect or seek from me in this place a full exposition of these words or of any others that we have proposed or might be proposing, except as much as the reason of the present topic requires as testimony of truth. And so the dawn and the moon have light, but they do not have heat. However, the sun is very powerful in both. For what has more light than the sun? What has more heat than the sun? Therefore you see that the ascension of the mind that is indicated in this passage of Scripture, and the end of which is compared to the sun—you see, I say, that it ends at some time in not just any kind of devotion but in supreme devotion, even though it begins from only the brightness and vivid representation of truth. For just as in that first instance mentioned previously the soul is found worthy to be raised up often to the contemplation of supreme truth on account of excessive heat of devotion, so in the second instance the soul is advanced little by little and at last is inflamed with supreme devotion on account of a sort of marveling and awed contemplation. Therefore, let us consider the greatness of the brightness and heat in the orb of the sun. From that let us infer the advancement of ascension and the consummation of advancement in a raising up of the mind such as this that begins from the dawn, as it were, and at last draws to itself at some time the similitude of the sun.

CHAPTER XI

That the second mode of ecstasy sometimes begins from wonder alone and continues in the same

We do not say that in this second ecstasy of mind the mode of human advancement always and everywhere has the same final consummation. We see in exterior things what we ought to think concerning interior things. For if you place a container of water in a ray of the sun, you soon will see that the water reflects the brightness of the light from itself into the heights and lifts the luminescence but not the heat into the heights. In this way many persons receive rays of divine showing. But from this, all do not advance equally to the same power of love. For in order that the Author of all goods might commend the gifts of His grace in us, He shows diverse effects from the same thing at diverse times and in diverse persons. I beg whoever reads or hears this to ponder from the proposed example what that ray of divine showing and eternal light effects in us and how it raises human understanding above itself by enlightenment from its infusion. Pay attention how the formula of this example being proposed to you, concerning which we now speak here, represents ecstasy of mind from the similitude of its quality. What does water mean, except human thinking that always flows to a lower place unless it is confined by a barrier of great strength? Water that has been collected in a container represents thinking that is directed towards meditation and fixed by intention. The gathering together of water represents meditation of the heart. A ray of the sun directs itself onto such water when a divine showing meets with meditation. But when the water receives in itself the ray of light from above, it sends a flash of light to the very heights, as has been said, and in a marvelous manner assuredly raises a ray of light from itself to that place to which it is not able to ascend in any way by itself. And although there is so much difference between water and light, nevertheless when water reflects a ray of light from itself, it impresses something of its similitude on the light so that by trembling it makes the light tremble; by being quiet; quiet; by being purer, purer; by being wider, wider. According to this similitude, when a showing of that inaccessible and eternal light irradiates the human heart, it raises human understanding above itself—nay above every human mode. And there, by an infusion of divine light and a rebound of wonder, the ray of understanding springs back from the lowest region to the highest, to which no sharp-sightedness of innate character, no activity of an art nor any human reasoning is capable of ascending. And the more deeply the brightness of divine brilliance penetrates the human mind shaken by the greatness of its state of awe and raised up by ecstasy, the higher it springs back to the very heights of divine secrets. However it ought to be completely evident that the more fully and perfectly the soul is able to compose itself in inward peace and tranquillity, the more firmly and tenaciously it will adhere to this raising up to the supreme light by means of contemplation. Without doubt the purer it is in integrity, and the wider it is in charity, then the more keen-sighted and capable it will be found for contemplation of supermundane and supercelestial things.

CHAPTER XII

That in the second mode of ecstasy, sometimes a divine showing meets with our meditation

Surely it ought to be noted that that brightness of divine showing sometimes meets with a preceding meditation while sometimes it precedes that human meditation. At one time it aids one who is seeking; at another time it incites one who is sluggish or wakes up one who is sleeping. Hence it is that the Queen of the South pressed King Solomon with questions, and by putting riddles to him she learned from him all those things which she put to him (3 Kings 10:1–3; RSV, 1 Kings 10:1–3). Hence it is that when Peter was in chains an angel roused him from the sleep of his sluggishness by visiting him with light (Acts 12:6–7). For what is said by Scripture concerning the Queen of the South who came to hear Solomon's wisdom except that Solomon answered for her all the questions that she put to him? Who is this Queen of the South, both inhabitant and lady of that warm region, who is kindled with longing to see Solomon? Who, I say, is this queen, except any holy soul who forcefully controls the senses and appetites of the flesh and the thoughts and affections of the mind; who burns with love for the supreme King and true Solomon; and who is afire with longing to see Him? Such a queen presses the King of highest wisdom by putting riddles and frequent questions to Him, when any devoted soul, confident of divine assistance, vigorously pursues with zeal the investigation of truth. She hears what she seeks, when the soul comes to know by a divine showing—often in the midst of the sighing of prayers—those things of which it is incapable by its own activity. Let us now see what the divine word proposes concerning this same queen, when by adding something it says: "However, when the Queen of Sheba saw all the wisdom of Solomon, the house which he had built, the foods of his table, the dwelling places of his servants, the order of his ministers and also their clothing, and the holocausts which he offered in the house of the Lord, she had no more Spirit" (3 Kings 10:4–5). It says, "When the Queen of Sheba saw." Behold she is now described as "seeing," who was first represented as "putting questions and asking." See what she saw; understand what she understood. It says "When the Queen of Sheba saw all the wisdom of Solomon, . . ." Behold how many things, behold what kind of things, are given for the devoted and zealous soul to know from divine showing. Consider what great things; pay attention to what marvelous things she shall come to know divinely by seeing. After seeing for a long time and marveling greatly, at long last on account of greatness of wonder she comes to the failure* of her spirit. Behold in what order she proceeds and to what conclusion she finally comes. First she asks and hears; next she sees and understands; finally she is struck dumb with astonishment and faints. She asks questions in order that she may learn; she contemplates in order that she may marvel; she is astonished in order that she may silence the mind and experience ecstasy of mind. The first is by meditation; the second, by contemplation; the third, by ecstasy. Behold, by what stages of advancement the soul is raised up. Certainly by meditation it is raised to contemplation; by contemplation, to wonder; by wonder, to alienation of mind. I think you already know by means of a clear example that a man

---

*The word *deficio* appears in this chapter in various forms. The translation is varied in context but generally is given as "faints," "failure," or "falls away."

comes to ecstasy of mind by greatness of wonder. For what else was it for that one not to have spirit except to experience ecstasy of mind? From what cause did this happen to her except from great wonder? In what way, I ask, was that queen without spirit, unless her spirit had been alienated from her? But at this point one recalls what another person said of himself: "I, John, was in the spirit" (Rev. 1:10). Behold, John bears witness that he himself was in the spirit; behold the Queen of the South is declared not to have spirit. What does this mean? Was the former in the spirit? Was the latter without spirit? Who is capable of understanding these things? If John was in the spirit, who can explain to me whether he was there according to the flesh or according to the spirit? But how could he be in the spirit according to the flesh, since the body is totally unable to exist except in a corporeal place? Therefore, if it is believed that he was there according to the spirit, who can explain how spirit is said to be in the spirit? What are we to say concerning the queen of the South? Did the body remain with the multitude when she began not to have spirit? Who could say this? Who except a mindless person would dare to construe it in this way? Therefore the body of the queen was not without spirit for this time since without spirit she would be completely unable to live. What now? Was spirit without spirit? Therefore, let whoever is able, in whatever way he is able, explain in what manner spirit is in spirit, and spirit is without spirit. If one is properly believed concerning John, the other is thought concerning the queen. Now perhaps this is what it means for spirit to be in spirit: to collect itself totally within itself, and to ignore completely for a while those things which concern the flesh and even those things which take place in the flesh. And possibly this is what it means for spirit to be without spirit: to pour itself completely outside of itself and above itself and to ignore completely for a while those things which are under it or in it and to go completely into that secret place of Divinity. Is it not rightly asserted that spirit is in the spirit when it forgets all exterior things, in like way is ignorant of all the things that are done corporeally in the body, and attends by memory or intellect to only those things which are acting in the spirit or about the spirit? Why, is not the spirit rightly said not to have itself when it begins to fall away from itself, and to pass over from itself to exist in a kind of supermundane and truly more than human state? By means of a marvelous transfiguration that spirit seems to fall away from the human into the divine, so that now it is no longer itself insofar as it begins from that time to cling more firmly to the Lord. For "he who clings to the Lord is one spirit" (1 Cor. 6:17). And he who is such a kind of person is able to sing: "My soul falls away into your salvation" (Ps. 118:81). And so, that one is in the spirit who ascends to the supreme part of mind; and that one falls away from the spirit, as it were, who goes beyond the highest part of mind. But let us leave the discussion of these matters for souls who are better instructed.

Chapter XIII

That in the second mode of ecstasy, divine showing sometimes comes even before our meditation

Let us now consider how divine revelation is accustomed sometimes to come even before the effort of our meditation and to lift up the human soul that has been cast down below even the common state of human liberty by the sudden violence of temptations. In this event the soul not only is lifted up to the usual state of stability but is even raised beyond the limits of human possibility. For often after receiving many honors for its exertions, the human mind is buffeted by the importunate force of temptations and after being shaken violently out of that ark of its sublime security and tranquillity is cast down. This happens lest it boast miserably and uselessly, as it were, concerning its own fortitude in the midst of a continuous succession of virtuousness. Hence it is that the blessed Peter, the leader of the apostles, after innumerable merits and sublime miracles, was taken, bound and imprisoned. But after the visit of an angel he is set free no less marvelously than he was earlier tortured cruelly by the administrators of cruelty (Acts 12:3–10). Do you wish to know about chains of this sort, which are sometimes accustomed to ensnare severely the minds of worthy persons and even of high-ranking persons? Who does not know the irritations of voluptuous desires that arise at one time from outside, at another time from within; from the outside, from delight; from within, from suggestion; by means of delight, in the flesh; by means of suggestion, in the mind? At one time the flesh is inflamed by foul titillation, while at another time the soul is befouled by filthy thoughts. Therefore, we meet darkness like that of a prison when, after being ensnared in these entwinings of concupiscence, we wish to turn away from the blindness of our confusion but we are not able to do it. But surely a showing of divine consolation is deserved by that mind which endures this darkness of its confusion not so much because of the personal listlessness of its sluggishness, but because of the wanton malice of another. Such a holy soul is set free by the coming of a divine ambassador, when from the grace of divine inspiration and the light of a showing it is relieved of the weight of its oppression. An angel is called a messenger. An angel doubtless is a messenger—not just any kind of messenger, but a divine messenger through whom we come to know the good pleasure of the divine will; a messenger through whom we are illumined for knowing eternal things and inflamed with longing for them. But do you know this messenger is only from heaven? Might he not be from earth? But how can he who knows the greater things be ignorant of lesser things? Surely that ambassador is good who suffices not only for teaching everything but also for persuading, insofar as He who sent him wishes it. Do you wish to hear what sort of ambassador the apostle John promised us when he said: "His unction will teach you concerning all things" (1 John 2:27)? What is this unction, except divine inspiration? This is that messenger whom we sought for a long time; this is a truly powerful ambassador, truly sufficient to lead the human soul to all truth and incline it to every good pleasure of the divine will. Therefore, why marvel if such a messenger, who immediately equally imparts knowledge and love of celestial and eternal things when he wills and as much as he pleases, sets an oppressed soul free from the involvements of its concupiscence and leads it from the darkness of its ignorance? He who said: "He sent from heaven, and he freed me" (Ps. 56:4) had experienced such messengers in his being set free. But perhaps you still seek to know of what sort that ambassador was, by whom he escaped from the captivity of his soul: "God sent his mercy and his truth and set my soul free" (Ps. 56:4–5). An angel coming with light means the working of divine compassion imparting truth. Mercy leading to truth means unction teaching. However, what does it mean for God to send mercy and truth and to set a man free from his captivity, except by the working of his mercy to inspire truth, and by the inspiration of truth to stabilize with respect to the strength of virtue? And who would ever completely escape the perils of his soul if he were not found worthy to experience the aid of this ambassador? Blessed is Peter, who was found worthy not only to be set free by the angel but also to follow the angel after he was set free. I think that not all of those who are set free by an angel even follow the angelic footprints. I read that when imprisoned, the apostles were led forth by an angel but they did not follow it (cf. Acts 5:19–20). Peter is taught by his own angel who set him free that he should follow him. What do we say that this means? How great a thing do we think it is to follow angelic footprints and go after celestial and winged creatures? Think, if you are able, what that departure or forward motion of the angel who precedes or follows means. Neither the custodian of the prison nor the iron door was able to prevent or retard the passage of this angel. Which of these is not new; which of these is not marvelous? It is truly angelic, and truly more than human, to go out from the darkness and terror of human suffering and to go beyond the difficulty and narrowness of ordinary impossibility. Think about that going forth which the first man had before he sinned and which man would now have if he had never sinned. By this going out, as often as it was necessary, he would have had easy passage from mundane things to supermundane things, from visible things to invisible things, from transitory things to eternal things, since he would be prepared to be present daily with celestial citizens by means of contemplation, to press freely into that place of divine secrets and to enter worthily into that inner joy of his Lord. Think how consequently, after sin, divine severity blocked and guarded with a door of terrible force and bars of impossibility that earlier easy passageway for going to and fro. Think about this, I say, and perhaps by this thinking you will discover what you ought to think and dare to affirm concerning that iron door. Yet if you are not capable of this, do not inquire of us, but rather inquire of those persons to whom perhaps this iron door is well known because of frequent passage and for whom perhaps it is often actually open, according to the similitude of Peter, having an angel going before and offering guidance. I think I have not spoken rashly, since he was far above man; since he withdrew far from himself and above himself; since he learned all of these things by means of experience. Otherwise there was no place from which he might afterward return to himself or of which it might rightly be written concerning him: "And Peter, having returned to himself, said: 'Now I know that the Lord in fact has sent his angel' " (Acts 12:11). There are many things that might have been said in this present chapter if we were obligated to say them in this place. But it is sufficient for us that we have set forth sufficiently from Peter's testimony in order to have proved how a divine showing sometimes is accustomed to precede the effort of our meditation and to incite our sluggish soul and even sometimes to lift the soul above itself after it has been cast down below itself.

Chapter XIV

That the third mode of ecstasy is accustomed to come from greatness of joy

It still remains for us to show in the third place how the human mind is accustomed to fall into ecstasy and to go out of itself on account of greatness of joy and exultation. This mode of ecstasy seems to me to have been expressed with sufficient suitableness in those words from the Song of Songs which we put in the third place: "Who is she," Scripture says, "who comes up from the desert, flowing with delights, leaning upon her beloved?" (Song of Songs 8:5). If by the desert is rightly understood the human heart, what will this coming up from the desert mean except ecstasy of the human mind? The human soul comes up from the desert, as it were, when it passes over above itself by means of alienation of mind, when deserting itself in the lowest place and passing upward to heaven it is immersed only in divine things by means of contemplation and devotion. But the cause of this kind of coming up is fitly associated with this passage, because she who comes up is described as "flowing with delights." What does it mean to be "flowing with delights" except to abound with the fullness of spiritual joys? What,

I say, is this flowing with delights except an abundance of true pleasure given from heaven and a joyfulness infused unrestrainedly? False riches are able to show neither an abundance of these delights nor true rejoicing. Moreover, they would not be false if they had really shown true delights—nay if they had been truly flowing with them. For those persons can be said really to have (I do not say to flow with) delights who, according to the judgment of the blessed Job, "reckon delights to be under thorns" (Job 30:7). Surely even the impious are able to have these exterior and false riches; nevertheless they are not able to have any joy at all, unless perchance we make into a liar that One whom we hear truly bearing witness through the Prophet: "It is not for the impious to rejoice, says the Lord" (Isa. 48:22; 57:21). And so, as often as you are without internal and true delights, even if you abound in exterior riches you can truly sing with the Prophet: "Since now I am needy and a pauper" (Ps. 85:1). Was it not a powerful king and a rich prince of the people who said these things? Therefore, of what sort are those riches and what sort of delights are they able to confer, in the midst of an abundance of which it is necessary to be needy and, in a different sense, to beg for true joy? "However, I am a beggar and a pauper; the Lord is solicitous for me" (Ps. 39:18). And so, this flowing with delights and abundance of true joys is not something for which you ought to hope nor something you are capable of possessing, except from that divinely infused inner joyfulness and sweetness of soul: "Who is she who comes up from the desert flowing with delights?" (Song of Songs 8:5). It does not say "having delights," but "flowing with delights," because not just any experience of these delights but only a flowing with them gives birth to and completes this sort of coming up that comes from the desert. However, it is evident that however much we advance, we cannot continually have these delights to this extent in this life. And so at the time when the soul is without such a flowing, she is not able to rise up to this coming up about which we are now speaking; for in her coming up she must be "flowing with delights." However, I think that it is one thing to come up flowing and another to flow coming up, just as it is another thing for the flowing to be the cause of the coming up. And so, flowing with delights appears then as the cause of coming up when, on account of that infusion of divine sweetness, the holy soul does not understand what she feels herself in the innermost place on account of rejoicing and exultation, so that by the greatness of her exultation and joy she pours herself outside of herself and is carried away above herself. In this way, when a forceful and unmeasurable joyfulness grows above a human mode, it raises one above humanity, and after raising him up above human things it suspends him in sublime things. We are surely able to see the form of such things daily, even in animals. In their play animals are often accustomed to make a kind of leap and to suspend their bodies in the air for a short while. In this way fishes often leap above the waters when they play in the water, and they go beyond the bounds of their natural habitation when they suspend themselves for a moment in the void. So without doubt when the holy soul is cut off from herself by a kind of internal applause of her dancing, when she is driven to go above herself by means of alienation of mind, when she is completely suspended in celestial things, when she is completely immersed in angelic manifestations—then she seems to have gone beyond the bounds of natural possibility. Hence there is that which is said by the Prophet: "The mountains exult like rams and the hills like the lambs of sheep" (Ps. 113:4). Who does not see that it is above nature, or rather against nature, that mountains and hills should make a kind of leap into higher things, rebound from the earth, and launch themselves through the void, according to a similitude of the playing of rams and lambs? Can earth be suspended above earth, when man is led above humanity, to whom it is said by the Lord's voice by way of reproach: "You are earth, and you shall return to earth" (Gen. 3:19)? Therefore, howevermuch he may grow by greatness of virtue, even though he rises to the heights according to a similitude of the hills or the mountains in general, in any case he is earth and can rightly be called earth as long as he inhabits a house of clay and has an earthly foundation. For this reason, this is said by Wisdom: "Why are earth and ashes proud?" (Ecclus. 10:9). If, therefore, we are content with a simple exposition, perhaps it suffices to say this: that this is the reason that mountains and hills exult according to the similitude of rams and lambs: In the highest and holiest men human nature ascends beyond human nature, and on account of an excess abundance of joy and exultation human nature goes above itself by means of alienation of mind. Behold, I think we have already taught by means of a clear example that sometimes a person attains ecstasy of the human mind on account of the greatness of exultation. But perhaps if that which we have said concerning the additional similitude of the sheep suffices less for that person, and he presses on with more curiosity concerning the expression of individual things, he should recall to memory those ninety-nine sheep the supreme Shepherd left in the heights when He came to earth searching for that one which had been lost. Therefore, let one who is able, think how great or what sort of thing it is that the mountainous regions of this earth of ours spring back into the heights with the impulse of their joy according to the similitude of these things, and that this nature of ours forms the applause of its exultation according to the dancing of an angelic similitude. However, if by rams we understand those highest orders of angels, and by lambs, the lower orders of the same, nevertheless since rams of such a sort (that is to say, the highest order of angels) go above themselves with that marvelous sport of their joy and ecstasy of contemplation when they suspend themselves in the higher things of themselves, we know well that they behold above themselves nothing other than the creative substance of everything nor do they find they are better able to contemplate or marvel at His power or wisdom in anything other than in themselves. But when those lower orders of angels, which seem to be indicated by the lambs, are brought above themselves, they certainly behold those spirits who surpass them by the marvelous prerogative of worth. In this raising up of themselves they now discover a kind of mirror, as it were, in which they marvelously discern the supreme majesty and now they have the advanced ability to see by a mirror, as it were. Therefore, if contemplative men are understood rightly by mountains, and speculative men by hills, you see how rightly mountains are said to exult according to the similitude of rams, and hills according to the similitude of lambs. For although contemplation and speculation are accustomed to be used with the same meaning and in this way often obscure and cover over the proper sense of Scripture, nevertheless we more aptly and expressly call something speculation when we see by a mirror; but we call it contemplation when we see the truth in its purity without any covering or any veil

335

of shadows. And so the hills exult according to the similitude of lambs when that immense dance of inner solemnity raises them above themselves to the extent that they are capable of seeing the hidden places of celestial secrets—at least by a mirror and in an enigma. (Cf. 1 Cor. 13:12.) But, in contrast, mountains exult as it were in resemblance to rams when in the ecstasies of their joy the greater ones see in pure and simple truth what the lesser, as has already been said, are scarcely able to see by a mirror and in an enigma.

CHAPTER XV

That any ecstasy of the mind goes beyond the mode of human activity and merit

Let no person presume that so much exultation or raising up of the heart is due to his own strength; nor should he attribute this to his own merits. Surely it is evident that this is not from human merit but from a divine gift. For this reason, every soul that is described as coming up from the desert is said to lean upon her Beloved. What does it mean for her to lean upon her Beloved except to be advanced by the virtue of that one and not by her own strength? I say, what is it for her to rely upon her Beloved, other than to presume that nothing at all connected with this part is due to her own virtue? As far as it seems to me, she is rightly presuming nothing is due to her own activity, nothing is due to her own prudence, especially in this place where she is coming up from the desert, but not even in the desert either when she is going through the desert. Surely the Beloved of this one knows this and for that reason leads her during the day in a cloud and during the whole night in a light of fire (Exod. 13:21). How could she sustain the burden and heat of the day, except in the shade of that One whom her soul loves? And what would be for her a place of safety from nocturnal fear, especially in a region of terror and vast solitude, unless He sent forth His light and His truth? Finally, she would have nothing whereby the heat of concupiscence might be moderated in her, unless the power of the Most High were to overshadow her. No less would she be lacking in that which would illumine the darkness of her ignorance, unless she saw light in His light. For this reason she says to Him: "For you light my lamp, O Lord. My God, illuminate my darkness" (Ps. 17:29). And so from the gift of her Beloved and from the kindness of her Spouse, the lover receives two remedies against two principal evils: the cloud of coolness against concupiscence of the flesh; the light of showing against ignorance of the mind. How often one knows the way of truth, yet does not follow it, as he is drawn away and allured by his concupiscence. Here he has for a while a day of knowing but does not have the cloud of cooling grace. How often many persons have zeal yet have nothing as far as knowledge is concerned. Perhaps these persons feel no heat of concupiscence for a while and are refreshed by the restful coolness of the night, as it were. And indeed the persons who are of this sort seem to have the night, but they do not have the fire of illumining grace. Therefore, it is good to hope in the Lord and not to presume concerning oneself. How blessed are those for whom He is in a covering during the day and in the light of the stars during the night, spreading out a cloud to protect them and a fire so that it might be a light for them during the night. For it is not of the one who wills, nor of the one who runs, but of God who shows mercy (Rom. 9:16). The lover knows this, and for this reason she leans upon her Beloved. For this reason it is rightly written concerning her: "Who is she who comes up from the desert, flowing with delights and leaning upon her Beloved?" (Song of Songs 8:5).

CHAPTER XVI

That especially in the third mode of ecstasy everything depends upon divine favor

Although this beloved of her Spouse always and everywhere is in need of the aid of her Beloved so that without Him she is unable to do anything, nevertheless she relies, or finds it necessary to rely, more strongly on the cooperation of the soul in no place more than in this place where she comes up from the desert, now especially at the time when she flows with delights. For if by desert is rightly understood the human heart, what will it mean to come up from the desert, except to go above herself? Therefore, what can a person do where one ascends above humanity, where human nature goes beyond the bounds of human possibility? Yet at no time does the holy soul lean more strongly on her Beloved than when she seems to flow with spiritual delights. Let us now think of a certain young and delicate girl, namely one who has been brought up in a great flowing of delights but is now a girl intoxicated with much wine, namely one who has been led into the wine cellar and has drunk from a rushing torrent of desire: On account of her very great youthfulness she is scarcely able to walk; on account of excessive inebriation she is completely unable to discern where she ought to be. Is not this one who is described as flowing with delights and leaning upon her Beloved presented to you for consideration under such a figure of speech? But why marvel if flowing with delights restores youthfulness? Do you wish to hear how it is accustomed to bring about youthfulness? She is raised almost above that which can be believed and finally to such a degree that no exterior delight can have the least savor for her, nor can any glory of the world bring any kind of consolation, so that she dares to say and to confess: "My soul refused to be consoled" (Ps. 76:3). This is because she truly feels and certainly says, "Because all flesh is grass and all the glory of it is like the flower of grass" (Isa. 40:6). At last her soul is wearied of its life as often as she is not given to have accustomed delights as she wishes. And so life itself turns into weariness for her—nay into something hated, as often as those rejoicings of her internal solemnity are withdrawn. Think, therefore, of what sort is the customary condition of those persons with such delights, who delight to have nothing in their own power. Without these delights, which she cannot acquire by her own activity or her own prudence, she cannot receive any consolation at all. Whatever is for her consolation, whatever is for her pleasure, depends upon the will of another and upon the favor of another. Therefore she rightly leans on the strength of that one upon whose generosity she can rightly presume completely for what she is hoping for, longing for, and loving. O how often in this state are those words which are said according to the warning of the Prophet turned into the word of the Lord for her: "Command, command again; command, command again; wait, wait again; wait, wait again; a moment here, a moment there" (Isa. 28:10). And so she is forced to wait and wait again, while her longing is deferred often and for a very long time, and while she is able neither to have her delights when she wishes nor to moderate her soul in such cravings. I think it is evident from these things how whatever is done or felt in this ecstasy of mind is far above humanity and goes beyond a human mode.

Chapter XVII

By what a person who has advanced to this third stage of such grace can be helped in himself

Nevertheless, when a person who has advanced to this grace now feels that it is being withdrawn from him more than is usual, there is something he ought to do, by which he can be assisted much in every way to regain this grace and by which he can form his soul in this undertaking as much as he is capable of doing. And so, the soul that is in such a situation ought to recover exultation of the heart in itself by its own meditations and to call back before the eyes of its recollection the costly gifts of divine kindness to it. On account of such recollection it ought to incite itself to a deep and devoted act of thankfulness and at last because of inner affection to set that internal organ of spiritual harmony free for divine praises. And so, when by such effort the inner affection of the heart is released with full devotion in the magnificence of divine praises, what is this other than that (if I may speak in this manner) an air hole is opened, by which an emanation of celestial sweetness and an abundance of divine pleasantness is poured into that small chamber of our heart? So it is that when Elisha the Prophet was asked for the word of the Lord, since he felt that he did not have the spirit of prophecy at that time, he had a minstrel brought to him. With the presence and singing of the minstrel, Elisha immediately drank in the prophetic spirit and soon opened his mouth with words of prophecy (4 Kings 3:15; RSV, 2 Kings 3:15). Perhaps some person may ask what it means to him that according to the historical sense a Prophet of the Lord sought a minstrel and received the spirit of prophecy because of his singing. Now, we do know this: that in an ordinary state of mind, a sweet harmony is accustomed to gladden the heart and to recall its joy to memory for it. Without doubt the more strongly anyone's love affects his soul, certainly the more deeply the harmony that is heard touches affection. The more profoundly he is touched by affection, the more effectively he is renewed with respect to his longings. Therefore, what else is it proper to feel about the prophetic man except that for him an external harmony brought back to memory that interior and spiritual harmony, and the melody that was heard called back and raised to customary joy the mind of the one listening? However, why should we not feel with respect to spiritual and true delight what we demonstrate by daily experience with respect to corporeal and empty delight? For who does not know how the mere memory of carnal delights can carry the carnal mind away into delight? Why should the delight of spiritual men not have the same—nay, rather a greater—effect in supreme things? And so the melody that was heard by the Prophet—what else was it other than a kind of ladder that raised him to customary joy? Although it is usually the cause of ruin for carnal persons, in this case the melody emerges as the cause of ascension. Let a person who is able think how profoundly, how intimately, that which carried him away above himself and restored the prophetic spirit and sense in the prophet's soul touched him on the occasion of someone's singing, on account of the memory of that supercelestial sweetness.

Chapter XVIII

What is especially accustomed to be effective for the renewal of grace of this sort

O soul, whoever you are, you who are accustomed to flow with spiritual delights of this sort, to come up often from the desert, leaning upon your Beloved, to be raised up to some contemplative ecstasies by a kind of sudden and unexpected—nay, even inconceivable—dance of rejoicing, and to be lifted up on high divinely by certain prophetic understandings and showings as it were: You, O soul, ought to learn from the example of the Prophet what you ought to do in order that in a time of great need you may have at hand, as it were, a way in which you are capable of restoring your soul to customary delights. Perhaps it would not be useless for you to summon a minstrel and listen to one who sings on the occasion of a similar need. But so that we may briefly bring to a close what we think concerning this thing, what else can we call that minstrel except the exultation of the heart in God? He who said: "Be joyful in the Lord and exult you just; glory all you upright of heart" (Ps. 31:11) wanted us to have such a minstrel present. However, what does it mean to summon a minstrel of this sort except to regain exultation of the heart by provident meditation and to awaken devotion of the heart by recollection of divine kindnesses and promises? Here without doubt we cause a minstrel to sing when on account of great dancing of the heart we shout in divine celebration and while rising up in thanksgiving we reecho in divine praises with a great shout of the heart from the innermost parts of ourselves. What does it mean to do these things, other than that we prepare the way by which we may receive the Lord when He comes and visits us? "The sacrifice of praise shall clothe me with honor, and there is the way by which I will show that one the salvation of God" (Ps. 49:23). And so, by singing and praising the way is prepared for the Lord, the way by which He judges it worthy to come to us and to show us some marvelous showings of His mysteries. Hence it is read in another place, "Sing to God, say a psalm to His name, make a way for Him who ascends above the west" (Ps. 67:5). Perhaps you seek to know what it means to ascend above the west.* Surely common usage agreed to call "west" that region of the earth in which the sun sets and light fades away each day.† Therefore, what can we more rightly understand by "west" than the failure of human understanding? For the sun of the under-

---

*In Ps. 67:5 and the sentences that follow, *occasus* is translated "west." Richard exploits a word play inherent in the Latin. *Occasus* may mean: "the setting of the sun"; "the west" as the quarter of the heavens in which the sun sets; "downfall or death." Setting sun, compass point, and the failure or "death" of understanding are all involved in this passage.

†The word *deficio* in varied forms reappears here. It is variously translated (e.g., fades away, failure). [See 5:12 above]

standing runs there towards the west, as it were, and hides the rays of its knowing, and the aforementioned light of day turns in a certain measure into the darkness of the land of night and draws everything away from human sight—when the human spirit falls into alienation of mind and knows nothing at all concerning what happens in it or around it when it fails with regard to ordinary sense and has been carried away outside of itself. However, what does it mean that the Lord ascends in the eyes of our consideration, except that by the showing of His greatness He increases the growth of our knowing? For the more He shows us the sublimer things concerning the loftiness of His greatness, the more He raises Himself to loftier heights in the view of our understanding. He truly ascends in the west when He carries a man above himself, draws away from his memory all those things which the man knows according to ordinary sense and manifests to him by means of ecstasy of mind this concerning the lofty height of His majesty, something that he would in no way be able to comprehend according to the ordinary state of this life and ordinary mode of human capacity. Therefore, let us strive with great quickness of mind to rejoice in the Lord; let us continually endeavor to sing with intimate devotion in His presence, so that it may be by these things that He will regard it as suitable to ascend in the west. In order to do this, it is necessary for us to summon a singer of this sort, just as it is also useful for us to hear someone singing. The spiritual soul is touched at the very core of its being because of the voice of a singer of this sort and it is spiritually affected when the spirit rushes into it. When the sense of understanding is opened to divine inspiration, in some way the grace of prophecy is renewed in it. And so, because of such psalmody and spiritual harmony, the contemplative soul accustomed to spiritual contemplations begins to dance and to make gestures in a certain way because of its excess of joy, to make some unique spiritual leaps, to suspend itself above the earth and all earthly things and to pass over completely to contemplation of celestial things by alienation of mind. Therefore, it is this, as we have said, that is effective for the renewing of the mind; it is this that is accustomed to be effective especially for the restoration of grace that has been lost.

Chapter XIX

By what stages ecstasy of the human mind increases

We have said by what causes alienation of mind is accustomed to happen. It seems that now we ought to be adding by what stages it ascends. Sometimes it ascends above corporeal sense; sometimes, above imagination; sometimes, above reason. However, who would dare to deny that which is above corporeal sense or that which is above reason, since apostolic authority clearly demonstrates that which is above reason: "I know a man, whether in the body or outside the body God knows, who was snatched up to the third heaven" (2 Cor. 12:2). Behold, how he who was totally unable to discern what was going on around him had passed beyond human reason by means of alienation of mind. But it is better to leave the more complete explanation of this passage to persons of more erudite talents than rashly to presume something above our powers with respect to such an important topic. In this matter we are better instructed by the practical knowledge of those persons who have advanced to the fullness of this knowledge not so much by the teaching of another person as from their own experience. And so to that summary of our matter which we set forth with concise brevity in the first book, we have added these things in the work that followed by way of a more complete treatment, where, as we have said above, we have been able to speak as a person at leisure to persons at leisure.

APPENDIX

Some Allegories of the Tabernacle of the Covenant
with a very brief recapitulation
of the contents of the foregoing work
concerning the grace of contemplation

By the tabernacle of the covenant
    we understand the state of perfection.

Where perfection of the soul is,
    there also is the habitation of God.

The more the mind approaches perfection,
    the more closely it is joined in a covenant with God.

However, the tabernacle itself
    ought to have an atrium around about it.

By atrium we understand discipline of the body;
    by tabernacle we understand discipline of the mind.

Where exterior discipline is lacking,
    interior discipline certainly cannot be observed.

But, on the other hand, without discipline of the mind,
    discipline of the body is certainly not beneficial.

An atrium lies uncovered under the open sky;
    discipline of the body is open for all to see.

Those things which are in the tabernacle
    are not open to the outside.

No person knows what belongs to the inner person
    except the spirit of humanity that is in him.

The *habitus* of the inner person is divided
　　into a rational and an intellectual *habitus*.

The rational *habitus* is understood by the exterior tabernacle,
　　　but the intellectual *habitus* is understood by the interior
　　tabernacle.

We call the rational sense
　　that by which we discern the things of ourself;

In this place we call the intellectual sense
　　　that by which we are raised up to the speculation of divine
　　things.

A person goes out from the tabernacle into the atrium
　　through the exercise of work.

A person enters into the first tabernacle
　　when he returns to himself.

A person enters into the second tabernacle
　　when he goes beyond himself.

When going beyond himself,
　　surely a person is elevated to God.

A person remains in the first tabernacle by consideration of himself;
　　in the second, by contemplation of God.

Behold, concerning the atrium, the first tabernacle and the second:
　　these places had five things for sanctification.

The atrium had only one thing,
　　so also the second tabernacle.

The first tabernacle had
　　the remaining three.

In the atrium of the tabernacle was
　　the altar of burnt offering.

In the first tabernacle were
　　the candelabrum, the table, and the altar of incense.

In the interior tabernacle was
　　the Ark of the Covenant.

The exterior altar is affliction of the body;
    the interior altar is contrition of the mind.

The candelabrum is
      the grace of discretion;
    the table is
      the teaching of sacred reading.

By the Ark of the Covenant
    we understand the grace of contemplation.

On the exterior altar the bodies of animals were burned up;
    by affliction of the body carnal longings are annihilated.

On the interior altar aromatic smoke was offered to the Lord;
    by contrition of heart the flame of celestial longings is kindled.

A candelabrum is a holder for lights;
    discretion is the lamp of the inner person.

On the table bread is placed;
    by it those who are hungry may be refreshed.

However, sacred reading certainly is
    the refreshment of the soul.

An ark is a secret place for gold and silver;
      the grace of contemplation lays hold of the treasury of celestial
    wisdom.

Good working pertains to
    the exterior altar.

Zealous meditation pertains to
    the candelabrum.

Sacred reading pertains to
    the table.

Devoted prayer pertains to
    the interior altar.

Contemplation of divine works pertains to
    the ark.

These are the five exercises

in which our justification is carried out and completed.

That is worthily called the ark of sanctification
    in which the consummation of our justification is represented.

You have what is a five-part undertaking
    in which all religion is exercised.

The exercise of good work pertains to
    discipline of the outer person.

It is agreed concerning the remaining things
    that they pertain to discipline of the inner person.

The altar of burnt offering bears
    the form of bodily exercise.

Therefore, it worthily stands in the atrium
    and is seen in the open.

The remaining things are in the tabernacle
    and are hidden away in a secret place.

By the Ark of the Covenant is understood the grace of
        contemplation,
    which is bestowed by the Lord as a kind of pledge of love, as it
    were, to his lovers.

Contemplation, however, is the free gaze of the mind,
    suspended with wonder in the manifestation of wisdom.

But there are six individual kinds of contemplation,
    each having distinct individual properties.

Two are engaged with visible creatures;
        two are engaged with invisible creatures;
    but the two highest are engaged with divine things.

Those to whom it is given to advance to two kinds only
    seem to have received wings like an eagle.

Those to whom it has been given to reach four kinds,
        you ought to think it said concerning such persons:
    "Four wings to one and four wings to the other."

Those who have advanced to all kinds of contemplation
    have received six wings as it were.

Therefore, you ought to think it said concerning these:
    "Six wings to one and six wings to the other."

The first four are engaged with created things, visible and invisible;
    the two remaining, with divine things.

The first four are represented in a symbolic figure by the ark;
      the last two are represented figurally in a symbolic figure
    by the angelic form.

Pay attention to how rightly the first are represented in a human
      construction;
    the last two are represented in an angelic figure.

To the first kind of contemplation seems to pertain
    the bringing of visible things into consideration and wonder.

It belongs to the second kind of contemplation
    to bring forth into light the hidden causes of things
    and to suspend the soul in wonder at them.

In the former we marvel with exultation at the
    multitude, greatness and usefulness of visible things;
    in the latter we examine with wonder the
    rational principle of visible things.

The first kind of contemplation is indicated
    in the arranging of pieces of wood.

The second kind of contemplation is indicated
    in the gilding of the pieces of wood.

What does the assigning of the rational principle of visible things
      mean,
    except a kind of gilding of pieces of wood, as it were?

Pay attention to how great a difference there is between wood and
      gold;
    that is, between these things that are connected with reason.

We examine the outer appearance of visible things by imagining;

we examine the causes of visible things by reasoning.

The ark is made of pieces of Setim wood, which are very
    incorruptible;
  a kind of true determination concerning corporeal things
    pertains to incorruptible wood.

Now the first kind of contemplation is divided into three stages:
  the first is in things,
  the second is in works,
  the third is in morals.

That consideration which is in things pertains to
  the length of the ark.

The consideration that is concerning works pertains to
  the width of the ark.

The consideration that is concerning morals pertains to
  the height of the ark.

Of course, length is naturally
  prior to width.

Moreover, height is naturally
  posterior to both of the others.

So surely things themselves are naturally prior to
  any of their workings whatsoever.

But if things and their workings are missing,
  then morals do not have a place.

Therefore it is agreed that:
  the first consideration pertains to the length of the ark;
  the second consideration pertains to the width of the ark;
  the third consideration pertains to the height of the ark.

Now, that consideration which concerns speculation of things and
    which has been said to pertain to the length of the ark
  is divided into three parts.

For it consists of considering:
  the matter of things;

the form of things;
the nature of things.

In the consideration of matter and form,
    our knowledge is able and accustomed to have a full cubit.

In the consideration of nature,
    our knowledge is in no way able to extend itself to a full cubit.

Our knowledge has a full cubit there, as it were,
    where it is informed to the full limit.

We easily perceive the matter and form of things,
    and with both we possess a cubit of certitude.

Knowledge of nature is only
    partially accessible to anyone.

Therefore, our knowledge is only able
    to have a half-cubit in this respect.

Concerning the length of our ark,
        it is clear how worthily it is said to have two and one-half
    cubits.

That consideration which is in workings and
        which we have already said pertains to the width of the ark,
    is divided into two parts.

One of these parts is the working of human activity;
    the other is the working of nature.

It is the work of human activity that we see in:
        pictures,
        carvings,
        books,
        and similar things;
    these things are works of nature:
        that herbs and trees grow;
        that they produce flowers, leaves and fruit.

Human knowledge is able and accustomed to have a full cubit of
    comprehension in the working of human activity;

otherwise, how could it discover what it was not able to
comprehend?

The evident effect of hidden causes lies open;
but we do not suffice to understand fully the hidden causes of
effects.

Therefore, it is clear
why the width of the ark is said to have a cubit and a half.

But that consideration which is in morals and
which we have already said refers to the height of the ark
is divided into two parts.

One part is engaged with human instructions,
the other is engaged with divine instructions.

Certainly where human instruction serves the divine,
on account of both, the soul and the structure of our ark both
rise up to the heights.

Certainly a man is able to comprehend
those human instructions which he is able to discover.

In the divine sacraments the exterior form that is outwardly
accessible is one thing;
that intrinsic power which lies deeply hidden is another.

And so, in divine instructions
we do not rise up at all to a full cubit of knowledge.

And so, the height of our ark consists of
a cubit and a half.

However, we ought to gild our ark and
to pursue as much as is possible the rational principle of things
that can be imagined.

Moreover, we ought to gild it not only on the outside,
but on the inside as well.

It is one thing to examine the physical causes of things;
it is another to think about the rational principle of justice
in the disposition of things.

The former pertains to external gilding;
    the latter pertains to internal gilding.

Our gilding ought to be done
    with the purest gold.

Let there be nothing false or trifling in the assertion of your
        conclusion
    and you have the purest gold.

When the gilding has been done,
    the crown of the ark must be made.

By the crown, as we have said, we understand the third kind of
        contemplation,
    just as the fourth kind is given to be understood by the
    propitiatory.

In the former it is a matter of invisible goods;
    in the latter it is a matter of invisible substances.

To the crown of the ark it pertains
    to seek what the crown of justice is;
    to seek what those goods are that are set aside for the saints.

It ought to be noted that the crown of the ark itself
    was fastened to pieces of wood.

So it surely is raised up from the similitude of visible things
    to the speculation of invisible things.

In the fourth kind of contemplation an enquiry is made
    concerning the supreme kinds of creatures.

However, from among every creature, none is more worthy
    than invisible and rational substance.

This kind of contemplation is rightly understood
    by the propitiatory which is placed over the ark.

But before we follow up more fully what is said concerning the
        propitiatory,
    it seems that those things which could be said concerning the
    rings ought to be inserted at this point.

For indeed, it is necessary for the ark of our speculation
    to have four rings of gold,
    two on each side of the ark.

By the ark, as we have said,
    we understand the grace of contemplation.

By all means we are able to bring into contemplation when we
    wish,
    the things that we know in whatever manner to be happening.

Among those things which are accustomed to occur,
    some happen for good, others for evil.

The former happen by the working of God;
    the latter happen by the permission of God.

Those which happen by the working of God
    pertain to one side of the ark;
    those which happen by the permission of God
    pertain to the other side in like manner.

Behold, let us see concerning the sides of the ark,
    and now concerning the rings of gold.

Among all metals nothing shines more than gold,
    nothing is more precious than gold;
    the wisdom of God shines more than all things.

Certainly the wisdom of God
    is simple and one.

Nevertheless, it is distinguished by various words,
    so that it can be more easily understood by us.

At one time it is called foreknowledge;
    at another, knowledge;
    at one time it is called predestination;
    at another, disposition.

If I am not mistaken, these are the rings
    that it is necessary to place on the sides of the ark.

A ring is turned back upon itself;
    for this reason neither beginning nor end can be found in it.

In every ordering by eternal wisdom,
    the beginning agrees with the end.

Therefore, in this fourfold distinction of wisdom,
    we are able with sufficient suitability to understand
      the above-mentioned golden rings.

On these rings the ark of our knowledge is
    directed toward the truth and
    advanced to distant and higher things.

Two of these rings are placed on one side,
    the remaining ones are placed on the other side.

Each one surely has a set place, as it were,
    and it clings most closely, as it were, there
      where more marvelous and more delightful
        things are manifest.

We have said that those things which happen
      by the permission of God
    pertain to one side.

The rings of knowledge and foreknowledge
    hang most closely on this side,
    where certainly the more marvelous things are manifest.

It is not so very marvelous
    that he foresees from eternity what he will do at some time.

But what sort of thing is it
    that he foresees from eternity
      what he gives over to the will of another;
    that he observes at every moment
      what is happening in the dark recesses of the heart?

But, on the other hand, those things which happen
    by the working of God
      have already been said to pertain to the other side.

The circles of predestination and disposition occupy this side
    where certainly the more delightful things are manifest.

What seems more delightful to a good heart

than that every divine disposition of predestination
    wages war for salvation?

It still remains for us to inquire
    which ring ought to be placed in which corner.

We have said that those things which happen
    by the permission of God
        pertain to one side of the ark,
    while those things which happen by the working of God
        pertain in like manner to the other side.

To the latter pertain those which belong to equity;
    to the former pertain those which belong to iniquity.

As the latter vary according to prosperity and adversity,
    so the former also vary.

Where iniquity and adversity meet,
    they form a corner, as it were.

In this corner reprobates are scourged by God,
    yet they are not reformed.

But why, I ask, does he bring them to the whips of his fatherhood,
    if he foresees that they cannot be reformed?

The ring of foreknowledge is placed on this corner,
    where a more marvelous thing is manifest.

Where iniquity and prosperity come together
    they form another corner.

In this corner reprobates observe the gifts of God,
    and they become ungrateful, always.

But surely this is not able to obscure the knowledge of God,
    nor does it cease to provoke those who prosper to the good of
        gratitude.

The ring of knowledge hangs closely to this corner,
    where so marvelous a thing shows itself.

In the meeting of fairness and prosperity,
    we understand the third corner.

Surely persons being saved from transitory things
    are prospering here,
        so that they are kindled with longing for eternal things.

What, I ask, is more beneficial than this speculation,
    or what is more delightful?

What does it mean, I ask, that He advances and favors with
    temporal goods
        those whom He has predestined to eternity?

And so the circle of predestination takes a place here,
    where a thing more delightful than all others is manifest.

The ring of divine disposition occupies the fourth corner,
    where there is a kind of running together of fairness and
        adversity.

Here good persons are busy with good things
    and pressed down by adverse things.

Here, nevertheless, according to God's disposing,
    this happens to them:
    They are kindled most passionately with love of God.

What sort of thing is it, I ask, that the more passionately they
    are kindled with love of Him,
        the more it seems that it ought to be extinguished?

Therefore the ring of divine disposition rightly takes a place in
    this location where a more magnificent thing is manifest.

It belongs to the third contemplation to ascend
    by means of visible things to speculation of invisible things.

This is a work that surely is incumbent
    upon the rings of divine wisdom, if we are not in error.

When the ark of understanding is suspended from these rings,
    it is carried about in any direction without any deviation of
        error.

The aforementioned rings ought to have rods inserted
    that one is not permitted to withdraw.

A multitude of wonder is in the rings of knowledge and
    foreknowledge;
    greatness of exultation is in the remaining two rings.

In divine knowledge and foreknowledge
    you will always find many things worthy of wonder;
    in the predestination and disposition of God
        the just heart always finds what is worthy of great
exultation.

Your admiration always ought to be in the former;
    your exultation always ought to be in the latter.

Nowhere else will you find what you can marvel at more worthily;
    nowhere else will you find what you can love more rightly.

There is nothing trifling in either;
    there is nothing false in either.

Each pole is gilded,
    so that they may shine all around with the splendor of truth.

On these poles the ark of understanding is carried forward at one
    time;
    it is lifted to higher places at another time.

As often as the heart of man is delighted marvelously
    by the wisdom of God,
    for that reason it is enlarged to an increased capacity
    for more and greater things.

By the propitiatory, as we have said,
    we understand the fourth kind of contemplation.

This kind uses the pure understanding for the first time
    and is engaged with supreme and intellectible creatures.

The propitiatory is made from purest gold
    and is placed in the highest place.

In these things we note the purity of understanding
    and the worth of supereminence.

Here the instrument of the reason is used
    without the service of imagination.

RICHARD OF ST. VICTOR

The propitiatory is placed in the highest place;
   the worth of the rational creature is placed before all others.

It ought to be noted that this work is called the propitiatory
      because by much thinking and consideration of the self,
   the Lord is rendered more merciful
      to the rational creature.

Now let us see what is said
   concerning the length and width of the propitiatory.

No less worthy of consideration is
   why he is silent concerning the height of the propitiatory.

We know that length is naturally prior to width
   and likewise that both are prior to height.

Therefore we understand by length
   those things which are for the beginning of the rational
      creature.

By width we understand
   those things which are for his advancement.

But by altitude we understand
   those things which are for his consummation.

The goods of his creation are for him for the beginning;
   the goods of justification are for advancement;
   the goods of glorification are for consummation.

Let the contemplative mind carefully exercise itself in these things
   so that its propitiatory can receive a proper measurement.

The rational creature receives three very marvelous things from
      creation:
   subtility of essence;
   discretion of good and evil;
   freedom of will.

The most notable characteristic of human beings is
   that they have freedom of will.

In our hearts we daily choose these things
   and in both we have a cubit of certitude.

But who, I ask, is able by any sense to see
    the substance of the soul itself?

I do not see yours;
    you do not see mine.

But accordingly neither is able to see
    either the other's or his.

In this instance, as long as we live
    we cannot extend our knowledge to a full cubit.

Therefore, the length of the propitiatory
    is rightly said to be two and one-half cubits.

We have already said that the making just of the rational creature
    pertains to the width of the propitiatory.

However, our justification is completed
    by divine inspiration and our own deliberation.

A person knows from experience
    what deliberation is.

But who, I ask, comprehends
    the way in which divine inspiration comes into us?

For the Spirit blows where it wills,
    and you do not know from whence it comes
        or to where it goes.

Therefore, in one thing we have a cubit of comprehension;
    in the other we are not able to have it.

You see how rightly the width of the propitiatory
    is said to have a cubit and a half.

Behold the length of the propitiatory;
    behold its width.

Those things which are for our glorification
    pertain to its height.

But who comprehends by any sense
    in what things our glorification consists:

What "eye has not seen, nor ear heard,
    nor has arisen in the heart of man" (1 Cor. 2:9)?

From this it is easily pondered
    why the height of the propitiatory is not appointed a measure.

The two last kinds of contemplation
    are engaged with divine things, as has been said.

Those things which are above reason yet not beyond reason
    refer to one kind.

Those things which go beyond the mode of its capacity
        are above reason;
    yet they are consistent with reason,
        although they cannot be understood by it.

The last kind of contemplation is engaged with those things
        which seem completely contrary to reason,
    and of such kinds to which reason would never acquiesce
        unless faith itself were to lead it in this.

These last kinds of contemplations
    are expressed by an angelic form.

It is certainly necessary that we assume an angelic form
    if we wish to fly to contemplation of eternal and divine things.

Now this angelic form is commanded
        to be of beaten work and of gold;
    so that it may be of gold,
        the mind of the contemplative should be cleansed of all
phantasies.

Beaten work is produced by striking;
    our cherubim are commanded to be of beaten work.

From this we clearly gather that we advance in such grace
    more by compunction than by investigation.

The excellence of these speculations is commended
    because they are called "cherubim."

For in this twin speculation

we are advanced to fullness of knowledge.

Beyond these, one cannot seek or discover
    anything for the augmenting of knowledge.

We said above that we ascend to contemplation of invisible things
    by means of visible things.

So we are surely raised up to speculation of the creatrix of nature
    by knowledge of invisible creatures.

Hence it is that the cherubim are commanded
    to turn the face toward the propitiatory.

Hence it is commanded that one stand on one side,
    the other on the other side.

In the speculation that is understood by the propitiatory,
    great similitude and great dissimilitude with the divine are
        found.

For the spiritual creature has been made
    according to the image and similitude of God.

Therefore, as it has been said before, one of the cherubim
    occupies the side of similitude,
    the other one of them occupies the side of dissimilitude.

The speculation having a greater agreement with reason
    stands on one side;
    the one that is in less agreement with reason
    stands on the other side.

The cherubim ought to spread out wings
    and cover the propitiatory.

What is the spreading out of wings,
    except a kind of preparation for flying?

The very preparation of the mind is turned
    into a veil of eternal things and into an umbrella;
    into an umbrella, I say, from the heat of the day
    and for security and hiding from wind and rain.

The cherubim ought to turn the face toward the propitiatory

and by examining the image of God
be taught more certainly
concerning the more sublime things of knowledge.

The aforementioned cherubim also ought to look mutually at each
other
and preserve in everything an agreement of assertion with
each other.

Let each one beware lest in that which it affirms
it contradicts the other.

The assertion of unity ought to be made by one
so that in it the confession of the Trinity is not negated.

The confession of the Trinity ought to be made by the other
so that in it the assertion of unity is not negated.

Let any prelate whomsoever hear how beneficial it is
to have the three last speculations in his possession.

"Whence," he says,
"I will speak to you."

He who strives with eagerness for a divine showing
endeavors to obtain these things.

The propitiatory is worthily called the mercy-seat
for the divine response was given from there.

The Lord speaks above the propitiatory
when He inspires spiritual things that go beyond our
conceptions of Him.

He is heard from between the cherubim as it were,
because the pair seem to agree in a matter.

The wings of the cherubim cover the propitiatory,
the propitiatory covers the ark,
since the knowledge of lower things is overshadowed
by the prerogative of the knowledge of higher things.

According to the precept of the Lord
a testimony must be placed in the ark.

Because we are taught what ought to be done in supreme things,
    we pass along the way of life firmly retaining them in the inner
        parts.

The principal precepts of God are called a testimony
    since they restore a testimony to the conscience of every
        person.

According to the manner of observance they restore a testimony to
    every person,
    as much as he loves his God.

I have narrated in a brief summary
    these things concerning the grace of contemplating,
    for I have discussed the same matter
    at greater length elsewhere.

By the table of the shew-bread
    we understand the teaching of sacred learning;
    food is placed on the table
    so that it can be taken for refreshment.

Some things are refreshment for the body;
    other things are refreshment for the spirit.

The former are of bodies;
    the latter are of spirits.

Worldly knowledge provides for the former;
    Divine Scripture provides for the latter.

In Divine Scripture refreshment of souls is set forth,
    for which reason it is worthily called a table of shew-bread.

However, the state of human life
    was one thing under hope of future redemption;
    it must of necessity be quite another thing
    under the faith of a redemption already accomplished.

It is the case of one in the Old Testament,
    of the other in the New Testament.

Sacred Scripture treats sufficiently of both,
    for which reason it is said to have two cubits of length.

RICHARD OF ST. VICTOR

Certainly either Testament is intended
    only for the care of souls.

It is silent concerning the care of bodies
    and leaves aside worldly knowledge.

In these things it is a case of a single and not a twofold care,
    for that reason it is said to have one cubit of width.

With respect to the manner of our restoration,
    it teaches sufficiently concerning the state of the present life.

However, it teaches few things concerning the future life;
    so its altitude has a cubit and a half.

It has a full cubit as far as it concerns the present life;
    it has a half cubit as far as it concerns the future life.

The table of shew-bread is made from wood,
    covered over with gold,
    encircled by a lip,
    embellished by two crowns.

By the work of wood we understand the historical sense;
    by the lip, the tropological;
    by the two crowns, the allegorical and anagogical.

The table is made of pieces of Setim wood,
    which is said to be very incorruptible.

Sacred history, alien from all falsity and foolishness,
    pertains to incorruptible wood.

The gilding of the table itself
    is the subtle and wise exposition of the letter.

Beautiful gilding is the commendation
    of prophetic divine judgments.

Surely it ought to be noted that the first work
    is of pieces of wood, but it is gilded.

But the other three works are not gilded;
    they are of gold.

That difference which is between wood and gold

is the difference between the historical and spiritual senses of
Scripture.

History holds first place
in Sacred Scripture.

But mystical understanding
is tripartite.

Tropology holds the lowest place;
allegory holds the middle;
anagogy holds the highest.

Why should that not hold the highest place
which is often employed concerning supreme and celestial
things?

Allegory is engaged especially with the sacraments of our faith
and with such things as are believed more than understood.

Tropology treats of those things which everyone understands
easily,
and for this reason it remains in the lowest place.

By the golden lip, therefore, I understand
spiritual and moral understanding.

Something great is intimated
since the form of this work is called a lip.

We know that every word of ours
is formed by the lips.

Perhaps it is given to be understood that
ordinary speech ought to be shaped by tropology.

A crown worked in low relief is placed upon the lip
because allegory is engaged with more subtle and sublime
things.

Work in low relief is accustomed to have certain ingenious
engravings;
why do you marvel that allegory is woven into history in a
marvelous manner?

For those things which can scarcely be believed and cannot be
    comprehended
    have been inserted there allegorically.

The crown worked in low relief has its surface
    flat in one place, concave in another, and pierced in another.

It is flat with regard to those things which are according to reason;
    concave with regard to those which are beyond reason;
    pierced with regard to those which seem to be against reason.

Now the situation of tropology is one thing;
    the situation of allegory is another.

For what is tropology except moral knowledge;
    what is allegory except the spiritual teaching of hidden things?

Honesty of morals has been inscribed naturally
    on the human heart.

But certainly no one presumes to understand the deep things of
    mysteries from his own sense,
    unless he does it thoughtlessly.

For this reason the height of the crown
    is said to measure only four fingers.

What, I ask, are the holy evangelists,
    except the fingers of the right hand of the Most High?

Allegorical teaching forms itself to the measure of these,
    when it agrees with their words in everything.

It should be noted that it is suggested that the crown itself be made
    before the lip,
    since the discipline of morals is observably and beneficially
    restored by the power of the sacraments.

By the aureole crown, as has been said,
    we understand anagogical teaching.

This teaching concerns supreme things,
    hence its large representation occupies the highest place.

For what shall we call anagogy,

except spiritual and upward-leading understanding?

In the aforementioned two senses,
    we seek teaching concerning morals and hidden things.

To anagogy belongs
    the foreseeing of hoped-for rewards.

Can it be the same that the crown is called an aureole,
    and if it is called modest and golden?

Whatever human power grasps concerning
      that which eye has not seen
      nor ear heard,
      nor has arisen in the human heart,
    is modest.

It should be noted that only Sacred Scripture uses
      allegorical and anagogical senses mystically,
    and among all the senses, it is crowned by this
      supereminent pair.

The holy teachers ought to study with great zeal
    so that they are always prepared when asked to give a reason
      for the faith and hope that are in them.

In public they ought to
    prove truth and disprove falsehood;
    exhort to just action and oppose unjust action by arguments.

Who knows this:
    What sort of rings was it necessary that he attach
      to the doctrinal table?

O what sort of rings these are for
    proof of truth and disproof of falsehood;
    exhortation to just action and opposition to unjust action!

Does reasoning not return again and make a circle
    when it demonstrates in the conclusion
      what it proposed at the outset?

From what has been said concerning one of these rings,

it is easy to understand what ought to be decided concerning
    them.

Now we see what those corners are
    in which such rings ought to be placed.

Where anyone doubts concerning what sacred Scripture proposes,
    in a certain way he runs toward a corner, as it were.

Doubt and hesitation make a corner
    where what ought to be decided does not come to mind easily.

Often one doubts whether a truth is true
    or whether something false is false.

Often one hesitates about doing something just
    or about doing or not doing something unjust.

However it is very easy to see which ring we ought to put at which
    corner
    and not be remiss in our placement of such.

It follows that now we ought to seek
    what ought to be thought concerning the feet of the table.

The whole body rests upon the feet
    and is held standing by them.

However, the more firmly we rely upon the divine commands,
    the more perfectly we shall be raised up to an upright position.

In accord with the four feet,
    give heed to a fourfold division of commands.

The first foot is a precept;
    the second, a prohibition;
        the third, an admonition;
            the fourth, a concession.

A precept has to do with those things
    the doing of which brings about merit;
    the not doing of which brings about guilt.

A prohibition has to do with those things

the doing of which brings about guilt;
the not doing of which brings about merit.

An admonition has to do with those things
the doing of which brings about merit,
while not doing them does not bring about guilt.

A concession has to do with those things
the not doing of which brings about merit,
although doing them does not bring about guilt.

We especially need:
assent with respect to precepts;
refusal with respect to prohibitions;
conviction with respect to admonitions;
resistance with respect to concessions.

It easily comes to light
why this should be carefully inquired about.

The duty of the true preacher consists of two things;
instruction in truth and exhortation to virtue.

By this twin influence the doctrinal table is carried about
and is transferred from one heart to another by them, as if by
some poles.

One pole is called keenness in instruction;
the other, keenness in exhortation.

Poles of this sort ought to be
made from the open testimony of the letter of Scripture,
from Setim wood, as it were,
and they ought to be gilded by the deeper senses of
the spiritual understanding of Scripture.

All sacred instruction ought to be relied upon
for proving truth
and disproving falsehood.

All sacred exhortation ought to be relied upon
for convincing about good
and advising against evil.

For this reason it is easy to give thought to
    which ring ought to have which pole.

It ought to be noted that:
    The witness of Scripture
        pertains to the poles
    while human reason
        pertains to the rings.

Since the depth of the hidden things goes beyond human reason,
    the rings properly receive a place below the crown.

BOOK THREE OF

THE TRINITY

Chapter I

That thus far we have treated the unity of the divine substance; hereafter we must inquire what we should hold concerning the plurality of divine persons

In those things which have been said thus far concerning the unity and attributes of the divine substance, we have discussed according to the way it seemed to us. Now for the remainder we have proposed to investigate what we ought to think concerning the plurality and properties of the divine persons.

First of all it seems that we should inquire whether there is true plurality in that true and simple Divinity and if, as we believe, the number of persons appears as a triad. Secondly, we should inquire how the unity of substance can be joined with a plurality of persons. In the third place it will be necessary for us to inquire, according to the teachings of our faith, whether there is only one person there who is from Himself, while each of the others proceeds from another. We should also see if there are other things we should inquire into related to this same consideration. If it should be granted to us to show these things clearly from reason it will finally still be necessary for us to inquire whether if in those two persons who proceed from another, rather than from themselves, there are different modes of preceeding, and which mode is proper to each and what follows in connection with the names of each according to the properties of each.

However, in those things remaining for us to inquire into, it is necessary to apply greater carefulness and to pursue more ardently as we find less in the writings of the Fathers from which we can show these things than from the testimony of reason (I do not speak of the testimony of Scripture). In connection with the proposal of my investigation, let him who wishes, laugh; let him who wishes mock—and rightly so. For, if I speak truth here, it is not so much knowledge that lifts me up, but rather the ardor of a burning soul that urges me to try this. What if it is not given to me to reach the goal I strive for? What if I falter in running the course? Well, I will rejoice that I totally ran, labored and sweated to the extent of my powers in seeking the face of my Lord. And if it should happen that I fail because of the excessive length, the roughness or difficulty of the way, I will have accomplished something at least, if I may truly say: I have done what I could do; "I have sought and not found him; I have called and he did not answer me" (Song of Songs 5:6). Behold Balaam's ass which delayed her rider on his journey. (Cf. Numbers 22:23–31.) In some mysterious way she impels and urges me to attempt to run the course I have begun. I hear one who still speaks and says to me: "He who could give to me to speak could undoubtedly give it also to you." But now let us turn our attention with all due care to that which we have proposed.

CHAPTER II

How fullness of goodness shows clearly from the nature of charity that in true divinity, plurality of persons cannot be lacking

We have learned above that in that supreme and altogether perfect good there is fullness and perfection of all goodness. However, where there is fullness of all goodness, true and supreme charity cannot be lacking. For nothing is better than charity; nothing is more perfect than charity. However, no one is properly said to have charity on the basis of his own private love of himself. And so it is necessary for love to be directed toward another for it to be charity. Therefore, where a plurality of persons is lacking, charity cannot exist.

But you might say, "Even if there were only one person in that true Divinity, nevertheless He could still have charity toward His creation—indeed He would have it." But certainly He could not have *supreme* charity toward a created person. For charity would be disordered if He loved supremely someone who should not be supremely loved. But in that supremely wise goodness it is impossible for charity to be disordered. Therefore a divine person could not have supreme charity toward a person who was not worthy of supreme love. However, in order that charity be supreme and supremely perfect, it is necessary that it be so great that nothing greater can exist and that it be of such a kind that nothing better can exist. However, as long as anyone loves no one else as much as he loves himself, that private love which he has for himself shows clearly that he has not yet reached the supreme level of charity. But a divine person certainly would not have anyone to love as worthily as Himself if He did not have a person of equal worth. However a person who is not God would not be equal in worth to a divine person. Therefore, so that fullness of charity might have a place in that true Divinity, it is necessary that a divine person not lack a relationship with an equally worthy person, who is, for this reason, divine.

Therefore see how easily reason clearly shows that in true Divinity plurality of persons cannot be lacking. Certainly God alone is supremely good. Therefore God alone ought to be loved supremely. A divine person could not show supreme love to a person who lacked divinity. However, fullness of Divinity could not exist without fullness of goodness. But fullness of goodness could not exist without fullness of charity, nor could fullness of charity exist without a plurality of divine persons.

CHAPTER III

That the fullness of divine happiness confirms what the fullness of goodness says concerning the plurality of divine persons

What the fullness of goodness clearly shows and proves concerning the plurality of persons, the fullness of happiness demonstrates by a similar reason. What one says, the other confirms. In one and the same confirmation of truth, the one speaks out and the other applauds.

Let each person examine his consciousness; without doubt and without contradiction he will discover that just as nothing is better than charity, so nothing is more pleasing than charity. Nature herself teaches us this; many experiences do the very same. Therefore, just as that than which nothing is better cannot be lacking in the fullness of true goodness, so also that than which nothing is more pleasing cannot be lacking in the fullness of supreme happiness.* Therefore, in supreme happiness it is necessary that charity not be lacking. However, so that charity may be in the supreme good, it is impossible that there be lacking either one who can show charity or one to whom charity can be shown. However it is a characteristic of love, and one without which it cannot possibly exist, to wish to be loved much by the one whom you love much. Therefore, love cannot be pleasing if it is not also mutual. Therefore, in that true and supreme happiness, just as pleasing love cannot be lacking, so mutual love cannot be lacking. However, in mutual love it is absolutely necessary that there be both one who gives love and one who returns love. Therefore one will be the offerer of love and the other the returner of love. Now, where the one and the other are clearly shown to exist, true plurality is discovered. In that fullness of true happiness, a plurality of persons cannot be lacking. However it is agreed that supreme happiness is nothing other than Divinity itself. Therefore, the showing of love freely given and the repayment of love that is due prove without any doubt that in true Divinity a plurality of persons cannot be lacking.

CHAPTER IV

That what is asserted in the above-mentioned two witnesses concerning the plurality of persons is confirmed by considering the fullness of divine glory

Certainly if we say that in that true Divinity there exists only one person, just as there is only one substance, then without doubt according to this He will not have anyone with whom He could share that infinite abundance of His fullness. But, how can this be, I ask? Would it be because even though He wished to, He could not

*Richard is reflecting the complex formula of Anselm's designation of God in the ontological argument; cf. *Proslogion*, 1–5.

have one who would share with Him? Or is it because He would not wish to, even if He could? But He who is undoubtedly omnipotent cannot be excused on the grounds of impossibility. But could not that which is not due to a defect of power be due to a defect of benevolence alone? But if He would be absolutely unwilling to have one to share with Him when He really could if He wanted, then observe, I ask you, what a defect of benevolence this would be in a divine person and how great it would be. Certainly, as has been said, nothing is sweeter than charity; nothing more pleasing than charity. The life of reason experiences nothing sweeter than the delights of charity; enjoys no pleasure more pleasing than this. He would lack these delights in eternity if He remains all alone on the throne of majesty because He lacks fellowship.

And so from these points we can realize what kind and how great the defect of such benevolence would be if He should prefer to keep for Himself alone in a miserly fashion the abundance of His fullness, which if He wished, He could communicate to another with such an accumulation of joy and such an increase of pleasure. If He were like this, He should quite rightly hide from the gaze of angels and of everyone. If such a great defect of benevolence were in Him, quite rightly He should blush with shame to be seen or to be recognized. But this is not proper! It is not proper that there be something in that supreme majesty in which He could not glory, for which He should not be glorified.

Yet where will fullness of glory be? For no fullness can be lacking there, as was proven above. However, what is more glorious, what is truly more magnificent than to have nothing that one does not want to share? And so it is evident that in that unfailing good and supremely wise counsel there can be no miserly holding back just as there can be no inordinate squandering. Behold, you plainly know, as you can see, that in that supreme and most exalted height, the fullness of glory requires that a sharer of glory be not lacking.

Chapter V

That the above-mentioned assertion of divine plurality is confirmed by a triple testimony

Behold, concerning the plurality of divine persons, we have presented our teaching with such transparent reasoning that whoever wishes to oppose such a clear confirmation would seem to suffer from the disease of folly. For who, except someone suffering from the disease of madness, would say that there is lacking in the supreme goodness that than which nothing is more perfect, and nothing better? Who, I ask, except someone weak in mind, would deny that there is in the supreme happiness that than which nothing is more joyful and nothing sweeter? Who, I say, except someone devoid of reason, would think that there could be lacking in the fullness of glory that than which nothing is more glorious and nothing more magnificent? Certainly nothing is better, nothing is more joyful, nothing is any more magnificent than true, sincere and supreme charity, which he knows does not exist without a plurality of persons.

And so the assertion of this plurality is confirmed by a triple testimony. For what supreme goodness and supreme happiness harmoniously declare concerning this matter, fullness of glory applauds by confirming and confirms by applauding. Behold concerning this article of our faith we have a triple testimony: the most supernal concerning supreme things; divine concerning divine things; the deepest concerning profound things; and the most open concerning hidden things. And we know that "in the mouth of two or three witness every word is established" (Matt. 18:16). Behold "a triple cord" that "is difficult to break" (Eccles. 4:12). Through the gift of the Trinity's wisdom, this cord firmly binds any frenzied attackers of our faith.

CHAPTER VI

It is utterly necessary that divine persons exist coeternally

As we can gather clearly from the above, see how the perfection of one person requires fellowship with another. We have discovered that nothing is more glorious, more magnificent than to wish to have nothing that you do not wish to share. And so a person who was supremely good would not wish to be without a sharer of His majesty. However, without doubt, whatever that One whose will was omnipotent willed to exist must exist; whatever that One whose will was unchangeable once willed, He always willed. Therefore, it is necessary that an eternal person have a coeternal person, for one is not able to precede the other nor is one able to follow the other. For just as nothing in that eternal and unchangeable Divinity is able to regress to an earlier condition, so nothing is able to come to a new condition. And so it is utterly impossible for divine persons not to be coeternal. For where there is true Divinity, there supreme goodness and full happiness exist. However, as has been said, supreme goodness cannot exist without perfect charity, nor can perfect charity exist without a plurality of persons. Indeed, full happiness cannot exist without true unchangeability, nor can true unchangeability exist without eternity. True charity demands a plurality of persons; true unchangeability demands a coeternity of persons.

CHAPTER VII

That in that plurality of persons both supreme equality and supreme similitude must exist

Surely it ought to be noted that as true charity demands a plurality of persons, so supreme charity demands equality of persons. Now supreme charity is not yet clearly shown to exist where the beloved is not truly loved supremely. But love is not discerning where one is loved supremely who should not be loved supremely. But in supremely wise goodness, just as the flame of love does not

379

burn otherwise than supreme wisdom prescribes, so it also does not burn more intensely. And so it is necessary that one who should be loved supremely according to that supreme abundance of charity without doubt should love according to that supreme rule of discretion. But the particular nature of love itself shows clearly that it is not sufficient for the one loving supremely if the one being loved supremely does not return supreme love. And so in mutual love, fullness of charity demands that each be supremely loved by the other and consequently, according to the previously mentioned norm of discretion, that each ought to be loved supremely. However where each ought to be loved equally, it is necessary that each be equally perfect. And so it is necessary that each one be equally powerful, equally wise, equally good, equally blessed. So supreme fullness of love demands supreme equality of perfection in those loved mutually. And so in true Divinity, as the particular nature of charity requires a plurality of persons, so the integrity of the same charity requires supreme equality of persons in true plurality. However, so that the persons may be equal in everything, it is necessary that they be similar in everything. For similitude can be possessed without equality, while equality is never possessed without mutual similitude. How are those persons able to be companions in wisdom who have no similitude in wisdom? However, what I say concerning wisdom, I say concerning power. Indeed, you will find the same in all the others, if you go through them individually.

Chapter VIII

According to a marvelous reasoning there is a substantial unity in that plurality and a personal plurality in that true unity of substance

We have sought and discovered that in the above-mentioned mutually loved and mutually loving persons, in order that supreme love might exist worthily, there must be in each both supreme perfection and the fullness of all perfection. And so in each there will be fullness of power, fullness of wisdom, fullness of goodness, fullness of Divinity. Behold, far above we made mention but did not define something: namely that the Divinity which we discovered could not be common to a plurality of substances; now here it clearly appears to be common to a plurality of persons. But if, as has been said, every perfection is common to those mutually loved, it is clear that if one is omnipotent, the other also will be omnipotent; if one is immeasurable, the other also will be immeasurable; if one is God, the other also will be God.

But as we have demonstrated with sufficient clarity in the above, only one can be omnipotent; only one can be immeasurable; only one can be God. What then? Certainly without any doubt each will be omnipotent in such a way that both together will be only one omnipotent; and each will be immeasurable in such a way that both together will be only one immeasurable; and without doubt each of them will be God in such a way that both together will be only one God.* "And who is fit for this?" (2 Cor. 2:16). But if Divinity itself, as we have said, is certainly common to both, certainly then divine substance will also be common to both; for as has been proved above, divine substance is nothing other than Divinity itself. And so it is shown clearly that each possesses one and the same substance in common—or if this sounds better: It is shown clearly that both are one and the same substance at the same time. And so why marvel if at the same time both are only one omnipotent, one eternal, one immense, only one God and Lord, when certainly both are only one in substance at the same time? Therefore, see how by what a wonderful reasoning there is substantial unity in that plurality of persons and a personal plurality in a true unity of substance, so that there is also "individuality in persons and unity in substance and equality in majesty."†

---

*Richard is here reflecting the formulation of the *Athanasian Creed*.
†*Athanasian Creed*.

Chapter IX

That in the divine nature there is plurality of persons in a unity of substance; and in human nature there is plurality of substances in a unity of person

Perhaps you who hear or read this marvel; you marvel, I say, how there can be more than one person where there is only one substance. But why marvel, why marvel, I say, if He who is marvelous in so many of His works is marvelous in Himself above everything? You marvel at how there is more than one person in the divine nature where there is not more than one substance. Yet you do not marvel equally at how there is more than one substance in human nature where there is not more than one person. For man consists of body and soul, and together these two are only one person. So a person has a basis in himself for how to observe and learn what he should, by way of contrast, think concerning his God.

If it is agreeable, let us gather in one place what reason discovers in the divine nature by reasoning and those things which experience finds in human nature. In both there is unity; in both, plurality. In the divine nature there is unity of substance; in human nature, unity of person. In the former there is plurality of persons; in the latter, plurality of substances. In the former, certainly, plurality of persons in unity of substance' but in the latter, plurality of substances in unity of person. Behold how human nature and divine nature seem to be related mutually yet as opposites, and the one seems to be oriented to the other in a contrasting way. So they are mutually related and should be mutually contrasted: created nature and uncreated nature; time and eternity; corruptible and incorruptible; changeable and unchangeable; the small and the immense; the bounded and the infinite.

CHAPTER X

How from the plurality and unity that he discovers in himself a man is taught what he ought to think, by way of opposites as it were, concerning those things which are proposed to him for believing with respect to his God

Let us add that in the plurality of persons in the divine nature there is full similitude and supreme equality. However, in the plurality of substance in human nature there is much dissimilitude and great inequality. For in the former plurality of persons, one is incorruptible and the other is incorruptible; one is unchangeable and the other is unchangeable; one is unbounded and the other is unbounded; the one and the other are equally powerful; the one and the other are equally wise, equally good, equally blessed. In the latter plurality of substances of which the human person is composed, one is corporeal, the other is incorporeal; one is visible, the other is invisible; one is mortal, the other is immortal; one is destructible, the other is indestructible; one is perishable, the other is imperishable. Nevertheless in the individual person they have been so joined into one that in experiencing and in being delighted with something, they cannot be severed (I do not say separated).

Behold, you have seen how great a dissimilitude and diversity of substances there are in human nature. You have seen, no less, how great a similitude and equality of persons there are in the divine nature. Explain to me, I implore you, how there is personal unity in so great a dissimilitude and diversity of substances, and I will tell you how there is a substantial unity in so great a similitude and equality of persons. You say, "I do not grasp it; I do not understand; but even if the understanding does not grasp it, nevertheless experience itself persuades me." Well said indeed and rightly too! But if experience teaches you that something exists in human nature that is above understanding, should it not also have taught you that something exists above your understanding in divine nature? And so a person can learn from himself, by way of opposites as it were, what he ought to think concerning those things which are proposed to him for believing concerning his God.

These things have been said on account of those who strive to define and determine the depth of divine secrets according to the mode of their own capacity—not according to the tradition of the holy Fathers, who, as it is known, have learned from and been taught by the Holy Spirit.

Chapter XI

How it is shown clearly from the integrity of charity that true Trinity is in true unity and true unity is in true Trinity

Now let us order what we have grasped; let us follow the mode of our reasoning. A plurality of divine persons has been established but not yet a Trinity of persons. For plurality can exist even where there is no Trinity. Indeed duality itself is plurality. And so, concerning the assertion of Trinity, let us question the same witnesses we brought forth above to testify for plurality.

If it is agreeable, first of all let supreme charity be asked what it testifies about this matter. Now, it is necessary that supreme charity be altogether perfect. Yet in order that it may be supremely perfect, just as it is necessary that it be so great that nothing greater can exist, so it is necessary that it be such that nothing better can exist. For just as in supreme charity what is greatest cannot be lacking, so what is clearly excellent cannot be lacking either. But in true charity, it seems excellent to wish another to be loved as one's self. Certainly in mutual and very fervent love nothing is rarer or more magnificent than to wish that another be loved equally by the one whom you love supremely and by whom you are supremely loved. And so the proof of perfected charity is a willing sharing of the love that has been shown to you. For the one loving supremely and longing to be loved supremely, surely the most excellent joy lies in the fulfillment of his own longing, namely in the attainment of longed-for love. So a person proves that he is not perfect in charity if he cannot yet take pleasure in sharing his excellent joy. And so it is a sign of a great weakness not to be able to allow a sharing of love, while to be able to is a sign of great perfection. If it is great to be able to allow it, it will be greater to undertake it with rejoicing; it will be greatest, however, to search for it with longing. The first is a great good; the second, a better one; but the third, the best. Therefore, let us offer to the supreme what is excellent; to the best, what is best. And in those who are mutually loved, who were earlier treated above, the perfection of each, in order to be completed, requires with equal reason a sharer of the love that has been shown to them. For if he does not will what perfect goodness demands, where will the fullness of goodness be? If he wills what cannot be done, where will fullness of power be?

Hence we gathered by clear reasoning that the most excellent level of charity, and therefore the fullness of goodness, cannot exist where a defect of will or a defect of a faculty excludes a sharer of love and a sharing of most excellent joy. Therefore it is necessary that each of those loved supremely and loving supremely should search with equal desire for someone who would be mutually loved and with equal concord willingly possess him. Thus you see how the perfection of charity requires a Trinity of persons, without which it is wholly unable to subsist in the integrity of its fullness. Thus, just as integral charity cannot be lacking, so also true Trinity cannot be lacking where everything that is, is altogether perfect. Therefore there is not only a plurality but also true Trinity in true unity and true unity in true Trinity.

CHAPTER XII

How supreme goodness and supreme happiness harmoniously proclaim the Trinity and confirm it by mutual witness

If anyone forcefully affirms that in true Divinity there exist only those whom reason discovered above who are loved mutually, what reason, I ask, will he be able to give for his claim? Will not each of them, I ask, be lacking a sharer in excellent joy? Will this be perhaps because both do not wish to have one, or because one wishes and the other does not? But if one does not wish what the other wishes, where will be that quality which is always found in true and perfect friends—and must always be present? Where, I ask, will be that unique sign of intimate love, namely the unanimity and intimate harmony of souls? And certainly, if anyone says that one wishes and another does not wish, then whoever concedes that in His will He is not able to prevail denies that He is supremely powerful. But if someone should say that neither is able to find repose in the sharing of the love that has been shown to them, how, I ask, will that person be able to excuse them of the defect of love mentioned above? Now we know that nothing can be hidden from those who are supremely wise. And so if they love each other truly and supremely, how will one of them be able to see a defect in the other and not grieve? For if one of the two sees a defect in the other and does not grieve, where will fullness of love be? If He sees and grieves, where will fullness of happiness be? However, it is the case that where a cause for grieving is never lacking, fullness of happiness cannot exist.

From this, therefore, we gather and grasp by indubitable reasoning that fullness of happiness excludes every defect of charity, whose perfection demands a Trinity of persons, as has been said, and furthermore shows clearly that it cannot be lacking. Behold how supreme goodness and supreme happiness harmoniously proclaim the assertion of Trinity and confirm it with mutual witness.

CHAPTER XIII

That the fullness of divine glory seems to shout out in conclusive witness of supreme goodness and happiness

No doubt, it is a great defect of mature charity to be unable to experience the fellowship of love. Who does not know this or who can cover it over? And so, if this defect mutually exists in those lovers often mentioned before, each not only has something to grieve over in the other, but at the same time something to be ashamed of in himself. For just as a true and intimate friend cannot see the defect of one who is loved intimately and not grieve, so surely in the presence of a friend he cannot fail to be ashamed over his own defect. But if there exists in that plurality of persons something of which one should rightly be ashamed, where, I beg you, will the fullness of glory be, which it is completely impossible to be without in true Divinity? But just as in supreme happiness there cannot be a cause of grieving, so in the fullness of supreme glory there cannot be matter for embarrassment. Indeed, who does not see what extreme madness it would be to suspect even weakly that there could be something in that supremely happy majesty which could overcloud even in the least the splendor of so much glory?

Behold how the fullness of divine goodness and the fullness of happiness and glory come together in one witness to truth. They clearly demonstrate what ought to be thought concerning the fullness of divine charity in that plurality of persons. Together, they condemn suspicion of any defect in that supreme charity; in accord they proclaim the fullness of all perfection. In order for charity to be true, it demands a plurality of persons; in order for charity to be perfected, it requires a Trinity of persons.

CHAPTER XIV

That a sharing of love cannot exist at all among less than three persons

However, if we concede that we cannot doubt after so many reasons have been set before us; if, I say, we concede that there exists in true Divinity some one person of such great benevolence that He wishes to have no riches or delights that He does not wish to share; of such great power that nothing is impossible for Him; of such great happiness that nothing is difficult for Him—it follows that it is necessary to acknowledge that a Trinity of divine persons cannot fail to exist. But so that this may be more apparent, let us gather into a unity what we have said more diffusely.

Certainly if there were only one person in Divinity, He would not have anyone with whom He might share the riches of His greatness. But conversely that abundance of delights and sweetness, which would have been able to increase for him on account of intimate love, would be lacking in eternity. But fullness of goodness does not allow the supremely good One to retain those riches greedily, nor does fullness of beatitude permit the supremely blessed One to fail to possess an abundance of delights and sweetness. And for the magnificence of His honor, He rejoices over sharing the riches as much as He glories over enjoying the abundance of delights and sweetness. On the basis of these things, consider how impossible it is for some one person in Divinity to lack the fellowship of association. If He were to have only one partner, certainly He would not lack one with whom He might share the riches of His greatness. But He would not have anyone with whom He might share the delights of charity. Nothing can be discovered that gives more pleasure than the sweetness of loving; there is nothing by which the soul is more delighted. He alone possesses the sweetness of such delights who has a partner and a loved one in the love that has been shown to Him.

And so sharing of love cannot exist among any less than three persons. Now, as has been said, nothing is more glorious, nothing more magnificent, than to share in common whatever you have that is useful and pleasant. But this cannot be hidden from supreme wisdom, nor can it fail to be pleasing to supreme benevolence. And as the happiness of the supremely powerful One and the power of supremely happy One cannot be lacking in what pleases Him, so in Divinity it is impossible for two persons not to be united to a third.

CHAPTER XV

That it is necessary for a pair of persons in the divinity to seek out a third person with equal desire and for a similar reason

Surely it ought to be noted in the divine persons that the perfection of one demands the addition of another and consequently in a pair of persons the perfection of each requires union with a third. For in a pair of persons, just as we have said elsewhere, in order that each may properly be supremely loved by the other, it is necessary that each be supremely perfect. And so, just as there is one wisdom and one power for both, so it is surely necessary that there be one supreme benevolence for both. Now it is a special characteristic of supreme and totally perfect benevolence that it shares in common the entire abundance of its fullness for everyone. However, where equal benevolence exists in either person it is necessary that each with equal desire and for a similar reason should seek out a sharer of his excellent joy. For when two persons who mutually love embrace each other with supreme long-ing and take supreme delight in each other's love, then the supreme joy of the first is in intimate love of the second, and conversely the excellent joy of the second is in love of the first. As long as only the first is loved by the second, he alone seems to possess the delights of his excellent sweetness. Similarly, as long as the second does not have someone who shares in love for a third,* he lacks the sharing of excellent joy. In order that both may be able to share delights of that kind, it is necessary for them to have someone who shares in love for a third.

When those who love mutually are of such great benevolence that, as we have said, they wish every perfection to be shared, then it is necessary, as has been said, that each with equal desire and for a similar reason seek out someone with whom to share love, and that each devotedly possess such a one, according to the fullness of his power.

CHAPTER XVI

That fullness of power and wisdom seems to be able to exist in a single person

There usually is this special difference between the delights of charity and those of wisdom: The delights of wisdom are capable of and are accustomed to be drawn from one's own heart, while the intimate delights of charity are drawn from the heart of another. Whoever loves intimately and craves to be so loved is made anxious rather than delighted when he thirsts if he does not draw from his beloved's heart the sweetness of love for which he thirsts. But the delights of wisdom delight much more when they are derived from one's own heart. Nothing is defined contrary to nature if fullness of wisdom is said to be able to subsist in a single person. For it seems that even if there were only one person in Divinity, nevertheless he could have fullness of wisdom. However, fullness of wisdom can-

---

*We have here translated *condilectus* as "someone who shares in love for a third." The word, which seems to have been Richard's own invention, represents a crucial element in Richard's Trinitarian theology and in his subtle and penetrating understanding of the nature of true charity, divine or human. Cf. his own detailed description of the meaning of the term in Chapter XIX.

not exist without fullness of power, just as fullness of power cannot exist without fullness of wisdom. For without doubt he would not have the fullness of wisdom who would not know how he could obtain what he lacked in omnipotence. Conversely, without doubt he who could unwillingly suffer some defect of wisdom would lack fullness of power. For fullness of one cannot be had without fullness of the other. Therefore it follows that we understand the same thing concerning power that we have said concerning wisdom. For if omnipotence cannot be lacking where there is fullness of wisdom, it certainly seems that fullness of power as well as fullness of wisdom can be possessed by a single person.

Chapter XVII

That the fulfillment of happiness does not seem to be able to subsist without a pair of persons

The fulfillment of true and supreme happiness does not seem to be able to subsist in any way without a pair of persons. This is clearer than the light of day from those things which we have said above. For if there were only one person in that true Divinity, He certainly would not have anyone to whom He might give supreme love, nor anyone who might return supreme love to Him. Indeed, whence would abound for him those supremely sweet delights which, as has been said, are accustomed to be drawn from the heart of another rather than from one's own heart? For, as we have already said, nothing is sweeter than these delights; nothing is more delightful; nothing is more healthful, more excellent or more pleasurable than this sweetness. Therefore, how could divine happiness, which always lacked supreme sweetness and supreme delight, obtain an abundance of complete fullness? And so happiness demands a pair of persons, as has been said, in order that it can subsist with the integrity of all fullness.

Chapter XVIII

How the consummation of true and supreme goodness does not seem to be able to subsist without the completion of the Trinity

Let it disturb no one, let no one be indignant if we speak in a human manner to provide a clearer understanding of the truth of divine and supermundane things. We adopt this manner of speaking at the point of our necessity all the more confidently, the more frequently we discover it in sacred Scripture.

The supreme level of goodness seems to exist there, when supreme love is given and nothing is obtained in return for the fullness of its own happiness. But, as is most evident from what we have already said, this level of supreme perfection cannot be found between only two persons who mutually love. For indeed, in this case, each of those who love gives love, and from this each undoubtedly draws those delights of love, flowing with honey. If each were alone and lived like a hermit he would not have anyone from whom he could draw this. And so a great accumulation of joy and pleasure builds up for anyone who gives and receives love in fellowship with another. From this, therefore, we clearly gather that the supreme level of that generosity would have no place in Divinity if a third person were lacking in that plurality of persons. Certainly in only a pair of persons there would be no one with whom either of the two could share the excellent delights of His pleasure. For this reason it is given to be understood that the consummation of true and supreme goodness cannot subsist without completion of the Trinity.

Chapter XIX

How a trace of the Trinity can be grasped by examining only the particular nature of shared love

What has been proved by the manifold witness of reason concerning the affirmation of the Trinity can be confirmed by a sufficiently brief and very evident consideration. Let us ponder with careful consideration the virtue and particular nature of shared love and we shall quickly discover what we seek. When one person gives love to another and he alone loves only the other, there certainly is love, but it is not a shared love. When two love each other mutually and give to each other the affection of supreme longing; when the affection of the first goes out to the second and the affection of the second goes out to the first and tends as it were in diverse ways—in this case there certainly is love on both sides, but it is not shared love. Shared love is properly said to exist when a third person is loved by two persons harmoniously and in community, and the affection of the two persons is fused into one affection by the flame of love for the third. From these things it is evident that shared love would have no place in Divinity itself if a third person were lacking to the other two persons. Here we are not speaking of just any shared love but of supreme shared love—a shared love of a sort such that a creature would never merit from the Creator and for which it would never be found worthy.

Who, I ask, should be able to explicate fitly how great is the virtue of supreme and totally perfect benevolence? Who, I ask, would suffice to estimate fitly what or how great is the worth of intimate and supreme harmony? If there is so much worth for each person in these two virtues on account of the virtue itself, what virtue, what worth, I ask, will there be where each is fashioned on account of the other, where one is greatly praised on account of the other, where one is brought to consummation on account of the other? However, what is intimate and supreme shared love, other than the mutual coming together of intimate benevolence and supreme harmony? Just as a virtue of so much worth and supereminent excellence cannot be lacking in the supreme and altogether perfect good, so it is not able to subsist without a Trinity of persons.

CHAPTER XX

That from shared fellowship with a third person in that Trinity it is argued that concordant charity and consocial love are never found anywhere in an individual

Consider now how union with a third person establishes concordant affection everywhere and brings about consocial love through all and in all. If you direct your attention to any one among these three persons, you will see that the other two love the third concordantly. If you turn your attention to the second, there in like manner you will find that the remaining pair unite with equal desire in love for him. If you bring the third of these into consideration, without doubt you will see that the affection of the others flows in equal harmony to the third. If creation is considered, there the cord of love is tripled so that where suspicion concerning a defect of love could arise more easily, certitude is made more firm by greater confederation. Behold how from shared fellowship with a third person in that Trinity it is argued that concordant charity and consocial love are never found anywhere in an isolated individual. Behold in the affirmation of the Trinity, so great, so firm a witness to truth occurs everywhere that a person for whom so much assurance is insufficient seems to be mad.

CHAPTER XXI

That there is supreme equality in that Trinity in which it is necessary for all to be equally perfect

What has been shown above concerning two can be inferred with equal reasoning also about the three, namely each one loving supremely and being loved supremely by each, because each is supremely perfect. The fullness of supreme happiness requires fullness of supreme pleasure. The fullness of supreme pleasure requires fullness of supreme charity. The fullness of supreme charity demands fullness of supreme perfection. And so where all must be equally perfect, it is necessary that all coincide in supreme equality. In all of them there will be equal wisdom, equal power, undifferentiated glory, uniform goodness, and eternal happiness, so that we may truly establish what the daily profession of Christian instruction teaches equally concerning the three: "the Divinity is one, glory equal, and majesty coeternal."* There no one is greater than another, no one is less than another; there no one is before another; no one is after another. And so it is established that in that Trinity all persons are coequal and coeternal together. For if they were not coeternal, for that reason they would not be coequal.

Chapter XXII

*That there is supreme simplicity in each person,
true and supreme unity in all together,
and marvelous identity everywhere*

In that supreme and totally perfect equality of persons, that supreme and supremely simple being is common to all. Thus it is the same for each one to exist as to live, to live as to understand, to understand as to be able. There wisdom does not differ from power, nor power from essence, and in this manner one comes to a similar conclusion in similar things. Thus you see that each thing is totally the same although it is in each person. But if supreme perfection is in that equality and supreme equality is in that perfection, will supreme fullness of wisdom be simultaneously in each individually and in all, and will supreme fullness of power be simultaneously in each individually and in all? But what is supreme and full power except omnipotence? However we know that omnipotence is called such because it is able to do everything. But if it is agreed that omnipotence is truly able to do everything, it will be able to carry out with ease what any other power would not be able to do. For this reason it is clear that only one omnipotence can exist. But it was proved above that omnipotence is the same as divine essence. Therefore, if it is common for all the persons to *have* omnipotence together—no, *rather* to *be* omnipotent, because there

---
*Athanasian Creed.

to be is not different from to have—it will also be common for all to be one and the same essence. For, like omnipotence, there can be only one divine essence. Not only is what each person is completely the same; but each one is what each other is. And so, supreme simplicity is in each; true and supreme unity is in all together; and marvelous identity is everywhere if you pay attention well.

Chapter XXIII

How the aforementioned equality ought to be understood in these persons where there is so much unity and such identity

We are able to understand in both a good way and a bad way what has been said concerning the equality of persons. Indeed, in so much simplicity and unity of persons there seems to be more identity than equality. We are able and accustomed to say that three golden statues are equal if they have the same purity and weight and the same similitude in everything. But such an equality is very different from that which exists in the Trinity of divine persons. For in that equality of statues the mass of gold in one statue is one thing and the mass of gold in another statue is another thing. According to this, one of the statues is one thing and the other is another thing. However, concerning that true and supreme Trinity we ought not to think that in it there are things that are different but equal among themselves. As has been shown already, whatever is in any one person of the Trinity, the same is also completely in any other person.

We do not unworthily say that three rational spirits are equal if they have the same power, the same wisdom, the same purity and goodness. But in this trinity of spirits, just as there are three persons, so it is evident that there are three substances. However, the supreme Trinity exists with unity of substance. And so, in that first trinity one thing and another thing, both equal, are found; but such equality is very different from the divine Trinity. But we say that persons are equal in that supreme Trinity for this reason: because that supreme and supremely simple being which belongs to one person in this fullness and perfection also belongs to each other person in this fullness and perfection.

Chapter XXIV

How incomprehensible supreme coequality is from every viewpoint

Certainly one and the same substance is not something greater or lesser, better or worse than itself. Therefore any one person in the Trinity will not be something greater or better than any other person in the Trinity, since one and the same substance is certainly in each. The very same substance is simultaneously in each and in everyone; for this reason any two persons will not be something greater or better than any one person alone; nor will all three taken together be more than any two or any one alone by itself. However, in that trinity of persons where there are many substances, one person alone is something less than two, and all three taken together are something greater than any two. Now observe how incomprehensible is that coequality of greatness from every viewpoint and in every respect in that Trinity where unity does not lack plurality and plurality does not go beyond unity!

Chapter XXV

That in that Trinity nothing is dissimilar to itself nor is it unequal to any other in anything

But in order that you may admire this equality of the divine persons more, pay attention to the fact that in all other persons there is in one and the same person neither individuality without plurality nor unity without inequality. I pass in silence over the fact that a person is able to increase or decrease and become unequal in himself. I pass in silence over the fact that his power is one thing, his wisdom is another, his justice is another, and that he is able to be greater with respect to one thing and lesser with respect to another, and likewise better or worse. Certainly his power alone is dissimilar to itself and his wisdom alone is unequal to itself. The very same thing happens in other cases. Observe his power and you will discover that one thing is easy for him, another is difficult and a third is impossible. And so his power is perceived as dissimilar and unequal to itself. In a similar way one thing is understandable to wisdom, while another is incomprehensible. For what human or angelic intelligence would ever be able to comprehend the very immensity of Divinity (I remain silent concerning other things)? While one and the same nature is more effective in some things, in other things it is less effective; in one respect it is less, in another it is greater, and is found to be dissimilar and unequal to itself. And so from these things we can gather that where there is no true simplicity, true equality cannot exist. However in that Trinity, nowhere is anything dissimilar to itself nor is it unequal to any other in anything. Surely where there is true eternity, there cannot be an earlier and a later; so also where there is unchangeable immensity, there cannot be a greater and a lesser.

In those who possess the same rational principle of eternity and immensity, no alternation or change of inequality can exist even partially because no "changing or shadow of change" is there (James 1:17). "There nothing is earlier, nothing is later; nothing is greater or lesser; but all three persons are coeternal and coequal with themselves."* Behold now we have proved by open and manifold reasoning how true that is which we are commanded to believe, namely, that we venerate "one God in Trinity and Trinity in unity."**

---

*Athanasian Creed
**Ibid.

SELECTED BIBLIOGRAPHY

EDITIONS AND TRANSLATIONS

Châtillon, Jean, ed. *L'Édit d'Alexandre ou les trois processions*, in Richard de Saint-Victor, *Sermons et opuscules spirituels inédits*, vol. I. Bruges, 1951.

Kirchberger, Clare, trans. Richard of St. Victor, *Selected Writings on Contemplation*. London, 1957.

Migne, J. P., ed. *Patrologiae latinae*, vol. 196. Paris, 1855.

Ribaillier, Jean, ed. Richard de Saint-Victor, *De Trinitate: texte critique avec introduction, notes et tables*. Paris, 1958.

Salet, Gaston, trans. Richard de Saint-Victor, *La Trinité*. Sources Chrétiennes, 63. Paris, 1969.

Wolff, Paul, trans. *Die Viktoriner: Mystische Schriften*. Wien, 1936.

STUDIES

Andres, F. "Die Stufen der Contemplatio in Bonaventuras Itinerarium mentis ad Deum und in Benjamin major des Richards von St. Viktor." *Franziskanische Studien* 8 (1921): 189–200.

Bonnard, F. *Histoire de l'abbaye royale et de l'ordre des channoines réguliers de Saint-Victor de Paris*, 2 vols. Paris, 1904–1907.

Bynum, Caroline W. "The Spirituality of Regular Canons in the Twelfth Century: A New Approach." *Medievalia et Humanistica* 4 (1973): 3–24.

Châtillon, Jean. "Autour des Miscellanea attribués à Hugues de Saint-Victor." *Revue d'ascétique et de mystique* 25 (1949): 299–305.

───── . "De Guillaume de Champeaux à Thomas Gallus: chronique d'histoire littéraire et doctrinale de l'École de Saint-Victor." *Revue du moyen âge latin* 8 (1952): 139–162, 247–273.

BIBLIOGRAPHY

——— . *Théologie, spiritualité et métaphysique dans l'owuvre oratoire d'Achard de Saint-Victor.* Études de Philosophie médiévale, 58. Paris, 1969.

——— . "Les trois modes de la contemplation selon Richard de Saint-Victor." *Bulletin de littérature ecclésiastique* 41 (1940): 3–26.

Chenu, M.-D. *La théologie au douzième siècle.* Ètudes de philosophie médiévale, 45. Paris, 1957.

Cousins, Ewert. "A Theology of Interpersonal Relations." *Thought* 45 (1970): 56–82.

Dickinson, J. C. *The Origins of the Austin Canons and Their Introduction into England.* London, 1950.

Ebner, Joseph. *Die Erkenntnislehre Richards von Saint Viktor.* Beiträge zur Geschichte der Philosophie und Theologie des Mittelalters, Band 19, heft 4. Münster, 1917.

Ethier, A.-M. *Le "De Trinitate" de Richard de Saint-Victor.* Publications de l'Institut d'Études médiévales d'Ottawa, 9. Paris-Ottawa, 1939.

Guimet, Fernand. "*Caritas ordinata et amor discretus* dans la théologie trinitaire de Richard de Saint-Victor." *Revue du moyen âge latin* 4 (1948): 225–236.

——— . "Notes in marge d'un texte de Richard de Saint-Victor." *Archives d'histoire litteraire et doctrinale du moyen âge* 14 (1943–1945): 361–394.

McGinn, Bernard. "Ascension and Introversion in the *Itinerarium Mentis in Deum,*" *S. Bonaventura 1274–1974.* Rome: Grottaferrata, 1974, III, pp. 535–552.

Peers, E. Allison. *Bernardino de Laredo, The Ascent of Mount Sion.* London, 1952.

Robilliard, J. A. "Les six genres de contemplation chez Richard de Saint-Victor et leur origine platonicienne." *Revue des sciences philosophiques et théologiques* 28 (1939): 229–233.

Smalley, Beryl. *The Study of the Bible in the Middle Ages,* 2nd ed. Oxford, 1952.

Weisweiler, H. "*Sacramentum fidei*: Augustinische und ps.-dionysiche in der Glaubenauffassung Hugos von St. Viktor." *Theologie in Geschichte und Gegenwart,* hsgb. von J. Auer und H. Volk. München, 1957, pp. 433–456.

Zinn, Jr., Grover A. "Book and Word. The Background of Bonaventure's Use of Symbols." *S. Bonaventura 1274–1974.* Rome: Grottaferrata, 1974), II, pp. 143–169.

——— . "Personification Allegory and Visions of Light in Richard of St. Victor's Teaching on Contemplation." *University of Toronto Quarterly* 46 (1977): 190–214.

INDEX TO PREFACE AND INTRODUCTION

love of, 47; return to, 45; and
virtue, 17; and world, 12.
Seraphim, 7, 23, 32, 33, 34, 35,
36, 45.
Sheba, Queen of, 17, 23, 41,
42.
Sichem, 18.
Simeon, 13, 18.
Sin, grief for, 13; penalty for,
18; shame for, 10, 18; and
virtue, 17.
Sinai, Mt. of, 34, 36, 43.
Smalley, Beryl, 11.
Solomon, 41.
Song of Songs, 23, 38, 40, 41.
Soul, and charity, 9; and
contemplation, 7, 28, 29; and
devotion, 40; and ecstasy, 41,
43; food for, 45; and
harmony, 31; knowledge of,
29; mirror of, 20, 21; nature
of, 30; powers of, 11;
preparation of, 38; rational,
11, 28, 31; Spirit in, 31;
spouse of, 14.
Speculation, 25-30, 34.
Spirituality, cf. also St. Victor,
Abbey of; ascent to, 27, 30,
43, 45, 46; life of, 17, 43;
quest for, 17, 18, 19; of
Richard, xi, 8; of 12th
century, 2, 4; works of, xii.
Symbol, and ecstasy, 40, 43;
and knowledge, 26-27; and

liturgy, 39; material, 16; and
Scripture, 11, 15, 17, 18, 19,
20, 23, 28, 32, 33, 42, 44,
45.

Tabernacle, 5, 23, 39, 43, 44,
45.
Tauler, 5.
Teresa of Avila, 5.
The Transfiguration, 10, 11,
20, 21, 22, 36.
Trinity, 24, 31, 32, 46-48.
Tropology, 7, 15, 21, 22, 23,
37, 40, 45.

Understanding, and ark, 35;
and contemplation, 24, 25,
29, 31, 32.

The Victorines, cf. St. Victor,
Abbey of.
Virtue, 6, 17, 18, 19, 31.

Weisweiler, H., 30.
William of Champeaux, 2, 3.
William of St. Thierry, 1.
Williams, Charles, 47.

Yankowski, S.V., xiii.

Zabulon, 17.
Zelpha, 12, 13, 16.
Zinn, Grover, xi, xii, xv, 4, 10,
44.

INDEX TO TEXT

contemplative, 288, 289, 302, 322, 335, 340; and desire, 318, 319, 320; and devotion, 316, 317-318, 320-322, 324; and divine favor, 337-339; and exultation, 316, 332-336, 339, 341; gift of, 305; of mind, 53, 139-141, 142, 143, 144, 228, 241, 268, 272, 276, 277, 278, 289, 301, 302, 304, 305, 306, 309, 312, 316-323, 325-328, 332, 335-337, 339, 342; modes of, 317-336, 337-339; and showing, 278, 319-322, 326-332; of soul, 267; and wonder, 316, 322-326, 327, 328.

Egypt, 145, 146, 147, 202.

Egyptians, 125, 187.

Elijah, 96, 136, 138, 139, 274, 276, 279, 281, 286.

Elisha, 339.

Emor, 106, 107, 110.

Ephesians, 2:20, 196.

Equity, cf. Justice.

Essence, difference of, 222, 270; divine, 270, 273, 289, 395; of God, 290, 291, 296; invisible, 219, 222; nature of, 240, 242; of soul, 235, 240, 249, 358; spiritual, 238, 242, 243; sublimity of, 239; of Trinity, 394, 395.

Eve, 200.

Evil, 54; bearing of, 54, 77, 80, 99, 113; consideration of, 60; and discretion, 128, 254; and disorder, 60; escape from, 232; external, 84; and fear, 118-121, 122; forgetting of, 95; forgiveness of, 64; future,

61, 68, 70, 80, 247; and good, 68, 94, 95, 232, 287; guard against, 247, 271; and guilt, 94, 113; internal, 84; and justice, 111, 118, 208; and patience, 78; reforming of, 206, 210; satisfaction for, 242; torments, 70, 71, 73, 80, 86, 94, 113, 209, 211, 213, 233, 355; and will, 73, 121, 247.

Exodus, 2:40, 270; 3:14, 304; 13:21, 336; 15:11, 270; 23:16-18, 311; 25:9, 267; 25:18-20, 259; 25:19, 269; 25:20, 271, 289; 25:22, 300; 25:40, 304; 29:37, 152; 32, 97.

Experience, of Christ, 138; and contemplation, 75, 131, 160, 287, 306, 310, 315; of joy, 90, 98, 333; and judgment, 71; and knowledge, 53, 98, 136, 162, 163, 166, 179, 191, 200, 202, 241, 242, 245, 261, 262, 315, 359, 382; sense, 78; of soul, 75, 130; teaching of, 53, 56, 59, 124, 125, 202, 240, 245, 332, 343, 376, 383; and understanding, 248; and will, 241.

Ezechiel, 169, 183.

Ezechiel, 1:6, 169; 1:14, 160; 1:16, 196; 28:12-13, 269; 40:26, 183.

Faith, 56, 141, 145, 184, 188, 189, 214, 218, 248, 262, 263, 279, 294, 296, 301, 360, 363, 365, 367, 373, 378.

Father, and Christ, 294; gifts

353-355, 357; love of, 60, 64, 65, 78, 79, 81, 90, 153, 197, 211, 212, 213, 257, 288, 289, 327, 356, 363; mysteries of, 341; nature of, 74, 296; offenses against, 83, 127, 210; peace of, 90; persons in, 141, 260, 292, 296, 301; pleasing of, 152; power of, 193, 237, 250, 291, 293, 335, 377, 386; predestination of, 206-212, 214-215, 217-218, 353-357; presence of, 81, 113, 224, 229, 250, 276, 292; retribution of, 113; revelation of, 228; secrets of, 315; serving of, 255; severity of, 211, 266; and shame, 116-117; simplicity of, 290, 291, 293; soldier of, 96; sons of, 101; and soul, 62, 63; Spirit of, 176, 228; substance of, 260, 292-297, 301; sweetness of, 63, 317; is truth, 65; unchangeable, 290, 291, 293; unity in, 141, 260, 293, 295, 296, 300, 301, 362, 381; union with, 259; vision of, 130; will of, 243, 244, 250, 256, 276, 298, 301, 379, 386; wisdom of, 74, 152, 187, 192, 206, 207, 211, 217-218, 237, 240, 291, 335, 353, 357, 377; works of, 175, 189, 197, 204, 206, 208, 233, 237, 244, 250, 257, 353-355; worship of, 112, 198.

Good, cf. Creation, God; confession of, 64; corporeal, 198; eternal, 74, 94, 101, 211, 212; and evil, 68, 94, 95, 232, 239, 287; and fear, 120-121, 122; fullness of, 374, 375, 376, 387; of future, 68, 70, 71, 74, 94, 194, 238; 255; highest, 95, 162, 192, 219; invisible, 71, 191, 192, 197, 198, 352; longing for, 74, 114, 223, 240; love of, 65, 122, 142, 143, 256; and moderation, 77; of neighbor, 109; perfection of, 374, 392; present, 71, 74, 79, 80, 94, 146, 211, 212, 243, 356; and prosperity, 206, 211, 212; spiritual, 89, 255; supreme, 375, 376, 378, 379, 380, 386, 391; true, 90, 146, 211, 223, 376, 391; uniformity of, 394; variety of, 255; and will, 121, 122; and wisdom, 375, 379.

Grace, 64, 97, 101, 128, 131, 225, 265; and ark, 152; and Christ, 294; of contemplation, 75, 129, 130-131, 142, 143, 146, 153-155, 172, 173, 205, 265, 267, 273, 274, 275, 277, 305, 307, 308-310, 314, 315, 339, 344, 346, 347, 353, 360, 363; cooperation of, 245, 256, 276, 305, 308, 310; desired, 277, 279; of discretion, 129, 346; of healing, 257; and knowledge, 337; of meditation, 146; prevenient, 135; regained, 339-343; of showings, 278, 279, 330; of similitude, 196; in soul, 231, 245, 279-284, 287; and teaching of others, 308, 309;

411

meditation, 71; and memory, 59, 66, 67; and mind, 165, 343; ordering of, 68, 69, 70, 80, 120; phantasies of, 219, 251, 263, 360; and reason, 57, 58, 66, 67, 68, 69, 70, 161, 162, 165, 166, 171, 172, 189, 190, 199, 203-204, 222, 263, 264, 348-349, 357; and speculation, 69-71; and sense, 58, 80, 174; and thinking, 156; and understanding, 69, 70, 146, 163, 167; and vice, 58-59; and visible things, 203, 204, 233.

Intellect, blindness of, 241; and invisible things, 234, 237; limits of, 241, 261; of man, 239; purity of, 219, 220; and reason, 65, 261; and spirit, 328; and third heaven, 233, 235.

Intention, changing of, 110-113; and discretion, 126, 254; enlarged, 276; of mind, 126, 127, 318; raising of, 284.

Isaiah, 269, 315.

Isaiah, 1:19, 244; 4:5-6, 272; 7:9, 189; 9:7, 255; 22:13, 243; 28:10, 13, 279, 282, 339; 38:13, 236; 40:6, 338; 40:17, 269; 40:31, 315; 48:22, 333; 55:10, 196; 56:12, 243; 57:21, 333; 60:4, 160; 60:8, 312; 64:4, 227; 64:6, 93.

Israel, 142; elders of, 307; God of, 154; people of, 105, 241, 244; tribes of, 72, 73.

Israelites, 142.

Issachar (Reward), 91-98, 107, 117, 122.

Jacob, 54, 75, 83, 111, 115, 116, 117, 123, 126, 127, 154; children of, 117; and Ruben, 118-123; sons of, 53, 59, 62, 90; wives of, 53, 55, 59, 60, 63, 68.

James, 135.

James, 1:12, 79; 1:17, 55, 290, 293, 397.

Jeremiah, 2:10, 313; 17:9, 233; 31:21, 313.

Jerusalem, 55; heavenly, 67, 70.

Jericho, 311.

Job, 126, 189, 240, 333.

Job, 5:6, 189; 19:4, 240; 27:6, 230; 30:7, 333.

John, 67, 135, 137, 140, 144, 328, 330.

John, 1:9, 192, 240; 3:8, 245; 3:12, 138; 3:20-21, 321; 14:6, 135; 15:5, 244; 15:15, 288; 17:3, 265; 17:5, 154.

1 John, 1:8, 101; 2:15, 60; 2:27, 330.

Joseph (Discretion), 124-130, 141, 145-147.

Joshua, 198, 307.

Joy, 117, 257; cf. Lord; and abstinence, 79; of beatitude, 78-79; birth of, 89-91; of conscience, 78, 89; of contemplation, 55, 75, 134, 135, 143, 144, 158, 163, 173, 198, 212, 215-216, 223, 227, 247, 250, 289, 316, 317, 340, 356; and ecstasy, 332-336; eternal, 80, 86, 91, 96, 101, 153, 175, 181, 203, 249, 394; exterior, 91, 143, 338; and fear, 122; fullness of, 375, 376, 377, 379, 386, 390;

and fear, 122, 202; of God, 60, 64, 65, 78, 79, 81, 90, 153, 197, 211, 212, 213, 282, 288, 289, 319, 327; joy of, 391; for justice, 54, 65, 88; and mind, 316; mutual, 376, 380, 381, 389, 391, 392; nature of, 63-65; of neighbor, 109, 119; ordering of, 60, 62-63, 65, 109, 123; of perishible things, 57; pledge of, 347; of praise, 82; of self, 109, 272, 273, 374, 375; and sensation, 58; shared, 387, 388, 389, 391, 392; singularity of, 288; in soul, 253, 316, 340; supreme, 375, 380, 386, 390, 391, 393; true, 266, 374; for truth, 321; of vainglory, 107, 108, 109; of virtue, 82, 256; for wisdom, 54, 299; of world, 60, 90, 118-119, 153, 273.

Luke, 1:52, 254; 6:25, 90; 6:37, 87; 10:42, 152; 15:7, 88; 15:17, 321; 16:8, 146; 24:26, 154.

Man, activity of, 178, 180, 181, 182, 184, 194, 225, 227, 244, 245, 308, 310, 311, 312, 314, 315, 336-337, 345, 350; instruction of, 181-182, 194, 308, 309, 351, 369; nature of, 76, 314, 315, 335, 338, 339, 382, 383; reformation of, 206, 210, 212, 213, 355; and sin, 200; Son of, 132; spirit of, 132, 197, 219, 225, 233; substance of, 382, 383; unity of, 382, 383.

Mamre, 320.
Mandrakes, 81-84, 90.
Martha, 153.
Mary, 152.
Matter, and speculation, 179-180, 182, 194, 349, 350.
Matthew, 3:17, 140; 5:4, 92; 5:5, 61; 5:7, 87; 5:8, 266; 5:10, 87; 5:16, 116, 225; 5:45, 187; 10:28, 91; 11:29, 103; 17:1, 135; 17:1-8, 311; 17:4, 134, 159; 18:16, 378; 22:37, 39, 60; 23:26, 225; 25:21, 90.
Meditation, 282; and contemplation, 57, 146, 155-158, 327; grace of, 146, 339; and imagination, 71; and joy, 288, 339, 341; and knowledge, 136, 230; and mind, 157, 158; and reason, 156; and showing, 325-332; and speculation, 75; zeal of, 346.
Memory, 188, 250, 251, 252; failure of, 140; of faults, 108, 110; and imagination, 59, 66, 67; and mortification, 168; and mysteries, 301; and spirit, 328; and vision, 220, 278, 285, 302, 306, 309, 310, 312, 340, 342.
Mercy, divine, 266, 276; Father of, 229; of God, 237, 330, 331, 337; of Lord, 187, 358; and patience, 87-88; in reproach, 102; works of, 220.
Mercy-seat, 362.
Michah, 2:1, 72.
Midianites, 96.
Mind, cf. Ecstasy; above itself,

321, 323, 329, 332; activity of, 315; affliction of, 115-116, 329; alienation of, 278, 288, 289, 303, 304, 309, 310-312, 316, 320, 321, 327, 332, 334, 335, 342, 343; and ark, 177, 329; and contemplation, 131, 141, 142, 146, 156, 157, 163, 192, 205, 228, 239, 246, 247, 276, 306, 310-312, 327, 347, 361; and corporeal things, 156, 204; corruption of, 113-115, 174; and discretion, 124, 126, 266; enlarging of, 310, 312-314, 323, 343; and fear, 119-120, 276; and future, 72, 113-114, 275-276; going out from, 320, 322, 332, 342; and higher things, 226, 277, 323; and hope, 113-114; and imagination, 165; intentions of, 126, 127; and judgment, 104; light of, 192, 273; limits of, 227, 228, 232, 249, 273, 302, 323; and meditation, 157, 158; perfection of, 344; piety of, 109; purification of, 266, 323; raising of, 276, 277, 303, 304, 306, 310-312, 315, 316, 318, 323, 324, 326, 327, 343; and reason, 162, 163; and shame, 106-109; and Spirit, 256; stability of, 92, 95, 175; and Trinity, 299; and understanding, 156, 162, 226, 310; unity of, 201; and virtue, 97, 109, 124; wanderings of, 142, 143, 266; and wonder, 322, 323, 327.

Miracles, 262, 263, 329.

Moab, 311.

Modesty, cf. Shame; and pride, 106; and zeal, 105.

Morality, and ark, 151, 178, 179, 349, 351; character of, 217, 232, 320; and discipline, 181; sense of, 151; and speculation, 178, 182; understanding of, 365, 366, 367; and works, 178-179.

Moses, 96, 136, 138, 139, 142, 143, 217; cf. also Ark; ark of, 151, 153, 155, 170, 173, 177, 206, 207, 259, 300, 302, 304, 305, 308; example of, 177, 231, 301, 305, 308; on mountain, 267, 268, 302, 303, 304, 306, 307, 308, 309, 311, 312; and tabernacle, 152.

Mutability, 169, 170, 217-218, 223, 277.

Mysticism, 70, 71, 172, 194, 195, 217, 259, 302, 323, 365, 367; cf. also Ark.

Naphtali (Conversion), 70-71, 74-77, 80, 86, 89.

Nature, cf. Divinity, God, Man; of angels, 269; and contemplation, 182, 350; corporeal, 190; hidden, 188; and philosophers, 186; of similitude, 269; and speculation, 179-182, 190, 238, 350, 361; spiritual, 238, 272; of soul, 240, 246, 249; transcending of, 334, 338; works of, 180-182, 194, 196, 245, 246, 350.

Nebo, Mt., 311.

200; 54:14-15, 203; 54:15,
202; 54:16, 203; 56:4, 330;
56:4-5, 330; 57:9, 236; 63:3,
229; 63:7, 176; 63:7, 8, 133,
315; 64:10, 92; 67:5, 341;
67:27, 142; 67:27-28, 142;
67:28, 53, 142; 68:6, 240;
68:10, 96; 69:6, 244; 72:1,
154; 72:22, 93; 72:25, 240;
75:6, 177; 76:3, 338; 76:7,
230; 78:9, 244; 80:14-15, 244;
82:2, 269; 85:1, 333; 85:8,
269; 91:5, 182; 93:19, 62;
103:24, 182, 185; 106:26,
160; 108:30, 64; 110:10, 60;
111:3, 89; 112:3, 175; 113:4,
334; 115:11, 312; 118:14, 88;
118:18, 234; 118:62, 236;
118:81, 329; 118:99-100, 229;
118:128, 96, 101; 118:139,
96; 126:2, 202; 131:8, 151;
132:2, 196; 138:9, 169;
138:22, 96; 142:5, 182;
142:10, 95; 144:3, 290; 144:9,
187; 144:13, 175.

Punishment, of body, 113; as
evil, 94; fear of, 61, 65, 74;
and love, 97, 98; of mind,
114; and shame, 104; and
sin, 72, 86, 114, 211, 213,
247.

Purification, of conscience, 225,
230, 248; of man, 188, 213;
and sanctification, 152, 153;
of soul, 56, 175, 220, 221,
241, 266, 286.

Rachel, 58, 59, 77, 120, 154;
children of, 53, 80; and
contemplation, 57; death of,
139, 140, 144, 145, 147; and

mandrakes, 82-83; and
reason, 66, 68, 69, 125, 130,
131; sons of, 72, 125; and
wisdom, 53-56, 65, 66.

Ramathaim, 152.

Reason, 69; cf. Showing;
above, 131, 132, 141, 145,
147, 161, 163, 166, 167, 173,
260-263, 270, 271, 278, 289,
290, 292, 343, 360; against,
163, 164, 172, 173, 261, 262,
271, 278, 290, 292, 293, 360,
366; agree with, 132, 172,
173, 263, 292, 360, 366;
below, 132; beyond, 145,
161, 163, 167, 172, 173, 260,
261, 263, 270, 271, 278, 289,
295, 343, 360, 366, 370; and
contemplation, 55, 57, 129,
132, 162-165, 167, 171-173,
189, 190, 203, 204, 221, 222,
227, 233, 261, 270, 271; and
discretion, 124-126, 129, 171;
divine, 261; and faith, 263,
294; *habitus* of, 345; and
imagination, 57, 67-70, 161,
162, 165, 166, 171, 172, 174,
189, 190, 199, 200, 357; and
knowledge, 65, 66, 129, 132,
136, 163, 199; limits of, 131,
140, 141, 163, 179, 248,
262-264, 278, 290; of man,
131, 140, 382; and
meditation, 156; ordering of,
69, 70, 82, 83, 203, 204, 222;
perfection of, 238; principles
of, 165, 166, 183, 184, 186,
188, 189, 193-198, 209, 213,
216, 222, 234, 269, 271, 298,
348, 351; and sense, 57, 58,
179, 180, 260, 261; and

Showing, cf. Divinity;
consolation of, 330; and
ecstasy, 139, 267, 278, 319,
320, 321, 329; end of, 216;
and grace, 153, 278, 279,
305, 307, 308, 309, 310, 318;
and knowing, 145, 157, 241,
262, 267, 268, 275, 278, 279,
285, 303, 304, 309, 312, 314,
315, 325, 329; and love, 288,
325; and mind, 141; of
mysteries, 341; and reason,
57, 146, 147, 260, 278; and
similitude, 325; and
speculation, 300-301; and
truth, 324; and witness,
138-139, 262; and work, 137.

Sichem, 106-111.

Sidon, 99, 100.

Simeon (Grief), 61, 113-115,
117, 122.

Similitude, 226, 316, 322, 324,
332, 334, 336; angelic, 260,
261, 267, 335; and
contemplation, 159, 162,
270, 298; corporeal, 190,
196, 198, 199, 200, 233, 234;
divine, 379-380, 383; and
God, 269, 270, 277, 298,
299; grace of, 196; and
invisible things, 193, 194,
198, 260; principle of, 193,
194, 195, 196, 269, 271, 298;
and reason, 262, 271, 297;
and showing, 325; testimony
of, 276; of visible things,
162, 193, 198, 199, 204, 228,
352; and will, 205.

Sin, 73, 107, 179; and anger,
96; condemned, 62;
denouncing of, 97, 102, 114;

fear of, 61; free of, 101, 102;
grief for, 202; hate for, 117;
and penance, 88, 282;
punishment of, 72, 86, 114,
211, 213, 247; shame for, 61,
102-103; state of, 225, 234,
331.

Sinai, 255.

Solomon, 231, 255, 326, 327.

Son, and Arius, 296; and
Father, 140, 141, 262, 292,
293, 299; and Holy Spirit,
292, 293, 299; incarnation of,
297, 299; of man, 132.

Song of Songs, 1:1, 76; 1:6,
236; 2:5, 76; 2:10, 281;
2:13-14, 281; 3:6, 317; 4:1-2,
77; 4:11, 76; 5:1, 288; 5:2,
280; 5:3, 280; 5:6, 280, 374;
5:10, 195; 5:15, 195; 6:9,
317, 322, 323, 324; 7:4-5, 77;
8:5, 317, 332, 333, 337.

Soul, cf. Essence, Grief, Joy;
activity of, 155, 157, 246,
247, 303, 305, 308; affections
of, 55, 58, 60, 65, 82, 110,
117, 127, 160, 246, 252-255,
287, 288, 318, 340; afflictions
of, 115, 119, 130, 252, 253,
279; alienation of, 272, 302,
310; ascent of, 128, 129, 132,
133, 182, 222, 223, 240, 252,
257, 303, 304, 315, 318, 324,
326, 329, 333, 336, 351; and
body, 113, 174, 199-201,
222, 240, 249, 382;
contemplative, 75, 156-158,
163, 191, 192, 220, 255, 274,
279, 300, 310, 315, 326, 342;
enemies of, 87, 100, 331;
eternal, 101, 249; and God,

62, 63, 237, 240; and grace, 231-232, 279-284, 339; holiness of, 257, 279, 318, 326-327, 330, 338; illumination of, 303; immortality of, 242, 243; and knowledge, 162, 201, 202, 223, 234, 251, 327; love in, 63, 74, 81, 130, 192, 216, 226, 253, 274, 279, 280, 286, 288, 319, 320, 336, 374; as mirror, 129, 130; nature of, 240, 246, 249; peace of, 78, 88, 203, 223, 227, 276, 284, 303, 304, 326; perfection of, 344; powers of, 69, 246; preparation of, 279-289; purification of, 56, 175, 220, 221, 241, 266, 286; qualities of, 247, 249; rational, 129, 130, 162, 163, 182, 190, 192, 252; refreshment of, 345, 363; and shame, 105, 106, 111, 115, 240; state of, 108, 278, 302, 306, 309-311; strengthening of, 81, 93, 96, 229, 240, 257; substance of, 241; transcending of, 286-289, 303, 318, 319, 332, 334; transformation of, 266-267; and virtues, 246, 247, 254, 255; and will, 246, 252, 276; and wonder, 75, 104, 160, 208, 216, 223, 240, 247, 255, 279, 304, 316, 348; zeal of, 97-101, 105, 190, 273.

Speculation, 160, 190, 282, 295, 350; cf. Nature; ark of, 353; and contemplation, 335-336; divine, 260, 264, 265, 298,

299, 345; and imagination, 69-77, 263; and invisible things, 67, 162, 171, 193, 199, 225, 242, 268, 352, 356, 361; and joy, 211-214, 356; kinds of, 222, 278, 300; and nature, 179-182, 190, 238, 350, 361; and reason, 162, 189, 196, 199, 260, 361; of self, 231-233; of soul, 242, 243, 247, 257, 258; stages of, 178-183, 192, 197, 237, 241; of Trinity, 292, 297; and understanding, 221, 232, 235, 244; and visible things, 67, 193, 199; and wisdom, 137; and wonder, 184, 210, 211, 216.

Substance, kinds of, 252; invisible, 197, 225, 352; plurality of, 382-386; spiritual, 241; of Son, 297; of soul, 241, 359; of Trinity, 141, 260, 292, 293, 295, 296, 297, 373, 380, 393; unity of, 141, 260, 292, 295, 296, 297, 301, 373, 376, 380, 382, 383, 393, 395, 396.

Trinity, 300; affirmation of, 391, 393; attributes of, 373; and charity, 374-380, 387, 389, 393; completion of, 391; equality in, 375, 379-381, 383, 393, 394, 395, 396, 397; essence of, 141, 395; faith in, 296; image of, 299; persons of, 141, 389, 390, 393, 394; of persons, 141, 164, 289, 290, 292, 293, 295, 296, 299, 301, 386, 387, 388, 392, 393,

395, 396; plurality of persons
in, 373-388, 390, 391;
processions in, 292, 293, 299,
373; substance of, 141, 292,
295-297, 373, 376, 380, 381,
395, 396; traces of, 299;
unity of, 292, 295-297, 362,
380, 382, 383, 394, 395, 396,
397; wisdom of, 378, 380.

Tropology, 364-366.

Truth, contemplation of, 153,
154, 206, 324, 335; highest,
153; instruction in, 369; joy
in, 90, 289, 357; of Lord,
135, 187, 336; love of, 321;
in man, 137; proof of, 367,
368, 369, 393; search for,
157, 158, 250, 324; and
similitude, 228; supreme,
298; teaching of, 53;
understanding of, 231, 256,
391; way of, 137, 187, 330,
331, 337; works of, 321.

Tabernacle, altar of, 345, 346,
347; atrium of, 344, 345,
347; building of, 152;
candelabrum of, 345; of the
covenant, 142, 152, 305, 306,
344; exterior, 345; first, 231,
306, 345; interior, 306, 307,
345; of Lord, 134, 135;
second, 306, 345; table of,
345, 363, 364, 368.

Temptation, 72, 73, 84, 96,
100, 125, 126, 128, 203, 314,
329.

Thaneos, 177.

Theology, 188, 226, 279.

Thought, 84; and affections,
110, 254; and contemplation,
155, 157, 285; governing of,

72, 85, 154; and knowledge,
228, 251; limits of, 260; and
meditation, 158; and reason,
143; and temptation, 84;
wandering of, 120, 156, 157,
216, 254, 266.

1 Timothy, 6:16, 74.

2 Timothy, 2:17, 100; 4:8, 214.

Understanding, ark of, 194,
356, 357; and contemplation,
75, 146, 156, 158, 162, 164,
171, 183, 220, 221, 252, 264,
267, 270, 274, 277, 303, 311;
and ecstasy, 228, 277;
enlarged, 231, 323; and faith,
188, 189; illumination of,
216, 303, 323; and
imagination, 70, 71, 146; of
invisible things, 119, 191,
234, 235, 264; lack of, 72,
188, 189; limits of, 245, 248,
262, 301, 341, 366, 383;
liveliness of, 250, 252, 310;
mystical, 365; pure, 65, 75,
146, 163, 165-167, 171, 220,
245, 266, 357; raising of,
191, 216, 267, 270, 274, 314,
325, 326, 342, 367; rays of,
221; and reason, 69, 70, 125,
165-167, 179, 234, 263, 278;
and showing, 278; and soul,
231; Spirit of, 128; spiritual,
70, 71, 75, 77, 119, 139, 231,
234, 367, 369; transforming
of, 145, 278.

Vice, 58, 85, 86, 96, 101, 103,
117, 123, 127, 128, 154, 218,
232, 240, 254, 255.

Virtues, and affection, 55,

speculation, 178-181; of virtue, 83, 105; of wisdom, 243.

World, cf. Creation; children of, 146; despising of, 80, 153, 175; end of, 169; forgetting of, 92; love of, 79, 118-119, 273; pleasures of, 78, 79, 101, 197, 338; prosperity of, 80, 86; tribulations of, 79, 80, 86, 92, 99, 120, 212; variety in, 298; wisdom of, 56, 177, 224.

Zabulon (Fortitude), 96-102, 105, 117, 122.

Zeal, excessive, 102; for purification, 225, 266; of souls, 97, 100-101, 105, 190, 273; true, 98, 101; for uprightness, 97, 98.

Zelpha, 58, 59, 78, 80, 81; and senses, 77; sons of, 72, 77, 84.

Zion, 240.